MY MISSION TO RUSSIA
AND OTHER DIPLOMATIC MEMORIES

MY MISSION TO RUSSIA
AND OTHER DIPLOMATIC MEMORIES

By The Right Hon.
Sir George Buchanan
G.C.B., G.C.M.G., G.G.V.O.
British Ambassador, Petrograd, 1910-1918

With an introduction by
John Van der Kiste

A & F Reprints

First published in two volumes in Britain by Cassell, London, 1923, and in USA by Little, Brown, Boston, 1923
First published in one volume in Britain by Royalty Digest, Ticehurst, 1997
This edition published by A & F 2020

A & F Publications
South Brent, Devon, England TQ10 9AS

Typeset 11pt Georgia

ISBN-13: 9781656048271

Front cover: Tsar Nicholas II and Empress Alexandra; Sir George Buchanan; St Petersburg, c.1910

Printed by KDP

CONTENTS

Introduction 8

Preface 11

Illustrations 15

1. 1876-1880
Vienna — Rome — My journey across America — Experiences in the U.S.A. — On the way to Tokio 16

2. 1880-1888
Tokio — Vienna again — Austro-Russian rivalry in the Balkans — Bulgarian situation reviewed — Prince Alexander's abdication and Prince Ferdinand's election 24

3. 1888-1900
Berne — Darmstadt and Carlsruhe — My personal relations with Queen Victoria 32

4. 1888-1903
Agent on the Venezuela Arbitration Tribunal — Counsellor at Rome and Berlin — Anglo-German Relations — Agent and Consul General at Sofia 39

5. 1887-1904
Review of Prince Ferdinand's reign — The Prince's marriage — The era of Personal Government — Conversion of Prince Boris — Bulgaria and the Macedonian Insurrectionary Movement 46

6. 1904-1908
My reception by Prince Ferdinand — Bulgaria's relations with Greece, Serbia and Roumania — Prince Ferdinand's visit to

London — German, Austrian and Russian influence — Better relations with Russia 53

7. 1908-1910
Bulgaria and the Young Turkish Movement — Prince Ferdinand recognized as King by the Powers — My mission to the Netherlands — My appointment as Ambassador at St. Petersburg 62

8. 1911
Russia's relations with Austria and Germany — My first conversations with the Emperor Nicholas — The Potsdam Agreement and its genesis — Persian crisis — Russia claims extension of her maritime jurisdiction — The Povage case 72

9. 1912-14
Visit of representative British Delegation to St. Petersburg — Improvement of Anglo-Russian relations — Persian question — Action of Russian Consuls in Persia — Conversation with the Emperor thereon — Trans-Persian Railway 82

10. 1912-13
Austro-Russian relations — Growing unrest in the Balkans — Serbo-Bulgarian Treaty of February, 1912 — Formation of the Balkan Confederation — Balkan crisis — Balmoral Meeting — First Balkan War — Russia's attitude regarding the Balkan States - Serbian port on the Adriatic — Danger of an Austro-Russian conflict— Prince Godfried Hohenlohe's mission to St. Petersburg — Tension relaxed— Albania — Conference on Bulgaro-Roumanian Frontier question 90

11. 1913-14
Review of Russia's policy during the First Balkan War -Lack of solidarity in Triple Entente, as compared with Triple Alliance — Sazonoff in favour of Anglo-Russian Alliance — I am offered the Vienna Embassy — Second Balkan War — Treaty of Bucharest — General Liman von Sanders' appointment to Command of First Army Corps at Constantinople 101

12. 1910-14
Internal situation of Russia — Political unrest in the Universities— M. Stolypin, M. Kokovtsoff, M. Goremykin — Growing gravity of the situation 110

13. 1896-1914
My relations with the Emperor and Imperial Family — The Empress Alexandra — First audiences with the Emperor, 1896 — His great personal charm — The Empress Marie — The Grand Duchess Marie Pawlowna— The Grand Duchess Victoria and the Grand Duchess Xenia — The Grand Duke Nicholas Michaelowich 120

14. 1914
German criticism of Entente attitude — Russia's and Great Britain's desire for good relations with Germany — Presentation of Austrian Ultimatum at Belgrade 128

15. 1914
Conversation at the French Embassy — Sazonoff urges war can only be averted by our declaring our complete solidarity with France and Russia — H.M.G. assumes role of Mediator — Russia's conciliatory attitude — Course of negotiations — Austria declares war — Russia's mobilization — Germany threatens Russia — Ultimatum and declaration of war 136

16. 1914
Rebuts statement respecting my attitude with regard to our participation in the war — Emperor's War Manifesto — The nation rallies round the throne — Patriotic scenes at Moscow — The offensive in East Prussia— Battle of Tannenberg — Campaign in Poland — Russian shortage of munitions and rifles — Count Witte's peace campaign 147

17. 1914-15
Turkey's entrance into the war — Closing of Straits — Russia asks sanction to eventual acquisition of Constantinople— My audience with the Emperor on the subject — Negotiations with Bulgaria— Serbia is asked to make concessions in Macedonia— Allies and Serbia — Political agreement reached with Roumania 156

18. 1915
Russians in Carpathians — German counter measures — Mackensen assumes command — Warsaw and other fortresses surrender — The Emperor assumes supreme command — Rasputin's influence, his life and character — Reactionary Ministers dismissed — The Duma — Union of Zemstvos favour a

Government possessing confidence of the nation — Peace overtures — I am given G.C.B 165

19. 1916
Improvement in military situation — Success of Brussiloff's offensive — Roumania intervenes too late — Stürmer appointed President of the Council — I receive the Freedom of Moscow 179

20. 1916
The Polish question — Sazonoff is dismissed — Stürmer appointed Foreign Minister — Sturmer and the pro-Germans — I speak to the Emperor about the internal situation 188

21. 1916
Anti-British campaign by Germans — Trepoff and Pokrowski appointed respectively President of Council and Minister for Foreign Affairs — Policy of the Empress and motives — Rasputin's assassination — Change of Government in England 197

22. 1917
Trepoff resigns — Prince Golitzin as President of the Council — My last audience with the Emperor — Meeting of Allied Conference and its outcome 206

23. 1917
My telegram reviewing Russian situation for information of Imperial Conference — Revolution begins — Rodzianko's telegram to the Emperor — Attitude of the Government and of the Duma — The Emperor decides to appoint a military dictator and to come himself to Petrograd — Appointment of an Executive Committee by the Duma — Formation of Soviet — Emperor's offer of concessions arrives too late — Delegates sent to Pskov to demand his abdication — Appointment of Provisional Government — Grand Duke Michael provisionally renounces the throne — Prikaz No. 1 215

24. 1917
The Emperor and the Empress placed under arrest — The Empress's fatal influence — Character and education of the Emperor — Review of his reign — His fatalism and firm belief in a controlling Providence 226

25. 1917
Our recognition of the Provisional Government — I am accused of having promoted the Russian Revolution 238

26. 1917
Order re-established at Petrograd — Discipline of Army undermined — The Provisional Government — Struggle between Government and Soviet — Kerensky's views — Lenin enters on the scene 249

27. 1917
Struggle between Miliukoff and Kerensky — War aims — Conflict with the Soviet — The Government wins a moral victory — Kerensky becomes Minister of War and of Marine — Socialism dominant — The Cadets — Social Revolutionaries — Social Democrats — Bolsheviks 259

28. 1917
Mr. Henderson's mission, its genesis and objects — Convocation of all Russian Council of Workmen's Delegates — Anti-war propaganda of the Bolsheviks — Tereschenko's proposal for Allied Conference — Bolshevik rising at Petrograd 270

29. 1917
Kerensky appointed Prime Minister — Stockholm Conference — Moscow Conference and its results 281

30. 1917
Rumours of a counter-revolutionary movement — Rupture between Kerensky and Korniloff — Kerensky declines to treat with Korniloff and declares him a traitor — Korniloff orders troops to advance on Petrograd — Collapse of the movement — Korniloff resigns 293

31. 1917
Soviet regains the upper hand — The Democratic Congress accepts a Coalition Government — Conversations with Tereschenko and Kerensky — The Government summons a Provisional Council as a Consultative Chamber — Russia's representation at the Paris Conference 301

32. 1917
Rumours of a Bolshevik rising — Defeat of the Government in the Provisional Council — The Bolsheviks strike — Kerensky escapes — Bombardment of Winter Palace — Arrest of Ministers — Bolsheviks form a Government — Kerensky utterly discredited — Bolsheviks become masters of the North 310

33. 1917
Trotsky's proposal for an Armistice — His attack on the Allies — Trotsky refuses to allow British subjects to leave Russia 319

34. 1917-1918
My interview with journalists with regard to our attitude towards the Armistice negotiations — Signature of Armistice — Lawlessness on the increase in Petrograd — Trotsky's appeals to Allied peoples — Bolshevik aims — Our last day at Petrograd 330

35. 1918-1922
Our journey home through Finland — War Cabinet's telegram — My unofficial Russian work — British Russia Club — My views on the Russian situation and on the policy of intervention — My appointment as Ambassador at Rome — Our two years in Italy — My wife's death 341

To

MY WIFE

In Memoriam. April 21-25, 1922.

She knew not Death was at the door,
    But lay transfigured, while her eyes
    Glowed with a light from Paradise,
Where her sweet soul so soon would soar.

She looked so radiantly fair
    And younger by a score of years,
    As, smiling at me through her tears,
She raised her hands in silent prayer.

With that smile lingering on her face,
    She passed into another land:
    I pressed a lily in her hand,
And laid her in her resting-place.

G. W. B.

INTRODUCTION

Born in Copenhagen on 25 November 1854, George was the youngest son of Sir Andrew Buchanan (1807-82), who served as ambassador in Prussia, Russia and Austria. He entered diplomatic service in 1876, and held posts in various cities including Tokyo, Vienna, Berne and Rome. In 1899 he was appointed Chargé d'Affaires at Darmstadt and Karlsruhe. After subsequent appointments at Berlin, Bulgaria, Netherlands and Luxembourg, in 1909 he was invested with the Knight's Grand Cross of Royal Victorian Order. One year later he was sworn of the Privy Council and became British Ambassador to Russia.

Remaining on the best of terms with Tsar Nicholas II (whom he called 'one of the most pathetic figures in history') and at the same time with some of the major advocates of liberal reform, he found his employment an increasingly thankless one as the internal situation in the empire deteriorated during the First World War. An active supporter of the Duma in its efforts to bring constitutional government to Russia, he tried to persuade the Tsar to grant reforms, but found his advice counted for nothing against the attitude of the Tsarina, who insisted that her husband was pledged to uphold the autocracy and could not share his power with anyone. In his final meeting with the beleaguered sovereign during the first few days of January 1917, he told him bluntly that:

> If I were to see a friend walking through a wood on a dark night along a path which I knew ended in a precipice, would it not be my duty, sir, to warn him of his danger? And is it not equally my duty to warn Your Majesty of the abyss that lies ahead of you? You have, sir, come to the parting of the ways, and you have now to choose between two paths. The one will lead you to victory and a glorious peace – the other to revolution and disaster. Let me implore Your Majesty to choose the former. (Chapter 22, p.208)

By that time it was too late to avert the impending disaster, and a few weeks later the curtain came down on three centuries of Romanov rule in Russia. The ambassador developed close relations with the liberal provisional government under George Lvov and then Alexander Kerensky, but feared that it would be eclipsed all too soon by the hardline leadership of the Bolsheviks. When that came to pass, he warned that the former empire would be engulfed in anarchy and disorder. After his forebodings were realized by the October revolution and the events that followed, he was widely – and unfairly – blamed for failing to ensure a passage from Russia to safety abroad of the former Tsar and his family, who were held captive in ever more degrading conditions until their execution at Ekaterinburg in July 1918. His health and that of his wife, Lady Georgina, had suffered under the strain, and the family left St Petersburg on 26 December 1918, arriving back in Scotland three weeks later. Following a period of recuperation in Cornwall, he was offered and accepted a two-year post as ambassador in Rome from 1919 to 1921.

His wife, Lady Georgina, had been responsible for the organization of the hospital for the Russian wounded created by the British colony in St Petersburg. When one of the provisional government's women's battalions, created in 1917 to shame the men into continuing the war, was seized by the Bolsheviks after participating in the defence of the Winter Palace in October 1917, it was largely owing to her firmness and courage that the safety of the women was assured. After they returned to England, she devoted no little effort to organising relief for Russian refugees. Yet she was already stricken with cancer by the time they left Rome and came home to England together for the last time, and she died in April 1922.

Her widower published the present work in two volumes in 1923, Chapters 1-18 comprising the first, Chapters 19-35 the second. As it was only five years since the massacre of the former Tsar and his family at Ekaterinburg, the controversy that had raged over their fate and the fact that they were not escorted out of Russia in time, he allegedly had to be circumspect in his account of the previous few years in Russia, or else risk losing his pension. He died at his home, 15 Lennox Gardens, London, on 20 December 1924. His obituary in *The Times* two days later wrote:

> Upright, urbane, tactful, and patient, imbued with the highest sense of duty, and perhaps for this very reason hyper-sensitive to ignorant or passionate criticism when it imputed to him any neglect of duty, he could make no enemies among all those who knew him well.

His daughter Meriel published several works, including *Recollections of imperial Russia* (1923), *The dissolution of an empire* (1932),

Queen Victoria's relations (1954), and *Ambassador's daughter* (1958), one year before her death.

Discreet though they may be, Buchanan's memoirs remain an invaluable record of the last few years of the Romanov era, as the upheavals of 1917 and beyond became ever more inevitable. This edition includes the full unabridged text of the original edition, apart from the index which has been omitted. My only modification has been to standardise the chapter numbering in western numerals throughout, instead of Roman numerals for headings throughout the text and western numerals on the contents page.

John Van der Kiste

PREFACE

Of the making of many books there is at present no end; any more than there was in the days of the Preacher. If I am now adding to their number, it is not so much for the purpose of recounting all that I saw and did during the forty-five years of my diplomatic life, as of endeavouring to throw fresh light on some of the great political events with which I have been either directly or indirectly associated. From the point of view of political work Sofia and Petrograd were my two most important posts, and, though I have given sketches of my earlier ones, it is with Bulgaria and Russia that the major part of this book is concerned. During my five years' mission to the former I assisted at the declaration of Bulgarian independence and the subsequent recognition of Prince Ferdinand as King. At the latter, where I spent rather more than seven years, I witnessed the outbreak of the Great War, the overthrow of the Empire, the rise and fall of the Provisional Government, and the Bolshevik Revolution.

It was while I was Second Secretary at Vienna that I first met Prince Ferdinand — then an officer in an Austrian cavalry regiment — and I was there when he, in 1887, offered himself as a candidate for the Bulgarian throne, which had become vacant in consequence of Prince Alexander's abdication. So few people now remember what happened in the Balkans forty years ago that I have briefly sketched the history of Bulgaria between 1885 and 1904 — the year in which I was appointed Agent and Consul-General at Sofia — in order that its later developments, as well as the mixed feelings of gratitude and suspicion with which Russia was regarded by many Bulgarians, may be the better understood. This sketch, and the chapters covering the period of my mission, are founded on the official reports written by me at the time, and I have adhered to the views expressed in those reports without allowing myself to be influenced by the part which Prince Ferdinand and his country played in the war. I have, indeed, followed this rule throughout my book, and in writing about Russia and the Russians I have been guided by the views recorded either in my official or in my private correspondence when I was at Petrograd.

I left Sofia in 1909, and after a year's interlude at The Hague I found myself once more drawn into the vortex of Balkan politics when I took up my appointment as Ambassador at Petrograd at the end of 1910. For the first year or so the Balkans remained more or less quiescent, and it was to questions affecting the maintenance of the Anglo-Russian understanding that I had to give my immediate attention. For the general reader the chapters dealing with the so-called Potsdam Agreement and the oft-recurring controversies about Persia may seem unattractive; but they are of historical interest, since there were, as I have shown, moments when those two questions threatened to shipwreck that understanding. Had they done so, the whole course of recent history might have been changed. The situation was fortunately saved, thanks to the untiring efforts of Sir Edward Grey and M. Sazonoff; and when, in 1912, the Balkan question once more entered on an acute stage, the two Governments worked wholeheartedly together for the maintenance of European peace.

I have passed in review each successive phase of that crisis: the Serbo-Bulgarian Treaty of Alliance of 1912, the formation of the Balkan Confederation, the first Balkan War, the rival claims of Austria and Russia that so nearly involved all Europe in the conflict, the conclusion of peace on terms that constituted the triumph of Slavdom and then the mad quarrel of the Balkan allies over the spoils, the second Balkan war and the Treaty of Bucharest which undid all that had been achieved by the first war. I have shown how Russia, torn between the wish of furthering Slav interests and the fear of international complications, more than once during the crisis had to readjust her policy; and, though loath to criticize my old friend and collaborator, I have pointed out certain mistakes which Sazonoff, in my opinion, committed.

I have, on the other hand, had the satisfaction of vindicating his conduct of the negotiations which followed the presentation of the Austrian ultimatum at Belgrade, and of being able, from personal knowledge, to affirm that he left no stone unturned in his desire to avoid a rupture. I have, at the same time, refuted the charges advanced by certain German writers and shown how utterly unfounded is their contention that Russia wanted war and that we egged her on by promising her our armed support. As regards the war itself, I have but outlined the course of the military operations so as to explain their bearing on the internal situation, more especially after the army, left almost defenceless before the enemy, had in 1915 suffered disaster after disaster.

It has been a melancholy task to trace the gradual decline of a great Empire – to contrast the enthusiasm and the promise of the early war-days with the depression and progressive collapse that followed; to picture a united nation rallying in loyal devotion round its Sovereign, and then to depict the same nation, weary of the sufferings and privations imposed on it by an utterly incompetent administration, turning against that Sovereign and driving him from the throne. Nor has it been less sad to follow in the Emperor's footsteps and to watch him, with his inbred fatalism, deliberately choosing a path that is to lead him and his to their doom. I have not attempted to screen his faults; but I have portrayed him as I knew him – a lovable man, possessed of many good qualities, a true and loyal ally, having, in spite of all appearances to the contrary, his country's true interests at heart. In explaining the rôle played by the Empress, I have shown how she, though a good woman, actuated by the best of motives, was instrumental in bringing about the final catastrophe. Her fatal misconception of the meaning of the crisis through which Russia was passing made her impose on the Emperor Ministers who had no other recommendation than that they were prepared to carry out her reactionary policy. Those of my readers who expect to find new and sensational revelations of Rasputin's doings at the Russian Court will be disappointed. I have told what I believe to be the truth about him without retailing all the unfounded gossip that has gathered round his name.

I have described in detail the progress of the Revolution, the constitution of the Provisional Government, its long-drawn-out struggle with the Soviet, its failure to arrest the demoralization of the army, its deplorable weakness in dealing with the Bolsheviks, its tactless handling of the Korniloff episode, and its final collapse before the Bolshevik onslaught. My work in treating this period has been facilitated by the permission, kindly given me by Sir Eyre Crowe, to consult my official correspondence in the archives of the Foreign Office; and by the valuable assistance which the librarian, Mr. Gaselee, was so good as to lend me in the matter. As the Provisional Government and the old Autocracy have both disappeared from the scene, I have been able to tell the story of my mission to Russia with far greater freedom than would otherwise have been possible. I have approached the subject from the objective standpoint, and have endeavoured, in my judgment of men and things, to play the part of an impartial observer, whose views on the great Russian tragedy may be of service to the future historian.

If I have given this book the form of memoirs, and have said much more about myself than I had originally intended, the responsibility lies with that great master-critic, my friend Edmund Gosse. He has shown such a kindly interest in the progress of my work, and has so impressed me with the importance of the personal equation, that I have recast some of the chapters so as to satisfy his craving for more personal touches." Though I could never induce him to put life into my poor prose with a touch of his magic pen, he has given me a much needed moral encouragement for which I shall always be grateful.

G.W.B.

January 25, 1923.

ILLUSTRATIONS

Sir George Buchanan 177

Lady Georgina Buchanan 177

Tsar Nicholas II and his family, 1913 177

Crowds outside the Winter Palace, St Petersburg, at the declaration of war, 1914 178

Barricades at Liteyny Prospekt, St Petersburg, during the revolution, 1917 178

CHAPTER 1
1876—1880

Though diplomats cannot, like poets, claim the distinction of being born and not made, I may in a certain sense be said to have been born into diplomacy, for I was born at the Legation at Copenhagen, where my father was then Minister. He had begun his career under Lord Stratford de Redcliffe, after the latter's appointment as Ambassador at Constantinople in 1825, and when, half a century later — in April, 1876 — the doors of the diplomatic service were opened to me, the great Elchi, mindful of the above fact, sent for me and gave me his blessing, wishing me God-speed on my journey through life. A strikingly handsome man in spite of his ninety years, he still retained that commanding personality which had, for good or for evil, made him so long the dominating factor in the Ottoman Empire.

In my day entrance into the diplomatic service was by nomination, with a qualifying examination that did not impose a severe tax on a candidate's intelligence, while the work allotted to a newly joined attaché during his preliminary training at the Foreign Office was of a purely clerical kind, such as the copying of despatches and the ciphering and deciphering of telegrams. It had, however, its compensations, for it was a novel and interesting experience to be admitted behind the scenes and to get a glimpse into the inner workings of diplomacy, more especially at a moment when the Eastern question was looming large on the horizon and when the famous Berlin Memorandum was being drawn up by Prince Bismarck without previous consultation with Her Majesty's Government. The Queen, I remember, was so indignant at the slight thus passed on her Government by Prince Bismarck that she gave vent to her feelings in the following minute, which I read at the time on a despatch from Berlin: "Prince Bismarck is treating England as if she were a third-rate Power, and this makes the Queen's blood boil."

I only remained at the Foreign Office for a few weeks, as my father, whose term of service as Ambassador at Vienna was drawing to a close, had asked for me to be attached to that Embassy. For a young attaché Vienna was then a delightful post, more especially when he had, as the Ambassador's son, the entree into its exclusive society, where one was either *Du und Du* with all one's contemporaries or else more or less ignored. The Viennese were so keen about dancing that I remember once going to a ball at Prince Schwarzenberg's which began at eleven o'clock in the morning and continued till six in the evening; but the dances then in vogue and the etiquette that had to be observed with regard to them would hardly appeal to the fox-trotters of the present day. At the Court balls even the trois temps was vetoed as being *peu convenable*, while at every ball there was a *Comtessin Zimmer*, into which no married woman was allowed to penetrate. There the girls gossiped with their partners between the dances, keeping a jealous and watchful eye on any erring sister who ventured to overstep the bounds of the most innocent flirtation.

Dancing engagements, moreover, were booked for the whole season, so that one always had the same set of partners at every ball; while if one was prevented going to any ball, one had to find a substitute to fulfil one's engagements.

But, despite some of its old world ways and customs, I shall always retain the pleasantest recollection of Austrian society, of its kind and generous hospitalities, and of its *Gemüthlichkeit* — that untranslatable Viennese expression that has no equivalent in English. Apart, moreover, from its pleasant social life, Vienna could boast of a number of theatres of a very high order, which to an ardent playgoer like myself were a source of endless enjoyment. The Burg Theater was then still in its old quarters, adjoining the Palace, where, in spite of the smallness of its old-fashioned house, the actors were far more at home and in their element than they afterwards were in the more spacious and sumptuous theatre that was built for them a few years later. Sonnenthal and Frau Wolter were still at the zenith of their fame as exponents of the dramatic art, and with them and with a whole *troupe* of consummate artists the Burg Theater was no unworthy rival of the great French theatre in the Rue Richelieu.

Nor were one's amusements confined to Vienna, for in the autumn my father and I frequently went to hunt at Gödollö, near Buda Pesth, where even a humble attaché like myself was brought into immediate personal contact with the Emperor and Empress and the ill-fated Crown Prince Rudolph. Count Andrassy and many of the Hungarian magnates were also constantly to be met in the hunting-field, so that my father combined business with pleasure, while I spent most of my evening ciphering the results of his conversations with the Emperor and the Chancellor. But of all the followers of the hunt it was the Empress, with her radiant beauty, her fine seat on a horse and her wonderful figure, who was the cynosure of all eyes. Horses and the care of her figure were her two chief interests in life, and she carried her love of equestrianism so far that she even practised circus-riding in her private riding school at Gödollö.

Horses, too, furnished her favourite topic of conversation, and on one occasion my stepmother, who was no respecter of persons, after listening for some time to what the Empress had to say on the subject, dryly remarked: "*Est-ce que Votre Majesté ne pense qu'aux chevaux?*" History does not record Her Majesty's answer, but I should imagine that the conversation was brought to a speedy close!

After serving a year as attaché at Vienna I returned to the Foreign Office, and in 1878 I was appointed Third Secretary at Rome, where I spent a happy year and a half under the best and kindest of chiefs! – Sir Augustus Paget.

Rome will always cast its spell over all who come within its walls, but the Rome of forty-five years ago was more entrancing even than the Rome of to-day. It had not yet become a great modem capital, and was still to a large extent the Rome of Papal times. The new town, which now encircles old Rome, was still in its infancy. The beautiful grounds of the Villa Ludovisi had not yet been transformed into countless streets of commonplace houses. The builder had not yet laid a sacrilegious hand on the domain of the Campagna, which then almost reached the walls. The excavations in the Forum, which have added so much that is of interest to our knowledge of classical times, had, it is true, hardly begun; but, from the purely aesthetic point of view, the Forum was even more picturesque than at present.

Our Embassy was already installed in its present quarters at the Villa Torlonia, but a parsimonious Government had not yet sold the lower portion of its delightful garden, which was half as large again as at present. Flanked on the one side by the Aurelian wall, it was within a stone's throw of Porta Pia, so that, riding out through that gate, one could reach the Campagna in a few minutes and gallop for miles over its vast plain. In the winter, too, not being overburdened with work, I could generally manage to hunt twice a week, though, as one often danced till five in the morning, an early start for a distant meet was not always an unmixed pleasure. For Rome was a very gay place in spite of the division of its society into Blacks and Whites. The great palaces of the aristocracy, most of which are now closed, were then the scene of constant entertainments, more especially during the ten days immediately preceding Lent, when the carnival was celebrated. Society danced and feasted every night, while in the afternoon King Carnival, who has long since died a natural death, made merry in the Corso. The whole street was hung with gorgeous draperies, and there, from one of the many balconies, one watched and took part in the battle of flowers and confetti, as the revellers, in every sort of fancy dress, passed in their gaily decorated cars. Then, when the Corso had been cleared, the festivities closed with the curious spectacle of a race of riderless horses known by the name of "Bárberi."

By the end of 1879 my term had come for service at a distant post, and I was appointed Second Secretary at Tokio. Sorry as I was to leave Rome, I was enchanted with the idea of seeing the Far East and of being able to spend a couple of months in the United States on my way there. Among the many good intentions, with which I have helped to pave the abode of the wicked in the nether world, is that of keeping a diary.

As, however, my journey to Japan was one of the few occasions on which I did carry out this good intention, I am able to record some of the impressions which the United States of forty years ago made on me. Washington, as a town, did not smile on me, though the Thorntons, with whom I stayed at the Embassy, were kindness itself. New York I found much more amusing. Its cafes, I noted, could compare favourably with those of Paris, and its social life was altogether more to my taste. I was given dinners, taken to theatres and dances and introduced to all the pretty young ladies. Like so many of my countrymen, I fell a victim to their charms, and in less than a fortnight I became engaged — but only for twenty-four hours. My prospective father-in-law, whom I had never seen till I was ushered into his bedroom, where he was laid up with a bad attack of gout, told me, on my asking for his blessing, that he had no use for me as a son-in-law. He added, however, that I would live to thank him — and I have.

After leaving New York I spent a few days with some acquaintances near Boston. America, unfortunately for me, had not then gone dry, and my host's idea of hospitality was to take me round the various clubs and bars where I had to drink cocktails with his friends. On one occasion — it was a national anniversary of some kind — I actually drank thirteen before lunch; or, to be accurate, in the course of the morning, for luncheon did not see me that day. From Boston I went to Niagara, where I was joined by my friend Sydney Campbell, who was travelling with me to Japan; and, after paying the homage of our unstinted admiration to the Horse Shoe Fall, we proceeded together to Chicago. Here we got into touch with the business side of American life and devoted our short stay to visiting its stockyards and granaries. Continuing our journey, we crossed the Mississippi and the Missouri and soon found ourselves in the open prairie — one enormous plain, without a sign of life save a few stray cattle grazing, with now and then a grove of trees and an occasional farmhouse. "It reminds me," I wrote in my journal, "of the Campagna on a large scale — but of the Campagna stripped of all its beauty — of its ruins, its aqueducts, of the hills lit up by the warm Italian sun and of that glorious dome with its background of deep blue sky. Here all is cold, grey and melancholy — and so monotonous. You wake up in the morning and seem to be just where you were the evening before. Last night it looked better, as there were several large prairie fires, which relieved the dreariness of the endless plain." After passing Cheyenne we got our first sight of the Rocky Mountains — a pleasant change after the prairie — and we kept on ascending till we reached Sherman, more than 8,000 feet above the sea. The scenery, on the rest of our journey to Ogden and Salt Lake City, was very picturesque, with much red sandstone and many fine rocks.

The following description of the Mormon city is taken from my journal: "It is a very clean, prosperous-looking place, with unpretentious, neat houses surrounded by gardens or orchards. On the morning after our arrival we took a carriage; and our driver, an Englishman, acted as our guide and informant. First we went to the Tithe House, where all Mormons, including even the ladies of the *demi-monde*, have to pay in the tenth of what they earn. We next visited the 'Temple' — a granite building which it will take another four or five years to finish — and then proceeded to the 'Tabernacle.' This is a long, ugly, wooden building, some two hundred and fifty feet long, of an oblong shape, with a low roof. It can hold twelve thousand people, and, so remarkable are its acoustic properties, that we could hear a pin fall which our guide dropped some seventy yards from where we were standing. All the roof is hung with festoons of leaves so as to prevent the slightest echo. After leaving the 'Tabernacle ' we called on Mr. Taylor, the president of the Mormons, at the Lion House. He is a man between sixty and seventy, with nothing remarkable about him. He received us very courteously and kept us talking for some twenty minutes. He comes from Westmorland, and was in prison with Joe Smith when the latter was killed by the mob at Nauvoo. He was fortunate enough to escape himself with only a gunshot wound.

"As president he is not regarded with the same feelings of awe and reverence as was his predecessor. Brigham Young, unlike Mr. Taylor, was a man of genius and iron will who, when he donned the prophet's mantle on the death of Joe Smith, conceived the idea of a great emigration to the West, where the Mormons could live in peace, safe from the persecution of the mob. To carry out this plan he had to lead them across the prairies of Nebraska, through the mountain paths of the Rockies, and over the great American desert. This he successfully accomplished, and in July, 1847, the promised land was reached, though not without the loss of many lives. In the choice of a settlement he again showed his wisdom, and the extraordinary prosperity which Salt Lake City has attained is due to his energy, shrewdness and powers of organization. He was an extraordinary man, but coarse and entirely unscrupulous as to the means which he employed to maintain his autocratic rule. Since his death the influence of the Mormon chiefs over the people has sensibly declined.

"Brigham Young had sixteen wives and about as many more who were 'sealed' to him — an expression which seems to mean that, though not his wives in the strict sense of the term in this world, they aspire to be so in the next. Thus a woman may be sealed to one husband for this life and to another for the life to come. At present no one seems to have more than four wives, and most people find two enough, as the expenses of keeping them is greater than it was owing to the 'Gentiles' having introduced a more expensive style of living than formerly. Where there are two wives in one house the house generally has two doors. and the two establishments are thus quite distinct. Our guide pointed out a house from which wife number one had driven wife number two and pursued her, flying down the street in her nightgown. Brigham Young built a very fine house for his last favourite, which is called, after her, the Amelia Palace, and which is the house in the city. Utah is not a State, but a territory, and the United States Government appoint a governor. It makes its own municipal laws, subject to the veto of the governor. Drunkenness is punished by a fine of from five to ten dollars, and in the event of the offender being unable to pay his fine he has to make up the amount due by working on the roads. Judging, however, by the state of the roads, there must either be very few poor people or very little drunkenness in the Mormon settlement."

Continuing our journey to San Francisco, we crossed the Sierra Nevada, where our train was blocked by the snow slides, and we had to spend sixteen hours in the bar room of a miserable little station, sleeping, or trying to sleep, on the bare planks. One of the curious sights of San Francisco in those days was the Chinese quarter, round which we were taken one night by a policeman. The Chinese lived there quite apart, in a town of their own, with their own butchers, bakers, chemists, jewellers, etc. Although it was past ten o'clock, we found all the shops still open, and after looking in at some of them we visited the temple, theatre and women's quarter.

On April 24 we started on a trip to the Yosemite Valley, in spite of being warned that we should be stopped by the deep snow. We slept the first night at Merced, and then, hiring a buggy and pair, drove to Mariposa, where we passed the night. There we left our buggy and crossed the mountain on horseback, and after breaking our journey at Hite's Cove, a little mining village, had a delightful ride through the Merced Canyon into the Valley. I append my impressions as recorded in my journal at the time:

"Our path lay through woods sloping down to the river, which was tumbling over the rocks fifty feet below. The grass was a brilliant green and sparkled in the sunlight, the trees were all bursting into life, flowers of every hue covered the ground, while a shrub with the appropriate name of 'Red Bud' gave life and colour to the woods. There were ranunculi of the most delicate yellow, campanulas of the forget-me-not blue, there were red flowers, white flowers, purple flowers, and flowers of every colour under heaven. The hillside across the river was one blaze of bright orange, but we were not near enough to distinguish the flower itself. As we approached the Yosemite the scenery became wilder, and we once more began to ascend a narrow stony path as the hillsides became steeper and rocks took the place of grass. At three o'clock we entered the valley. My first impression was one of disappointment. I could not see what there was to rave about in those great rocks rising up so straight to heaven; they were grand and savage, but where was their charm? I failed at first even to realize their size. I soon, however, learned to understand and appreciate their unique beauty. It grew on me hour by hour, especially in the evening light. At the part of the valley where Bernard's Hotel is, one feels rather oppressed and imprisoned by the hills, but some two miles down the river the valley broadens. There we got on to a little sand island, at the foot of 'El Capitan,' and laid down for an hour after dinner. Lying there, looking up at that gigantic rock rising over three thousand feet straight into the air, faced on the other side by rocks of almost equal grandeur — the two forming a sort of frame to the landscape beyond — with the dark pines, standing out against the pale blue of the sky, so 'thick inlaid with patines of bright gold,' I felt how wrong my first impressions had been and how all that has been said of the valley falls short of the reality."

Re-reading the above description of the Yosemite after a lapse of more than forty years, I ask myself whether, could I be transported there once more, I should be equally impressed by its beauty and whether I should be prompted to give expression to my feelings in the same poetic language as when I was young. Sainte Beuve once wrote:

Il existe, en un mot, chez les trois quarts des hommes,
Un poète, mort jeune, à qui l'homme survit.

Alfred de Musset replied in a sonnet in which he contested the truth of this dictum, and after hiking Sainte Beuve to task for having blasphemed "*dans la langue des Dieux*," told him to remember

qu'en nous il existe souvent
Un poète endormi, toujours jeune et vivant.

I fear, nevertheless, that as a rule the poet born in us sleeps so soundly as we grow older that only some deep emotion, be it of joy or grief, ever rouses him from his slumber. For, worn by the battles and sorrows of life, we most of us find

That nothing can bring back the hour
Of splendour in the grass, of glory in the flower.

On leaving the valley we tried to return to Merced by another route across the mountains, but the snow was so deep that we had to get off our horses, and after leading them for three hours uphill at a snail's pace we gave up the attempt. Owing to the time thus lost we only reached the foot of the mountain that separates the Merced valley from Hite's Cove late in the evening, and had to make our way as best we could up a narrow bridle path, skirting the edge of a precipice which in places went sheer down for some two thousand feet. It was so pitch dark when we got to the top that we drove our horses before us and followed them on foot, as they seemed to be able to find the path easier than we could. We only got to Hite's Cove at eleven at night, dead tired and half famished.

CHAPTER 2
1880-1888

Leaving San Francisco on board the *City of Pekin*, we reached Yokohama on May 24, after a tedious and uneventful voyage of twenty days. Japan was then in a transition period. Though she had already started on the road that was to lead her, in such an incredibly short time, to the high position which she now holds among the Great Powers of the world, she was not so Europeanized and retained more of the picturesque charm of the Old Japan than at present. Save for the Tokio-Yokohama line, railways were non-existent. Though the area of one's travels was thus circumscribed, one saw what one actually did see of the country at much greater advantage travelling by jin-rickshaw and on foot than one could possibly have done by rail. During the long excursions which I made into the interior every summer I spent a night on the top of Fuji-Yama, that peerless mountain that rises for more than 12,000 feet so majestically from the plain; ascended Asama Yama, the great active volcano; went to Kioto, the ancient capital; visited Nikko as well as other shrines; shot the rapids on some of the rivers, and walked hundreds of miles across country, wherever my fancy took me, occasionally coming to places where Europeans had never been seen. Except on one occasion, when the keeper of a tea-house displayed the old anti-foreign feeling by refusing to take us in, we met with the most friendly reception, and the best rooms in the villages where we slept were always placed at our disposal. My native cook and manservant accompanied me on these expeditions, and, though when at home they never walked a yard, they were never too tired to provide me with an excellent repast even when, as on the occasion of our ascending Asama Yama, we had been seventeen hours on the move owing to our guides losing their way and bringing us down on the wrong side of the mountain.

When I was at Tokio the King, then Prince George of Wales, and his elder brother the late Duke of Clarence, who were midshipmen on board the *Bacchante*, came to Japan. The entertainments arranged in their honour were on much the same lines as those given the Prince of Wales during his recent visit. They included the, to us, novel sport of catching wild duck in butterfly nets as they rose from the water trenches into which they had been lured by decoy ducks; Japanese polo; dinners *à la Japonaise*, and a garden party at the palace. The Mikado also paid them the special compliment of going, if I am not mistaken, for the first time, on board a foreign ship of war as guest at a luncheon on the Bacchante. One expedition on which I accompanied them was to the famous bronze Buddha at Kamakura, some fifteen or twenty miles from Yokohama. We rode out a numerous party, but after a sumptuous picnic luncheon no one except the two young princes cared to make the return journey on horseback, so I had the honour of riding back alone with them in the evening.

Life in Japan was very cheap in those days, and, among other luxuries, I had a small stud of racing ponies. At Yokohama, where the British and other foreign colonies resided, there were two meetings every year, with separate races for Japanese and Chinese ponies, as the latter are far the better of the two. The Japanese, who were very keen on racing, always tried to prevent foreigners buying any of their best ponies; but at the Autumn Meeting of 1882 I was lucky enough to win the Champion Japanese Race, for the third time in succession with the same pony, and to keep the £100 Challenge Cup. At the same meeting I won the heavyweight race, riding myself, while my best China pony would have won the Champion China Race had he not been fouled by a Japanese jockey. On my appealing to the stewards of the Jockey Club, the latter questioned the offending jockey and, as he protested that he had not fouled my pony on purpose, awarded him the race.

Sir Harry Parkes, who was then our Minister at Tokio, was a very able man with a long record of distinguished services, and had, when attached to Lord Elgin's Mission in 1860, been treacherously arrested by the Chinese and kept in heavy chains for eleven days. He refused to purchase his liberty on terms that might compromise the success of Lord Elgin's negotiations, and was condemned to be executed. On the seizure of the Summer Palace the order for his execution was countermanded and he was released. Appointed Minister to Japan in 1865, he rendered the Mikado great assistance during the early years of the new regime and more than once narrowly escaped assassination. His temper, however, was not of the best, and he sometimes made things very unpleasant for his staff. On one occasion — it was before my arrival — they could not find a despatch which he had asked for. He thereupon went fuming into the Chancery, pulled all the papers out of the archive press, threw them on the floor, kicked them about the room, and then, turning to the secretaries, exclaimed:

"That will teach you to keep the archives in proper order and to find despatches when I want them." He was absent on leave when I arrived in Tokio, and had, when in London, been given a hint by the Foreign Office to treat his staff with greater consideration. On his return he completely changed his tactics and, in all his dealings with me, he was courtesy itself. He showed me much kindness, and he never gave me any cause for complaint save as regarded the length of his despatches. After copying one that covered more than four hundred pages of foolscap I felt inclined to remind its author of what Sheridan said to Gibbon, when the latter thanked him for having spoken in the House of "that luminous writer Gibbon" — "Not luminous; I said voluminous!"

I left Japan early in 1883 and returned home, stopping on the way at Hong Kong, Ceylon, Cairo, Malta and Gibraltar. After taking a long leave I once more went to Vienna, where I had been appointed Second Secretary, my pleasure in returning to my old post being enhanced by the fact that the Pagets were about the same time transferred there from Rome.

In the following year I became engaged to Lady Georgina Bathurst, in spite of dear Sir Augustus's warning that for a poor man like myself to marry would spell ruin for my career. Marriage is always a great adventure, and to embark on it on £1,000 a year in one of the most expensive capitals in Europe was no doubt a somewhat rash proceeding; but, fortunately, Sir Augustus proved a false prophet, for my marriage gave me a helpmate, who not only made my life an ideally happy one, but who, by her personality and by her happy gift of inspiring friendship, largely contributed to such success as I have achieved in my career. How we managed to live for three years at Vienna without falling seriously into debt is still somewhat of a mystery to me. We had a charming little apartment within a few minutes' walk of the Embassy, and we went everywhere and did everything, thanks chiefly to the kindness of our many friends. The Pagets always took us with them to balls and parties, so that we were spared the expense of keeping a two-horse *fiacre* — for one-horse carriages were tabooed in society— while other friends drove us to the races and placed their boxes at the opera and theatres at our disposal. One of the most expensive items in our budget was that of country-house visits for shooting and hunting, on account of the tips which they entailed, but we paid many such visits to the Kinskys, Larisches, Apponyis and other friends.

Princess Pauline Metternich, whose husband had been Austrian Ambassador in Paris under the Second Empire, was then the recognized leader of Viennese society. She had taken the Rothschilds under her special protection, and it was thanks to her influence that they were for the first time admitted within its charmed circle. She organized Blumen-Corsos in the Prater, which so captivated the pleasure-loving Viennese that they sang her praises in the following quatrain:

> *Es giebt nur eine Kaiserstadt,*
> *Es giebt nur ein Wien;*
> *Es giebt nur eine Fürstin,*
> *Metternich Pauline.*

But amongst all the entertainments which she organized in our time the one which I remember best was a musical revue given at the Palais Schwarzenberg, entitled the *Götterdämmerung in Wien*, in which the gods and goddesses, bored with Olympus, come to Vienna in various disguises in search of Hebe, who had fled there. After visiting all the sights of the capital and assisting at a variety entertainment that included scenes from the *Wiener Walzer*, *Excelsior*, and the *Zigeuner Baron*, they eventually find Hebe in the Wurzel Prater and return rejuvenated to Olympus. Princess Metternich had herself, in collaboration with Baron Bourgoing, a former French diplomat, written the libretto, and had, by enlisting the services of all the most beautiful women of the Austrian aristocracy, including Prince Kinsky's two daughters, Princess Montenuovo and Countess Wilczek, Countess Czernin, Countess Amelie Podstatsky, Baronin Bourgoing and Countess Irma Schönborn — who afterwards married Prince Fürstenberg, the Emperor William's friend — converted the final apotheosis into a dream of fair women.

Politically speaking, Vienna as a post derived its main interest from the conflicting ambitions of Austria and Russia in the Balkans; and as I shall have so much to say about the Balkan question in subsequent chapters, a brief review of the acute crisis through which it was then passing may help to explain its later developments. The aim of Russia's policy ever since the War of Liberation had always been to make Bulgaria a Russian province, and with this end in view she had placed the Government of the principality under the control of specially selected generals. Whenever Prince Alexander ventured to dispute their authority he was reminded that he was but the instrument of the Tsar, till, finding his position intolerable, he effected a reconciliation with the Liberal party, in the hope of emancipating his adopted country from Russian domination.

In September, 1885, a successful coup d'état at Philippopolis had resulted in the proclamation of the union of the province of Eastern

Roumelia with the principality, and in the assumption by Prince Alexander of the title of Prince of Northern and Southern Bulgaria. This was such a flagrant violation of the Treaty of Berlin that Europe could not condone it off-hand, while Russia at once declined to recognize a union which had been effected without her intervention. The Tsar marked his disapproval by striking Prince Alexander's name off the roll of the Russian army and by recalling all the Russian officers from Bulgaria. At the same time, through his ambassador at Constantinople, he encouraged the Sultan to restore the status quo ante in Eastern Roumelia by force of arms. The idea of such a Turkish execution found favour with Russia's associates in the *Drei Kaiser Bund*, and the execution was only stayed by the firm attitude of Her Majesty's Government, who recognized the advantage of having a strong Bulgaria as a bulwark against future aggression.

Had Austria adopted a bolder attitude and recognized the union as an accomplished fact she might have supplanted Russia at Sofia ; but Count Kalnoky's one desire was to avert the danger of a breach with Russia, while he was afraid that by supporting Bulgaria he might weaken Austria's influence at Belgrade. Meanwhile Greece and Serbia, disturbed by the idea of Bulgaria's aggrandisement, were actively preparing to assert their claims to territorial compensation; and though, thanks to the intervention of the Powers, the former was forced to hold her hand, the latter declared war on Bulgaria in November, 1885. The position of the Bulgarian army, disorganized by the recall of its Russian officers, and stationed for the most part in Eastern Roumelia, seemed almost desperate. A small number of troops had, however, been posted near the Serbian frontier, and by forced marches Prince Alexander succeeded in bringing up the rest of his army to their support and in routing the Serbian army after a three days battle at Slivnitza. Following up his victory, he occupied Pirot; but his march on Belgrade was arrested by an Austrian ultimatum to the effect that, if he attempted to advance any farther, he would find himself face to face with the Austrian army. Finally, after prolonged negotiations, a conference of the Powers at Constantinople adopted a formula conferring on the Prince of Bulgaria in the abstract, instead of on Prince Alexander personally, the Governor-Generalship of Eastern Roumelia for a term of five years, in accordance with Article xvii of the Treaty of Berlin, under which the consent of all the Powers would be required for its renewal.

The fact that this union ,was but a personal one was at once exploited by Russia to undermine the power of the prince and to represent him as the one bar to the real union which Russia was prepared to confer on Bulgaria, and a few months later a military conspiracy, working under her auspices, brought about his abduction and enforced abdication. Recalled almost immediately by a counter-revolution, the Prince landed at Roustchouk and addressed a last but fatal appeal to the Tsar in a telegram which, after announcing his return, concluded with the words: "Russia gave me my crown. I am ready to return it into the hands of her Sovereign." The Emperor's reply was a crushing one. He disapproved of the Prince's return and declared that he would abstain from all intervention in the affairs of the principality so long as His Highness remained in Bulgaria. Despairing of being able to reign in the face of Russia's opposition, and alarmed by the discovery of the widespread character of the recent plot. Prince Alexander abdicated and, after appointing a regency composed of Stambuloff and two others, left Bulgaria on February 8, 1886.

There followed a prolonged crisis fraught with danger to the peace of Europe. Russia refused to recognize the regency and despatched General Kaulbars to Sofia, with the mission of terrorizing the Bulgarians into submission. Tn spite, however, of his declaring the elections invalid, the Grand Sobranje met and occupied itself with the difficult task of finding a prince willing to accept the thorny crown which Prince Alexander had laid down. Prince Waldemar of Denmark was eventually elected, but declined the honour, while the Prince of Mingrelia, Russia's candidate, whose name had been submitted by the Porte, was categorically vetoed by Stambuloff.

Austria, meanwhile, though the most directly interested of the Powers, had observed an expectant attitude, as Count Kalnoky cherished the hope that Russia, if left to herself, would end by estranging Bulgaria for all time. Her Majesty's Government, on the other hand, were seriously preoccupied by the prospect of an eventual Russian advance on Constantinople, and Sir Augustus Paget was consequently instructed to sound the Austrian Government as to the steps to be taken to avert the danger of Bulgaria's falling completely under Russian influence and to urge the importance of the two Governments acting in concert. Count Kalnoky received these overtures in a friendly spirit, but contended that so far there had been no violation of the international status of Bulgaria, and that only when this happened would the time for intervention have arrived. Her Majesty's Government replied by citing all the illegal acts committed by General Kaulbars in support of their view that the time had already come for united European action.

Count Kalnoky, however, did not place sufficient confidence in the material support, which he was likely to receive from Great Britain, to commit himself to a policy of active intervention; and, though both

Governments acknowledged the identity of their interests, no regular understanding was arrived at. He was, nevertheless, somewhat reassured by Lord Salisbury's statement at the Guildhall Banquet on November 9, that, if British interests were directly threatened. Great Britain would know how to defend them with her own right arm, and that in questions in which she was only indirectly interested the attitude adopted by Austria would largely contribute to shape the policy of Her Majesty's Government. Fortunately about this time the situation was somewhat eased by Kaulbars breaking off diplomatic relations with the Bulgarian Government; and the regents profited by his departure to send a delegation to the various capitals with a view to ending the interregnum. On their arrival at Vienna, Prince Ferdinand of Coburg, on his own initiative and prompted by motives of personal ambition, offered himself as a candidate for the vacant throne, though neither the Emperor nor Count Kalnoky approved of his doing so. The latter, indeed, remarked in the course of a private conversation that the Prince had too much the airs and manners of a *vieille cocotte* to make a suitable successor to Prince Alexander.

Prince Ferdinand had at first attached a condition to his acceptance of the princely crown that was almost equivalent to a refusal, namely, that he should be confirmed by the Porte and approved by the Powers, and it was only six months later, in July, 1887, that he was formally elected Prince of Bulgaria. Russia objected to his election as being an infraction of Article III of the Treaty of Berlin, which stipulated that the Prince should be "freely elected"; whereas, according to her contention, he had been elected under the dictation and tyranny of the regency, itself an illegal body, by an assembly illegally constituted, owing to the presence in it of deputies from Eastern Roumelia. Count Kalnoky's attitude was very similar to that of Her Majesty's Government. He considered that the Grand Sobranje had acted strictly within its legal rights, but regretted that its choice had not fallen on a better candidate. A few days before Prince Ferdinand's departure for Sofia he urged him to adhere to his original intention and to await the assent of the Powers, pointing out that, if he went without that assent, he would be acting the part of an adventurer and would enjoy no legal status. Germany's attitude was one of theoretical support of Russia. In Prince Bismarck's opinion it was desirable that there should be an understanding between Austria and Russia as to their respective spheres of influence in the Balkans, and that, while the former should be predominant in Serbia, the latter should be allowed to regain in Bulgaria the position which she had held prior to 1885. His one object was to deprive Russia of any pretext of ill-humour against Germany, and he held that, considering the innumerable mistakes which Russia had made in the political handling of the Bulgarian question, the larger the scope allowed her for action the more certain would she be to dig her own grave. The keynote to his policy lay in his conviction that France would never attack Germany unless the latter was at war with Russia, and he was therefore prepared to go all lengths to maintain friendly relations with the latter country. He told Count Kalnoky, however, that he need not *prendre au sérieux* such theoretical support as he (Prince Bismarck) might give to any proposals put forward by Russia, as his only object was to keep on good terms with her, while he was confident that no Russian proposal would ever materialize if seriously opposed by Austria, Great Britain and Italy. His confidence in the energetic action of those Powers was, nevertheless, not sufficient to tempt him to run the risk of offending Russia.

CHAPTER 3
1888–1900

In the summer of 1888 I exchanged into the Foreign Office and worked there till the end of the following year, when I was transferred to Berne, and at the end of 1892 I was promoted Secretary of Legation and offered the post of *chargé d'affaires* at Coburg. A hitch, however, occurred with regard to my appointment, as for reasons connected with the past life of the then Duke, the Queen objected to a married man being sent to Coburg. While the question was still under discussion between Her Majesty and the Foreign Office the sudden death of our Minister at Darmstadt provided a way out of the dilemma, and I was appointed to Darmstadt with the rank of *chargé d'affaires*.

Darmstadt was in every respect a more desirable post, as, owing to its central position and to its proximity to Frankfurt and Homburg, one could keep in touch with the outside world and extend the circle of one's acquaintances beyond the confines of what was virtually but a small garrison town. In spite, however, of its limited social resources Darmstadt as a residence had much to commend it. One could ride for miles on end in the surrounding woods ; one could, at no great distance, get excellent shooting of almost every kind of game – stags, roebucks, wild boar, pheasants, partridges, hares, and even capercailzie; and when not otherwise engaged one could spend one's evenings at the Court theatre, where plays and operas were given on alternate nights. The theatre, which was largely subsidized by the Grand Duke, was of a very high order, and it was there that I learned to appreciate and to understand Goethe's *Faust*. It was admirably put on the stage and admirably acted, the whole representation being extended over three nights, the first concluding with the scene in the *Hexen Küche*, the second being devoted to Gretchen's tragic love story, and the third comprising the whole of the second part in an abridged form. The social life, too, which centred round the Court was pleasant enough with its constant little dinners and informal dances; but what I look back to with the most pleasure were the days which I spent with my friend, Baron Max von Heyl, partridge shooting near Worms and stalking deer and chamois in the Tyrol.

Though, after the marriage of Princess Alice of Hesse to the Emperor of Russia, Darmstadt acquired a certain political importance in consequence of the frequent visits of their Russian Majesties, it was only what is commonly termed a "family post." Both the Grand Duke and the Grand Duchess were the grandchildren of Queen Victoria, the former through his mother, the Princess Alice, and the latter through her father, the Duke of Edinburgh and Coburg. The Queen, who had arranged this marriage, took a lively interest in all that concerned them, and during the six years which I passed at Darmstadt I had the privilege of being in direct correspondence with Her Majesty and of being honoured, together with my wife, with invitations to Windsor and Osborne whenever we were in England. There was, however, a *revers de la médaille* that rendered my position far from an easy one. The Grand Duke and Grand Duchess, like most young married couples, no matter what their station in life, liked to go their own way, and were apt to leave undone many things .which they ought to have done, and to do many things which they had better, perhaps, have left undone. Whenever anything of this kind happened, and more especially when they had omitted to answer letters or to pay befitting attentions to any of their elderly relatives who happened to be in their neighbourhood, the onus of remonstrating with them invariably fell on my shoulders. I was, moreover, expected to keep the Queen fully informed of all their doings and misdoings — a very invidious task, in view of the great kindness which their Royal Highnesses constantly showed' us and of the terms of intimate friendship on which they admitted us into their family circle. We were constantly invited to dine with them at the palace and to stop with them for weeks on end at their summer residence at Wolfsgarten, while they frequently honoured us with their presence at dinner.

Unfortunately their marriage, on account of incompatibility of character and temperament, did not prove a happy one, and as they gradually drifted apart it was no easy matter for my wife and me to try and smooth over difficulties and to prevent the complete separation which took place shortly after our leaving Darmstadt. We were both devoted to the Grand Duchess, who, in addition to the gift of beauty, had a wonderful personal charm and a way of saying things that was most attractive; and, as reason and right were on her side, she had our fullest sympathies. But this did not prevent my being perfectly frank and outspoken in the advice which I tendered, and as she realized that I only did this in her own interest she never resented it, and regarded me, as she said on one occasion, as "My kind schoolmaster."

During the summer months Homburg, with its cosmopolitan crowd of water-drinkers, was a never-failing resource, as one was sure to find among them friends and acquaintances from almost every country in Europe. It was at Homburg that I had the privilege of being brought into close relations with the Prince of Wales (afterwards King Edward VII), and it was thanks to His Royal Highness's kindness in representing to the Queen that my chances of advancement in the service would be seriously prejudiced were she to keep me indefinitely at Darmstadt that she eventually consented to my being given another post. The Empress Frederick, whose beautiful *schloss* at Cronberg was only a few miles distant from Homburg, was also most kind to us and often invited us to stay with her. Those visits were always as interesting as they were delightful. In the morning I generally rode with Her Majesty, and in the afternoon we all took long drives and walks among the Taunus Hills.

In the course of our conversations the Empress would often unburden herself on the subject of the anti-British feeling in Germany and of the difficulties with which she was consequently beset. As the mother of the future Queen of Greece she was naturally intensely interested in the critical situation in which that country found itself placed after the Turkish War, and I used sometimes to serve as the channel through which Her Majesty communicated her views on this question to Queen Victoria. But what interested me most was when the Empress, who was extremely well read, turned her conversation on to literary subjects and discussed the respective merits of some of the great English and German poets. One day, however, her memory played her false and she made a slip which rather embarrassed me. I had happened to quote some lines from the "Ancient Mariner," and Her Majesty at once said: "Oh yes. I remember them quite well. They are from Longfellow's 'Ancient Mariner.'" Though it was Hardly a courtier-like proceeding to contradict her, I could not help saying: "Your Majesty, I think, means Coleridge's 'Ancient Mariner.'" A somewhat heated argument followed that ended in a drawn battle, as neither of us would admit that the other was right. Our last visit to Cronberg was saddened by the knowledge of the fatal illness to which the Empress succumbed in the following year, but the courage and patience with which she bore her sufferings did but enhance the admiration and respectful sympathy which I had always entertained for Her Majesty.

Among the many Royal personages, whom we frequently met during our visits to Cronberg, were the Duke and Duchess of Sparta (afterwards King and Queen of Greece) and Prince and Princess Frederick Charles of Hesse - Princess Frederick Charles, who, like the Duchess of Sparta, was a daughter of the Empress Frederick, had married a younger brother of the Landgraf of Hesse, and the latter's name recalls to my mind an incident which is typical of the mentality of some Germans. The Prince of Wales had charged me with the mission of representing him at the christening of one of the Princess's children, of whom His Royal Highness was the godfather, and I accordingly proceeded on the appointed day to the Landgraf's schloss, where the ceremony was to take place. Some forty persons were present at the luncheon that followed the christening, and knowing how punctilious Germans are, I was careful, as I thought, to get presented to all of them. After luncheon the Landgraf engaged me in conversation and finally asked me whether I liked shooting. On my replying in the affirmative he said: "Then come and shoot pheasants here in December," without, however, fixing any particular day. As it happened, I had already arranged to go home on leave at the end of November, and I was trying to explain this, with many expressions of my regret, when he turned his back on me, saying: "You may go to h—." I was naturally somewhat taken aback, and as I saw a gentleman standing near me, whom I took for his equerry, I went up to him in order to explain and expostulate. As bad luck would have it, not only was this gentleman not his equerry, but he was also the one person out of the whole company to whom, by some oversight, I had not been presented. After looking me up and down, he interrupted my explanations by frigidly remarking: "Sir, in Germany it is customary that a gentleman does not speak to another gentleman without first being presented to him by a third gentleman." He then also turned his back on me. I was quite dumbfounded by this lesson in German manners, when the Princess's lady-in-waiting came up to me and said: "Mr. Buchanan, I have by chance overheard what passed in both your conversations, and all that I can say is that I am ashamed of my countrymen." The Princess afterwards sent for me and apologized in the most charming way for what had happened.

The Court of Carlsruhe, to which I was also accredited, was in all respects the direct opposite of that of Darmstadt. While, in the latter, etiquette was more honoured in the breach than in the observance, it was in the former rigidly enforced and reduced almost to a fine art. When invited to luncheon with the Grand Ducal family, one had to don an evening coat, with a black tie; and on the occasion of the celebration of the Grand Duke's seventieth birthday I remember beginning the day at eight o'clock in the morning in my blue dress coat, with brass buttons, and only discarding it at seven o'clock in the evening in favour of my full uniform. But the most trying ordeals were the interminable circles which followed a dinner at the palace, when one had to stand for two or three hours while the Grand Duke and Grand Duchess went the round of their guests. Nor was one always left in peace when one got to one's hotel, for on one occasion I was woke at eight o'clock by a royal lackey knocking at my bedroom door to tell me that, as I was no doubt going to the English church service at ten-thirty, the Grand Duchess had given orders for me to be shown over an adjoining hospital at ten o'clock; and as this amounted to a royal command, I had no choice but to submit.

If ever lambent dullness played around a Court, it was surely round that of Carlsruhe, and the town itself reflected the dullness of the Court.

Matters were not improved by the fact that during the concluding years of the nineteenth century, more especially after the outbreak of our war in South Africa, public feeling throughout Germany was strongly anti-British, and one was constantly exposed to having unpleasant things said about one's country. The Grand Duke of Baden was himself far too much of a gentleman ever to do this. A grand seigneur of the old school, he was courtesy itself; and if in the course of our conversations he alluded to the somewhat strained relations between Germany and Great Britain, he spoke rather in sorrow than in anger, and attributed our misunderstanding to the irresponsible language of the British and German Press. He even on one occasion put forward the somewhat fantastic suggestion that, in order to render the Press less potent for evil, the Powers should agree not to allow themselves to be influenced by what the Press of foreign countries might say about international questions, and not to use their own Press as the channel for their official utterances on such questions. He was, unfortunately, possessed with the idea that the important position secured by Great Britain in the world was due to the long-sighted and Machiavellian policy pursued by successive British Governments. Nor did he take me seriously when I remarked that His Royal Highness was paying our diplomacy an unmerited compliment, for British Governments were not, as a general rule, in the habit of looking far ahead. They rather, I added, adapted their policy to the requirements of the moment, and their practice of muddling through as best they could had on the whole proved most successful.

The Grand Duchess, who was a daughter of the old Emperor William, was, on the other hand, far less considerate and gave free expression to her feelings. As an ultra-German she held that Germany could do no wrong and that, consequently, Great Britain was entirely to blame if the relations between the two Governments were not so good as they should be. It was in vain that I tried to persuade her that there might be faults on both sides and that, if our two countries were to remain friends, they must each show due consideration for the other's national interests. On one occasion — either immediately before or immediately after the outbreak of the Boer War — she lectured me before the whole Court and marked her displeasure by not giving me her hand to kiss, as was usual at such an official reception.

I happened shortly afterwards, on going on leave to England, to be invited to Osborne for a couple of nights, and to be placed at dinner one off the Queen, when, much to my surprise, Her Majesty, who had been talking of the anti-British feeling in Germany, turned to me and said: "The dear Grand Duchess of Baden is the only friend whom we have in Germany." I ventured to reply that if Her Royal Highness had represented herself as our friend she had been careful to mask her true feelings; and I then proceeded to tell Her Majesty of my recent visit to Carlsruhe and how the Grand Duchess had gone out of her way to let me know that she fully shared the views then prevalent in Germany with regard to Great Britain. The Queen was quite taken aback at hearing this, and on my going on to describe how, both at Carlsruhe and Darmstadt, the crowds in the streets gloated over the telegrams announcing our reverses, which were posted up in the windows of the post office. Her Majesty said: "We shall not forget."

In July, 1898, Lord Salisbury offered me the post of British agent on the Venezuelan Arbitration Tribunal, that had become vacant by Michael Herbert's appointment as Ambassador to Washington. As it was the Queen's wish that I should nevertheless continue to act as *chargé d'affaires* at Darmstadt, I paid a flying visit to London, in order to settle how I could best combine the discharge of the duties of my new post with those of my old one. It was characteristic of Her Majesty's thoughtfulness that, knowing how short my stay in England was to be, she should have sent the following telegram through the Foreign Office; "The Queen wishes Mr. Buchanan to come to Osborne any day he likes." Sovereigns are not, as a rule, in the habit of showing such consideration for the convenience of one of their subjects, more especially when that subject happens to be but a junior member of the diplomatic service; but, judging by my personal experience, no Sovereign was ever more thoughtful for others or more grateful for the smallest service rendered than was Queen Victoria.

I had been fortunate enough from the outset to win Her Majesty's confidence. After the first rather alarming interview, when, on my appointment to Darmstadt, I had to wait in the gallery at Osborne for

Her Majesty to pass on her way to dinner and to fall on one knee and kiss her hand, I was never again afraid of her. I fell at once under the charm of her wonderful smile, and was always perfectly natural and frank in all my conversations with her. I nearly always found the Queen very easy to talk to and easily amused. On my telling her once that by a curious coincidence not only was November 25 the common birthday of the Grand Duke and Grand Duchess of Hesse, but mine as well, Her Majesty asked: "And were you born in the same year as they were?" I replied, with a smile, that that was an honour to which I could not aspire, as I was, unfortunately, old enough to be the Grand Duke's father. "How very stupid of me!" replied the Queen, laughing heartily at her mistake. There were, however, occasions when it was not so easy for me to reply to Her Majesty's questions with regard to affairs at Darmstadt. I remember more especially how embarrassed I was at a long audience, which I had during a Saturday to Monday visit to Windsor early in 1898, when I could no longer conceal from Her Majesty the growing tension in the relations of the Grand Duke and the Grand Duchess. After listening to what I had to tell her the Queen remarked: "I got up that marriage. I will never try to marry anyone again," and then proceeded to ply me with questions. When, however, I ventured to say that I had always tried to do my duty both by Her Majesty and by the Grand Duke and Grand Duchess, and that I trusted that she would understand how difficult it was for me, after being confided in by their Royal Highnesses, to betray their confidence by repeating what they had told me. Her Majesty at once said: "I quite understand, and I am very grateful." Both my wife and I had several further conversations with the Queen during this visit, and before leaving I received a charming letter from Her Majesty, enclosing two Jubilee Medals, which "She hopes they will accept as a mark of her gratitude for their great kindness to her grandchildren."

The last time that I saw the Queen was at Balmoral in October, 1900, on my relinquishing my appointment as *chargé d'affaires* at Darmstadt, when Her Majesty conferred on me the C.V.O. — a decoration which at that time was but rarely given. A few months later the great Queen, who had always inspired me with feelings of veneration and devotion, as well as of intense gratitude for the kindness and consideration which she had constantly shown me, entered into her rest.

CHAPTER 4
1888—1903

Few people, I imagine, now remember anything about our dispute with Venezuela respecting the boundary between her territory and that of the British Colony of Guiana, though it constituted at that time one of the burning questions of the day. It derived its importance from the fact that in 1895 President Cleveland had, in a message to Congress, espoused the cause of Venezuela, with the result that the question threatened to embroil our relations with the United States of America. It was to avoid this danger that, after prolonged negotiations, a treaty was signed at Washington in February, 1897, between Her Majesty's Government and the Government of Venezuela, under which the question of the territory in dispute was to be submitted to arbitration.

When in July, 1898, 1 took up my appointment as British Agent to the Arbitration Tribunal, the two contracting parties had already exchanged their cases and counter cases; and at the end of the year the respective arguments, which summed up the documentary evidence, were also exchanged. After a preliminary meeting held early in the New Year to settle certain questions with regard to procedure, the tribunal assembled at Paris on June 15, 1899. The court was composed of two British arbitrators (Lord Chief Justice Russell and Lord Justice Henn Collins) and of two American judges (the Hon. Melville Webster Fuller, Chief Justice of the United States, and the Hon. David Brewer, a Justice of the Supreme Court), with the well-known Russian jurist, M. de Martens, as president. The leading counsel on our side were the Attorney-General, Sir Richard Webster (afterwards Lord Alverstone and Lord Chief Justice) and Sir Robert Reid (afterwards Lord Loreburn and Lord Chancellor), assisted by the present Lord Askwith and the present Mr. Justice Rowlatt, while Venezuela was represented by General Harrison (an ex-President of the United States) and other eminent American lawyers.

The history of the territory in dispute went back as far as the end of the sixteenth century. As heir to Spain, Venezuela claimed the whole territory between the Orinoco and the left bank of the Essequibo — a claim which we contested on the ground that the greater part of that territory had for more than two centuries been successively under the control of the Dutch and British, and that since our formal occupation of the colony in 1814 it was by Great Britain and not by Venezuela that it had been developed. Counsel for Venezuela further contended that though, according to Article 4 of the Treaty of Washington, adverse holding or prescription legalized a title, that rule had been intended to apply to the fifty years prior to 1814 and not to the fifty years immediately preceding the signature of the treaty. This would have constituted such a serious modification of the conditions on which Her Majesty's Government had consented to arbitration that, had the arbitrators accepted the American interpretation of the article in question, we should have refused to proceed with the arbitration.

The Attorney-General, who was the first to address the court, presented the British case in a masterly speech that occupied thirteen sittings, marshalling all the facts of our case with extraordinary ability. He made the mistake, however, of dealing with it too much in detail and, as I ventured to remark at the time, he pulled down our house in order to show of what good bricks it had been built. This gave counsel for Venezuela the opportunity of seizing on the weak points in our argument and of demonstrating the inferior quality of some of our boasted bricks. When Sir Robert Reid rose to reply to two of the counsel for Venezuela, who had spoken for twenty-two days, the outlook was by no means promising; but, in a short and brilliant speech, he raised the discussion to a higher level and concentrated into it the very essence of the British case. He succeeded, moreover, in throwing ridicule on the plea of the prior right of Spain that formed the corner stone of the Venezuelan argument, and in drawing a telling contrast between the action of the Spaniards and the Venezuelans on the one hand and of the Dutch and the British on the other. Mr. Askwith next spoke and was followed by General Tracy on behalf of Venezuela. The Attorney-General then summed up for Great Britain, while General Harrison brought the oral argument to a close with a speech which, despite its force and eloquence, failed to make any serious impression on the court. The absence, indeed, of any affirmative evidence forced the General to found the Venezuelan case almost entirely on the contention that, as successor to Spain, Venezuela was vested with a prior and paramount title to the territory in dispute and to supplement this argument with criticisms of the British case.

Had the case been tried by an impartial court of justice, that would have decided it in the light of the evidence laid before it, the whole of the territory in dispute would in all probability have been awarded us. As it was, the boundary line fixed by the award did not entail the sacrifice of any serious British interests, though the mouth of the Barima was not left, as we had hoped, in the absolute possession of Great Britain. But with an arbitral tribunal, in which the litigant parties are represented by arbitrators appointed by themselves, the neutral president is naturally tempted to find some compromise that will secure a unanimous decision. Such unanimity had been lacking in all the arbitral awards that had been delivered between that on the Alabama claims in 1873 and that on the Behring Sea Fisheries some twenty years later, and Monsieur de Martens had special reasons for desiring to break through this rule in the case of the Venezuelan arbitration. The first Peace Conference, convoked on the initiative of the Emperor Nicholas, had met at the Hague in the month of July, and he was anxious to second his Sovereign's efforts in the cause of peace by securing a unanimous award that would go far to encourage other States to submit their differences to arbitration. Such a desire was laudable in itself, but the means which he employed to give effect to it were not above criticism. Having decided in his own mind on a boundary line that would constitute a fair compromise between the conflicting claims of the parties to the dispute, he approached their respective arbitrators in turn, and intimated that if either side declined to accept it he would give his easting vote in favour of the opponent's extreme claim.

The oral argument had occupied fifty-four sittings of the court, and, if the proceedings were unduly prolonged, the responsibility lay with the counsel for Venezuela, who had spoken for ten days more, than with our counsel. Though the most cordial personal relations were maintained throughout, there were, as was but natural, many sharp passages of arms between the opposing counsel. The Attorney-General, in spite of his able conduct of the case, did not like facing a difficult situation, and would always try to get round it by returning an evasive answer to any awkward question that was addressed to him. These tactics so annoyed General Harrison that on one occasion he rose and caused considerable amusement in court by remarking: "The Attorney-General reminds me of a large bird that has alighted on a branch too weak to hold him, so he spreads out his wings and goes flap, flap with them to keep himself in position." The General at the same time was moving his arms up and down like a bird's wings, and every time the Attorney-General tried to burke a question he quietly rose and repeated this pantomimic action.

It was with some diffidence that I had accepted the post as agent, as, apart from the novelty of the work, the position of an agent on a big arbitration case is rather an anomalous one unless he is prepared to be a mere cipher. The preparation and the conduct of the case were naturally in the hands of the great lawyers employed on it, and, though I took part in all their discussions, my role was rather to keep the Government informed of the result of their deliberations and of the line of argument which it was proposed to adopt. The Attorney-General, however, was always ready to listen to anything which I had to say, and when, as sometimes happened, I was not in entire agreement with him on some important question, I did not hesitate to say so, and on more than one occasion I succeeded in carrying my point. During the sittings of the court at Paris our respective positions were never quite clearly defined. While the Attorney-General was in the habit of speaking of me as "my agent," Lord Justice Collins resented his dubbing the Government's representative *his* agent, and urged me to retort by referring to "my Attorney-General" — a piece of advice which I naturally did not follow.

Besides having to arrange for the housing of all the members of the British delegation at Paris, I had to settle with the Treasury the amount of their salaries and subsistence allowances. This was rather an ungrateful task, as we are all inclined to rate our services at a somewhat higher figure than the Government attaches to them; but by making graceful concessions to the Treasury in minor matters I generally succeeded in getting what I wanted. To quote but one instance. The Lord Chief Justice protested that five guineas a day was not sufficient to enable him to live in Paris in a style befitting his high office, and pressed me to raise his own subsistence allowance to six guineas and that of his clerk from twenty-five shillings to thirty shillings. In submitting his request to the Treasury I said that I considered that Lord Russell's claim reasonable, but that I could not conscientiously support his request for an extra five shillings for his clerk. The Treasury thereupon not only granted his lordship the six guineas which he had asked for, but remarked, much to my amusement, that it was refreshing to deal with someone like myself who had the public's interest at heart. The clerk, however, did not suffer in the end, as on the conclusion of the arbitration I secured for him a bonus of fifty pounds.

My most difficult task at Paris was preparing for the Foreign Office a report of each successive sitting of the court, as, in such a lengthy and complicated case, it was no easy matter to summarize in a despatch the speeches of counsel and to appraise the value of their respective arguments. The labour which I bestowed on these reports was, however, amply rewarded by the Government's cordial appreciation of my services. I was given the C.B. and offered the choice of a small Legation or the post of counsellor of embassy. As I was anxious to get back to political work I opted for the latter, and at the end of 1900 was appointed to Rome, where Lord Currie was then our ambassador. During four out of the eleven months I spent there I was in charge of the embassy; but Rome in those days was a very easy post. Political interest centred round the Cretan question, which was dealt with in a conference of the representatives of the Powers more immediately interested under the presidency of the Italian Minister for Foreign Affairs, Signor Prinetti. *Tempora mutantur* – and in these days of storm and stress one looks back with envy to the time when such a question as the Government of Crete was one of our chief preoccupations.

In the autumn of 1901 I was transferred to the embassy at Berlin, the post which I had originally asked for. I was anxious to go there not only because Frank Lascelles, our ambassador, was a very old friend, but because Berlin was at that particular moment the most important of all our embassies. All who have read Baron Eckhartstein's remarkable revelations will remember how the repeated attempts made by our Government to come to an understanding and to conclude some sort of defensive alliance with Germany had been frustrated by the folly and insincerity of the Anglophobe clique in the Wilhelmstrasse. Great Britain was then at the parting of the ways, as the time had come when it was impossible for her to pursue any longer her policy of splendid isolation. She had either to range herself on the side of the Triple Alliance or to throw in her lot with France and Russia. During the Boer War Anglo-German relations had been strained almost to the breaking point by such incidents as the holding up and searching of the German steamers *Bundesrath*, *General* and *Hertzog*; and, while the excitement produced by these incidents in Germany was intense, the threatening attitude adopted by the Imperial Government had provoked a counter-irritation in official circles in London. In spite of this, however, the idea of a defensive arrangement with Germany was not altogether abandoned by His Majesty's Government, and as late as the spring of 1901 the question was once more broached by Lord Lansdowne. The reception, however, accorded to this tentative proposal by the Wilhelmstrasse was not encouraging, and the negotiations which followed only served to convince our Government that it was hopeless to look on Germany as a possible ally.

Shortly after my arrival in Berlin in October, 1901, Sir Frank went on leave, and I was consequently left in charge of the embassy. It was a moment of acute tension. In the Press calumnies of every description were being circulated respecting the conduct of our troops in South Africa, while in the Reichstag the latter were being denounced as mercenaries and accused of fighting behind a screen of women and children. In a speech which he delivered at the end of October repudiating these unfounded charges, Mr. Chamberlain cited incidents in the War of 1870 which were not to the credit of the -German army. These counter-charges did but add fuel to the flames and provoked a fresh anti-British campaign in the Reichstag, to which Count Bülow, who had recently succeeded Prince Hohenlohe as Chancellor, contributed a speech criticizing Mr. Chamberlain in the strongest terms.

A *chargé d'affaires* has but few opportunities of seeing so exalted a personage as the Imperial Chancellor; but Count Bülow, to whom I had been recommended by my friend and colleague at Rome, Baron Jagow, was good enough to ask me to dine, and I took advantage of a conversation which I had with him after dinner to refer to the recent debates in the Reichstag. I was, I proceeded to say, prepared to admit that, as a fighting force, the British army did not bear comparison with the German army. The navy was our first line of defence, and our army was, relatively speaking, a small one; but this fact did not prevent our being proud both of it and its great traditions. We resented its being treated as an army of mercenaries, and we resented still more the calumnious charges that had been made against it in the Reichstag. Men who volunteered for active service, men who were ready of their own free will to lay down their lives for their king and country, were, in my opinion, on a higher plane than men who were forced to do so under a system of obligatory service. His Excellency, I .was convinced, did not himself give credence to the stories which had been told about our troops in the Reichstag. I would therefore appeal to him, in the interest of the maintenance of good relations between our two countries, to intervene in the debate and to put matters right by explaining that the Reichstag had been misinformed as to the conduct of our troops. Count Bülow admitted that he did not personally credit the truth of these stories, and spoke with his characteristic charm and courtesy. But he was not a strong enough man to swim against the current, so he turned a deaf ear to my appeal, declaring that he could not interfere with the Reichstag and that it was impossible for him to say anything.

In December, 1901, the Marquis Ito arrived in Berlin on his way to London, and, as Japan was still hesitating between an alliance with Russia and an alliance with Great Britain, I was naturally anxious to ascertain what had passed between him and Count Witte during his stay at St. Petersburg. I had known the Marquis when I was a secretary at our Legation at Tokio in 1880, and, on renewing acquaintance with him at a party at the Japanese Legation, I tried to draw him by turning the conversation on to the subject of his journey. Japanese statesmen, however, are never very communicative. The Marquis, who had throughout our conversation maintained an attitude of studied reserve, declined to be drawn and eventually silenced me with the crushing remark: "I have had a most interesting journey, but I never allowed myself to be interviewed."

The Anglo-Japanese Treaty, which was signed some six weeks later, and the final abandonment of the idea of any defensive alliance with Germany, paved the way for the understanding with France which was to follow two years later. This new trend in British foreign policy did not help to improve our relations with Germany, and, though ostensibly normal and friendly, those relations became marked by a growing feeling of mutual distrust. Apart from the question of her naval programme, that constituted a direct challenge to our supremacy on the seas, repeated friction was caused by Germany's provocative action in China. This was more especially the case in the autumn of 1902, when I was in charge of the embassy, and I remember being hurried back from a flying visit to London, where I had gone in order to attend my wife's operation for appendicitis — an operation of so serious a character that her life was only saved by Sir Frederick Treves' consummate skill — in order to "rub in" the very bad impression which some recent step, taken by Germany on the Yangtse, had made on His Majesty's Government. I did so with such effect that the Foreign Secretary, Baron von Richthofen, who as a rule was the most courteous of men, lost all control of his temper and gave vent to his feelings in a torrent of angry words that did not serve any useful purpose. On reading the telegram in which I had reported this heated conversation King Edward was good enough to commend my outspoken language and to tell Sir Frank, who happened to be staying at Sandringham, that he had got a very good locum-tenens.

Of all my posts Berlin, despite its political interest, was the one which I liked the least, and as I had been sent there at my own special request, I sometimes felt, with Charles Kingsley, that I had been "cursed with the burden of an answered prayer." As a town it was unattractive and, except for a small circle of intimate friends who showed us much kindness, the social life, with its tedious afternoon receptions and stiff official dinners, was boring in the extreme. I was therefore not sorry to leave it on being appointed at the end of 1903 agent and consul-general at Sofia with the personal rank of Minister.

CHAPTER 5
1887-1904
REVIEW OF PRINCE FERDINAND'S REIGN

On August 14, 1887, Prince Ferdinand had taken the oath before the Grand Sobranje at Tirnovo, the ancient Bulgarian capital, and in a proclamation issued on the same day had informed "our free people" that he had mounted the throne of the glorious Bulgarian Tsars. The circumstances under which he had been elected have been already explained, and I propose in the present chapter to give a brief sketch of his career as a Balkan prince down to the date of my arrival at Sofia early in 1904.

For the first seven years he reigned and Stambuloff governed, and it was only after the fall of his all-powerful Minister in 1894 that he took the reins of power into his own hands. The first of these two periods was marked by the open hostility of Russia, by the ever-present danger of a Russian occupation, and by a succession of plots against his life. With his recognition in 1896 and the consequent resumption of diplomatic relations, Russia abandoned her openly hostile attitude, and endeavoured to regain by more insidious means the position which she had lost by her own folly. One feature there was common to both periods — on the one hand, the wounded pride of Russia claiming, by virtue of her sacrifices in the war of liberation, the right to direct the course of Bulgarian policy into her own channels; and, on the other, a young, virile and democratic nation struggling to maintain its independence and determined to shape its own destinies without the interference of any foreign Power. Prince Ferdinand was from the first anxious to reconcile these conflicting forces, as he was persuaded that neither Bulgaria nor her ruler could exist in the long run without the good will of Russia. He had, even before proceeding to Sofia, made advances to her through the Russian ambassador in Vienna, but without success. Russia was implacable, and twice in the next six months she endeavoured to make the Porte insist on his vacating the throne of which he had taken illegal possession.

Fortunately for Prince Ferdinand, Great Britain, Austria and Italy were alive to the danger of the establishment of a Panslavist regime in Bulgaria, and they not only discouraged the Sultan from taking a course that might have led to the employment of force by either Russia or Turkey, but they even empowered their representatives at Sofia to enter into private and unofficial relations with him. Though he thus continued to reign as a *de facto* Sovereign, with the unofficial support of the so-called friendly Powers, his position was long a precarious one. The army had never really transferred its allegiance to him, and the spring of 1890 was marked by the discovery of an extensive military conspiracy to dethrone him. The doubtful loyalty of the army made Stambuloff anxious to secure the Prince's recognition by the Sultan, but, in the face of Russia's opposition, his overtures at Constantinople met with no response. He did, however, succeed in obtaining *berats* for the appointment of Bulgarian bishops to the sees of Ochrida, Uskub, Veles and Nevrokop. He was the one strong man on whom the whole situation depended, and he dictated the Government's policy. While not hesitating when occasion demanded it to work on the Sultan's fears by means of veiled threats, he pursued a conciliatory policy. He restricted his demands to that measure of autonomy, to which Macedonia was entitled under the Treaty of Berlin, in the conviction that, were that autonomy once granted, the union of Macedonia with Bulgaria would follow as naturally and as irresistibly as the union with Eastern Roumelia.

Meanwhile the risk of assassination, to which the Prince might at any time be exposed in consequence of the plots of the Russophil party, rendered it more than ever desirable that he should marry and found a dynasty. In 1892 negotiations were opened with the Duke of Parma for the hand of his daughter. Princess Marie Louise. As the Duke insisted that the children of the marriage should be brought up in the Catholic religion, Stambuloff undertook to secure the revision of Article 32 of the Constitution, according to which the heir to the throne had to belong to the Orthodox religion. Russia at once entered a protest against a step which she held to be contrary to the religious sentiments of the Bulgarian people. In the country itself the idea was unpopular; but so indispensable did Stambuloff consider it for the Prince's marriage that, taking all the odium of the measure on his own shoulders, he forced its adoption on the Sobranje. Prince Ferdinand's marriage was celebrated in the spring of 1893, and, followed as it was at the close of that year by the death of his only rival, Prince Alexander, greatly strengthened his position. It at the same time rendered him impatient of the tutelage of a man who could brook no opposition to his will, even from his own Sovereign. Feeling that he was now strong enough to stand alone, he determined to get rid of a Minister whom he regarded as the chief obstacle to his official recognition by the Powers. The tension that had so long existed between them was brought to a climax by an incident connected with the resignation of the Minister of War, and Stambuloff tendered his resignation, which was at once accepted.

The fall of Stambuloff marked a turning point in the constitutional history of Bulgaria and inaugurated an era of personal government by the Prince, more especially in the domain of foreign affairs. He was succeeded by M. Stoiloff, the leader of the Conservative party, as head of a coalition government; but the Prince at once made it clear that he intended to be his own Foreign Minister. One of his first steps was to pave the way for a rapprochement with Russia by an exchange of telegrams with the Emperor Nicholas on the occasion of the death of the Emperor Alexander III in November, 1894, and by sending a deputation, under the Archbishop Clement, to St. Petersburg in the following July to place a wreath on the late Emperor's tomb. The reception accorded to the deputation was distinctly cool, and the only result obtained was an intimation to the effect that the admission of Prince Boris into the Orthodox Church would be agreeable to the Emperor and that a request for the despatch of a Russian agent to Sofia would be favourably entertained. But while he was thus endeavouring to regain the good will of Russia, his treatment of Stambuloff lost him the sympathy formerly felt for Bulgaria at Vienna and in London. Though repeatedly warned of the danger to which that statesman's life was exposed, the Prince's Government had not only taken no measures for his protection, but had even refused him permission to go to Carlsbad, and the cynical indifference which they displayed after his assassination in July, 1895, laid them open to the charge of being morally, if not directly, responsible for his murder.

Another cause of difference between the Western Powers and Bulgaria was the attitude of tolerance, and even of actual encouragement, which the latter Government had, since Stambuloff's fall, adopted towards the insurrectionary Bulgarian movement in Macedonia. That movement, in contradistinction to those of the Greeks and Serbs, was essentially Macedonian in its origin. It was a protest against the geographical limitations placed by the Treaty of Berlin on the national aspirations, which had been awakened not only by the Treaty of San Stefano, but also by the recommendations of the conference held at Constantinople on the eve of the Russo-Turkish War. In the *Projet du Règlement pour le Bulgarie* Europe had recognized the ethnographical claims of the Bulgarian race as comprising the three northern kazas of the Adrianople vilayet, the principality as afterwards constituted by the Treaty of Berlin, the Sanjaks of Uskub, Monastir (with the exception of its two southern kazas), the three northern kazas of Serres, and the kazas of Strumnitza and Kastoria. The publication of the provisions of the Treaty of Berlin was immediately followed by two ineffectual risings in the valley of the Struma, and in 1880 a conspiracy of a more ambitious character was discovered at Ochrida. No further risings were attempted for more than a decade, though the brigand bands, which had always existed in Macedonia, showed occasional signs of activity. The movement, however, did but slumber, and the idea of an eventual, if distant, emancipation was kept alive by the steady stream of emigration which soon set in towards the principality. The national sentiment, moreover, had been stimulated by the spread of the influence of the Exarchist Church. Prior to 1870 the Patriarchate had been supreme in all ecclesiastical and scholastic matters, while politically it had been a potent instrument of Hellenization. Since the last vestige of a Bulgarian Church had disappeared with the suppression in 1767 of the see of Ochrida, all Orthodox Christians had necessarily been Patriarchists, and allegiance to the Patriarchate was reputed, though quite erroneously, to carry with it the implication of Greek nationality. By the Firman of 1870, however, the Exarchate had acquired the right to appoint bishops to certain specified dioceses as far south as Fiorina, as well as to others where two-thirds of the Orthodox inhabitants acknowledged its jurisdiction. This right was from the first strenuously contested by the Patriarchate, and the conflict which ensued soon developed into one of races and politics rather than of churches and religion. The Exarchate, supported by Stambuloff, had aimed at establishing the preponderance of the Bulgarian element by means of bishops, priests and schoolmasters; but in 1898 a group of young Macedonians, finding the methods of the schoolmaster too slow, founded the "Internal Organization." While in Macedonia itself it could only exist as a secret committee, it established a regular political organization among the Macedonians in Bulgaria. So long as Stambuloff was in power the action of the latter was kept well in hand, but shortly after his fall its activities became more pronounced, and in 1895 the Macedonian Central Committee was founded at Sofia. Its methods were openly revolutionary: it collected money, enrolled hands and preached insurrection, while the Government remained a passive spectator, doing nothing to arrest the movement till compelled to do so in consequence of the serious representations of the Powers.

Meanwhile the feeling in favour of a reconciliation with Russia was gaining ground, and the question of the religion of the heir apparent was being openly discussed. In thus allowing Prince Boris's conversion to become an article of a political programme, Prince Ferdinand had neither gauged the strength of the religious objections of his wife's family nor foreseen the political pressure which eventually induced him to give effect to it. As a result of his having taken the reins of 'Government into his own hands, the attacks of the opposition were now directed against his person, and he had come to be regarded as an obstacle to the realization of the national wish. Plots for his assassination were discovered, and extraordinary precautions had to be taken for his safety. A ministerial crisis was threatened, and the Sobranje voiced the desire of the nation that Prince Boris should pass into the Orthodox Church. Before taking a final decision. Prince Ferdinand went on a pilgrimage to Rome in the hope of persuading the Pope to release him from the engagement which he had contracted on his marriage. His Holiness, however, was inexorable, and on his return to Sofia Prince Ferdinand, after first feigning to contemplate abdication, signed a proclamation providing for Prince Boris's confirmation according to Orthodox rites. The Emperor Nicholas accepted the office of godfather, while M. Tcharikoff was accredited as Russian diplomatic agent at Sofia. The Sultan at the same time recognized His Royal Highness as Prince of Bulgaria and as Governor-General of Eastern Roumelia; the other Powers gave their assent, and Prince Ferdinand's position was formally regularized. The recognition of the Powers had, however, been purchased by a moral sacrifice which, though imposed on him in great measure by reasons of high policy, was none the less prompted by motives of personal ambition. In breaking the solemn engagement which had alone rendered his marriage possible, or, as he preferred to put it, in sacrificing his child for the welfare of Bulgaria, he had loosened the ties which bound him to his own family and to the Western Powers. "The West," Prince Ferdinand told the Sobranje, "has pronounced its anathema on me; the day dawn of the East spreads its rays around my dynasty and illuminates our future."

But to return to Macedonia, where the Internal Organization had not been idle. The period of secret preparation, at which they had been working for five years, was in 1897 brought to a close. A period of action was inaugurated, while the committee was transformed into a terroristic organization whose decisions were executed by the bands. Every year that passed witnessed fresh excesses on the part of the Turks and fresh reprisals on the part of the committees. The attitude of successive Bulgarian Governments towards the insurrectionary movement differed only in degree, and, while condemning its criminal practices, they one and all sympathized with its aims. Whenever a crisis seemed imminent representations were made by the Powers at Sofia. Austria and Russia, however, did not always act cordially together, and the attitude of M. Bakhmeteeff, the Russian diplomatic agent, and of the Panslavist agents in the Balkans did not tally with the assurances of the official Russia at St. Petersburg. The presence of a Russian Grand Duke and of General Ignatieff at the fetes held in the autumn of 1902 to commemorate the taking of the Shipka Pass was not, moreover, calculated to damp the ardour of the Macedonian committees, and the language held by General Ignatieff was a direct incentive to action.

In December Count Lamsdorff himself paid a short visit to Sofia, during which he made it clear that Russia had no intention of allowing the committees to drag her into an armed intervention in the Balkans. On his journey home via Vienna he elaborated with Count Goluchowski a scheme of reforms, of which the principal feature was the appointment of Hilmi Pasha as inspector-general of the three Macedonian vilayets. This scheme, which came into force in February, 1903, was not far-reaching enough to satisfy public opinion in Bulgaria, and the Stambulovist Government — which came into power shortly afterwards — determined to resume its party's traditional policy of cultivating good relations with Turkey, while endeavouring to extract concessions by working on her fears of foreign intervention. The Russian Government, however, were opposed to a direct understanding between vassal and suzerain, and the Bulgarian mission that had been despatched to Constantinople for the purpose of effecting such an understanding returned empty-handed. Meanwhile in Macedonia preparations for a general rising were being hurriedly pushed forward, and in August the signal was given.

The Bulgarian Government were not prepared for war, and, despite the intense resentment aroused by the methods of repression to which Turkey had recourse, they so mistrusted the drift of Russia's policy that they were anxious to avoid an open rupture with Turkey. Russia, they believed, was playing a double game. While the Russian Ambassador at Constantinople was advocating a stern repression of the insurrection, the Russian agent at Sofia was supporting the cause of the insurgents — and both seemed bent on causing a breach between Bulgaria and Turkey that would furnish Russia with a pretext for intervention. The only result attained by the insurrection was to bring home to Europe the gravity of the situation as well as the necessity of adopting measures of a more thoroughgoing and practical kind. Thanks in great measure to Lord Lansdowne's initiative, an extensive reform scheme was concerted by Count

Lamsdorff and Count Goluchowski at Mürzteg in October. The principal points in this scheme were the appointment of an Austrian and Russian civil agent as assessors to Hilmi Pasha, the reorganization of the gendarmerie by a staff of foreign officers, the reform of the judicial administration, financial provision for the return of the refugees and so on.

Though some of its provisions were received with satisfaction by the Bulgarian Government, the scheme as a whole was vitiated in their eyes by the fact that the control of its application was vested in Austria and Russia, the two most reactionary and self-interested members of the European Concert. Such was the position of affairs when the outbreak of the Russo-Japanese War caused the Bulgarian Government to reconsider their attitude. Despite their apprehension of Russia's designs, they had always cherished the comforting conviction that, should they meet with a crushing disaster in a war with Turkey, Russia would come to their assistance; while, apart from the fear of finding themselves isolated in the hour, of defeat, they were preoccupied by the idea that Austria might take advantage of Russia's embarrassments to occupy the northern districts of Macedonia. Negotiations for a direct understanding with Turkey were therefore resumed, and in April, 1904, an agreement was signed that served to place the relations between vassal and suzerain on a more friendly footing, though, owing to Russian opposition, it failed to secure the extension, so much desired by Bulgaria, of the Mürzteg reform scheme to the Adrianople vilayet.

It was while these negotiations were still in progress that I arrived in Sofia, shortly after the outbreak of the Russo-Japanese War.

CHAPTER 6
1904-1908

So far as my personal relations with the Prince were concerned, I began my mission under favourable auspices, for, in signifying his agreement to my appointment as His Majesty's agent and consul-general. Prince Ferdinand had, in one of those well-turned phrases of which he was a past master, written: "*Enchanté de recevoir le fils de son père, qui était l'ami du mien.*" On the other hand, the official relations between the two Governments had for some time past been marked by a certain coolness owing to the extreme Russophil policy initiated by His Royal Highness. Nor had these relations been improved by an incident, which had led to a personal estrangement between the two Courts. On receiving the news of Queen Victoria's death Prince Ferdinand had called at the Legation and, in announcing his intention of attending the funeral, had stipulated that he should be given the precedence due to him as Ruler of Bulgaria instead of being treated, as he had been at the time of the Diamond Jubilee, as a cadet of the House of Coburg. The Prince had been informed in reply that this was not a fitting occasion to raise such a question, and that no change could be made in the procedure already sanctioned. His Royal Highness thereupon countermanded the arrangements made for his journey. He sent a deputation to represent him, but he himself spent the day of the funeral at Philippopolis, where he celebrated Prince Boris's birthday with a review and a gala luncheon to which the Russian representative at Sofia was specially invited. This "painful episode," as Prince Ferdinand termed what he regarded as a personal slight, had naturally seriously indisposed King Edward against him.

I had always looked on Bulgaria as the most important factor in the Balkans and, in view of the new situation created by the Russo-Japanese War, I was more than ever anxious to wean her if possible from too great dependence on Russia. I had, therefore, when presenting my letters of credence, laid stress, with Lord Lansdowne's sanction, on the sympathetic interest with which His Majesty's

Government had followed her moral and material progress under Prince Ferdinand's rule, and had emphasized their feelings of friendship for her people. With a Prince, however, who was careful to keep the direction of foreign affairs in his own hands and who was, moreover, naturally drawn towards any Power that understood how to flatter his vanity, a better understanding between the two Governments could only be arrived at by placing his personal relations with the Court of St. James's on a more intimate footing.

Before leaving England I had had the honour of being invited to Windsor for a couple of nights, and I had then endeavoured to induce King Edward to charge me with a friendly message to Prince Ferdinand that would tend to promote the success of my mission. The King, however, was not to be moved. "You may tell the Prince," he said, "that I have not forgotten the fact that he is my cousin, but that, so long as he pursues his present double-faced policy he cannot count on my support." Such a caustic message was not encouraging, and I was rather at a loss what to say when, at a dinner given me at the palace shortly after my arrival at Sofia, I had to reply to the King's health which the Prince had proposed in very friendly terms. I did not dare disturb the harmony of the evening by giving His Majesty's message in its entirety, as that would have had the effect of a bombshell. I therefore took for my text His Majesty's reference to the *liens de parenté* existing between him and the Prince, and after embroidering this theme, concluded by saying a few nice things about the Prince and Bulgaria without making it clear whether I was expressing the King's feelings or my own personal views.

On my sitting down Prince Ferdinand shook me warmly by the hand and remarked: "Things are then not as bad as I thought." After a moment's pause he looked at me and said: "*Feu Lord Salisbury m'a toujours traiti en assassin de Stambuloff!*" I began to protest feebly, when it fortunately occurred to me to repeat to the Prince, in an amended and more palatable form, a story which Lord Sanderson had once told me about His Royal Highness's visit to London in the Diamond Jubilee year. Lord Salisbury, I said, had rather a poor opinion of his fellow men and was not given to wasting his time on what he considered as unprofitable conversations. On its being suggested that he ought to call on His Royal Highness he had raised every sort of objection, and it was only after considerable pressure had been brought to bear on him that he had eventually consented to do so. He had returned, however, in quite another frame of mind, and in conversation with Lord Sanderson had, like Napoleon after his interview with Goethe, said of His Royal Highness: "Voilà un homme." The Prince was delighted and made no further reference to his supposed complicity in Stambuloff's assassination. But he would not have been so pleased had I told him that, though Lord Salisbury did really say: "There's a man," his lordship had added: "but I would not like to be his Prime Minister."

Though the signature of the Turco-Bulgarian agreement had helped to relax the prevailing tension, the atmosphere at Sofia was constantly charged with electricity, and never did a winter pass without the oft-repeated warning that, when the snows melted in the Balkans we should witness the outbreak of the long-talked-of war. For the moment, however, the Bulgarian Government were anxious to give the promised reforms a chance, and were, for other reasons, disposed to exercise a restraining influence on the insurgent leaders. The state of exhaustion, to which the Bulgarian element in Macedonia had been reduced by the disorganization reigning in the ranks of the committees, had encouraged the Greeks to recruit bands in Crete and Greece which, thanks to the connivance of the local Turkish authorities, were able to strike crushing blows at their Bulgarian rivals. Their crowning exploit — the destruction of the village of Zagorichani in the spring of 1904 and the massacre of the majority of its inhabitants — provoked a serious anti-Greek movement in Bulgaria that resulted in the seizure of many of the Greek Patriarchate churches.

On the other hand, Bulgaria's relations with Roumania showed signs of improvement. Though both were exposed to the common danger of Russian aggression, the good understanding, which had been established while Prince Alexander was on the throne, had not been maintained during the reign of his successor. It would indeed have been strange had men of such entirely different characters as King Charles and Prince Ferdinand remained friends; as it was, each of the two Sovereigns disliked each other personally, and each distrusted the other's policy. The fall of Stambuloff had completed the breach. Roumania was credited by the one with a wish to extend her frontier to a better strategical line at the expense of the principality, and Bulgaria was believed by the other to have designs on the Dobrudja and to resent the attempt being made there to Roumanize the Bulgarian population. King Charles blamed Prince Ferdinand for allowing himself to be entangled in the meshes of his old enemy Russia and for deserting his former friends Austria and Roumania; while Prince Ferdinand, who regarded with suspicion Roumania's military convention with Austria, spoke of King Charles as a puppet in the hands of the Austrian and German Emperors and as their watchman on the Danube. The King, moreover, was strongly opposed to the idea of any territorial aggrandisement which would disturb the balance of power in the Balkans, and had even on one occasion told the Prince that if the Bulgarian army crossed the Rhodope the Roumanian army would occupy Silistria. Since 1902, however, when King Charles had paid his long-deferred return visit to Sofia, the personal relations between the two Sovereigns, as well as the official relations between the two Governments, had improved, and recent events in Macedonia — where both Koutzo-Vlachs and Bulgarians were exposed to the attacks of Greek bands — had helped to bring the two countries nearer together.

Though an understanding with Serbia was beset with still greater difficulties, an interview which Prince Ferdinand had with King Peter at Nisch in the summer of 1904, and an official visit paid by the latter to Sofia later in that year, paved the way for somewhat better relations. During this visit I unwittingly incurred the Prince's serious displeasure, and it manifested itself in a very characteristic fashion. His Majesty's Government had not yet recognized King Peter, so that I was debarred from attending the State banquet given in his honour; but on the day of His Majesty's arrival curiosity prompted me to watch the royal procession from the balcony of a friend's house. As he drove past on his way to the station Prince Ferdinand waved his hand in friendly greeting. On returning to the palace with the King he again looked up at the balcony, and failing to make me out, as I had kept well in the background till the procession had passed the house, he turned round in his carriage and, catching my eye, smiled and winked. I was so taken aback that my face probably expressed my blank astonishment, but I thought no more of the incident.

On the following day the Bulgarian agent in London happened to be dining with me. As I had heard that at the dinner at the palace on the pre ceding evening the Russian representative had been treated as if he were on quite a different plane from the representatives of the other Powers, I took the opportunity of protesting against such a differential treatment, and remarked that if Prince Ferdinand accorded M. Bakhmeteeff the position of a Russian viceroy, he need not look to His Majesty's Government for sympathy and support. Two days later M. Tsokoff, who had, as I learnt later, repeated these remarks to the Prince, was sent to tell me that His Royal Highness regarded the look which I had given him on the day of King Peter's arrival as a personal insult. Such was Prince Ferdinand's way of marking his displeasure with my outspoken language to M. Tsokoff. I had, however, to take his message seriously, so I wrote him a private letter expressing my painful surprise at this unfounded charge and saying that I could only ask pardon for an offence which I had not committed. The situation was rendered all the more piquant by the fact that I had, a few days previously, invited the Prince to dine on the King's birthday, while he was, apparently, contemplating asking for my recall. In the end he accepted my invitation, and nothing was said at the dinner about our little misunderstanding. On the contrary, we paid each other compliments and exchanged pretty speeches, for with a character such as his one could, as Lord Beaconsfield put it, lay flattery on with a trowel.

It was not long, however, before I was once more in his black books. Prince Ferdinand had, in the summer of 1904, met King Edward at Marienbad, and in an audience which I had on going to London in the following February I had suggested that His Majesty should put the seal on this reconciliation by inviting His Royal Highness to pay him a short visit at Buckingham Palace. The King agreed, and in authorizing me to convey an invitation to the Prince added: "Tell him only to bring a small suite, as the smaller the Prince the larger the suite." Knowing how touchy Prince Ferdinand was on all matters of etiquette, I, with much difficulty, obtained the King's permission to go to meet him on his arrival at Dover, and to make other arrangements for his reception. At the dinner given in his honour at Buckingham Palace the Prince told my wife that this was the first time that he had been received with the honours due to his rank, and that he would never forget all that I had done for him. The next day there was the usual exchange of decorations, and His Royal Highness showed his gratitude by sending me a Bulgarian order of the second class, being piqued at the fact that the King had, after consulting me, only given the Bulgarian agent the K.C.V.O. On my representing to the King that, as most of my colleagues at Sofia had Bulgarian orders of the first class, I would prefer not to accept this decoration, His Majesty caused a communication to be made to the Prince that resulted in my receiving the Grand Cross in time for me to wear it at the dinner given by the Prince of Wales at Marlborough House. On leaving the dining-room after dinner the King said to me in passing, "I am so glad that it's all right"; but Prince Ferdinand, who had overheard this remark, was not so pleased, and, putting his eyeglass in his eye and looking up at the ceiling, cut me dead. Though he had to put up with my company on his journey to Dover, he did not speak to me for six months after my return to Sofia. The visit, nevertheless, served a useful purpose in spite of his not being altogether satisfied with his conversations with Lord Lansdowne, who, he complained, was too "*boutonné*."

Meanwhile Prince Ferdinand had succeeded in establishing better relations with both Austria and Germany. Austria's one desire was to dissociate Bulgaria from Serbia and to induce her, by motives of self-interest, to renounce all idea of a political or economic alliance with that kingdom. It was in consequence of the pressure which she had brought to bear at Belgrade that the so-called Serbo-Bulgarian Customs Union Treaty, negotiated in 1905, was never ratified by the Skuptschina, although it had been voted, by acclamation, by the Sobranje and although Prince Ferdinand had even undertaken to make common cause with Serbia should the latter be drawn into a tariff war with the Dual Monarchy. The result was that Bulgaria, who had been on the verge of a rupture of commercial relations with Austria, arranged a modus vivendi with that Empire on the basis of the most favoured nation treatment; while Austria abandoned her attitude of cold reserve and adopted one of friendly interest in the principality. Germany had also become alive to the fact that Bulgaria, as the most promising of the Balkan States, was worthy of her serious attention. The German Emperor went out of his way to be civil to the Prince, and the German Government posed as her disinterested friend. A German bank was established at Sofia, mountain guns and artillery ammunition were supplied to the army, and German capital was encouraged to assist in the economic exploitation of the country. Prince Ferdinand, on the other hand, hoped to enlist the services of German diplomacy on his side and to use the influence of the Sultan's friend in support of Bulgaria's claims in Macedonia. His leanings towards Berlin were, moreover, prompted by the belief that Russia was, for the moment, powerless to help him. It had been fear rather than love of Russia that had, ever since Stambuloff's fall, been the keynote of his policy, as he had always been haunted by the dread of sharing the fate of his predecessor or of falling a victim to some plot for his assassination. The enfeeblement of that Empire, owing to the turn which events had taken in the Far East, had therefore afforded him a welcome relief. Russian influence, indeed, had been on the wane ever since the fall of the Russophil Daneff Government in 1903; and the following incident, which, though trivial in itself, gradually assumed an international character, shows how low the prestige of the Russian agency had fallen in 1905.

I happened to be president that year of the Union Club, and M. Bakhmeteeff — who had more than once tried to make things unpleasant for me — wrote to me one day saying that he had torn up that week's copy of *Simplicissimus* on account of a caricature which it had published of the Emperor Nicholas. He concluded by requesting me, as president, to stop its being any longer taken in by the club. I replied that other Sovereigns had been frequently caricatured in *Simplicissimus*, and that if, in an international club like the Union, members were at liberty to tear up any paper that displeased them, there would not be many left intact in the reading room. Had he, I added, sent me the caricature in question and requested me to have the *Simplicissimus* suppressed, I would have submitted the question to the committee, and I was even now prepared to do so if he would admit that he had acted incorrectly. He declined, however, to do this, and rejected other overtures which I made him with the object of providing a golden bridge over which he might beat a graceful retreat. He even told me that he had but to hold up his little finger and all the Bulgarian members of the club would support him. Finally, after the incident had lasted some ten days, he wrote requesting me to strike his name and the names of all his staff from the list of the members of the club over which I presided. As I had no wish to expose myself to the charge of having purposely forced the staff of the Russian agency to leave the club, I at once sent in my resignation as president — an example that was followed by all the members of the committee. A general meeting had consequently to be held to elect a new president and a new committee, and after I had briefly stated the facts of the case we were all re-elected, with but one dissentient voice — that of a secretary of the Greek Legation. M. Bakhméteeff was naturally furious and cut me ever afterwards. He was, fortunately, transferred to Tokio in the following year, and after the appointment of M. Sementowski as Russian diplomatic agent in 1907 my relations with the Russian agency, more especially after the Reval meeting, were of a most cordial character.

It is by no means an easy matter to follow the course of Prince Ferdinand's foreign policy, for he always made it a rule not to commit himself to any definite line of action. An opportunist, inspired solely by regard for his own personal interests, he preferred to pursue a politique de bascule and to coquette first with one and then with another of the Powers as he deemed best for the advancement of those interests. When in 1907 Serbia's persistent efforts to divide up Macedonia into spheres of influence had brought the two countries to the verge of war, it was to Austria that he turned, as he had no wish to see the eventual march of the Bulgarian army on Belgrade arrested, as it had been in 1885, by the intervention of a second Count Khevenhüller. His advances were met in a benevolent spirit; but as the war scare passed away his thoughts were diverted into another channel.

Prince Ferdinand had long cherished the ambition of converting the principality into an independent kingdom, and the twentieth anniversary of his accession to the throne, which was to be celebrated at Tirnovo by the convocation of a grand national assembly composed of all deputies who had ever sat in the Sobranje, seemed to furnish a grateful nation with a fitting occasion for offering their Prince a royal crown. His Royal Highness, as was his wont on occasions of this sort, kept carefully in the background and allowed others to do the necessary spade-work. The foreign representatives were sounded and feelers were put out with a view to preparing the public for what was coming. Though the idea of thus gratifying the Prince's vanity appealed but to a few interested generals and politicians, it was nevertheless generally expected that he would be acclaimed King at one of the many banquets by which the anniversary would be celebrated, and that he would yield to this *douce violence*. Austria, however, whose plans for the annexation of Bosnia and Herzegovina had not yet matured, considered that the pyschological moment had not yet come for such an open violation of the Treaty of Berlin. She therefore demanded a categorical answer to the question whether or not independence was about to be proclaimed, and warned the Prince that the Emperor would not recognize such a change in the status of the principality. His Royal Highness, who happened to be abroad, at once published a manifesto, assuring his subjects that their Prince "*s'est imposé d'autres devoirs envers la nation et ne saurait s'occuper de vaines questions de formalités, de titres et de satisfaction personelle.*" He subsequently repeated these assurances both to the Emperor at Ischl and to Baron Aehrenthal at Vienna, while the Tirnovo fetes were countermanded and his Jubilee celebrated on a modest scale at Sofia. In vetoing the proclamation of Bulgarian independence the Emperor of Austria had been careful to gild the pill by conferring on the Prince the colonelcy of an Austrian regiment; but this compliment did not soothe his wounded feelings. He had, he confided to a friend, been treated "*d'une manière indigne*," and he would take care, when he found a favourable opportunity for declaring Bulgaria's independence, that nobody should have an inkling of his intentions an hour beforehand.

While Prince Ferdinand had been thus coquetting with Austria, he had not neglected Russia. The Emperor had, at the orthodox New Year, appealed to the weak side of the Prince's character by conferring on him the brilliants of the Order of St. Andre, and in the following September His Majesty deputed the Grand Duke Vladimir to inaugurate the statue erected by the Bulgarian nation at Sofia to the memory of the Tsar Liberator. The political importance of this visit lay chiefly in the fact that it was the first sign which Russia had given since her war with Japan of the revival of her active interest in the affairs of the Near East and of her desire to reassert her influence in Bulgaria. The welcome given the Russian visitors by all classes of the population was also symptomatic. For it showed that, in spite of the intrigues by which Russia had in the past endeavoured to undermine the independence of the principality, the salient fact alone remained that, as it was to Russia that Bulgaria had owed her emancipation, so it was to Russia that she must look for the realization of her dreams of the Greater Bulgaria projected in the Treaty of San Stefano. On the other hand, the astonishing progress accomplished by the principality and the efficiency of her army were a revelation to the Grand Duke and his staff, who realized for the first time that Bulgaria, though founding her hopes for the future on Russia, was now a factor with whom Russia would have to count and was no longer necessarily dependent on her. The astute mind of the Prince had, moreover, not been slow to grasp the fact that both Russia and Austria had need of his co-operation, and that it was to his interest to keep them apart so as to be free to side with whichever of them was prepared to pay the highest price for that co-operation.

Early in the following year Prince Ferdinand decided to part with his Stambulovist advisers, who during their five years' tenure of office had amassed small fortunes, and to allow one of the other parties to have, as he put it, a bite at the bone. He chose the democrats, under Malinoff, as their successors; but insisted, as was his wont, on the appointment of two outsiders to the Ministries of War and of Foreign Affairs, in order to keep the control of those two ministries in his own hands. The result of the elections, which followed the dissolution of the Sobranje, was a complete victory for the new ministry; but the methods of constitutional government as practised in Bulgaria may be gauged by the fact that the Stambulovists, who had been in a majority of two to one in the late chamber, were unrepresented in the new one, while the Democrats, who had previously but two parliamentary representatives, won 173 out of a total of 203 seats.

CHAPTER 7
1908-1910

In the spring of 1908 His Majesty's Government had put forward a far-reaching scheme of reforms for Macedonia that had caused intense satisfaction in Bulgaria; and the somewhat negative attitude which Russia adopted towards it did but make her turn more than ever towards Great Britain. A new factor, however, had suddenly appeared on the scene in the shape of the constitutional movement in Turkey which took Europe by surprise at the end of July. The first impression produced at Sofia was one of scepticism, and the revival of the Constitution of 1876 by Imperial Decree was regarded in the light of a ruse to gain time for the purpose of nullifying the new reform scheme. It was for this reason that the overtures, made at the outset by the Young Turks to the Macedonian committees, were rejected; but as the constitutional movement gathered force the question as to how Bulgarian interests would be affected by the new order of things had to be seriously considered. On the one hand, it was felt that a constitutional regime, if honestly applied, would enable the Bulgarian element in Macedonia to develop both politically and materially; on the other, it was feared that it might seriously compromise the realization of Bulgaria's national aspirations in Macedonia. The Government, at a loss whether to support or to oppose it, adopted an attitude of reserve; but, while it was thus searching for a policy, an event occurred at Constantinople that determined its choice. The Turkish Minister for Foreign Affairs had omitted to invite the Bulgarian agent to a banquet, given the heads of missions in honour of the Sultan's birthday, on the ground that the dinner in question was confined to representatives of Foreign Powers, and that, if in the past M. Gueshoff had ever been treated as a member of the diplomatic body, it had been owing to an over sight on the part of a Court official. M. Gueshoff was, in consequence, at once ordered to return to Sofia. This incident, though trifling in itself, raised the whole question of Bulgaria's international status; and the Government felt that, if they now yielded on a point of etiquette, they might later on have to surrender other rights and privileges, acquired by a series of precedents, despite the provisions of the Treaty of Berlin. The nominal rights of suzerainty vested in Turkey had, they held, but proved a constant source of friction in the past, and they, therefore, decided to sever the connecting link. The moment was well chosen for such a step. Austria-Hungary, they were aware, was also contemplating the annexation of Bosnia and Herzegovina, and, as Prince Ferdinand was about to visit the Emperor of Austria at Buda-Pesth, it would not be difficult to arrange that the two acts should proceed on parallel lines. An opportune strike on the Oriental railway, and the consequent stoppage of all traffic in South Bulgaria, provided them further with a plea that appealed much more to the national sentiment than had the Gueshoff incident; and they at once proceeded to occupy the Bulgarian section of the line. The retention of the railway was so essential to the success of the campaign in favour of independence that, though the strike had terminated, the Government, in spite of the representations of the Powers, decided on September 28 not to restore it to the company. Events were now moving fast, and on October 4 a Cabinet Council, held under the presidency of the Prince, who had just returned from Hungary, finally decided in favour of independence. On the following day His Royal Highness was solemnly proclaimed Tsar of the Bulgarians at Tirnovo, their ancient capital.

I had, at the end of August, been offered the post of Minister at The Hague, but had subsequently, in view of the growing gravity of the situation, been asked to stay on at Sofia and to see the crisis through, a request which I complied with all the more readily as it was accompanied by the assurance that I should not be a financial loser by this arrangement. I had not unnaturally interpreted this assurance to mean that I should receive my Hague salary, which was some £2,000 more than that of Sofia; but, when after eight strenuous months of incessant work, with a chancery composed of a single vice-consul, reinforced by the voluntary services of my wife and daughter, I claimed the fulfilment of this promise, I was met with a polite *non possumus*.

The negotiations that ensued after the Declaration of Independence centred round the two questions of the Oriental railway and the East Roumelia tribute; and it was only thanks to the energetic intervention of Great Britain, France and Russia – for the Powers of the Triple Alliance did but little to prevent a rupture – that peace was preserved. The majority of Bulgarians were strongly opposed to the idea of paying for independence in hard cash, and, though Prince Ferdinand had, in October, in a telegram to the President of the

French Republic, acknowledged Turkey's claim to compensation, his Ministers had contested his right as a constitutional Sovereign to make such a declaration without consulting them. Both Great Britain and Russia had strongly disapproved of the Declaration of Independence, made, as it was, in collusion with Austria; and Russia more especially resented what she regarded as an act of treason on Prince Ferdinand's part in allowing Austria to preside over what ought to have been a *fête de famille Slave*. British public opinion, on the other hand, was warmly on the side of the Young Turks, and the British Press not only manifested its sympathy with the aggrieved parties, but was loud in its denunciation of Bulgaria. I, personally, nevertheless, espoused the cause of the latter and acted throughout the whole crisis as their advocate with His Majesty's Government, for the Young Turks, with whose delegates I had become acquainted at Sofia, inspired me with neither sympathy nor confidence. My Russian colleague, M. Sementowski, took the same line; and Russia, through fear of being completely supplanted by Austria, eventually adopted a strong pro-Bulgarian attitude which was not quite compatible with the view taken by His Majesty's Government of the inviolability of treaties.

From the very outset Bulgaria had declared that she would not expend more than 82,000,000 francs on account of the railway, and that she would pay no tribute for East Roumelia for the period subsequent to the Declaration of Independence. She knew what she wanted, and was determined to get it, and, as I told the Foreign Office, she had got her back to the wall and would not sign a blank cheque for the Powers to fill in. On two occasions — in January and in April, 1909 — she risked a war with Turkey because the negotiations were proceeding too slowly for her, and in the end she got what she wanted. It was, however, in great measure due to the pressure brought to bear on the Porte by His Majesty's Government, that the Turco-Bulgarian protocol recognizing independence was signed on April 19, 1909. Russia, as was but natural, wished to be the first Power to recognize the new order of things, and on April 21 the Emperor Nicholas addressed a telegram to King Ferdinand, congratulating him on the independence of his country. Two days later the French agent and I conveyed to the Bulgarian Government the official recognition of our respective Governments, and on the 27th the Austrian, German and Italian agents followed our example.

During all these months of crisis I had had to refrain from any official intercourse with Prince Ferdinand, and such unofficial communications as passed between us had to be made through his Chef de Cabinet. As an unrecognized King he was more than ever sensitive to anything in the nature of a personal slight, and, though he had never reason to complain of any want of respect on my part, he on one occasion sent his Chef de Cabinet to draw my attention to some facetious comments which an English illustrated paper had appended to a picture of his triumphal entry into Sofia after the Proclamation of Independence. The Prince, who was never quite happy on horseback, had failed to arrive at the time fixed for his entry, and, as nearly an hour passed without his putting in an appearance, some wag remarked: "Perhaps His Majesty has been pleased to part company with his horse." For some reason best known to himself, Prince Ferdinand suspected my daughter of having written the peccant paragraph, and, in spite of my indignant denial, he only withdrew the charge on discovering shortly afterwards that the real culprit was a well-known journalist. After his recognition as King by His Majesty's Government our relations were of a most cordial character, and at a dinner which he gave us on the eve of our departure for The Hague, he bade us farewell in almost affectionate terms.

I have already called attention to certain sides of Prince Ferdinand's character and to his very questionable conduct at various stages of his career; but, before leaving the subject, I must sum up my general impressions of him.

His parting with Stambuloff and his subsequent treatment of his fallen Minister; his breach of faith with his wife's family on the question of the religion of the heir to the throne; and his attitude of almost abject prostration before Russia after Prince Boris's conversion, all reveal to us a man dominated by strong personal ambitions and not much troubled with scruples as to the mode of their attainment. But an impartial critic, reviewing the first twenty-two years of his reign — for with the period subsequent to my departure from Sofia I am not at present concerned — would have to make allowances for the exceptional difficulties with which he had been confronted and to place certain things to his credit. When, as a young lieutenant in the Austrian army, he elected to face the risks attendant on his acceptance of the Bulgarian crown, he was generally regarded as an adventurer embarking on a forlorn hope that could only end in failure. But Prince Bismarck was right when he said: "*Der Coburger wird sich doch durchfressen*" ("The Coburger will worry through"). Unrecognized by the Powers for the first eight years of his reign, he was, as he said of himself, "the pariah of Europe," and it required no small moral courage on his part to brave not only the open hostility of Russia, but her still more dangerous secret machinations, as well as frequent plots for his assassination. During those trying years he developed talents and capacities with which no one had credited him, and proved himself beyond all expectation a successful ruler of a somewhat turbulent Balkan State. It was thanks to his restraining influence that the principality had not yet embarked on war with Turkey, and it was largely due to his initiative and foresight that it had advanced so rapidly on the path of progress. "*Je remplis ma mission philanthropique*," Prince Ferdinand once said to me, and if for "philanthropic" he had substituted "civilizing" he would not have been far from the truth.

In spite, however, of the services which he had rendered his adopted country, the Prince never won the affections of his subjects, for he was not endowed with those special qualities that arouse popular enthusiasm, while the pomp and paraphernalia of royalty, with which he loved to surround himself, did not appeal to a simple-minded and democratic people like the Bulgarians. He had, none the less, succeeded in inspiring a certain respect for his person that bordered on fear in the case of those whose official positions brought them into immediate contact with him, and stories are told of members of his household, who had incurred his displeasure, hiding in the palace garden in the hope of escaping from the wrath to come. His intellectual gifts were many and varied. He was master of some seven or eight languages, was well read, was a distinguished botanist and ornithologist, and, when he pleased, the most charming of *causeurs*. He was very *journalier*, but if he was in a good humour he would keep me at an audience for an hour or two talking on every possible subject in the most perfect French, or lapsing occasionally into English or German if he could not find in French an appropriate phrase to give expression to his thoughts. Vanity and love of theatrical effect were the weak points of his character; but I should be lacking in gratitude were I to be oblivious of the sympathy and kindness which he showed me on more than one occasion. His talents as a diplomatist were of no mean order; but his conduct of foreign affairs suffered from his love of intrigue and from over-confidence in his ability to outwit others. Prince Ferdinand was, in a word, an interesting and complex personality who, as he himself told me, had been happily described by King Edward, when presenting Lord Haldane to him at Marienbad, as "*l'homme le plus fin en Europe*."

Early in 1908 Prince Ferdinand had married, *en secondes noces*, Princess Eleonora of Reuss-Köstritz, a lady who, unlike her husband, had succeeded in winning the affections of the Bulgarians by the kindly interest which she showed in everything that concerned their welfare, and more especially in the working of the hospitals, which were in a very backward state. The Princess had served with the

Russian Red Cross in the Japanese War and had gained much experience as a nurse, an experience by which I benefited when, as the result of a riding accident, I was laid up for weeks and weeks with a broken leg and ankle. Not only did she make all the necessary arrangements for my being carried on a stretcher to one of the hospitals, where the fractures were photographed with Röntgen rays, but she discussed with the doctors the best means of relieving the pain which was causing me sleepless nights, and she often came and sat with me, bringing me flowers and showing me a kindness which I can never forget. Her life with the Prince was far from a happy one, but she was a real mother to his children, who were all devoted to her. Prince Boris — the present King — was then a very attractive but a rather shy boy who stood in perpetual fear of his father, as the latter's natural affection for his son was tempered by the unpleasant misgiving which he did not always conceal, that his heir might one day supplant him. He even told me on one occasion that, if the Bulgarians imagined that, were they to force him to abdicate, they could keep Prince Boris as his successor, they were much mistaken, as, in the event of his having to leave the principality, he would take good care that his son accompanied him into exile. Prince Ferdinand's personality so overshadowed that of others that I have not thought it necessary to speak of his Ministers, with whom I had to transact business, as they were for the most part but puppets whose movements were governed by the strings which he held in his hand. There were, however, a few exceptions to this rule, and among them I would cite M. Petkoff and M. Stancioff — for both of whom I had a sincere personal regard. The former was a striking figure. The son of a peasant, he had in early life been a revolutionary and an intimate friend of Stambuloff. During the Russophil reaction that followed the latter 's assassination, he conducted a violent Press campaign against the Prince, with whom, however, he became reconciled in 1899. He eventually became Prime Minister and was the most trustworthy and patriotic of Bulgarian statesmen, being one of the few who ventured to express his views openly to his Sovereign. He was, unfortunately for his country, assassinated in 1907. M. Stancioff, on the other hand, was a highly cultured man who had served successively as diplomatic agent at Bucharest, Vienna and St. Petersburg, and who took a far broader and more cosmopolitan view of things than the majority of his compatriots. My relations with him, when he was Minister for Foreign Affairs, were always of a most cordial kind, and it was in great measure due to his conciliatory attitude that the negotiations which I had to conduct for the conclusion of a treaty of commerce ended satisfactorily. Later on he was Bulgarian Minister in Paris and, after the outbreak of the Great War, had the courage to warn King Ferdinand, with whom he had always been a favourite, against the fatal step which he was about to take, in language which lost him his Sovereign's favour and led to his complete disgrace. His appointment as Bulgarian Minister in London has given me a welcome opportunity of renewing our old friendship.

When I left Sofia at the end of May, 1909, I received from public men of nearly all parties so many marks of the sympathy entertained for my country and of the gratitude which they felt for the services rendered Bulgaria by His Majesty's Government during the recent crisis, that, had I then been told that, in less than a decade, Bulgaria would be at war with Great Britain, I should not have believed it possible. Entente diplomacy during the intervening years cannot, however, as I shall endeavour to show later, be held entirely blameless in this matter.

On my arrival in London I was received in audience by King Edward, to kiss hands on my appointment to The Hague, when His Majesty, after referring in very flattering terms to my work at Sofia, handed me the insignia of the G.C.V.O. I was further given the K.C.M.G. as a mark of the approval of His Majesty's Government, while Sir E. Grey expressed his appreciation of my services in the following official dispatch:

I desire to take this opportunity to convey to you the high appreciation entertained by His Majesty's Government of the manner in which you have filled the post of British representative at Sofia since the date of your appointment in November, 1903, and their entire approval of your action during the recent crisis.

Your interesting and able reports on the situation proved invaluable to His Majesty's Government in their efforts for the maintenance of peace, and the moderating influence which you successfully exerted on several occasions largely contributed to the attainment of their object.

After such a storm centre as Sofia, The Hague was a very haven of rest — whose calm waters were unruffled by any political convulsion that might be taking place in the distant Balkans. With the exception of an occasional conference on such a stirring topic as bills of exchange, or the meeting of an arbitral tribunal, there was but little work to do. I had, however, while in Bulgaria had such a surfeit of constantly recurring crises, with their attendant war scares, that I was glad to have leisure to devote to the study of a country so interesting as Holland; to visit its picturesque old towns, its art treasures, its storied monuments; and to revel in that sea of ever-changing glorious colours into which its fields are transformed when the tulips are in bloom. For myself, too, The Hague, and especially the Legation — a beautiful old house that had been the residence of the Spanish Ambassadors in the seventeenth century — had a special attraction, associated as they were in my memory with bygone years, when my father had been accredited as Minister to Queen Sophia, and when I had lived there as a small boy.

As the Legation had to be refurnished from top to bottom, it was from Clingendaal, under whose hospitable roof so many an Anglo-Dutch friendship has been cemented, and under the auspices of our almost lifelong friend Baroness (Daisy) de Brienen, that we made our debut in Dutch society, a society in which we soon found ourselves quite at home, thanks to the warm welcome extended to us. Many of its members, I am glad to think, still remain our friends, and among them none have given us more constant proofs of their friendly feelings than the present Netherlands Minister in London and his wife. Jonkheer van Swinderen was Minister for Foreign Affairs during all the time that I was at The Hague, and it was a real pleasure to me to have to transact my official business with a man of his quick intelligence, mother wit and conciliatory disposition.

It was at the van Swinderens' house, where we were frequent guests, that I had the good fortune to meet ex-President Roosevelt, who was then making a tour of the European capitals. Our hostess — to whose sympathetic and attractive personality I would pay a passing tribute — had told him, in the course of luncheon, that I had recently translated the first part of *Faust* into English verse. On hearing this, Mr. Roosevelt at once engaged me in conversation across the table, and, beginning with the early English ballads, passed in rapid review all the great writers of English verse down to modern times. On my remarking that I considered Swinburne the greatest poet of our generation, he exclaimed: "There I am with you. When I was a young man," he went on, "I would walk in the woods after my day's work and recite that glorious chorus from 'Atalanta in Calydon,'" some half-dozen lines of which he then recited. Not to be outdone, I replied: "Well, Mr. Roosevelt, when I was a young man, crossed in love, I would declaim the lines in 'Dolores':

> Time turns the old days to derision,
> Our loves into corpses or wives."

"And," interrupted Mr. Roosevelt, without giving me time to finish:

> "Marriage and death and division
> Make barren our lives."

"What young man," he continued, thumping the table with his fist, "has not, when suffering the pangs of despised love, given vent to his feelings in those words?"

As one could dine at the Legation and breakfast in London it was easy to pay flying visits to friends in England, and I remember more especially one visit which we paid the Berkeley Sheffields for the Doncaster Meeting in September, 1909 — for it was at that meeting that I saw King Edward for the last time. His Majesty had sent for me after the running of the Leger, in which his horse Minoru, though a warm favourite, had been beaten, and, with the kindly interest which he had always shown in my career, asked me about our life at The Hague. After saying how happy we were there, I remarked that life in the Dutch capital was so calm and peaceful that I was afraid that I should end like Rip Van Winkle in Sleepy Hollow, and sleep away the remaining years of my diplomatic life. "You must not think that," said His Majesty, laughing. "Something is sure to turn up." It was but a few months after King Edward's death that the something which His Majesty had predicted *did* turn up and that I received the following letter from Sir Edward Grey:

FOREIGN OFFICE.
July 16, 1910.

MY DEAR BUCHANAN, — Sir Arthur Nicholson's transfer to the Foreign Office will make a vacancy at St. Petersburg. The place is one of great importance, as, though our relations with the Russian Government are happily cordial, there are questions which present difficulties for both Governments, which require constant tact and skill on the part of the Ambassador at St. Petersburg.

I am confident, from all I myself have seen and from all that I have heard from those who have had still longer experience of the Diplomatic Service than I have had, that you would fill the post of Ambassador with success, and, if it would be agreeable to you, I should be very glad to recommend you for it. — Yours sincerely, E. GREY.

I had never dared aspire to such an important Embassy, and, in thanking Sir Edward for this signal proof of his confidence, I could but express the hope that I should prove worthy of it and that I should not disappoint his expectations. I had, fortunately, four months in which to work up the various questions with which I should have to deal; and it was only at the end of November, 1910, that I kissed hands on my appointment. King George, who had such a warm affection for the Emperor Nicholas, charged me with many messages for His Majesty and continued throughout the whole of my mission to honour me with his confidence and support.

CHAPTER 8
1911

Though the relations between the two Governments were, as Sir Edward Grey had pointed out in his letter to me, cordial, Russia and Great Britain were friends over whom still hung the shadow of past differences and misunderstandings. They had not yet cast aside the mutual suspicions with which they had for more than half a century regarded the trend of each other's policy. The Anglo-Russian understanding dated from the year 1907. It was founded on a somewhat loosely-worded document which, while binding the two Powers to maintain the integrity and independence of Persia and denning their respective spheres of interest in that country, said nothing about their relations in Europe. Framed with the immediate object of preventing Persia becoming an apple of discord between them, it nevertheless served to bring them nearer together and indirectly paved the way for their future collaboration in European questions. It proved, indeed, in the end more successful in promoting an understanding, that was outside the purview of the written agreement, than in reconciling their conflicting interests in Persia, which up to the very eve of the Great War occasioned constant friction.

On my arrival at St. Petersburg early in December, 1910, the international outlook, though giving no cause for immediate anxiety, was not altogether reassuring. The Bosnia and Herzegovina crisis, in which M. Isvolsky had been worsted in his duel with Count Aehrenthal, had created in Russia a bitter feeling of resentment against Austria — a resentment that had been intensified by the former's personal dislike of Count Aehrenthal; while the danger of complications in the Balkans, that might bring Russia's interests into direct conflict with those of Austria, could not be overlooked. M. Sazonoff, who had just succeeded M. Isvolsky at the Russian Foreign Office, had, fortunately, no personal grudge against Count Aehrenthal, and even held that it might be better that he should remain in office for fear of his being succeeded by a Minister more amenable to German influence. All that he could do under the circumstances was to refrain from giving a hostile turn to his policy and to work for the gradual re-establishment of more normal relations between the two Governments. But what struck me most about the then existing situation was the fact that, though Russia's relations with Germany had been seriously strained ever since the Emperor William had in 1909 donned his shining armour in support of his Austrian ally, and though it was thanks to Germany that Count Aehrenthal had won the day, the Russian public took a more tolerant view of her action and did not harbour the same rancorous resentment against her as against Austria.

M. Sazonoff, whom I had known when he was counsellor of embassy in London, gave me a most cordial welcome on my paying him my first official visit, and we soon became fast friends. A Russian of the Russians when it was a question of defending his country's interests, he was always a staunch friend of Great Britain; and down to the last day of his tenure of the post of Foreign Minister — down to the end of July, 1916, when the Emperor, unfortunately for himself and for Russia, was so ill-advised as to replace him by M. Sturmer — I ever found in him a loyal and zealous collaborator for the maintenance of the Anglo-Russian understanding. We did not, as was but natural, always see eye to eye in the many intricate questions which we had to discuss during the next five years and a half, but he never resented my frank, outspoken language and invariably did all he could to smooth over difficulties. He had but recently returned from Potsdam, where, in his desire to relax the tension existing between the two Governments and to secure Germany's recognition of Russia's predominant position in Persia, he had been inveigled into negotiations about the Bagdad railway which were not in keeping with the understanding on which the other members of the Triple Entente had hitherto acted. This so-called Potsdam Agreement was the first of the many thorny questions which I had to discuss with Sazonoff. It also formed the subject of my first conversations with the Emperor. On presenting my letters of credence I had, after emphasizing the King's earnest wish to see the Anglo-Russian understanding maintained and consolidated, told the Emperor that His Majesty's Government were following the course of these Russo-German negotiations with some anxiety. His Majesty had assured me, in reply, that his Government would conclude no arrangement with Germany without first submitting it to His Majesty's Government, and that the latter could always count on his assistance whenever they stood in need of it. He repeated these assurances in a further conversation which I had with him a few weeks later, and added that the pending negotiations with Germany would in no way affect his attitude towards Great Britain.

Though the Emperor was acting in perfect good faith, he failed to grasp the fact that the concessions which his Government were making to Germany with regard to the Bagdad railway were incompatible with the support which they were pledged to give their partners in the Triple Entente. It was not, as I subsequently endeavoured to impress on M. Sazonoff, that we had the slightest objection to Russia cultivating good relations with Germany, but that we were afraid that she was about to do so at our expense. Anxious as we were ourselves to come to an understanding with Germany on the subject of armaments, we should never, I assured him, think of taking any step that might entail the sacrifice of our friendship with Russia and France. We trusted, therefore, that the Russian Government would, in its dealings with Germany, show a like consideration for our interests.

In view of the historical interest attaching to them, I append a short account of the long-drawn-out negotiations which ensued between the Russian and German Governments. They entailed constant intervention on my part, as, had not the former Government realized in time that there was a point beyond which they could not go, the latter would have succeeded in causing a serious split in the ranks of the Entente Powers.

At the beginning of December, 1910, Sazonoff had submitted to the German Ambassador a draft agreement embodying the substance of the Potsdam conversations. By the first of its articles Russia engaged not to oppose the realization of the Bagdad railway, nor to put any obstacle in the way of the participation of foreign capital in that enterprise, on the condition that she would not be required to make any pecuniary or economic sacrifices. By the second, she undertook to link up the Bagdad railway with the future North Persian railway system. By the third, Germany engaged neither to construct nor to give her material or diplomatic support to the construction of any railway in the zone situated between the Bagdad line and the Russian and Persian frontier to the north of Khanikin; while, by the fourth, she declared that she had no political interests in Persia; that she would but pursue there objects of a commercial character; that she recognized Russia's special political, strategical and economic interests in North Persia, and that she would not seek for any concession of a territorial character to the north of a line running from Kasri Chirin by Ispahan, Yezd and Khakh to the Afghan frontier, in the latitude of Ghazrik.

The engagement taken by Russian in the first article was, Sazonoff contended, to apply only to the Koniah-Bagdad section of the railway, and left the Russian Government free, as far as the Gulf section was concerned, to co-operate with Great Britain in the future, as in the past. Early in January the *Evening Times* published the text of the draft agreement, and in order to prove that this version was unauthentic the two Governments agreed to recast the whole text. The negotiations now turned mainly on the question of the linking up of the two railway systems, as Germany was anxious to bind Russia to commence the construction of the linking-up line as soon as a branch line from Sadijeh had reached Khanikin. This question was complicated by the fact that Russian public opinion proved to be opposed to the expenditure of money on a railway that was to open the Persian markets to German trade, before provision was made for the construction of a railway from Enzeli to Tehran that would render a similar service to Russian goods. In order to get over this difficulty M. Sazonoff suggested that British and French financiers should finance the construction of both the Enzeli-Tehran and the Khanikin-Tehran lines; but, in the absence of any guarantee from the Russian Government, this suggestion could not be entertained. The only other alternative — that of allowing the Germans to build the railway — was opposed by us on the ground that the Germans would then get the control of the railway into their own hands, with the result that they might use it for the transport of troops. On February 21 Sazonoff handed the German Ambassador a revised draft, under which Russia engaged to obtain a concession for the linking-up line as soon as the Sadijeh-Khanikin branch line had been completed, while the text of the first article of the original draft was modified so as to restrict Russia's engagement — not to oppose the realization of the Bagdad railway — to the Koniah-Bagdad section. Russia also stipulated that, in the event of her ceding her rights in the linking-up line to any third party, all the other clauses of the agreement should still remain in force.

The negotiations were interrupted, owing to the serious illness that incapacitated Sazonoff for over nine months, but were resumed later on by the acting Foreign Minister, M. Neratoff, who in July submitted a further amended draft.

The progress of the negotiations was now somewhat accelerated, as both Governments had special reasons for bringing them to a speedy conclusion. Germany, on the one hand, was engaged in a delicate conversation with France on the subject of Morocco, and considered the moment well chosen for the publication of an agreement which would, she hoped, demonstrate the intimate character of her relations with France's ally. Russia, on the other hand, was anxious — in view of the internal conflict that had broken out in Persia — to secure a declaration of Germany's *désinteressement* in that country, so that she might have a freer hand to deal with the situation should intervention become necessary. Germany declined to accept the restricted interpretation placed by Russia on the term "Bagdad Railway" or to consent to the retention in the agreement of Article ill of the original draft, under which she was to engage not to construct any railway in the zone north of Khanikin. The German Ambassador did, however, give a categorical verbal assurance, on the part of the Emperor William, that Germany would only construct in that zone such railways as she was entitled to build under the Bagdad railway concession. She further claimed the right to obtain for herself the concession for the Khanikin-Tehran railway, should Russia, or the finance syndicate to whom she might cede her rights, fail to commence its construction within two years of the completion of the Sadijeh-Khanikin branch line. All her demands were, in the end, conceded, and the agreement as finally signed was a diplomatic victory for Germany. The initial mistake committed by Sazonoff, in allowing himself to be entrapped during his conversations with M. Kiderlen-Waechter into giving verbal assurances, of which he did not at the time realize the full significance, was never retrieved. He had pledged Russia, without previous consultation with Great Britain and France, to withdraw her opposition to the Bagdad railway scheme, and, though he subsequently endeavoured to restrict this engagement to the Koniah-Bagdad section, it was clear from the outset that Germany would hold him to the strict letter of his bond.

Whether, in thus accelerating the final stage of these negotiations, the Russian Government were prompted or not by the desire to be relieved of all apprehensions as to Germany's attitude in the event of their embarking on a policy of active intervention in Persia, the signature of the Russo-German agreement was shortly followed by a change for the worse in their relations with that country. This change was primarily due to the fact that the Persian Government had, in spite of Russia's repeated remonstrances, taken Mr. Shuster and other American advisers into their service. One of Mr. Shuster's first acts was to entrust Major Stokes (at one time British military attaché at Tehran) with the task of organizing a treasury gendarmerie. The appointment of a British officer to the command of a gendarmerie, whose operations were to extend over the whole of Persia, including the Russian sphere in the north, was resented by the Russian Government as a violation of the Anglo-Russian understanding; and it was only by making strong representations at Tehran, which resulted in the appointment being left in abeyance, that we were able to convince them of our good faith.

But hardly had this incident been happily closed when Mr. Shuster's disregard of Russia's privileged position in Persia provoked a still more serious crisis. Bent, as he was, on securing for himself an absolutely free hand with regard to loans and railway concessions, he gave her serious offence by appointing an Englishman (Mr. Lecoffre) as treasury agent at Tabriz; and in November he brought matters to a head by seizing a property belonging to Shoa es Sultaneh that had been mortgaged to the Russian bank, and by replacing the Persian Cossacks on guard there by treasury gendarmes. The Russian Government at once presented an ultimatum demanding an apology and the reinstatement of the Persian Cossacks within forty-eight hours; and, as the Persian Government, in order to avoid compliance with these demands, resigned, orders were given for the despatch to Kaswin of a force sufficiently strong to enable a detachment being eventually sent to occupy Tehran.

It was in vain that I endeavoured to impress on the acting Minister for Foreign Affairs the serious consequences which an occupation of Tehran might have for the maintenance of the Anglo-Russian understand ing. While assuring me that Russia had no intention of violating the principle of Persian integrity, he not only refused to cancel the orders already given, but told me that, unless the Persian Government complied with the terms of the ultimatum before the Russian troops landed on Persian territory, further demands would be presented. With M. Kokovtsoff, who had recently succeeded M. Stolypin as President of the Council, was more successful; and, after Neratoff's uncompromising language, I was agreeably surprised to receive from him the unqualified assurance that, as soon as the two original Russian demands had been conceded, the Russian troops would be recalled. M. Kokovtsoff, however, had counted without his colleagues in the Government. The Russian troops having, meanwhile, landed at Enzeli, a second ultimatum was despatched, demanding a refund of the cost of the military expedition, the dismissal of Mr. Sinister and Mr. Lecoffre, and an engagement that the Persian Government would not in future take any foreigners into their service without the previous consent of the Russian and British Governments.

The despatch of this second ultimatum, in the teeth of the categorical assurances given me by the President of the Council, naturally evoked a protest from His Majesty's Government; and in my conversations with M. Neratoff I once more endeavoured to dissuade him from an occupation of Tehran, which would, as I reminded him, be regarded in England as a blow struck at the independence of Persia, and consequently at our understanding with Russia. Neratoff, notwithstanding, remained obdurate on this point, and at the same time declined to sanction a statement being made in the House of Commons to the effect that the two Governments had agreed under no circumstances to recognize the ex-Shah Mohammed Ali, who had recently returned to Persia. It was only after Sazonoff had, towards the middle of December, resumed the direction of foreign affairs that the tension between the two Governments relaxed and that the Russian demands as the result of further negotiations, were toned down. They were accepted by the Persian Government before the end of the year, though, owing to the outbreak of serious disturbances in North Persia, the promised recall of the Russian troops from Kaswin had to be postponed.

I have recorded the above incidents in order to show how difficult it sometimes was for the two Governments to act in concert owing to the diametrically opposite standpoints from which the situation was viewed by public opinion in their respective countries. In Russia the despatch of troops to Kaswin and the contemplated occupation of Tehran were regarded as measures which it was incumbent on her to take for the vindication of her outraged honour. In England, on the contrary, they were condemned as an unjustifiable attempt to bring a weak country into subjection and as a violation of its integrity and independence. So acute was the divergence of views that, had not the Persian Government yielded before the order was given for an advance on Tehran, the Anglo-Russian understanding would with difficulty have borne the strain. Fortunately, both Sir Edward Grey and M. Sazonoff were statesmen endowed with the gifts of tact, patience and forbearance, so necessary for the conduct of delicate negotiations; and, though it is now the custom to depreciate the services of the Old Diplomacy, I doubt whether the vaunted New Diplomacy would have been equally successful in saving the Anglo-Russian understanding from the shipwreck with which it was more than once threatened.

My personal efforts were naturally directed to reconciling as far as possible the conflicting views and interests of the two Governments; but I was hampered in this task by the absence of any solidarity or collective responsibility between the members of the Russian Cabinet. The categorical assurances given me by the President of the Council respecting the recall of the Russian troops were, as already stated, disregarded by his colleagues, and the reason for this very unusual procedure was only made clear to me a few months later, when a Blue Book on Persia was about to be presented to Parliament.

In submitting to Sazonoff, in accordance with diplomatic usage, the proofs of my despatches, I had been careful to tone down the reports of my conversations with M. Kokovtsoff so that it should not appear that he had failed to give effect to his promises. Sazonoff, who was fully acquainted with what had passed in the course of those conversations, at once took me to task for having appealed to the President of the Council in a matter which only concerned the Ministry for Foreign Affairs.

As the Minister, or, in his absence, the acting Minister for Foreign Affairs, was alone responsible to the Emperor for the direction of Russia's foreign policy, Sazonoff strongly objected to the publication in a Blue Book of despatches reporting conversations with another Minister about the affairs of a department with which that Minister was in no way connected. I had been wrong, he declared, in discussing the Persian question with the President of the Council, and the latter had exceeded his powers in giving me assurances which he was not competent to give. I objected that the Russian Ambassador in London frequently discussed foreign affairs with the Prime Minister, and that, when it was a question which vitally affected the relations of our two countries, it was but natural that I should consult the President of the Council, more especially as an acting Minister for Foreign Affairs, not being a member of the Cabinet, could not speak with the same authority as the head of his Government. Though Sazonoff had never objected to my taking this course when his brother-in-law, Stolypin, was at the head of the Government, he merely replied that Russia was not a parliamentary country like Great Britain, and that the President of the Council had no control over Russia's foreign policy.

Of the other questions with which I had to deal during the course of the year, by far the most important was the right claimed by Russia to extend her maritime jurisdiction from three to twelve miles. In January and March bills had been introduced in the Duma forbidding foreigners to fish within twelve miles of the coasts of the Archangel Government and of the Pri Amur respectively, and as this claim was contrary to recognized practice and to the generally accepted principles of international law, I was instructed to protest. In their reply to this protest the Russian Government contended that the question of the extent of the territorial waters of a State was determined either by international treaties or by internal legislation; that, when it was determined in the latter manner, the limit fixed might differ in the case of customs, fisheries, criminal or civil jurisdiction, according to the requirements of their several interests ; and that, as Russia was not bound by any treaty obligations, the extent of her territorial waters, from the point of view of international law, could only be determined by the range of the coastal guns — a range which exceeded twelve miles. They suggested, however, that the question might be submitted to the third Peace Conference, which was to meet at The Hague in 1915. While expressing our willingness to discuss in an international conference the limits within which territorial jurisdiction could be exercised by any State over the waters adjacent to its shores, we attached the condition that, until such a conference had arrived at a decision, the Russian Government should not interfere with British vessels outside the existing three miles limit without a previous agreement with us. In a conversation which I had with him on the subject, Stolypin declared that this was a condition which the Russian Government could not accept, as in the opinion of their law officers there was no rule in international law that precluded Russia from acting as she proposed. He could not, therefore, promise to do more than to endeavour to adjourn the discusssion of the bills in the Duma till the autumn session.

The arguments advanced by the Russian Government in support of their claim were refuted in a succession of notes, in one of which they were reminded that they had themselves, in an official note addressed to Lord A. Loftus in October, 1874, recognized three miles as the limit of the maritime jurisdiction of a State, and had admitted that the question of such jurisdiction "*rentre dans la catégorie de celles, qui dans l'intérêt des bonnes rélations Internationales, il serait désirable de voir réglées par un commun accord entre les Etats*."

The Pri Amur bill was passed, both by the Duma and the Council of Empire, in June, with the result that Japan at once entered an official protest against its application; but the discussion with regard to the Arch-angel fisheries bill was not pressed to a division. While declining to withdraw it, the Government did nothing to accelerate its passage, and as a considerable number of deputies were unwilling to press a measure that was calculated to cause friction with Great Britain, the bill eventually died a natural death.

In one of my conversations with the President of the Council in which, after discussing Russia's claim to an extension of her maritime jurisdiction, I had taken occasion to press for the settlement of two other pending questions, M. Stolypin exclaimed: "*Vraiment, M. l'Ambassadeur, vous n'êtes pas en veine! Voilà la troisième question désagréable que vous me posez aujourd'hui*." M. Stolypin was right. I had fallen on troublous times, for during this, my first, year at St. Petersburg there was a constant succession of disagreeable questions about which I had to make representations to the Russian Government. One of them — a typical one — deserves a passing reference.

Early in April the Russian Press published the report of the trial of a former employee in the Ministry of Marine accused of having sold a secret signal book to Captain Calthorpe, naval attaché to His Majesty's Embassy, in 1903, and of having subsequently, in 1909, communicated a further signal book, together with other secret documents, to his successor, Captain Aubrey Smith. In the course of his examination this man, Povagé, admitted that he had tried to sell a signal book to Captain Calthorpe, who had, however, declined to take it. He declared, however, on oath that he had never seen Captain Smith in his life. The court found him guilty on all counts, but as, owing to the lapse of time, he was exempted by statutory rules from punishment on the first count, he was condemned on the second to twelve years' hard labour.

I at once entered a strong protest. I pointed out that the judicial authorities had failed to inform the Embassy, as they ought to have done, that a trial was about to take place in which serious charges were to be brought against the British naval attaché; and, after giving my word of honour that there was not a particle of truth in the whole story, I requested the acting Minister for Foreign Affairs to publish an official *démenti* of certain unfounded statements made by some of the witnesses for the prosecution. While admitting that the judicial authorities ought to have given the Embassy notice of the impending trial, and while promising to inform the Emperor of all that I had said, M. Neratoff, instead of publishing an official *démenti* on behalf of the Russian Government, merely communicated to the Press a statement that the British Ambassador had denied in the most categorical manner that Captain Aubrey Smith had ever had any dealings with Povagé. The Emperor, who happened to be receiving Colonel Wyndham, our military attaché, in audience the following day, said that he was completely satisfied with my assurances and that, so far as he was concerned, the incident was closed. In spite of the repeated remonstrances which I addressed to the Russian Government on behalf of His Majesty's Government, and in spite of the fact that we could prove that Captain Smith had been absent from St. Petersburg on two occasions when Povagé was said to have visited him in his flat, this was the only satisfaction which Captain Smith ever received.

CHAPTER 9
1912-1914

In spite of the critical phases through which our understanding with Russia had passed in 1911, the two countries were nevertheless gradually being drawn nearer each other, and the warm welcome accorded to an influential and thoroughly representative British delegation, which visited St. Petersburg and Moscow in February, 1912, marked a fresh milestone on the road to Anglo-Russian friendship. Unfortunately the Speaker of the House of Commons, Mr. Lowther (now Lord Ullswater), who was to have headed the delegation, was at the last moment prevented coming, owing to his father's death, but his place was ably filled by Lord Weardale.

On the night of their arrival I gave a dinner at the Embassy, to which I invited all the members of the Government, representatives of the army and navy, and the leaders of the constitutional groups in both the Duma and the Council of Empire, with the exception of the leader of the cadets, M. Miliukoff, whom some of the Ministers declined to meet. In my speech welcoming them to Russia, I laid stress on the fact that it was not on diplomatic acts, but on the surer foundation of mutual sympathy, friendship and confidence, and on a community of interests, that we must endeavour to build up a real and lasting understanding with Russia. This was the keynote of nearly all the speeches delivered at the successive banquets given in their honour. On one or two occasions, however, and notably at the dinner given by the Duma and the Council of Empire, the speakers on either side went considerably farther. At the last-named dinner I was asked by the President of the Duma to return thanks for the toast of the Crimean veterans that was to be proposed by a Russian general, but excused myself on the ground that there was but one reply that I could make to such a toast, namely, that we had in the Crimean War learned to respect each other as brave and generous foemen, but that, should we ever be engaged in another war, we would, I trusted, find ourselves fighting shoulder to shoulder against the common enemy. It was with much difficulty that I induced President Rodzianko to entrust the duty of replying to this toast to someone who had not to weigh his words with the same care as myself. Sir E. Bethune's name was eventually coupled with it, and the gallant general, rushing in where I had feared to tread, delighted the Russians by replying in almost the identical words which I had forecasted, and was, in consequence, taken severely to task by the German Press.

It was not, however, so much by its speeches that the British delegation promoted a better understanding between the two countries, as by the personal contact which those of its members, who represented the Church, the parliament, the army and the navy of Great Britain established with the Russian naval, military, parliamentary and ecclesiastical authorities; for between nations, as between individuals, personal contact helps more than anything else to establish good relations. In the same way, the visit which M. Sazonoff paid in September to the King at Balmoral, and the conversations which he had there with Sir Edward Grey, laid the foundation for that close collaboration between the two Governments, which alone prevented the Balkan conflagration of 1912-13 spreading over Europe. Before, however, attempting to follow them through the various stages of the Balkan War, it will be well first to clear the ground of all the other questions which engaged their attention down to the outbreak of the Great War.

Though with the return of M. Sazonoff in restored health to the Ministry for Foreign Affairs at the close of 1911, the Persian question lost much of the acuteness which had characterized it during the latter half of that year, it continued, nevertheless, to provoke constant friction and misunderstandings between the two Governments. In speaking to me of the situation early in 1912, the Emperor remarked that the Persian Government was so weak, and the country in such a state of anarchy, that order would never be restored without the assistance of Russian troops in the north and of British troops in the south. When once they had accomplished this task they could be replaced by a small Persian army capable of maintaining the order which they had established. His Majesty further expressed his regret that the sincerity of the assurances given by his Government was doubted in certain quarters in England, adding that, when he gave his word that Russia would not annex any Persian territory, His Majesty's Government might rest assured that that word would not be broken.

But while both the Emperor and M. Sazonoff were really anxious to re-establish normal and correct relations with Persia, the Russian consuls in that country favoured a forward policy and acted in an entirely contrary spirit. The consul-general at Meshed, Prince Dabija, was directly responsible for the bombardment and desecration of the shrine of that town ; while his colleagues at other places, such as Tabriz, did not hesitate to provoke disorders that might serve as a pretext for Russian intervention. In their reports to their Government they so successfully misrepresented the origin and character of these disturbances that Sazonoff even threatened that Russia would have to take over the administration of Northern Azerbaijan, if the Persian Government failed to maintain order at Tabriz. How difficult it was for the two Governments to work together in Persia will be seen from the following extract from a private letter, which I wrote to Sir Edward Grey after having been instructed to warn the Russian Government of the serious consequences which might ensue from any such action on their part:

As Sazonoff could not see me yesterday, I communicated to him, in a private letter, what you had instructed me to tell him respecting a possible assumption by Russia of the administration of Northern Azerbaijan.

You will have already learned from the telegraphic report of the conversation, which I had with him this morning, that this is a step which he only contemplated taking in the very last resort, and that he trusts that it may be averted altogether if the Persians will consent to leave Shuja ed Dowleh at Tabriz as deputy-governor.

After giving me the above explanation, Sazonoff proceeded to speak with some heat of what you had said with regard to the Anglo-Russian understanding. That understanding, he remarked, was the Alpha and Omega of his policy, and he only regretted that it had been Isvolsky, and not himself, who had put his signature to it. Its maintenance was essential to the vital interests of the two countries, and, were it to break down, German hegemony would at once be established in Europe. In order to maintain it and to meet the wishes of His Majesty's Government, he had, in defiance of Russian public opinion, stopped the advance of the Russian troops on Tehran, facilitated an amicable arrangement with the Persian Government, consented to the joint advance of £200,000, sacrificed the ex- Shah, and, in fact, done everything which we had asked him to do.

I here interrupted him by remarking that, while fully appreciating the loyal manner in which he had co-operated with us, I must remind him of the very difficult position in which you had been placed by Russia's action in Persia. Public opinion in Russia was a very different thing to what it was in a constitutional country like England, where it was voiced in Parliament; and I could tell him that there was a moment when there was such a strong feeling against the military measures undertaken by Russia in Persia that, in spite of your earnest desire to maintain the

Anglo-Russian understanding intact, you had almost despaired of being able to defend it.

Sazonoff replied that I made a mistake in underestimating the weight of public opinion in this country and the difficulties with which he had been confronted. Not only had he been attacked in the Press, but he had been reproached in other quarters with sacrificing Russia's interests at our dictation. He had had to overcome considerable opposition in the Council of Ministers, and after the attacks made on the Russian troops at Tabriz last December he had received three letters telling him that he was not fit to direct Russian foreign policy and threatening his life. He was determined to maintain the principle on which the Anglo-Russian understanding was based, and he had not the least desire to assume the administration of Northern Azerbaijan; but if the Russian troops were again attacked he would be forced to do it. We must have more confidence in each other, and His Majesty's Government must believe that, whatever provisional measures Russia might be forced to take in self-defence, she had not the slightest intention of annexing a single yard of Persian territory. Each of the two parties to the agreement of 1907 must, while adhering to its general lines and principles, be allowed a certain latitude as to the measures which either might judge it necessary to adopt in its respective sphere of influence, for Russian public opinion would be estranged did it become known that its Government was being lectured like a child at every step which it took to safeguard its interests.

I told Sazonoff that I fully recognized the difficulties of his position, but that, in my opinion, the principal cause of the misunderstandings which occasionally arose between us lay in the fact that, while the two Governments were doing their best to act loyally together, the Russian consuls in Persia acted in a contrary spirit. When, as had more than once been the case, he had told me that disorders had broken out at Meshed or at Tabriz that had necessitated the intervention of Russian troops, I had never felt quite sure, in my own mind, whether those disorders had not been wilfully provoked by one or other of the consuls in order to provide an excuse for intervention.

Sazonoff declined to admit this. He declared that Müller, his consul at Tabriz, who is now on leave, was an excellent man, and contended that the version given by Dabija of the Meshed incident was correct. I disputed this, and said that Sykes had reported that some eight men had been killed in the sacred chamber itself by maxim fire, and that he had, by a personal visit to the tomb, corroborated the fact of shots having been fired within the shrine itself. Sazonoff replied that he could show me the reports which he had received that stated the exact contrary. The dome of the shrine had alone been injured, and the action of the Russian troops in attacking the sanctuary, outside the shrine, had been amply justified by the fact that the agitators had used it as a base of operations against them. The Emperor, he added, had been much annoyed by the manner in which this incident had been distorted.

Finally, Sazonoff said that he had shown his good intentions by recalling Pokhitonoff, and that he would have no objection to recalling Dabija at the first suitable opportunity. He could not, however, do so immediately, as otherwise it would appear as if he were acting under pressure. He would much prefer, however, that Sykes should be moved at the same time.

We shall never, I fear, be able to work harmoniously with Russia till several changes are effected in the Russian consular service in Persia ; but Sazonoff is not strong enough to effect these changes unaided. He is obliged to consider his own position, which is none too secure, and I therefore think that it would be politic on our part to offer to move one or two of our consuls as an act of reciprocity. The Persian Minister here has repeatedly told me that he has implicit confidence in Sazonoff's loyalty and good intentions, but that he is too heavily handicapped owing to the manner in which the consuls, as well as some of the subordinate officials in his Ministry, disobey his instructions.

Persia was naturally one of the questions discussed by Sir E. Grey and M. Sazonoff at Balmoral. Though they were agreed in principle as to the necessity of establishing a strong government at Tehran with a properly organized force to maintain order, the subsequent negotiations came to nothing owing to the difficulty of finding the right man to place at the head of such a government, as well as of providing the funds necessary for the formation of a gendarmerie under foreign officers. Meanwhile the Russian consuls continued to arrogate to themselves more and more administrative powers, while the representations which I had to make on the subject did but serve to accentuate the divergence of views held in London and St. Petersburg with regard to the interpretation to be placed on the 1907 agreement. Russia, on the one hand, desired more elbow room and freedom of action in North Persia, where she had thousands of subjects or protected subjects, and where the trade was entirely in her hands. She was willing to allow us to do what we liked in our own sphere provided that we refrained from exercising a sort of inquisitorial control over her actions in the Russian sphere. She also thought that the time had come for what would virtually have amounted to the partition of the neutral zone, and suggested that the clause relating to it should be modified by an exchange of secret notes. His Majesty's Government, on the other hand, had constantly in view the maintenance of Persia's integrity and independence. While naturally concerned with the protection of British economic interests in the neutral zone, they had no wish to enlarge the sphere of their own responsibilities or to see Russian political influence extended over its northern portion. They therefore merely expressed their readiness to take into consideration any proposals which the Russian Government might submit with a view to effecting a clearer definition of British and Russian interests in that zone.

The situation created by the action of the Russian consuls at last became so serious that I was instructed at the end of June, 1914, to ask for an audience in order to impress on the Emperor the grave preoccupation which it was causing His Majesty's Government.

On His Majesty's inquiring whether their anxiety had been caused by anything that had happened recently, I replied that I had already, a year ago, advocated a frank exchange of views between the two Governments, as I .was even then afraid that the trend of events in North Persia would end by creating a situation that might prove fatal to the Anglo-Russian understanding. Events had since been moving fast, and North Persia was now to all intents and purposes a Russian province. We did not, I proceeded to say, for a moment doubt His Majesty's assurance that he would not annex any portion of Persian territory. We were but recording actual facts. Unforeseen events had led to the occupation of certain districts in North Persia by Russian troops, and, little by little, the whole machinery of the administration had been placed in the hands of the Russian consuls. The Governor-General of Azerbaijan was a mere puppet who received and carried out the orders of the Russian consul-general, and the same might be said of the Governors at Resht, Kazwin and Julfa. They were one and all agents of the Russian Government and acted in entire independence of the central government at Tehran. Vast tracts of land in North Persia were being acquired by illegal methods, large numbers of Persians were being converted into Russian-protected subjects, and the taxes were being collected by the Russian consuls to the exclusion of the agents of the Persian financial administration. The above system was being extended to Ispahan and even to the neutral zone. We had not the slightest desire to dispute Russia's predominant interests and position in the north, but we did take exception to the methods by which that predominance was being asserted and the attempts which were being made to extend it to the neutral zone. I concluded by reminding the Emperor that, without the support of Parliament, no British Government could maintain the Anglo-Russian understanding, and that, unfortunately, the sympathies of Liberals and Conservatives alike were being alienated by what was happening in North Persia.

The Emperor, after listening attentively to what I had said, replied that the present situation in North Persia had been brought about by circumstances which the Russian Government could not control. It had originated with the troubles caused by the Fedais in Tabriz and by the necessity which had subsequently arisen of safeguarding Russia's interests in the north. No one regretted this necessity more than himself. In the first place he could give me his word of honour that he sincerely desired to withdraw his troops, and, in the second, he felt that he was laying himself open to the suspicion of acting contrary to his assurances. He quite understood the motives which had prompted the representations of His Majesty's Government, and he would welcome a frank exchange of views as calculated to remove the danger of any possible misunderstanding in the future. The first thing, however, to be done was to control the action of his consuls, and he would cause the whole matter to be inquired into by a committee at the Ministry for Foreign Affairs.

The Emperor then turned the conversation on to the question of the neutral zone, remarking that the simplest manner of defining our respective positions with regard to it was to partition it. On my replying that, though I quite agreed that the two Governments ought to come to an understanding as to what they were respectively entitled to do in that zone, His Majesty's Government had no desire to extend their responsibilities, the Emperor said that it might in any case be necessary to revise the agreement of 1907. He was quite ready to consent to this if His Majesty's Government desired it. As I took leave of His Majesty at the close of my audience, the Emperor said: "I can only tell you, as I have so often told you before, that my one desire is to remain firm friends with England and, if I can prevent it, nothing shall stand in the way of the closest possible understanding between our two countries."

I, personally, was strongly in favour of a revision of the 1907 agreement, as nothing was more calculated in my opinion to create tension between the two countries than to leave the neutral zone a debatable land. To do so would but occasion constant bickerings and mutual recriminations in the future. As it was, their respective economic interests in it were constantly clashing, more especially as regarded the construction of railways. While British syndicates were anxious to obtain concessions for certain lines, the Russian Government objected to the construction of any such railways near the Russian zone, for fear that the Persian markets would be flooded with seaborne British goods to the detriment of Russia's trade.

On the other hand, the Russian Government strongly favoured the idea of a Trans-Persian railway that, when linked up with the Russian and the Indian railway systems, would serve as a transit route between Europe on the one side and India and Australasia on the other. Early in 1912 they submitted a scheme for such a railway to His Majesty's Government, who accepted it in principle under certain reserves, with the result that a Société des Etudes was eventually formed to consider the questions of alignment and finance. During the two years which followed there were intermittent conversations between the two Governments on the subject of the alignment. No agreement was, however, reached, as, while His Majesty's Government insisted on the line entering the British sphere at Bunder Abbas via Ispahan and Shiraz, and on its not being prolonged to Karachi without their formal consent, the Russian Government held out for the more direct route via Tehran and Kerman to Chahbar, which they maintained was the only point on the South Persian coast where a good harbour could be constructed. But leaving the alignment question out of account, the chances of raising the necessary capital were so remote that, even had the war not intervened, it is very doubtful if the scheme would have materialized.

CHAPTER 10
1912-1913

Events were, meanwhile, moving fast in the Balkans, where the Turco-Italian War had engendered an unrest which proved to be but the precursor of a general upheaval. The crisis which ensued not only brought the interests of Russia into direct conflict with those of Austria, but threatened on more than one occasion to endanger European peace.

The death of Count Aehrenthal, and the appointment of Count Berchtold as his successor, had effected a distinct improvement in Austro-Russian relations, for the latter had, as Austrian Ambassador at St. Petersburg during the Bosnia crisis of 1908-9, acquitted himself of his difficult mission with such tact and discretion that the sins of his Government were not visited on him. Though destined to play so fateful and uncompromising a part in the negotiations which preceded the Great War, he was a *persona non grata* at the Russian Court, and this fact had helped to relax the existing tension. The very question, moreover, which was at the root of their mutual jealousies served, curiously enough for a time, to bring the two Governments into closer contact till, as it became more acute, their relations again grew dangerously strained.

In an audience, which I had with the Emperor early in 1912, His Majesty told me that he was seriously preoccupied by the situation in the Balkans, as, though anxious to maintain friendly relations with Turkey, he could not remain a disinterested spectator of a war between that Power and one of the Balkan States. He therefore suggested that the Powers of the Triple Entente should consult together beforehand so as to be prepared with a united plan of action, in the event of their being suddenly confronted with a Balkan war or with a forward movement on the part of Austria. No practical steps were taken to give effect to this suggestion; for, as I told the Emperor, we wished to avoid taking any step that might split up Europe into two hostile camps. We should, I added, prefer to see Austria and Russia, as the two Powers most directly interested, come to some agreement to which all the other Powers could become parties. Russian diplomacy, meanwhile, was not idle, and in February, 1912, as I learned later in the year, Bulgaria and Serbia signed a treaty of defensive alliance guaranteeing the integrity of their respective territories in the event of either of them being attacked by Austria, Roumania or any other Power. By a secret military convention attached to this treaty provision was made for the number of troops to be furnished by each of the two contracting parties in such a defensive war, as well as for the disposal of their respective armies and for the plan of campaign to be adopted in the event of their both being engaged in war with Turkey.

By a further secret "annexe" they determined their respective spheres of influence in Macedonia, while they agreed that any difference respecting the execution or interpretation of the treaty should be referred to Russia for decision. The presence of members of the Greek and Montenegrin royal families at the coming of age festivities of the Crown Prince Boris, which were celebrated shortly afterwards at Sofia, prepared the ground for the conclusion of treaties of a somewhat similar character with Greece and Montenegro. With the signature of these treaties the Balkan Confederation, for which Russia had so long been working, became an accomplished fact. For it was at her inspiration that Serbia and Bulgaria had concluded a treaty of alliance, that was to bring together two Slav races who had for years past been cutting each other's throat in Macedonia, and that the Balkan Confederation had been finally constituted. It would, she fondly believed, prove a docile instrument in her hands and serve the double purpose of maintaining peace in the Balkans and of barring an Austrian advance to the Ægean.

It was not long, however, before the hopes which she had founded on it as an instrument of peace were rudely shaken. Early in July the first note of warning was sounded by the Russian Minister in Sofia, who reported that the military conspiracy in Turkey and the Albanian insurrection had given rise to a dangerous movement in Bulgaria in favour of armed intervention. Proposals for allaying the threatening storm were successively submitted by M. Sazonoff and Count Berchtold; but, though the latter's programme, in so far as it was based on the maintenance of the territorial status quo and on the pacific development of the Balkan States, did not fail to evoke an official expression of satisfaction from St. Petersburg, the Russian Government were anything but pleased with the initiative thus taken by Austria. She was suspected of wishing to pose as the patron of the Balkan States, a rôle to which Russia laid an exclusive claim. By September the attitude of the Bulgarian Government had become so threatening that they were warned that, if they attacked Turkey, Russia would consider her historic mission at an end and leave Bulgaria to her fate. Sazonoff at the same time made, with the support of His Majesty's Government, strong representations at Constantinople urging the Porte to lose no time in initiating reforms of a far-reaching character.

Curiously enough, however, on his proceeding to Balmoral at the end of the month, Sazonoff never once, despite the growing gravity of the situation, suggested our bringing stronger pressure to bear on the Porte, while the official *communiqué* recording the purport of his conversations with Sir Edward Grey, made but a passing reference to the Balkan crisis. The consequence was that the Russian public, who had founded all their hopes on the Balmoral meeting, most unjustly attributed the subsequent serious turn of events to the lack of support which Russia had received from Great Britain. Even, however, had their hopes been realized and had the Balmoral meeting led to the adoption of some more drastic action at Constantinople, it would have been too late. Be fore Sazonoff had left London the order for the mobilization of the Bulgarian army had been issued, and before he reached St. Petersburg war had been formally declared.

All the efforts of the Russian Government were now directed to localizing the war and to averting an Austrian occupation of the Sanjak, a breach of neutrality that would inevitably have entailed Russia's intervention. They at once announced their determination of upholding the principle of the territorial *status quo*, while they gave the most positive assurances at Vienna that Russia would not intervene if Austria abstained from doing so. Austria, on her part, engaged to restrict her action to the concentration of troops near the Serbian frontier, so that the two Governments were for a time able to act more or less in concert. The policy thus enunciated was not, however, long maintained. Towards the end of October the Emperor, who was entertaining a shooting party at Spala that included the Grand Duke Nicholas and other generals, sent for Sazonoff and said that he desired to afford the Balkan States all the assistance in his power short of involving Russia in any serious entanglements. This audience marked a turning point in the attitude of the Russian Government. They had at first viewed with a certain apprehension the idea of a Bulgarian expansion eastwards and had insisted that the future Turco-Bulgarian frontier should be drawn to the north of Adrianople. They had even approached His Majesty's Government with a proposal for mediation and had submitted a programme of the reforms to be eventually introduced into European Turkey; but before either of these proposals could materialize, the battle of Lule-Burgas had been fought and won and the Balkan Allies had declared that they would not return home empty-handed.

The task of championing the far-reaching claims of the Balkan States was now assumed by Russia; and M. I. Sazonoff, early in November, formulated his views respecting the prospective changes in the territorial status quo as follows:

Turkey to retain possession of Constantinople, with the territory comprised within the Enos-Midia line, and the rest of her European provinces to be divided by right of conquest among the Balkan States; Serbia to acquire, in accordance with the terms of the Serbo-Bulgarian Treaty of 1912, Uskub and a slice of territory extending down to Lake Ochrida, to secure possession of San Giovanni di Medua, and to obtain access to the sea by means of a corridor that would give her direct access to that port; Albania to be made an autonomous province; Montenegro to be given the Sanjak; Roumania to be compensated for her neutrality by a rectification of her frontier on the side of the Dobrudja; Salonica to be converted into a free port, and Mount Athos to be neutralized as a purely monastic settlement.

In drawing up this programme Sazonoff had hoped that Bulgaria would consent to compensate Roumania by a slight concession of territory and that Austria's opposition to a Serbian port on the Adriatic could be bought off by a guarantee of her economic access to the Ægean. Both these expectations proved fallacious, and the latter question was unfortunately allowed to assume proportions which at one moment were fraught with danger to the peace of Europe. The Russian Government had, moreover, given their unqualified support to Serbia's claims under the erroneous impression that, even were Austria to prove troublesome, Germany was so bent on peace that she would not support her ally in any action likely to provoke international complications. Germany's relations with Russia were still referred to in all official utterances as those of traditional friendship, and in spite of the part which she had played in the Bosnia crisis, the Emperor Nicholas did not, as he himself told me, regard her with mistrust. Confidence in Germany's pacific intentions had been further strengthened by the meeting of the two Emperors at Port Baltic, where the personality of the German Chancellor had so favourably impressed both the Emperor and Sazonoff that too large an interpretation had been placed on M. Bethmann-Hollweg's assurances that Germany would not support Austria in a forward policy in the Balkans.

It was, therefore, an unpleasant surprise for the Russian Government when the German Ambassador, after inquiring whether Russia proposed to treat the question of a Serbian post as a *Kraftprobe* (trial of strength), used language that left no doubt as to what Germany would do in the event of an Austro-Russian war. Sazonoff, in reply, reminded Count Pourtales that there had been such trials of strength both in 1909 and 1911, and that, if Germany contemplated acting towards Russia in the spirit of her Agadir policy, the consequences might be very serious. The Russian Government, however, had no wish to push matters too far, as they realized that, were Austria to attempt to expel Serbia from any port of which she had taken possession, Russia would be compelled to intervene. They therefore gave counsels of moderation at Belgrade and in formed the German Ambassador that, though Serbia must be emancipated from her position of dependence on other Powers, the question of how this result was to be achieved might be left over for discussion by the Powers. Thanks to Sir Edward Grey's intervention it was eventually agreed that a conference of Ambassadors should be held in London to discuss the question of Serbia's access to the sea, Albania, the Ægean Islands and Mount Athos, leaving the question of the conditions of peace to stand over till the end of the war.

Down to the meeting of this conference, at the end of 1912, the aim of Russia's policy had been the maintenance of European peace, provided always that her vital interests could be safeguarded by pacific means. On the other hand, it must be admitted that her Government more than once jeopardized the cause of peace by failing to grasp certain salient features of the situation. Neither they nor the Austrians had anticipated the victories on which Serbia had founded her claim to access to the sea, and it was only when they realized that to insist on this claim would mean war with Germany as well as with Austria that they withdrew from an untenable position. Their successive changes of front reflected the views which for the moment found favour with the Emperor. His Majesty was divided between his desire to support the claims of the Balkan States and his wish to keep clear of international complications, and Sazonoff had consequently to vary his language according as either the one or the other of these conflicting purposes held temporary sway over the Emperor's mind. Apt as the Emperor was to be influenced by his immediate surroundings, the presence of the Grand Duke Nicholas and other generals at the Imperial shooting party at Spala at the end of October had tended to give a chauvinistic turn to his policy; while, on returning to Tsarskoe early in December, he once more got into direct touch with Sazonoff and Kokovtsoff, neither of whom desired war. It had been due to their intervention that the partial mobilization desired by the Minister of War had not been carried out, though in consequence of the number of troops which Austria had massed near the Serbian frontier, and of the reinforcements which she had sent to Galicia, Russia had been obliged to retain 350,000 time-expired men with the colours. But whether it was owing to the advice tendered him by his Ministers or to apprehension of a recrudescence of the revolutionary movement should the Russian arms meet with a serious reverse, the pacific trend of his policy at the end of the year came at a most opportune moment. Public opinion was incensed against Austria, and in many quarters the feeling in favour of war was gaining ground.

Fortunately, too, at this conjuncture, the Emperor of Austria made what was regarded in Russian official circles as a *geste pacifique* by sending Prince Godfried Hohenlohe, formerly military attaché at St. Petersburg and a *persona grata* at the Russian Court, with an autograph letter to the Emperor Nicholas. The object of the Prince's mission was not so much to discuss in detail any of the pending questions as to remove the misunderstandings existing between the two Governments. In this he was to a certain extent successful, and the reply of the Emperor Nicholas to the Emperor of Austria's letter was couched in very friendly terms. It laid stress on the concession which Russia had made in consenting to the creation of an autonomous Albania, and concluded by expressing the hope that, by mutual concessions, an arrangement satisfactory to both Governments might be arrived at. The next step taken by the Austrian Government was to suggest that Russia should dismiss her reservists, on the understanding that the Austrian troops on the Galician frontier should be reduced to a figure somewhat below the normal peace effectives of Russian regiments.

As owing to the political outlook Austria would not reduce the number of her troops on the Serbian frontier, the Russian Government urged that the *communiqué* announcing the dismissal of the Russian reservists should contain an assurance that Austria harboured no aggressive designs against Serbia. After a week of fruitless negotiations the Austrian Ambassador eventually took upon himself to authorize the publication in the *Rossia* of a *communiqué* to the above effect; but, by an unaccountable oversight, he omitted to inform his Government of his having done so. The *Rossia's communiqué* was, in consequence, repudiated by the Vienna Telegraphic Agency. Count Thurn subsequently telegraphed to Vienna explaining how the mistake had arisen; and, as M. Sazonoff did not wish to do anything to injure his career, the incident was passed over in silence by the Russian Press. Count Berchtold thanked M. Sazonoff for the considerate manner in which he had acted, and at the same time published an official *communiqué* disclaiming all responsibility for the various statements made on the subject in the Vienna Press. Count Thurn was, nevertheless, shortly afterwards recalled.

In the meantime Adrianople had fallen, and on April 16 an informal truce was concluded at Chatalja; but so great were the fears entertained by the Russian Government of a Bulgarian advance on Constantinople that it was only after the Bulgarians had definitely renounced all idea of forcing the Chatalja line that they withdrew their proposal for the despatch of an international fleet to the Dardanelles. Negotiations for peace were now resumed, and on May 30 the Treaty of London was signed.

Two other questions in which Russia was directly interested — the delimitation of the future Albanian State and Roumania's claim to a rectification of her frontier on the side of the Dobrudja — had at the same time been passing through a succession of acute phases, which had more than once threatened to involve her in war. In consenting to the creation of an autonomous Albania the Russian Government had counted on its being composed of the territory comprised within a line which, starting from Khimarra on the coast, would skirt the shores of Lake Ochrida and follow the course of the rivers Drin and Boyana to the Adriatic. When, therefore, Austria put forward the unexpected demand that Scutari, which Russia desired to see assigned to Montenegro, should be incorporated in its territory, there ensued a deadlock which was rendered all the more perilous owing to the fact that Austria's attitude had been stiffened by the knowledge that she could count on Germany's support. Though warned not to commit themselves too far with regard to Scutari, as His Majesty's Government could not give them more than diplomatic support on a question which was, after all, but of secondary importance, the Russian Government were so afraid that Austria wanted to make Scutari the capital of an almost independent Albania and to exercise a predominant influence over it through its Catholic tribes, that they declined to give way unless complete satisfaction were given to Serbia in the matter of the five towns of Tarabosch, Luma, Radomir, Djakova and Dibra. In the course of the subsequent negotiations they allowed the first three of the above- named towns to be assigned to Albania, but they made a firm stand as regarded Dibra and Djakova, declaring
Two other questions in which Russia was directly interested — the delimitation of the future Albanian State and Roumania's claim to a rectification of her frontier on the side of the Dobrudja — had at the

same time been passing through a succession of acute phases, which had more than once threatened to involve her in war. In consenting to the creation of an autonomous Albania the Russian Government had counted on its being composed of the territory comprised within a line which, starting from Khimarra on the coast, would skirt the shores of Lake Ochrida and follow the course of the rivers Drin and Boyana to the Adriatic. When, therefore, Austria put forward the unexpected demand that Scutari, which Russia desired to see assigned to Montenegro, should be incorporated in its territory, there ensued a deadlock which was rendered all the more perilous owing to the fact that Austria's attitude had been stiffened by the knowledge that she could count on Germany's support. Though warned not to commit themselves too far with regard to Scutari, as His Majesty's Government could not give them more than diplomatic support on a question which was, after all, but of secondary importance, the Russian Government were so afraid that Austria wanted to make Scutari the capital of an almost independent Albania and to exercise a predominant influence over it through its Catholic tribes, that they declined to give way unless complete satisfaction were given to Serbia in the matter of the five towns of Tarabosch, Luma, Radomir, Djakova and Dibra. In the course of the subsequent negotiations they allowed the first three of the above-named towns to be assigned to Albania, but they made a firm stand as regarded Dibra and Djakova, declaring that they would never consent to the incorporation in a Moslem State of places where there were Slav religious institutions. Thanks to Sir E. Grey's good offices, Austria was induced to yield on the question of Dibra, but Djakova still barred the way to a complete settlement. The situation was, moreover, rendered all the more acute by the persistence with which the King of Montenegro was pressing the siege of Scutari. King Nicholas had recently incurred Russia's displeasure by a letter in which he had informed the Emperor that, though he had hitherto always obeyed his commands, he would be unable, after the sacrifice of so many Montenegrin lives, to withdraw from Scutari when it was once taken, even should His Majesty order him to do so. Sooner than give it up he would release Russia from all her obligations to Montenegro.

The Emperor, in reply, told the King that he had already released Russia from her obligations by breaking the agreement under which he was bound to undertake no military operations without Russia's permission; that, in the opinion of Russia's friends and allies, Montenegro's claims to Scutari were ill-founded; and that, as Russia would find herself isolated were she to promise him her support, she must decline to give it. In view of the growing gravity of the situation, the Russian Government were now invited to join the other Powers in making energetic representations at Belgrade and Cettinje for the purpose of raising the siege of Scutari and securing the evacuation of the territories assigned to Albania. As they would only agree to do this on the express condition that Djakova was ceded to Serbia, Count Berchtold, on March 21, agreed to abandon his claim to its incorporation in Albania provided that steps were taken to enforce the immediate cessation of hostilities and the evacuation by Serbia and Montenegro of the territories allotted to that province. Unfortunately, owing to the dilatory action of the Russian Minister, there was some delay in making the necessary notification at Belgrade, and the Austrian Government, in consequence, presented an ultimatum at Cettinje demanding that the civil population should be allowed to leave the town within three days.

Much as this isolated action on the part of Austria was resented at St. Petersburg, the orders given by King Nicholas for a general assault on the town caused such offence that the Russian Government informed the Powers that they would raise no objection to a collective naval demonstration at Antivari, though Russia would not be able to participate in it. The Emperor at the same time addressed a personal telegram to King Nicholas telling him, in terms which amounted to a command, that he must bow to the decision of the Powers. In consequence of the language held by Russia at Belgrade, the Serbian troops received orders on April 10 to abstain from any further active operations against Scutari, but on the 23rd the town surrendered to the Montenegrins. The situation was thus rendered extremely critical, as, unless some coercive measures were taken by the Powers collectively, Austria, it was feared, would have recourse to isolated action, and such action on her part might easily involve Russia in war. In order to prevent this the Russian Government appealed to France and Great Britain to put in an appearance, even if they did not fire a shot, should coercive action of any kind be decided on. There were, however, difficulties in the way of their doing so. Fortunately, when the outlook was almost desperate — for there was a moment when I thought war inevitable — King Nicholas on May 4 announced his intention of surrendering Scutari to the Powers. Ten days later the town was occupied by an international naval force.

The second question — that of Roumania's claim to territorial compensation — had already been raised at the first Peace Conference in London, but owing to the tactless manner in which it had been treated by the Bulgarian delegate, Dr. Daneff, no settlement had been reached. The Roumanians had now put forward a claim to all the territory comprised within a line drawn from Silistria to Baltchik, and had, in doing so, placed Russia in a very difficult position. By a convention concluded in 1902 she had guaranteed the integrity of Bulgaria's territory, and she had, therefore, to give Roumania a friendly warning not to attempt to occupy any portion of it by force of arms. About the middle of February the unexpected announcement that Roumania contemplated occupying Silistria fell like a bombshell at St. Petersburg, causing a profound feeling of depression in official circles as well as a sharp fall on the Bourse. Much, however, as the Emperor resented what he regarded as an unjustifiable attempt to deprive Bulgaria of territory which Russia had won for her by the War of Liberation, he was so bent on maintaining peace that, while using all his influence to stay Roumania's hand, he caused Bulgaria to be informed that she must be prepared to make some concession. Were she to refuse to do so she might involve not only Russia but Europe in war; and His Majesty therefore gave her clearly to understand that if she desired his support she must cede Silistria to Roumania.

This question formed the subject of a somewhat heated conversation between the German Ambassador and M. Sazonoff in which Count Pourtales, after pointing out the serious consequences that might ensue from an active intervention by Russia, suggested that, were Bulgaria and Roumania to come to blows, the Powers should stand aside as they had in the Balkan War. The question was, however, one in which Russia was too directly interested for her to take such an engagement. The Black Sea was not the Adriatic, and as M. Sazonoff warned Count Pourtales, circumstances might arise which would compel her to act as her interests dictated. He nevertheless took the opportunity of suggesting that Bulgaria and Roumania should leave the whole question in the hands of the Powers, and it was eventually agreed to refer it to a conference of the Ambassadors at St. Petersburg.

That conference held its first sitting on March 31, under the presidency of M. Sazonoff, and its discussions were throughout conducted on purely party lines — the Ambassadors of the Triple Alliance taking the side of Roumania, while the cause of Bulgaria was pleaded by M. Sazonoff, M. Delcassé and myself. The former based Roumania's claims to Silistria and to the territory comprised within a line drawn from that town to Baltchik, on the ground of its strategical importance for the defence of the Dobrudja. They dwelt more especially on the fact that it was in consequence of the assurances given by the Powers that there should be no change in the territorial status quo, that Roumania had maintained her attitude of reserve during the war, and that now that the Balkan States were to acquire a large accession of territory, Roumania was entitled to some compensation. They also argued that Silistria would certainly have been given to Roumania in 1878 had Bulgaria then acquired the new territories about to be assigned to her.

The representatives of the Triple Entente, on the other hand, contended that the Bulgaro-Roumanian frontier had been definitely fixed by the Treaty of Berlin; that as, owing to her geographical position, Roumania could not participate in the redistribution of Turkey's territory, it was only at Bulgaria's expense that she could receive any territorial compensation, and that no principle of international law entitled a State to demand a cession of territory from one of its neighbours on the ground of the latter's aggrandisement in another direction; that the only principle which Rou mania could invoke was the right of the strongest; and that, while fully appreciating the correctness of her attitude, they considered that she could only claim the cession of certain strategical points to render her frontier more secure on the Bulgarian side.

After prolonged and heated discussions the conference decided that Silistria, together with the territory comprised within a radius of three kilomètres, should be assigned to Roumania; that Roumania should indemnify all Bulgarian subjects who within six months expressed their desire to emigrate from the said territory; and that Bulgaria should erect no fortifications along the frontier between the Danube and the Black Sea. The only interest attaching to this award, which was so soon to become a dead letter, was the whole-hearted support given Bulgaria by M. Sazonoff, as it was in such marked contrast to the attitude which he adopted to her a few months later. It had, however, an unpleasant sequel for myself. Owing to my having held the rank of Ambassador longer than my French colleague, I had been deputed by M. Sazonoff to open the case for Bulgaria, and I did so on the lines indicated above. My language was reported to Bucharest, with the result that when, a few months later, the present Queen of Roumania — then only Crown Princess — whom I had met frequently at Darmstadt, came to St. Petersburg, I was severely taken to task as the supposed inspirer of the Triple Entente's attitude. Her Royal Highness began by remarking that she felt inclined not to speak to me, and then proceeded to ask how I had dared to say that Roumania had no right to any territorial compensation. I replied that I had merely expressed the views which I had formed after a careful study of the question, though those views might have been biased by the fact that Roumania moved in the German orbit. Were Roumania, I added, to enter the fold of the Triple Entente, she would always find in me a warm defender of her interests.

CHAPTER 11
1913-14

During the protracted crisis caused by the first Balkan War Russia's role had been a very difficult one, and the course of her policy had naturally fluctuated with its successive developments. She had in the spring of 1912 succeeded in reconciling the conflicting claims of Bulgaria and Serbia in Macedonia and in calling into being a Balkan confederation that was to bar Austria's access to the Ægean. She had imagined that this confederation would dance to her tune, whereas it disobeyed her express injunctions and declared war on Turkey. As the natural protector of the Balkan Slavs, she was expected to take charge of their interests and to see that they were not deprived of the fruits of their victory by the intervention of other Powers. In undertaking to champion their cause she was brought face to face with Austria, and in the diplomatic duel which ensued she was seconded by Great Britain and France, and Austria by Germany and Italy. It was mainly due to the untiring efforts of Sir Edward Grey, who acted throughout as mediator and peacemaker, that the two rivals did not have to settle their differences sword in hand and that the European war, which more than once seemed almost within sight, was averted for a time. It was thanks to him that Russia was able to retire without too much loss of prestige from the position which she had taken up on the questions of a Serbian port and of Scutari; and it was again thanks to his intervention that Austria yielded on the subject of Dibra and Djakova — the two points on which Russia was determined to make a firm stand. Though Russia more than once suffered a rebuff, she could well afford to make concessions on matters of secondary importance, as she could console herself with the thought of all the advantages that would accrue from the final settlement of the Balkan question on the lines laid down by the Treaty of London. Turkey was to be virtually banished from Europe, and her European possessions, with the exception of Albania, were to be divided between Russia's clients; while the Balkan confederation was to be converted into a new international factor with which both Germany and Austria would have to count. The Slav world had, therefore, every reason to rejoice, though, as subsequent events proved, its joy was destined to be short-lived.

As Sir Edward Grey's mouthpiece at St. Petersburg, my role throughout the crisis had been to tender counsels of moderation; and both the Emperor and Sazonoff were, fortunately, so bent on maintaining peace so far as was consonant with Russia's honour and interests, that they did not turn a deaf ear to such counsels. The situation was, however, complicated by the fact that Germany had stiffened Austria's attitude by promising to support her should she find herself involved in war with Russia. The Triple Entente was, moreover, at a disadvantage owing to the lack of solidarity between its members. As Sazonoff more than once pointed out in the course of our conversations during the Balkan crisis, as well as during the crisis which followed the appointment of General Liman von Sanders to the command of the Constantinople army corps — to which reference will be made later on — Germany and Austria were allies, while Great Britain and Russia were only friends. Russia, he asserted, was not afraid of Austria, but she had to reckon with Germany as well. If Germany supported Austria, France would make common cause with Russia; but no one knew what Great Britain would do.

This uncertainty as to our attitude encouraged Germany to exploit the situation. Great Britain was the one Power that could strike a mortal blow at her, and if Germany knew that Great Britain would stand by France and Russia she would think twice before taking any action that would place them in a position from which they could not recede with honour. When, in the following year, Austria presented her ill-fated ultimatum at Belgrade, Sazonoff held much the same language, contending that the situation could only be saved by our declaring our complete solidarity with France and Russia. It was then too late, as nothing that we might have said or done could have averted war; but it is a moot question whether an earlier conversion of the Triple Entente into a formal alliance would have exercised any influence on Germany's attitude. The Emperor took the same view of this question as M. Sazonoff, and held that the fact of our not being Russia's ally prevented us giving her the same effective support as France. While realizing how difficult it would be for His Majesty's Government to take such a step, he could not, he said, understand the apprehensions with which such an alliance was regarded in England. It would be restricted to one of a purely defensive character, and would not entail on us any greater risk of war than we ran at present.

Referring to the question in a private letter addressed to Sir E. Grey in February, 1914, I wrote:

Impracticable as is, from our point of view, the idea of an alliance at the present moment, there is no doubt a good deal of truth in Sazonoff's contention that, if Germany knew beforehand that France and Russia could count on England's support, she would never face the risks which such a war would entail. The uncertainty which exists with regard to our attitude enables us, no doubt, to influence both sides to maintain peace, but it places the Triple Entente at a disadvantage in its dealings with the Triple Alliance. Should war, unfortunately, ever break out, it will be almost impossible for us to stand aside and not take part in it.

But what really barred the way to an Anglo-Russian alliance was the fact that it would not have been sanctioned by public opinion in England.

In another respect, too, the Triple Alliance was in a better position than the Triple Entente, as its members had, as a general rule, to take their orders from Berlin ; whereas, whenever some important step was about to be taken by the latter, so much time was lost in the preliminary exchanges of views that by the time the desired formula had been agreed on the psychological moment had often passed or the situation had so changed that the contemplated action had to be modified. Unity of command is often as necessary in the field of diplomacy as it is in the conduct of military operations; and during the Balkan Wars, as subsequently during the Great War, Entente diplomacy was often handicapped by divided counsels, whereas the policy of the Triple Alliance was dictated by its predominant partner. The course which that policy was to take — whether for good or evil — was not, moreover, hampered, as was sometimes the case with us, by a divergence of views among the members of the Cabinet. In this connection the following little story is instructive. I had been invited — I think in the summer of 1912 — by Mr. and Mrs. Asquith to meet the newly-appointed German Ambassador (Baron Marshal von Bieberstein) and his wife at a luncheon given in their honour at No. 10 Downing Street. After the departure of the other guests our hostess took the Marshals and me to see the room where the Cabinet councils are held. Looking at the long green table, with a score or so of chairs ranged in order around it, the Ambassadress asked, "How many Ministers are there in the Cabinet?" After answering this question, Mrs. Asquith, turning to the Ambassador, said, "And how many are you at Berlin?" "*One*," was the curt reply.

In the spring of 1918 I had the offer of a change of post. The Russian climate, coupled with the strain of so much responsible work, had seriously affected my health, and at the end of April Sir Edward, who was always the most considerate of chiefs, wrote me the following letter:

FOREIGN OFFICE.
April 27, 1913.

MY DEAR BUCHANAN, — Increasing physical infirmity will make it impossible to renew Cartwright's term at Vienna, which comes to an end in November.

I know that your health has not been good at St. Petersburg, and if you really think a change necessary I would submit your name for Vienna.

At the same time, I should like to make it very clear that, unless your health requires it, I do not think it is at all in the public interest that you should leave St. Petersburg. You have done the work there so well that I should regret any change. Whoever your successor might be, it would be some time before he could get the position that I believe you have made for yourself at St. Petersburg.

To put it shortly, I should like you to remain at St. Petersburg; but if St. Petersburg is really injuring your health, I do not think it right or fair that Vienna should be filled up without asking you whether you would like that post for yourself. If you think you can stay at St. Petersburg, I shall not only be satisfied but relieved. — Yours,

(Signed) E. GREY.

The offer was a very tempting one, and as I was on the point of going to England on leave, I asked for time to consider it. The day after my arrival in London I was received in audience by the King, and on His Majesty graciously repeating the offer I virtually accepted it. On the following day, however, I had to confess to Sir Edward that my doctor, whom I had seen in the morning, had told me that I could, in his opinion, face St. Petersburg for another two years without serious injury to my health. Sir Edward therefore proposed that I should remain on there subject to the conditions that if my health broke down before the two years were over I should exchange with Sir Maurice de Bunsen, who would go to Vienna, while if I was able to see the two years out I should succeed Sir E. Goschen on the termination of his appointment as Ambassador at Berlin. I agreed, and I actually remained on at St. Petersburg for another five years. I should, however, never have been able to have done this had it not been for the timely discovery that the neuritis and other ailments from which I had been suffering were caused by pyorrhoea. Thanks to my friend Sir Kenneth Goadby's skilful treatment of that insidious complaint, I recovered my health, and was able to bear the strain of four strenuous years of war work without once returning home.

On the conclusion of the first Balkan War Sir Edward was also good enough to submit my name for the G.C.M.G.

But to return to more serious matters. The Treaty of London had re-established peace with Turkey, but had not ended the Balkan crisis, which did but pass from one dangerous phase to another. The victors were busy quarrelling over the division of the spoils, and as under the treaty of 1912 both Serbia and Bulgaria had engaged to submit to Russia's arbitration any differences which might arise between them as to the interpretation of its terms, Sazonoff now called on the two Governments to fulfil this engagement. Serbia, he was aware, would not accept an arbitration based solely on the strict interpretation of that treaty, as in such case the award was bound to be given in Bulgaria's favour. He therefore, while recognizing that the latter's claims in Macedonia were based on both ethnographical and historical grounds, endeavoured to induce her to make certain concessions. As no satisfactory reply had been received from either Government, the Emperor (early in June) addressed a strongly worded telegram to the Kings of Serbia and Bulgaria, expressing surprise that no effect had yet been given to his proposal for a conference of the four allied Prime Ministers at St. Petersburg, and warning them that, were they to embark on a fratricidal war, Russia would reserve her full liberty of action whatever might be the outcome of that conflict.

King Peter's reply was more or less satisfactory, though it insisted that Serbia's claims could not be restricted to the terms of the treaty of 1912 ; but King Ferdinand merely observed that he had already appealed to Russia's arbitration, and that Serbia was endeavouring to deprive Bulgaria of the fruits of her victories. On June 25 the Bulgarian Minister informed Sazonoff that his Government could not accept arbitration except on the basis of the 1912 treaty, and that they had, moreover, decided to recall their Minister from Belgrade. As this was regarded at St. Petersburg as tantamount to a declaration of war and as a betrayal of the Slav cause, Russia formally denounced the treaty of 1902, under which she had guaranteed the integrity of Bulgaria's territory against an attack on the part of Roumania. A few days later the Bulgarian Government accepted Russia's arbitration without insisting on their former conditions, but at the last moment the departure of their delegates for St. Petersburg was countermanded, and on June 29 General Savoff ordered an advance along the whole line.

In Russian military circles the impression had at first prevailed that the Bulgarians would be strong enough to defeat the combined armies of Greece and Serbia, and though such a result would have had the advantage of precluding any danger of Austria's intervention, the prospect of a too powerful Bulgaria was regarded with a certain apprehension that was, not unnaturally, strengthened by Bulgaria's utter disregard of Russia's wishes and advice. Both the Emperor and Sazonoff, moreover, had listened sympathetically to Prince Nicholas of Greece, who had come to St. Petersburg for the express purpose of inducing Russia to use her influence at Bucharest in favour of Roumania's intervention in the coming war. The appeal for assistance which Bulgaria now addressed to Russia fell, therefore, on deaf ears, and, so far from exercising a restraining influence on Roumania, Russia indirectly encouraged her to take the field. There was an exchange of friendly messages between the Emperor and King Charles in which the identity of Russia's and Roumania's interests was emphasized.

Though Russia may at the outset have been prompted to adopt this line by the hope of maintaining peace, the idea of checkmating Austria by detaching Roumania from the Triple Alliance and of preventing Bulgaria establishing her hegemony in the Balkans was not altogether absent from her mind. No attempt was even made to restrict Roumania's action to the occupation of the Turtukoi-Baltchik line, and her advance on Sofia deprived Bulgaria of all possibility of retrieving her initial reverses. Under the terms of the Treaty of Bucharest, which was signed on August 10, 1913, she had to submit to seeing Macedonia divided between Serbia and Greece and to ceding to Roumania some eight thousand square kilometres of territory. The original idea of the Russian Government had been that, while the belligerents should be allowed to draw up their own treaty of peace, that treaty should be subject to revision by the Powers; but all idea of revising the Treaty of Bucharest was dropped after the publication of the telegram in which the Emperor William congratulated King Charles on the results of his wise and statesmanlike policy.

Meanwhile Turkey, following the example set by Roumania, had moved her troops across the Enos-Midia line and had occupied Adrianople. Russia at once protested, and informed the Porte that she could not allow an emancipated Christian population to be replaced under Ottoman rule. She was not, however, prepared to back up this protest by any military action, more especially as, so far as her material interests were concerned, she had no objection to Adrianople remaining in Turkey's hands. It was different when Turkey went a step farther and ordered her troops to cross the

Maritza. Sazonoff was then at once authorized by the Emperor to recall the Russian Ambassador from Constantinople and to concert with his colleagues as to the further measures which Russia should take. This time Russia was really in earnest, and had not the Turkish Government yielded and recalled their troops across the Maritza effect would have been given to the Emperor's orders. As a result of the subsequent negotiations between Turkey and Bulgaria, the former recovered the greater part of Thrace, of which Bulgaria had been in occupation for some six months.

The outbreak of the second Balkan War had created an entirely new situation and had revealed, not for the first time, the little respect with which orders emanating from St. Petersburg were treated at Sofia and Belgrade. Intoxicated with the wine of their victories and suffering from an acute form of megalomania, the Balkan allies were one and all intent on retaining possession of whatever territories their respective armies had wrested from Turkey. Bulgaria had borne the brunt of the war; she had had to face, on the eastern front, the bulk of the Turkish army, while her losses in killed and wounded far exceeded those of her allies. As a result of her victories she was to annex the large and fertile province of Thrace. Such an extension of her territory towards the east had never been contemplated when, in 1912, she and Serbia had determined their respective spheres of influence in Macedonia. Greece and Serbia, therefore, contended that she ought to renounce her rights under that treaty in favour of her allies. It was their armies that had liberated Macedonia from the Turkish yoke, and Serbia, moreover, would, by the proposed creation of an autonomous Albania, be deprived of certain districts that had been allotted to her.

They failed, however, to take into account the fact that Bulgaria had, ever since the short-lived Treaty of San Stefano, had her eyes constantly fixed on Macedonia as her lawful inheritance, and had during all the intervening years been gradually consolidating her position in that province. Bulgaria, on the other hand, was ill-advised enough to insist on the strict execution of the treaty of 1912, and refused to make concessions which were but reasonable under the altered circumstances, more especially as it was in order to satisfy her territorial ambitions in Thrace that the first Balkan War had been unduly prolonged contrary to the wishes of her allies. She, moreover, regarded the military convention that had been concluded between Greece and Serbia as a direct provocation, framed with the express purpose of forcing her to renounce her long-coveted prize. Finally, she committed the colossal blunder of placing herself in the wrong and her rivals in the right, in the eyes of the civilized world, by attacking Serbia.

After the manner in which Bulgaria had flouted her advice it was but natural that Russia's sympathies should be on the side of Serbia, but in encouraging Roumania to intervene in the conflict she, in my opinion, steered a course which, as I told Sazonoff at the time, was fraught with danger for the future. If, as I readily admitted, Bulgaria was responsible for the opening of hostilities, Greece and Serbia could hardly be acquitted of what almost amounted to deliberate provocation. Prince Nicholas of Greece had, during his visit to St. Petersburg, urged me to persuade my Government to use all their influence to bring not only Roumania, but even Turkey, into the war which he regarded as imminent. The fact that Greece, who without the victories won by Bulgaria over the Turks would have played but a sorry part in the first Balkan War, was prepared to call in the old enemy of the Balkan Christians to crush her former ally, revealed the general spirit of unscrupulous aggrandizement that produced the second Balkan War. But it was not on such ethical grounds, but on considerations of what the Germans call *Real Politik*, that I tried to dissuade M. Sazonoff from listening to Prince Nicholas. Bulgaria, despite her heavy losses in the first Balkan War, was still a very important factor in the Balkans, while neither Roumania nor Greece could be counted on to fly to Serbia's assistance should she be attacked by Austria. For us to take a step that would alienate Bulgaria for all time and drive her into the arms of the Triple Alliance would, I urged, break down the barrier which Russia had been at such pains to erect against an Austro-German *Drang nach Osten*.

The Treaty of Bucharest was hailed with satisfaction by the Emperor William, and with good cause. For that treaty undid all that had been accomplished by the first Balkan War and created a situation which Germany turned to good account when the Great War broke out. After its signature King Ferdinand is reported to have said, "*Ma vengeance sera terrible*," and he kept his word.

I was absent from Russia on sick leave during the greater part of the autumn of 1913, and on returning to St. Petersburg at the end of the year I found the Russian Government greatly exercised by the question of the appointment of General Liman von Sanders to the command of the Turkish army corps at Constantinople, as well as by the engagement of a large number of German officers to hold executive posts in the Turkish army. Such an appointment would, in their opinion, place Constantinople and the key of the Straits in the hands of a German general. We had promised the Russian Government our diplomatic support on this question, but at their request the representations which were to have been made by the

Ambassadors of the Triple Entente had been temporarily postponed. It was only, indeed, after the publication of an Imperial trade appointing General von Sanders to the command in question that they asked us to take action.

From information which we had received in the meanwhile we had reason to believe that the importance of this command had been exaggerated, and we were, moreover, seriously hampered by the fact — on which the German Government had laid great stress — that the executive command of the Turkish Fleet was held by a British admiral. We were not, therefore, prepared to go quite as far as M. Sazonoff wished. The instructions originally sent to Sir Louis Mallet had consequently to be toned down. On hearing of this, M. Sazonoff expressed the keenest disappointment. His contention was that, as this was almost the first question seriously affecting her interests on which Russia had appealed to Great Britain for support, it was in the nature of a test case in which the Triple Entente was on its trial. The Entente, he urged, constituted a stronger combination of Powers than the Triple Alliance, and if only Great Britain, France and Russia would let Turkey see that they were in earnest the latter would give way and Germany would do nothing. Instead, however, of acting firmly together, they were always proclaiming their nervous dread of war, and by so doing would one day find that they had brought war upon themselves.

There was a grain of truth in the above contention. During the Balkan Wars Russia had had on more than one occasion to recede from positions which she had somewhat rashly taken up, and the impression that she would never fight had gained such ground at Constantinople that the Turks had even told the German Ambassador that he need have no apprehensions of any action by Russia. M. Sazonoff had, however, been mistaken when he hinted that the Triple Entente had on this occasion proved a failure. For Sir E. Grey had again successfully intervened as mediator, adding one more to the many services which he had already rendered Russia and Europe in the cause of peace. It was, indeed, as M. Sazonoff himself gratefully acknowledged after wards, thanks to the firm language which he used to Prince Lichnowsky, that a settlement was eventually reached under which General Liman von Sanders, while being accorded the rank of a Turkish field-marshal and remaining at the head of the German military mission, relinquished the command of the Constantinople army corps.

CHAPTER 12
1910-1914

I have in the preceding chapters dealt exclusively with questions affecting Russia's international position and her relations with foreign Powers; but, before proceeding further and before entering on a review of the fateful year that was to witness the outbreak of a world war, I must devote a few pages to the consideration of her internal situation.

When I arrived in Russia at the end of the year 1910 it was among the students of the universities and of the high schools that the prevailing political unrest was most marked. In many of them strikes had been declared and lectures suspended, while recourse was had to noxious gases and other terroristic measures to prevent students who desired to continue their studies putting in an appearance. On the other hand, vigorous measures were taken by the Government to restore order; but the professors, as a rule, delivered their lectures to almost empty benches under the protection of the police. In a conversation which I had with him early in March M. Stolypin told me that the Government had not suspended the autonomy of the universities, but had left it intact as far as regarded ordinary matters of administration.

They could not, however, accord to a number of hot-headed youths the right, which no other class of Russian subjects possessed, of holding political meetings without the sanction of the competent authorities. Nor could they permit a return to the state of things that had existed in 1905, when a professor delivered a lecture on the subject of the manufacture of bombs. As neither the peasants nor the army were any longer disposed to listen to revolutionary propaganda, the universities, according to M. Stolypin, were almost the only field left open to the machinations of the committees that, in Paris and other capitals, were endeavouring to organize a fresh rising through the agency of the students. The strike, having accomplished its object — that of calling public attention to the state of Russian educational institutions — was shortly afterwards countermanded. In the Duma, however, the disciplinary measures which the Government had adopted, as well as the expulsion of a number of students and of several leading professors, had but increased the hostility with which their general policy was regarded by a large section of that Chamber. During the debate on the Budget violent speeches were made in condemnation of their habitual recourse to exceptional laws and of their system of administrative exile.

But it was from an unexpected quarter, during the debate in the Council of Empire on a Local Government bill for the six western provinces, that an attack was delivered which placed the Government in a minority. The object of this bill was to limit the influence of the large Polish landowners. In order to accomplish this it was proposed that the election of representatives of the proprietary class to district and provincial councils should take place in two curiae, the one Russian and the other Polish, while the number of Polish members to be elected was to be fixed by law. The bill represented, in fact, the idea of nationalism which had of late years been one of the fundamental principles of the Government's policy. It might, therefore, have been expected to appeal to those parties on the right, who were never weary of propounding the doctrine of "Russia for the Russians." They had, however, long been seeking a favourable opportunity for encompassing the fall of M. Stolypin; and a cabal, under the leadership of M. Trepoff and M. Durnovo, succeeded in getting the measure defeated by a majority of 24 votes.

On the following day — March 18 — M. Stolypin tendered his resignation, and at one moment it was believed that the Emperor had accepted it. Thanks, however, to the intervention of the Dowager Empress, a Ministerial crisis was averted and M. Stolypin withdrew his resignation. Two days later the *Official Messenger* published an Imperial ukase suspending, by virtue of Article XCIX of the Fundamental Laws, the sittings of the Duma and of the Council of Empire for three days. It was at the same time announced that M. Trepoff and M. Durnovo, the leaders of the attack on M. Stolypin's bill, had been granted leave of absence from their duties from January 1-14. The personal satisfaction thus given M. Stolypin met with but little criticism save on the part of the friends of these two gentlemen; but it was different with regard to the ukase suspending the sittings of the two Chambers.

The object of that ukase had been to enable the Government to promulgate the Western Governments bill by administrative decree under Article LXXXVII of the Fundamental Laws, according to which the Government was at liberty to publish such decrees in cases of urgency when the Duma was not in session. As had been generally expected, the Western Governments bill was immediately promulgated by an Imperial ukase ! in the form in which it had left the Duma, and, as had equally been expected, the head of the Octobrist party, M. Guchkoff, at once resigned the presidency of that Chamber. He was succeeded by M. Rodzianko. The Government's organs in the Press defended M. Stolypin's action on the ground that the right to determine whether circumstances were abnormal or not rested solely with the supreme authority, and that that authority could alone decide whether circumstances justified the application of Article LXXXVII of the Fundamental Laws. It cannot, however, be contested that M. Stolypin had not only made an unwarranted and unconstitutional use of that article, but that he had also committed a grave tactical blunder. Had he been contented with the satisfaction afforded him by the suspension of his two principal opponents, and had he had the patience to wait a few months till the bill had become law, as it most certainly would have, in the normal constitutional course of its re-introduction in the Duma, he would have won over the great majority of that assembly to the side of the Government. As it was, he alienated the sympathies of his principal supporters in that chamber at the very moment when he had thrown down the gauntlet to the reactionary party in the Council of Empire. He tried, but utterly failed, to persuade M. Guchkoff and the Octobrists that, in acting as he had done, he was but defending the rights of the Duma, whose bill had been rejected by the Upper Chamber. Resolutions condemning his action were subsequently passed in both chambers.

The term of two months, within which the Government was obliged by law to submit to the Duma any bill that had been promulgated by Imperial ukase, expired on May 26. On that day, and only on that day, was the Western Government bill laid before that chamber; but in order that there might be no risk of its being rejected, the Duma was at the same time prorogued till the autumn. It would undoubtedly have constituted the one great contentious measure of the autumn session had it not been for the deplorable tragedy that had in the meanwhile removed M. Stolypin from the scene.

On September 9 the Emperor with the Imperial family had left Peterhof for Kieff, where His Majesty was to unveil a statue of Alexander II. On the evening of the 14th the Emperor with the young grand duchesses attended a gala representation at the Opera House. The President of the Council and some of his colleagues who were in attendance occupied seats in the first row of the stalls. During the second *entr'acte* M. Stolypin was standing, with his back to the orchestra, facing the audience, and was talking to a colleague when a young man dressed in evening clothes approached him, coming down the gangway between the stalls from the rear of the house. M. Stolypin seems to have looked at him interrogatively as if to ask him what he wanted, when the young man drew a revolver and fired two shots point blank at His Excellency. A scene of indescribable confusion ensued, during which the assassin almost succeeded in escaping. The Emperor, who at once advanced to the front of his box, was enthusiastically acclaimed, and the National Anthem was, on the demand of the audience, sung by the whole opera company kneeling on the stage. M. Stolypin was removed in an ambulance to a neighbouring hospital, where he expired four days later.

The assassin, a Christianized Jew, Mordko Bogrov by name, had in 1906-7 been a member of the Revolutionary Committee of Student Delegates, and had, as such, undergone on more than one occasion short terms of imprisonment. Like the famous Azef, he had at the same time acted as an agent of the secret police, whose confidence he secured by the betrayal of some of his associates. Bogrov, it appears, had recently been living with a married brother in St. Petersburg, and only arrived in Kieff on the day preceding his crime. He at once called on Lieutenant-Colonel Kuliabko, the chief of the secret police in that town, and informed him that the St. Petersburg Social Revolutionary Committee had decided to kill the President of the Council and the Minister of Education, and that they were employing as their instruments a woman called Nina Alexandrovna and a man known by the name of Nicholas. Colonel Kuliabko placed implicit confidence in all that Bogrov told him and even entrusted him with the mission of watching over M. Stolypin's safety and of securing the arrest of the intending murderers. He at the same time warned M. Stolypin's secretary of the plot, adding that all the necessary precautions had been taken. The Governor of Kieff, which was known as a hotbed of the revolutionary movement, in which Jews had always played a prominent part, was said to have issued an order to the effect that no Jews were to be admitted to the theatre. In spite of this, however, Bogrov was given a pass and was not even subjected to a personal examination to see if he carried any weapon on him. Considering that the most minute precautions had been taken to prevent the entrance of any suspicious persons, it seems incredible that Colonel Kuliabko should have taken no steps to have Bogrov watched and that he should have placed implicit reliance on the word of a man who, he knew, had at one time been in close relations with the revolutionary party.

M. Stolypin had been appointed President of the Council in July, 1906, at a moment when Russia was still in the throes of revolution and when government on constitutional lines had been rendered almost impossible by the irreconcilable attitude of the cadets and of the parties of the extreme left. Though it was he who gave effect to the Imperial ukase dissolving the first Duma, it was not on his advice that the Emperor had signed it. In his "Souvenirs de Mon Ministère," published in the *Révue des Deux Mondes*, the late M. Isvolsky tells us how M. Stolypin, who was at that time Minister of the Interior, had been in favour of a Coalition Government in which the Duma and the Council of the Empire were to be largely represented; how the President of the Council, M. Goremykin, who had apparently heard of the *pour-parlers* already initiated with certain prominent members of the Duma, had suddenly told his colleagues that it was his intention to submit for the Emperor's signature an Imperial ukase dissolving that assembly; how he had asked them to meet him the next evening on his return from his audience, and how he had then electrified them by announcing that he had brought back the Imperial ukase duly signed, but that the Emperor had at the same time deigned to relieve him of his functions as President of the Council and to replace him by M. Stolypin.

The step thus taken by the Emperor, in the hope of mitigating the bad impression which the dissolution of the Duma was bound to create, did but exasperate all parties alike. The reactionaries were indignant at M. Goremykin's summary dismissal, while Liberals of all shades of opinion saw in the dissolution of the Duma the first step towards the eventual abrogation of the 1905 charter. In a crisis like that through which Russia was then passing, M. Stolypin had no choice but to accept the mandate with which the Emperor had charged him, involving though it did the dissolution of the Duma. The dissolution was immediately followed by renewed efforts on the part of the cadets and their allies to foment disorders. The Viborg proclamation calling on the people to refuse to serve in the army or to pay taxes was issued; the peasantry were incited to agrarian outrages; the houses of landed proprietors were pillaged or burnt"; terrorist crimes followed each other in quick succession; and finally M. Stolypin's summer residence was blown up, his daughter maimed for life, and some fifty persons killed or wounded.

The second Duma, which met in the spring of 1907, was more moderate than the first, but the revolutionary doctrines preached by the Social Democrats forced Stolypin to ask the Chamber to consent to judicial proceedings being taken against fifty-five members of that party. On an attempt being made to avoid a direct answer to this request by referring it to a Commission, he obtained from the Emperor a ukase dissolving the Duma.

Stolypin then decided that the only course open to him was to restrict the franchise. His object was to secure the representation of the best classes and to give to the landed proprietors and to those who had material interests at stake a preponderating voice in the representative Chamber. A new electoral law was accordingly promulgated under which sweeping changes were effected with a view to introducing as many Conservative or moderate Liberal elements as possible and of eliminating or reducing the representation of all non-Russian nationalities.

This new departure exposed Stolypin to the reproach of having deprived the Duma of its character of a representative assembly; but his accusers were too apt to forget the difficulties with which he was confronted. On the one hand, the party of reaction was clamouring for the abolition of all forms of parliamentary institutions on the ground that they had been tried and found wanting. On the other hand, he could not hope to draw from an ignorant peasantry, hungering for land which did not belong to them, who had not a thought for anything beyond their own personal interests, the material wherewith to build up a Chamber that would help him to stamp out anarchy and to elaborate reforms of a moderate but beneficial character. In his desire to promote the nationalist policy, of which he had made himself the champion, he inclined too much towards the right, and, as has already been shown, he committed the grave mistake of making an unconstitutional use of Article LXXXVII of the Fundamental Laws.

Stolypin had such confidence in himself — such an iron determination to do what he considered best for his country without any regard for his own safety or interests, that he was too prone to govern with a strong hand. He relied too much on the police and suppressed any manifestation of discontent without attempting to remove the causes which had given rise to it. His faults and mistakes were, however, largely outweighed by the services which he had rendered. Though he failed to destroy the seeds of unrest that continued to germinate underground, he rescued Russia from anarchy and chaos; and, though forced to place her newly granted representative institutions on a narrower foundation, he saved them from the destruction which at one moment threatened them. He was a true patriot and, despite his faults, a great Minister. He combined with rare strength of character a simple, gentle nature that charmed and attracted me. From the moment of my arrival he held out the hand of friendship, which I was not slow to grasp, and up to the day of his death I was in constant touch with him. He was an ideal Minister to transact business with. Frank and outspoken, he always went straight to the point and, what is unusual in a man who, like himself, possessed to an extraordinary degree the gift of oratory, he never wasted time in words. When he once pro mised a thing it was always done. His death was an irreparable loss not only to his own country but to ours; for, had his life been spared, and had he been at the head of the Government when war broke out, many of the disasters which have since befallen Russia would have been avoided.

He had achieved one signal success by initiating a scheme of agrarian reform which had conferred inestimable benefits on the peasantry. With the abolition of serfage by Alexander II, the Russian peasantry had not only secured their own personal liberty, but had at the same time been endowed with grants of land. The Government, however, in its desire to prevent the formation of an agrarian proletariat, had not allotted these lands to the peasants individually, but had divided them among the different communes to be held under a system of collective communal ownership. Each commune, or *mir*, then apportioned out the lands assigned to it in separate lots among its members for a fixed term of years, at the end of which these lots were redistributed afresh. Such a system was incompatible with the requirements of modern agriculture, as it deprived the peasants of all incentive to develop the land of which they were but temporary tenants. In order to give the peasants a personal interest in their lands, and with a view to creating a conservative class of peasant proprietors, Stolypin introduced a series of agrarian reforms which had for their object the gradual conversion of the communal lands into individual holdings. He further facilitated the purchase by the peasants of lands belonging to the State and to the Imperial apanages by the institution of peasant banks. The success of Stolypin's agrarian policy surpassed all expectations, and at the time of his death nearly 19,000,000 acres of land had been allotted to individual peasant proprietors by the land committees.

M. Kokovtsoff, who succeeded Stolypin as President of the Council, was a man of a very different stamp, representing as he did the best type of the old Russian bureaucracy. Honest, hardworking and remarkably intelligent, he had, as Minister of Finance, effected an extraordinary improvement in Russia's financial position; and it was in great measure thanks to his able administration, as well as to the progressive development of Russia's industries and agriculture, that in 1914 her ordinary revenue, which during the preceding years had been rapidly expanding, was estimated at over £370,000,000, and that the gold reserve amounted to £150,000,000. The only serious blot in the Russian Budget was the fact that £95,000,000 of the ordinary revenue were derived from the Government's alcohol monopoly. M. Kokovtsoff was on better terms with the Duma than either his predecessor or the majority of his colleagues. He had on more than one occasion evinced a desire to work in harmony with it ; but in an official statement, published shortly after his appointment as President of the Council, he made it quite clear that, while there could be no question of the abrogation of any of the existing institutions of Government, Stolypin's policy must be carried out in its entirety and would not be changed owing to the acts of terrorists.

In foreign policy M. Kokovtsoff was a firm supporter of the Anglo-Russian understanding. I had a great personal regard for him, and our official relations were always of the best. Unfortunately, while possessing, like M. Stolypin, great natural eloquence, he had not the latter's gift of being able to compress what he had to say into a few words, and, after my conversations with him, I had often to ask myself: "*Was ist der langen Rede kürzer Sinn*?" ("What, briefly, is the long oration's gist?"). He had not, moreover, Stolypin's commanding personality, and, as he was not always able to impose his own views on his colleagues, his assurances did not carry the same weight.

Stolypin's assassination had naturally drawn public attention to the extraordinary and anomalous methods of the Okhrana, or secret police – that darkest of all dark blots in the history of the old régime. Though it seems almost incredible, it is a fact that the Government was in the habit of employing creatures like Azeff, who, acting as the *agents provocateurs*, incited to crime and murder and then delivered over into the hands of the police their unsuspecting victims. They kept these men in their employ even when they knew them to be active revolutionaries who had themselves played a prominent part in the assassination of high-placed State officials. During the autumn session of the Duma the drastic reform of the Okhrana was urgently but vainly demanded.

During the year 1912 there was, with the exception of a number of strikes of a distinctly political character, no open manifestation of the prevailing discontent on the part of the proletariat, while the peasants were engrossed by the task of securing for themselves the benefits accruing from Stolypin's agrarian reforms. The revolutionary organizations were, nevertheless, quietly but actively carrying on their subterranean work, with the result that mutinies broke out in the Baltic and Black Sea fleets as well as among the troops at Tashkent, which had to be suppressed by force. In September the third Duma was dissolved after a life of four and a half years. The new elections, however, effected but little change in the composition of that chamber.

The Octobrists, though somewhat diminished in numbers, still held the balance between the parties on their right and on their left; but they were so dissatisfied with the continual postponement of all constitutional reforms that they were gradually adopting an attitude of greater independence towards the Government. The increasing gravity of the internal situation was, indeed, one of the causes that contributed to the determination of the Government not to depart from a pacific attitude during the acute stages of the Balkan crisis.

In June of the following year — 1913 — the Duma by a large majority passed a resolution censuring the Government for prolonging the state of exceptional law and for delaying the introduction of measures of constitutional reform. The continual postponement of these reforms, together with the severity of the administrative regime that had been accentuated by M. Maklakoff, the newly appointed Minister of the Interior, had so incensed all the law-abiding classes that, as M. Guchkoff remarked, there had never been a time when Russian society and the Russian people had been so deeply permeated with the revolutionary spirit. The legislative work of the Duma continued to be hampered by the constant rejection or radical amendment of its bills by the Council of the Empire and by the failure of the Government to submit for its consideration measures of importance.

To quote but one instance of these. A bill for the reform of the municipalities in Poland that had been voted by the Duma was amended by the Council of the Empire so as to prohibit the use of the Polish language in the debates of the municipal councils. Though the President of the Council had himself supported the proposal to allow the use of Polish, he was successfully opposed by the reactionary Ministers of Justice and of the Interior and by the Procurator of the Holy Synod. The reactionary party in the Government was rapidly gaining the upper hand, and during all the ensuing months till the outbreak of war the situation grew steadily worse. M. Kokovtsoff was summarily dismissed and M. Goremykin, who had been responsible for the dissolution of the first Duma, was once more appointed President of the Council. An amiable old gentleman with pleasant manners, of an indolent temperament and quite past his work, he had not moved with the times, and still looked upon the Duma as an unimportant factor that could be safely ignored. With the consummate skill of the born courtier he had ingratiated himself with the Empress, though, except for his ultra monarchical views, he had nothing whatever to recommend him. The record of his tenure of office in 1906, on the other hand, extinguished all hope of constitutional reforms so long as he enjoyed the confidence of the Emperor. Discontent became so general and so acute, strikes succeeded each other in such rapid succession and assumed such dangerous proportions, that it was hardly surprising that the German Ambassador should have predicted that the declaration of war would start the revolution.

CHAPTER 13
1896-1914

I have in previous chapters reported some of my conversations with the Emperor Nicholas, and it is time that I should give a brief account of my personal relations with His Majesty and with the Imperial family in general. Though I am only dealing at present with the pre-war period, I shall occasionally have to anticipate and to refer to events of a later date.

My relations with the Imperial family date back to the days, some sixteen years before my appointment as Ambassador at St. Petersburg, when I was accredited as *chargé d'affaires* to the Empress's brother, the Grand Duke of Hesse. Princess "Alix" — the name by which the Empress was best known before her marriage — was then a beautiful girl, though shy and reserved; but when once this barrier of reserve was broken down, one realized how charming she could be. Her natural kindness of heart manifested itself in many ways, and in our case more especially by the ready sympathy which she more than once showed us when we were in trouble. Her face was a very striking one, with, at times, a sad and pathetic expression — an expression which Koppay has reproduced to the life in the portrait which he painted soon after her marriage. I remember remarking, when I first saw an engraving of this picture, that there was something in it that suggested the idea of impending tragedy.

It was during a visit which Their Majesties paid to Darmstadt in 1896 that I first had the honour of being presented to the Emperor. It was in one of the *entr'actes* of a gala performance given at the Court theatre, and under ordinary circumstances such a presentation would not have alarmed me. But I had been charged by Lord Salisbury with a somewhat delicate mission, and I was afraid that I should not get in what I wanted to say in the course of a few minutes' conversation. Lord Salisbury had, during the Emperor's recent visit to Balmoral, spoken to him about the Armenian question, which was then passing through one of its acute phases, and the Emperor Nicholas, who was about to visit Paris, had promised to communicate to him, through our Ambassador, the result of the conversations which he was to have on the subject with members of the French Government.

As the Emperor in his conversation with Lord Dufferin had said nothing about Armenia, I had been instructed to endeavour to ascertain whether any decision had been arrived at in Paris. I had hoped, by an indirect reference to the Balmoral meeting, to remind the Emperor of his promise without having to violate the rules of Court etiquette by myself introducing the subject; but this hope was doomed to disappointment. The Emperor, after saying how much he had enjoyed his visit to the Queen, of whom he spoke in the warmest terms, proceeded to speak of matters of local interest, and disconcerted me by saying that he had heard that I had a charming daughter. I confess that for the moment I wished my daughter anywhere, as the mention of her name had deprived me of my last chance of giving the conversation the turn which I desired. I had, therefore, no choice but to tell the Emperor straight out, as he was on the point of dismissing me, that Lord Salisbury would be glad to know what, if any, decisions had been taken at Paris. Much to my relief, he at once reassured me by requesting me to inform Lord Salisbury that during his short stay at Paris his time had been so taken up with other matters that he had had no opportunity of discussing the Armenian question with the French Ministers.

In the autumn of the following year the Emperor and Empress spent several weeks with the Grand Duke and Grand Duchess at Wolfsgarten, and we were occasionally invited to meet them there or at the Darmstadt tennis club, where the Emperor sometimes played while the Empress sat and looked on. The Emperor also received me in private audience, when he talked to me on a variety of subjects. He began with tennis and then went on to shooting, telling me all about the elk, stag, buffaloes and wild boar which he had recently shot in Poland, and saying that his best day's pheasant shooting was 1,400 head, which he considered quite enough. As the conversation became more political in character I remarked that, according to the German Press, His Majesty's Government were pursuing a long-sighted Machiavellian policy with the intent of provoking a European war; whereas, if the truth were known, they had no definite policy at all and were not in the habit of looking far ahead. The Emperor laughed and said that one of the disadvantages of parliamentary government was that the policy of the Government of the day might be reversed by the Government of the morrow. There could thus be no continuity in its foreign policy. Foreign Governments could not, therefore, place implicit reliance on our friendship, though in view of our insular position it was no doubt to our interest to preserve our liberty of action and to keep aloof from all hard-and-fast alliances.

With regard to what I had said about the German Press, His Majesty observed that nothing interested him more than to read what people thought of him and his Government. He then asked me how things were going on the Indian frontier, and on my saying that order was gradually being restored there, he proceeded to speak of our relations in Asia. He did not, he said, believe in buffer States, unless they were strong and independent; and Persia, with its effete and corrupt Government, was too weak to play the role of such a State with advantage. Russia had already quite as much territory as she could manage, and he did not desire to acquire more; but he personally thought that our relations would be far more friendly and satisfactory were there no Persia between us. He feared, however, that British public opinion was hardly yet prepared to see England and Russia neighbours, though our old distrust of his country was, he rejoiced to say, gradually waning. During the rest of the audience the Emperor talked about the Klondike and Siberian mines, about his own journey through Siberia and about its climate and vegetation.

I little foresaw when I took leave of His Majesty how many audiences I was to have with him in years to come, and how eventually I should have to hold language such as no Ambassador before me has, I imagine, ever held to an autocratic Sovereign. The tact, however, that my wife and I were personally known to the Emperor and Empress was a considerable asset in our favour when we went to St. Petersburg.

I had, as already stated in Chapter 8, assumed charge of the Embassy at a moment when the Anglo-Russian understanding had been somewhat strained in consequence of the Potsdam Agreement, and I made it a rule from the first to be perfectly frank and outspoken in my conversations with the Emperor. His Majesty, who was most anxious to maintain that understanding intact, appreciated this frankness and honoured me with his confidence. During the years which followed my relations with him gradually assumed a more intimate character, and I personally became devotedly attached to him. His Majesty had such a wonderful charm of manner that when he received me in audience he almost made me feel that it was a friend, and not the Emperor, with whom I was talking. There was, if I may say so without presumption, what amounted to a feeling of mutual sympathy between us. Knowing, as he did, that my language with regard to international questions was inspired by my desire to promote Anglo-Russian friendship, while that as regarded the internal situation I had what I conceived to be his true interests at heart, he never once resented my outspoken language.

At official ceremonies, with the exception of the New Year's diplomatic reception, the Emperor seldom spoke to any of the Ambassadors. He would shake hands with them without engaging them in conversation, and would then go from one group of Russians to another, talking with whom he would. On one occasion — it was at a dinner given at Peterhof in 1911 in honour of the King of Serbia — he placed me in rather an embarrassing position. I was the only Ambassador present, having been invited to meet Prince Arthur of Connaught, who happened to be on a visit to the Emperor and Empress. His Royal Highness, however, had at the last moment been told by the Emperor that the dinner would not amuse him, and that he had better go out stalking. There was thus no *raison d'être* for my presence at the dinner, and I remember poor Stolypin — who was assassinated a few weeks later — asking me what I was doing "*en cette galère.*" After dinner one of the Court chamberlains came up to me and begged me to stand on one side of the room where the Emperor was about to pass, as His Majesty would doubtless wish to speak to me. I accordingly did so; but as His Majesty passed without apparently seeing me, my friend once more placed me in another favourable position for catching His Majesty's eye — with the same unfortunate result. As he was about to repeat the experiment a third time I remarked that if His Majesty wished to speak to me he could always send for me, but that I was not going to run after him. It was only as he was about to retire that the Emperor, as he passed, shook hands with me and bade me good night. The fact was that he had forgotten, when he sent Prince Arthur out shooting, that I had been invited to the dinner, and consequently felt somewhat embarrassed by my presence.

Only once had I the courage to approach the Emperor at a public ceremony and to speak to him without being sent for. It was during the war, at the launching of a battle cruiser. His Majesty was standing alone, watching the preliminary proceedings, and as I had something which I particularly wished to say to him I went up and spoke to him. He received me very graciously and kept me in conversation till the ceremony was about to commence.

It is a curious fact that, in spite of the long-established ceremonial and the traditional etiquette of the Imperial Court, Ambassadors were sometimes treated rather cavalierly. So much was this the case that at a meeting of Ambassadors convoked shortly after my arrival the doyen was charged to make certain representations on the subject. According to the unwritten law governing such questions, an

Ambassador who is invited to lunch or to dine at the palace lunches or dines at the Sovereign's table. When, therefore, on the eve of my first audience I received a telephone message from Tsarskoe saying that I was to remain to luncheon, I naturally imagined that I was to lunch with the Imperial family. I was, however, mistaken, as at the conclusion of my audience I was taken off to lunch with the household. I said nothing at the time, as I felt that it hardly became a new-fledged Ambassador to be too punctilious.

In the following year, on being invited to Tsarskoe to present to Their Majesties the members of the recently arrived British delegation, I was once more constrained to lunch with the household in spite of my having tried to excuse myself. As my colleagues and I had agreed not to accept such invitations in future, I thought it time to protest. As soon, therefore, as the luncheon was over I spoke to the grand master of the ceremonies. He had, I said, placed me in a very embarrassing position. I had come to the palace in my official capacity as His Majesty's Ambassador, and he must know as well as I did that under such circumstances it was contrary to all etiquette to invite me to lunch with the household. I therefore trusted that he would not repeat such invitations in future, and that he would arrange for me to return to St. Petersburg as soon as my audiences were over. Count Hendrikoff had to admit that I was right, and on all subsequent occasions I was given a special train, which waited for me at the Tsarskoe station till I was ready to return to town.

Ever since the revolutionary outbreak that had followed the Japanese War the Emperor and Empress had lived in comparative retirement at Tsarskoe Selo, and only came to St. Petersburg when some State function or religious ceremony necessitated their presence there. The Court no longer played a part in the social life of the capital, and the splendid balls, of which the Winter Palace had so often been the scene, were a tradition of the past. From time to time, on such occasions as that of the Romanoff Tercentenary, there were gala performances at the opera, when the house presented a wonderful sight with the parterre one mass of gorgeous uniforms and the boxes filled with smartly dressed ladies resplendent with jewels.

But only once during the whole period of my mission were the doors of the Winter Palace opened for anything beyond the formal New Year's reception and the ceremony of the Blessing of the Waters at the Epiphany. It was during the winter of 1913-14 that the heads of missions and the leading members of Russian society were invited to witness a performance of *Parsifal* in the private theatre in the Hermitage that had been built by the Empress Catherine. It was in every respect a beautiful performance, and one of which the great

Catherine might herself have been proud. I, personally, am not musical, and I was afterwards reproached by the Empress Marie and the young Grand Duchesses with having slept peacefully through the performance; but, as I assured them, I had but closed my eyes the better to listen to the music. The dinner, however, that was served in the Winter Palace during one of the *entr'actes* hardly came up to one's expectations after all that one heard of the splendours of such entertainments in the past. Neither from a spectacular nor from a gastronomic standpoint could it compare with a State banquet at Buckingham Palace.

In their retreat at Tsarskoe the Emperor and Empress led a simple domestic life, and the latter discouraged the idea of allowing outsiders to intrude into their happy family circle. They entertained but little, and it was only on very rare occasions — such as the arrival of General Sir Arthur Paget on a special mission; the visit of Admiral Sir David Beatty (as he then was) with the First Battle-cruiser Squadron; the meeting of the Allied Conference at Petrograd on the eve of the revolution — that I had the honour of lunching or dining with the Imperial Family. Once — in 1916 — I was invited to witness a private representation at Tsarskoe of the films showing the part which the British army and navy had played in the war; but though I sat between the Emperor and Empress during the representation, which lasted till past eight o'clock, I was not invited to remain to dinner. Nor was the French Ambassador, who was invited a few days later to witness a representation of French war films. As Ambassador, therefore, I had but few opportunities of any serious conversation with the Emperor unless I could find some excuse for asking for a special audience.

With the Empress Marie it was very different. Her Majesty liked to see people, and, though since the death of the Emperor Alexander III she had not entertained on a large scale, she gave small, informal luncheons to which I often had the privilege of being invited. Her whole personality was so attractive and sympathetic that she was loved by all who approached her, and she had the great gift of putting everybody at their ease. Her sense of humour also did away with all constraint on the part of the guests, so that the conversation at these luncheons never flagged and was as a rule very amusing. I had, more than once, occasion to discuss with Her Majesty the internal situation, which, as the war progressed, caused her ever-increasing preoccupation. Realizing as she did the danger of the course which the Emperor was steering, she repeatedly tendered counsels of moderation, and, had her advice been followed, Russia might have been spared much suffering. But Fate had willed it otherwise.

Among the other members of the Imperial family the Grand Duchess Marie Pawlowna, the widow of the Grand Duke Wladimir, took the first place. In her palaces at St. Petersburg and Tsarskoe Her Imperial Highness held a little Court of her own. It had, indeed, socially speaking, become a substitute in miniature for what the Imperial Court had been before it underwent all but total eclipse owing to the retired life led by the Emperor and Empress. A *grande dame* in the best sense of that term, but without any pretensions as regards the strict observance of Court etiquette, the Grand Duchess was admirably fitted to play the part of hostess and to do the honours of the Court. With great conversational gifts, she was not only herself full of *verve* and *entrain*, but possessed the art of inspiring them in others. Her entertainments, no matter what form they took, were never dull, and no one was ever bored. At her dinners and receptions one met many of the younger members of the Imperial family and the élite of Russian society, more especially the "smart set," as well as a sprinkling of the official and artistic worlds. For the Grand Duchess, though very fond of society, had other and more serious tastes, and was President — and a very active one — of the Russian Academy of Arts. During the war she devoted herself entirely to Red Cross work, while she was exceptionally well-informed on all political and military questions, in which she took active interest.

The Grand Duchess Victoria — the wife of the Grand Duke Cyril — who, when she was Grand Duchess of Hesse, had befriended us at Darmstadt, and the Grand Duchess Xenia, the Emperor's sister, whose kindness to us I shall never forget, also entertained a good deal; and many were the pleasant evenings which we spent at their informal dinners and dances. One of the most attractive traits in the Russian character was — for I cannot speak of the present — its extreme simplicity; and all the members of the Imperial family were as simple and natural as could be. They never stood on their dignity and disliked being treated with too much ceremony. When they came to the Embassy it was always by preference to some informal entertainment, and what they liked the best of all was a *diner dansant* at round tables, where they could talk unreservedly to their friends. No one could have been more simple and natural than the Emperor himself. I remember how, at the diplomatic reception on New Year's Day, 1912, after speaking to me about some political question, he said: "My sisters tell me that they are going to your house to-night. Are you giving a ball?" On my replying that it was not a regular ball, but that we were giving a dinner of about a hundred and fifty persons at round tables and were going to dance after wards, His Majesty exclaimed: "What fun that will be." I longed to ask him to come too, but knew that it would be useless, as neither he nor the Empress ever went into society.

Of the Grand Dukes whom I met in society or at the Yacht Club, where I occasionally dined, the Grand Duke Nicholas Michaelowich was the one whom I knew the best. A liberal-minded and cultured man, he was distinguished alike as an author — he had written an admirable history of the reign of Alexander I — and as a collector of pictures and miniatures, of which he was an expert judge. He honoured me with his friendship, and I shall have later on the opportunity of paying a tribute of my affectionate regard to his memory. He always drove about in an ordinary "isvostchik" (cab), and his advanced political views, as well as his democratic ways, had earned him the sobriquet of "Philippe Egalité."

CHAPTER 14
1914

In his book on the war the late Herr von Bethmann-Hollweg asserts that by joining the Entente Great Britain encouraged France and Russia in their warlike designs. Such a contention is absolutely unfounded. In the first place Russia, with whom I am alone concerned, did not desire war, and throughout the protracted Balkan crisis of 1912-13 the preservation of peace had been the keynote of her policy. In spite of occasional errors of judgment on the part of his Government, the Emperor, when faced with a situation involving the question of war or peace, never hesitated to throw the whole weight of his influence on the side of peace. So far did he carry his pacific policy, so ready was he to make concessions, if only by so doing he could avert the horrors of war, that at the end of 1913, as I have shown in Chapter XI, the impression had gained ground that Russia would never fight, an impression that unfortunately encouraged Germany to exploit the situation. In the second place, the idea that His Majesty's Government ever incited Russia to embark on a policy of adventure is refuted by facts. The exact contrary was the case. No one ever worked harder than did Sir Edward Grey to preserve the peace of Europe during those two critical years; and it was thanks mainly to his untiring efforts, to his restraining influence and to the counsels of moderation, which he gave both at St. Petersburg and Vienna, that war was averted. If anyone was to blame it was Germany herself; for it was her policy of piling up armaments wherewith to impose her will on Europe that forced Great Britain, France and Russia to concert together for the protection of their respective interests. Nor is it true that the aim of the Entente Powers was to encircle Germany with an iron ring. In concluding an agreement that was to remove as far as possible any cause of further misunderstanding between them, Russia and Great Britain had not been inspired by any feeling of hostility to Germany. They, on the contrary, gave repeated proof of their desire to cultivate friendly relations with her — Russia, by concluding the Potsdam Agreement, and Great Britain, by entering into negotiations with her — with the object of placing Anglo-German relations on a better footing. I would supplement what I have already said on this subject by recording the conversations which I had with the Emperor on the international situation between the years 1912 and 1914.

On February 23, 1912, I had an audience in which, after informing the Emperor that the main object of Lord Haldane's recent visit to Germany was to create a better feeling between London and Berlin, I received the emphatic assurance of the satisfaction which the news of this visit had caused His Majesty. Russia, he said, had concluded an arrangement with Germany that had greatly improved her relations with that empire; and it was not only natural, but necessary, in the interest of the world's peace, that relations of a similar friendly character should be established between Germany and Great Britain. A nation might be attracted to one nation more than to another, but this was no reason why it should not live on good terms with the latter. His Majesty then proceeded to say that he had no reason to mistrust Germany except with regard to her Turkish policy. If the Ottoman army were ever to take the field it would be either against Russia or against one of the Balkan States; it was not, therefore, a friendly act on Germany's part to supply it with military instructors. It was thanks to those instructors that that army was acquiring a high degree of efficiency; but though he had more than once questioned the Emperor William on the subject, he had never received a satisfactory answer.

In another audience — April 14, 1918 — during the discussions which were taking place on the subject of Scutari, the Emperor said that he fully realized that Germany would make common cause with Austria, and that he had no intention of embarking on a war with those two empires about a wretched Albanian town. In supporting the claims of the Balkan States with an insistence which, he feared, had sometimes caused His Majesty's Government considerable embarrassment, Russia had but fulfilled her historic mission as the protector of those States. The crisis had, he was glad to say, brought the two Governments nearer together, and he was more especially grateful for the services which Sir Edward Grey had rendered the cause of peace. On my observing that, while desirous of giving Russia all the support in their power, His Majesty's Government were at the same time anxious to maintain good and friendly relations with Germany, His Majesty said that he quite understood this and that he desired to do the same. He was leaving shortly for Berlin to attend the Royal wedding, and was looking forward with the greatest pleasure to meeting the King there. During this visit he would, no doubt, as on former occasions, be plied with questions and proposals by the Emperor William. He would in that case listen patiently to what the Emperor had to say and be careful not to commit himself, as he always found that this was the safest course to pursue.

Returning once more to the subject of the Balkan War, the Emperor told me that as regarded the contemplated occupation of Constantinople by the Bulgarians, the latter had originally intended to offer it to Russia as a token of gratitude for their liberation from the Turkish yoke. He had given them clearly to understand that Russia could not possibly accept such a gift, and he had urged them to renounce all idea of attempting to occupy it.

As the conversation then turned on the German Army Bill and the counter-measures being taken by France to meet the new military situation, I asked the Emperor whether he thought that the financial strain thus imposed on the two countries would be so severe that one or other of them might lose patience and precipitate a war, and whether, if this danger really existed, it would be possible for the Powers to do anything to avert it. The Emperor replied that in 1899 he had taken the initiative in convoking the Peace Conference at The Hague, but his action had been misrepresented as aiming at a general disarmament. He was not, therefore, tempted to repeat the experiment, and would abstain from putting forward any proposals on the present occasion. He quite understood the reasons which had prompted the proposed increase of the German army, but the German Government must be aware that they were but setting an example which other States would be bound to follow. They would probably have no difficulty in finding the men, but whether the country would for long be able to bear the increased taxation was another question. Russia, on the other hand, had unlimited resources to draw on i with regard both to men and money; and just as His Majesty's Government had fixed the relative strength of the British and German fleets at sixteen to ten, so he was determined to maintain the same ratio between the Russian and German armies. It was impossible to foresee what would happen, but it was very necessary to prepare beforehand to meet the danger should it arise.

The Emperor spoke of Austria without any bitterness, but as a source of weakness to Germany and as a danger to peace, owing to the fact that Germany was bound to support her in her Balkan policy. He further expressed the opinion that the disintegration of the Austrian Empire was merely a question of time, and that the day was not far distant when we should see a kingdom of Hungary and a kingdom of Bohemia. The Southern Slavs would probably be absorbed by Serbia, the Roumanians of Transylvania by Roumania, and the German provinces of Austria incorporated in Germany. The fact that Germany would then have no Austria to inveigle her into a war about the Balkans would, His Majesty opined, make for peace. I ventured to observe that such a recasting of the map of Europe could hardly be effected without a general war.

In March, 1914, public attention was drawn to Russia's international position by the publication in the *Novoye Vremja* of a series of conversations with a Russian statesman in whom it was easy to recognize Count Witte. The gist of these conversations was to the effect that the only hope of permanent peace lay in a regrouping of the Powers. Count Witte had always regarded a close understanding with Germany as the mainspring of Russia's foreign policy, and had consequently denounced the Anglo-Russian agreement as a mistaken sacrifice of her freedom of action. Very similar views were held by the German party at Court, who contrasted the material advantages to be derived from an alliance with Germany with the somewhat problematic benefits which an understanding with Great Britain had to offer. Even persons who were well disposed towards us were beginning to ask themselves of what practical value was an understanding with a country whose support could not be counted on in the event of war.

I was not, therefore, surprised when, in an audience which I had on April 3, the Emperor himself broached the subject of Anglo-Russian relations. We had been talking of the views expressed by Count Witte in the *Novoye Vremja*, and His Majesty had ridiculed the idea of a regrouping of the Powers. Much as he desired to live on good terms with Germany, an alliance with her was, he declared, out of the question, as, apart from other reasons, Germany was endeavouring to acquire a position at Constantinople that would enable her to keep Russia shut in altogether in the Black Sea. After remarking that with Europe divided into two camps the international situation was disquieting, the Emperor said: "What I should like to see is a closer bond of union between England and Russia, such as an alliance of a purely defensive character." On my remarking that this was, I feared, impracticable at present, the Emperor then suggested that we might at any rate conclude some arrangement similar to that which existed between France and England. Though he was not acquainted with the terms of that arrangement, he believed that if we had not actually a military convention with France we had discussed and agreed on what each country was to do in certain eventualities. I said that I knew nothing about our arrangement with France, but that it would, for material reasons, be impossible for us to send troops to co-operate with the Russian army. "I have men enough and to spare," replied the

Emperor, "and such an expeditionary force would serve no useful purpose; but it might be advantageous to arrange beforehand for the co-operation of the British and Russian fleets. Our understanding," His Majesty continued, "is at present confined to Persia, and I am strongly of opinion that it ought to be extended, either by some sort of arrangement such as I have just suggested, or by some written formula which would record the fact of Anglo-Russian co-operation in Europe."

I told the Emperor in reply that much as I should personally welcome any arrangement that would tend to consolidate the Anglo-Russian understanding, I could but ask myself whether, supposing that England had in 1913 been the ally of Russia, she could have rendered her any more effective service than she had done as her friend. On several occasions during the prolonged Balkan crisis she had been able to play the role of mediator at Berlin and Vienna. It was thanks, moreover, to her friendly intervention that a more or less satisfactory settlement of the Serbian port question had been arrived at, and that Austria had yielded about Dibra and Djakova, which were blocking the way to a settlement of the all-important question of Scutari. It was, I thought, doubtful whether we should have been so successful either at Berlin or Vienna had we approached those two Governments as the ally of Russia instead of as a friend who might be turned into an ally should Germany and Austria force war on Russia. While admitting that there might be some force in the above argument, the Emperor said that he would nevertheless prefer to see the Anglo-Russian understanding assume a more precise and definite character.

I recently came across the following passage in Admiral Tirpitz's "Memoirs" (English edition, Vol. I, p. 256): "During the visit of the English Fleet to Kiel at the end of June, 1914, the British Ambassador at St. Petersburg, Buchanan, announced the conclusion of an Anglo-Russian naval convention." It would appear from the context that I had intended this announcement to act as a sort of counterblast to the friendly gesture implied in the despatch by His Majesty's Government of a British squadron to Kiel. If Admiral Tirpitz has ever read Sheridan's play *The Critic*, he will remember how the Governor of Tilbury Fort interrupted his daughter, who was descanting on all that she saw on the approaching Armada, by remarking:

> The Spanish fleet thou canst not see — because
> It is not yet in sight.

In the same way I may reply that I did not announce the conclusion of an Anglo-Russian convention — because no such convention ever existed. I may further inform the gallant admiral that I never even entered into negotiations with the Russian Government for the conclusion of a naval convention, and that, if Great Britain eventually became Russia's ally both by land and sea, that alliance owed its being to Germany's violation of Belgium's neutrality.

I have recorded the above conversations in order to show how utterly unfounded are the charges of chauvinism brought by so many highly placed Germans against both Russia and Great Britain. Not one word did the Emperor ever utter that betrayed a desire on his part to adopt an aggressive attitude towards Germany. On the contrary, he never missed an occasion of expressing his earnest wish to live on good terms with her. It was only when he realized the trend of her policy and the meaning of her ever-growing armaments that he took steps to guard against possible future eventualities. He increased the number of his peace effectives, and he suggested the conversion of the Anglo-Russian understanding into an alliance of a purely defensive character. On the other hand, the language which I used when the Emperor made this tentative suggestion is, I think, a sufficient answer to those who accuse His Majesty's Government of having encouraged Russia to steer a warlike course. Germany, it must not be forgotten, had in 1913 raised £50,000,000 by a levy on capital for military purposes, and Russia had to take counter-measures in self-defence. I remember how M. Delcassé, who was then Ambassador at St. Petersburg, warned me at the time that Germany would never have had recourse to such a drastic measure of finance were she not determined on war in the near future. I passed on the warning to London, but it fell on deaf ears, for no one believed Germany capable of such criminal folly. The general impression seems to have been that, as a friend wrote to me, the "financiers," who were opposed to war, would put the brake on. The German Emperor was at the same time credited with the wish of going down to posterity as the keeper of European peace. The view taken by German writers of Russia's military preparations reminds me of what a witty Frenchman wrote many years ago: "*Cet animal est bien méchant. Quand on l'attaque, il se défend.*"

The last audience which I had with the Emperor before the outbreak of war has already been recorded in Chapter 9. The questions discussed in it had reference exclusively to such countries as Persia, Thibet and Afghanistan, where British and Russian interests were likely to clash. The Emperor said nothing about Germany, but urged that the conversations proceeding between our two Governments with reference to the aforesaid countries should be brought to as speedy a conclusion as possible, "in order that," as His Majesty remarked, "we might be able to sleep comfortably in our beds without fear of any breach being made in the Anglo-Russian understanding."

This last audience took place on June 15, after the luncheon given by the Emperor at Tsarskoe to Admiral Beatty and the officers of the First Battle-cruiser Squadron, which had just arrived at Cronstadt on a complimentary visit to Russia. The welcome accorded them by the Emperor, as well as by the general public, was of the warmest, while the naval and municipal authorities entertained them with true Russian hospitality. The Emperor paid a visit of inspection to the squadron, which was composed of the *Lion, Queen Mary, Princess Royal* and *New Zealand*, and, together with the Empress and his four daughters, honoured Admiral Beatty with his presence at luncheon on board his flagship. Never have I seen happier faces than those of the young Grand Duchesses as they were escorted over the *Lion* by a little band of middies specially told off for their amusement; and when I think of them as I saw them that day, the tragic story of their deaths seems like some hideous nightmare.

On July 20 the President of the French Republic, M. Poincaré, arrived on an official visit to the Russian Court. There were the usual reviews, banquets and toasts. The international outlook, which was not reassuring, naturally formed the subject of their private conversations, but the Emperor, though preoccupied, still believed in the pacific intentions of the Emperor William. On the 21st the President held a reception of the heads of foreign missions. While I was awaiting my turn to be conducted to the room where he was receiving the Ambassadors, the Serbian Minister engaged me in conversation. Speaking with considerable emotion, he called my attention to the threatening attitude of Austria, and said that Serbia was faced with the gravest crisis in her history. M. Poincaré, to whom I repeated what M. Spalaikovitch had told me, afterwards broached the subject in his conversation with the Austrian Ambassador, but failed to elicit any satisfactory assurance as to Austria's attitude. On the evening of the 23rd the President started on his homeward journey.

As several weeks had elapsed since the assassination of the Archduke Franz Ferdinand without any move on Austria's part, there seemed reason to hope that she had renounced the idea of any punitive action. I had myself been granted leave of absence and had already taken tickets for our journey to England. As I was sitting in my study the next morning (the 24th) musing on all that I was going to do during my approaching holiday, I was roused by the ringing of the telephone. "Who's there?" I asked. "I, Sazonoff," was the reply. "Austria has presented an ultimatum at Belgrade couched in terms which mean war. Please meet me at the French Embassy in an hour's time as I must discuss matters with you and Paléologue."

CHAPTER 15
1914

Austria had carefully timed the presentation of her ultimatum so that it should coincide with the departure from St. Petersburg of the President of the French Republic and the President of the French Council of Ministers on their return journey to France, a journey that would take at least four days. I knew that Austria's action would be regarded at St. Petersburg as a direct challenge to Russia, and I was not sorry, therefore, to have an hour wherein to reflect on its possible consequences, more especially as I foresaw that the conversation of the French Embassy would turn on the crucial question of British solidarity with France and Russia.

Nor was I mistaken. After pointing out how utterly unacceptable were some of her demands, M. Sazonoff remarked that Austria would never have presented such an ultimatum unless she had assured herself beforehand of Germany's approval and support. Could Russia, he proceeded to inquire, equally count on the support of her partners in the Triple Entente? The French Ambassador, to whom he first addressed this question, assured him that France would give Russia her diplomatic support and would also, if necessity arose, fulfil all the obligations entailed by her alliance. "And your Government?" next inquired M. Sazonoff, turning to me. I replied that though I could not speak in the name of His Majesty's Government, I had no doubt that they would give them all the diplomatic support in their power. I could not, however, hold out any hope of their making a declaration of solidarity that would entail an unconditional engagement to support France and Russia by force of arms on behalf of a country like Serbia, where no direct British interests were involved. Such an engagement would not be sanctioned by British public opinion; and, unless backed by public opinion, no British Government could take upon themselves the responsibility of pledging their country to war. To this M. Sazonoff objected that we must not forget that the Serbian was but a part of the general European question and that, in view of the vital interests at stake, we could not afford to efface ourselves altogether. I replied that I gathered that he wished us to join Russia in making a communication to Austria to the effect that we would not tolerate any active intervention by her in the internal affairs of Serbia; but, supposing that Austria nevertheless took military measures against Serbia, was it, I asked, the intention of the Russian Government forthwith to declare war on her? While expressing the personal opinion that Russia would have to mobilize, M. Sazonoff said that the whole question would be considered by a Council of Ministers over which the Emperor would preside. I therefore urged that the first and most important thing to do was to endeavour to induce Austria to extend the time limit of forty-eight hours and, at the same time, to find out how far Serbia was prepared to go to meet the demands formulated by Austria in her note. M. Sazonoff agreed, saying that some of the Austrian demands could doubtless be accepted by Serbia.

The conversation, which had begun at noon, was continued after luncheon, when M. Sazonoff and M. Paleologue once more pressed me to declare British solidarity with Russia and France. Apart from the fact that it was quite outside my province to make any declaration that would bind His Majesty's Government, I was determined not to say one word that could be interpreted as an encouragement to Russia to declare war on Austria. To do so might not only have diminished any chance of a pacific solution of the question, but would, I knew, be seized on by Germany as an argument to prove — as she is still endeavouring to prove — that we had egged on Russia into war. I therefore confined myself to saying that His Majesty's Government might, I thought, be prepared to make strong representations at Berlin and Vienna, pointing out that, as an Austrian attack on Serbia would bring Russia into the field, it would be difficult for Great Britain to stand aside were the war to become general. This did not satisfy M. Sazonoff, who contended that we should render war more likely if we did not at once make common cause with Russia and France.

On receiving my telegraphic report of this conversation, Sir Edward Grey replied: "You spoke quite rightly in very difficult circumstances as to the attitude of His Majesty's Government. I entirely approve what you said and I cannot promise more on behalf of the Government."

To give an account of all the conversations held at the different capitals and of all the telegrams exchanged during the critical days which followed the presentation of the Austrian ultimatum would require a book in itself. I shall, therefore, content myself with recording those which have a special bearing on Russia's attitude, and on the advice which we tendered at St. Petersburg, in order to show how unfounded are the statements of certain German writers who have endeavoured to throw on Great Britain and Russia the responsibility for the war.

To take but two of them — Herr von Bethmann-Hollweg and Baron von Schoen, who was Ambassador at Paris at the time. The former, in his "Betrachtungen zum Weltkriege," asserts that while Germany was doing all she could to restrain Austria, we refrained from giving counsels of moderation at St. Petersburg. The latter, in his "Memoirs of an Ambassador," goes a good deal farther. He accuses Russia of having brought about the war in order to stave off the danger of internal complications, and he accuses us of having never shown the slightest inclination to work for the maintenance of peace at St. Petersburg. He represents us as having, on the contrary, frustrated Germany's efforts to bring about a direct conversation between St. Petersburg and Vienna by encouraging Russia in her attitude of "intransigeance." He further states that it was the knowledge that she could rely on our support that determined Russia to mobilize.

On the other hand, his vindication of the course pursued by his own Government is so enlightening that I am tempted to reproduce it. Austria, he states, was competing with Russia for supremacy in the Balkans, while Germany stood behind her ally and protected her out of regard for her own interests. The Austrian Government were determined to exact ample atonement for the Serajevo murder, which had demonstrated the necessity of crushing once for all at their centre (Belgrade) the subversive activities at work in the south eastern portions of the Hapsburg monarchy. In order to secure really effective guarantees for the future the terms of the ultimatum had been made as harsh as possible, so that Serbia had either to make complete submission to Austria, to sacrifice some of her sovereign rights and to renounce her connexion with Russia — or to face the consequences. Germany, on being consulted, recognized that it was but a question of striking at the root of dangers which directly threatened the existence of her ally and indirectly her own. She could not reasonably refuse her consent and support, for were Austria, as a result of the undermining work being carried on by the Serbs, to fall to pieces, she would be of no further use to Germany as an ally. Germany, therefore, announced her intention of loyally adhering to her alliance and of preventing any disastrous intervention from outside. She proposed localizing the conflict, but her proposal was checkmated by Russia acting as Serbia's protector and declaring that the conflict could not leave her indifferent. Finally Baron von Schoen blames Sir Edward Grey for having proposed a conference of the four Powers not immediately interested, as, in doing so, he had contravened the principle of non-intervention on which Germany laid such stress. In a word, Germany, according to Baron von Schoen, undertook to keep the ring while Austria made Serbia her vassal, although she knew, from what had passed during the Balkan crisis, that Russia would never tolerate an Austrian attack on Serbia.

The following summary of my successive conversations with M. Sazonoff will show how different from this was the attitude of the Russian and the British Governments.

On July 25 we resumed our conversation of the preceding day. Austria, Sazonoff contended, aimed at establishing her hegemony in the Balkans, and the action which she had taken at Belgrade was directed against Russia. Germany's attitude, on the other hand, would be determined by ours. So long as she believed that she could count on our neutrality she would go all lengths; but if only we took our stand firmly by France and Russia there would be no war. If we failed them, rivers of blood would flow and we would in the end be dragged into the war. Though I feared that his prediction was likely to come true, I could but repeat what I had said to the Emperor in one of the audiences recorded in the preceding chapter, that we could play the role of mediator to better purpose as a friend who, if her counsels of moderation were disregarded, might be converted into an ally, than if we were at once to declare our complete solidarity with Russia. I, at the same time, expressed the earnest hope that Russia would give His Majesty's Government time to use their influence as peacemaker and that she would not precipitate matters by mobilizing. Were she to do so Germany would, I warned him, not be content with a counter-mobilization, but would at once declare war on her. Russia, M. Sazonoff replied, could not allow Austria to crush Serbia, but I might rest assured that she would take no military action unless absolutely forced to do so.

On the following day — July 26 — he informed me that he had, in conversation with the Austrian Ambassador, suggested a direct conversation between Vienna and St. Petersburg for the purpose of finding a formula that, while giving satisfaction to Austria as regarded her principal demands, might prove more acceptable to Serbia. He had, he said, told Count Szapary that he quite understood the motives which had prompted Austria to present her ultimatum, and that if only she would consent to revise certain of its articles it would not be difficult to arrive at a satisfactory settlement.

In reply to a question which he addressed to me in the course of our conversation I told him that the language which I had held to him on the 24th had been approved by Sir E. Grey as correctly defining the attitude of His Majesty's Government. They would, I added, use all their influence to avert war; but if their efforts were to be successful it was essential that Russia should not mobilize save in the very last resort.

On my communicating to him on July 27 Sir E. Grey's proposal for a conference of the four Ambassadors in London, M. Sazonoff replied: "I have begun a conversation with the Austro-Hungarian Ambassador under conditions which I think may be favourable for a revision of the Austrian ultimatum to Serbia. Should direct explanations with Vienna prove impossible I am ready to accept Sir E. Grey's proposal or any other proposal of a nature to bring about a favourable solution of the conflict."

In consequence of the threatening international outlook orders had been given to the British fleet, concentrated at Portland, not to disperse for manoeuvre leave. In informing the Russian Ambassador of the above fact Sir Edward Grey was careful to explain that this must not be taken to mean anything more than a promise of diplomatic action.

On July 28 things took a decided turn for the worse. Not only did Count Berchtold decline M. Sazonoff's proposal for a direct conversation between the two Governments, but Austria declared war on Serbia. No assurance which Austria might give as to the integrity and independence of Serbia would, M. Sazonoff told me, satisfy Russia, and the order for mobilization against Austria would be given on the day that the Austrian army crossed the Serbian frontier. I, nevertheless, once more urged him to refrain from any military measures which might be construed as a challenge by Germany.

I repeated the gist of this conversation to my French colleague, whom I found in the ante-room awaiting his turn to be received, and begged him to speak in the same sense. The situation, I said, was becoming critical. Russia was in earnest and would never allow Austria to crush Serbia. But if war was forced on Russia it was important that she should not give Germany any pretext for representing her as the aggressor. For, unless convinced that the whole responsibility for the war rested with Germany, British public opinion would never sanction our participation in it.

Baron von Schoen, in his "Memoirs," translates a passage from "La Russie des Tsars dans la Grande Guerre," in which M. Paléologue records my above-mentioned remarks, and reads into them a meaning which they do not possess. He makes me say: "Russia is determined to go to war. We must, therefore, saddle Germany with the whole responsibility and initiative of the attack, as this will be the only way of winning over public opinion in England to the war." He goes on to represent me as egging on Russia to fight, while endeavouring to throw all the blame on Germany. This is a wanton misrepresentation of my attitude, as I had — as I have already shown — said all that I possibly could to discourage mobilization, knowing that it would furnish Germany with the pretext which she wanted for declaring war on Russia.

The German Ambassador at St. Petersburg had all along been under the impression that the Russian public had not been greatly stirred by the Austro-Serbian conflict and that only a small clique of chauvinists was endeavouring to give it an acute character. As he happened to be lunching with me at the Embassy on the 28th I took the opportunity of opening his eyes to the growing danger of the situation. He had asked me to impress prudence on Sazonoff, and I told him that I had done so from the outset. It was, I added, time for the German Ambassador at Vienna to speak seriously to Count Berchtold, for, if Germany allowed Austria to attack Serbia, a general war would be the inevitable result. Count Pourtales, who was greatly upset by this remark, protested that Russia and not Germany was responsible for the existing tension. He was, I believe, personally anxious to avert war, and had probably been kept in the dark as to the real intentions of his Government. But his attitude was not calculated to smooth over matters. He held that Austria had to administer a severe chastisement to Serbia, while Russia had to look on quietly and maintain the passive rôle of a disinterested spectator. Were she, on the contrary, to carry out her projected mobilization, she would, he contended, be endangering the peace of Europe. It was in vain that I argued that Russia had shown her pacific intentions by accepting the proposal for a conference *à quatre*, and by declaring her readiness to abide by any decision which that conference might take, that had the approval of France and Great Britain. Nor would he listen to me when I reminded him that Austria had not only partially mobilized but had actually declared war on Serbia. "I cannot," he replied, "discuss anything that Austria has done."

Though Austria had already begun mobilizing against Serbia on the 26th, it was only on the 28th that Russia took any preliminary steps for a mobilization in the military districts of Kieff, Odessa, Kazan and Moscow. Between one and two o'clock on the afternoon of July 29 Count Pourtales had an interview with M. Sazonoff, in which he reminded the latter that, in the event of such a partial mobilization, Germany's treaty of alliance with Austria would automatically cause German mobilization. About seven o'clock the same evening Count Pourtales again called at the Ministry for Foreign Affairs and communicated to M. Sazonoff a telegram from the German Chancellor stating that any further development of Russia's military preparations would compel Germany to take counter-measures and that this would mean war.

As such language was almost tantamount to an ultimatum, and as the Russian War Office had, meanwhile, received information of the extensive military preparations that Germany was secretly making, as well as of the Austrian general mobilization, the whole situation had to be reconsidered. In the course of the evening the Emperor, yielding to the pressure brought to bear on him by his military advisers, unwillingly consented to order a general mobilization. A few hours after doing so he received the following telegram from the German Emperor:

"I believe that a direct understanding between your Government and Vienna is possible — an understanding which my Government is endeavouring to promote. Naturally military measures by Russia, which might be construed as a menace by Austria-Hungary, would accelerate a calamity which both of us desire to avoid."

To this the Emperor Nicholas replied:

"Thanks for your telegram, which is conciliatory, while the official message, presented by your Ambassador to my Foreign Minister, was conveyed in a very different tone. I beg you to explain the difference. It would be right to submit the Austro-Serbian question to the Hague Conference. I trust in your wisdom and friendship."

After despatching this telegram the Emperor Nicholas successively rang up on the telephone the Minister of War and the Chief of the General Staff and countermanded the general mobilization. That mobilization had already commenced, and to stop it would, as both the generals protested, throw the whole military machine out of gear. The Emperor, nevertheless, insisted ; but in spite of his categorical orders the military authorities allowed the general mobilization to proceed without his knowledge.

Meanwhile the German Ambassador had learned what was going on, and at two o'clock on the morning of July 30 called at the Ministry for Foreign Affairs. Seeing that war was now inevitable, he broke down and appealed to Sazonoff to make some suggestion for him to telegraph to his Government. Sazonoff thereupon drew up the following formula:

"If Austria, recognizing that the conflict with Serbia has assumed the character of a question of European interest, declares herself ready to eliminate from her ultimatum the points which violate the principles of Serbia's sovereignty, Russia engages to stop all military preparations."

Sazonoff, who had been informed by the Chief of the General Staff of the telephonic conversation which he had had during the night with the Emperor, had an audience with His Majesty early in the afternoon of the 30th. Before proceeding to Peterhof he had received the news of the Austrian bombardment of Belgrade and of the refusal of the German Government to consider the formula which he had given to Count Pourtales. He found the Emperor greatly perturbed by a telegram which he had just received from the German Emperor. "My Ambassador," the latter stated, "has instructions to direct the attention of your Government to the dangers and serious consequences of mobilization. I have told you the same in my last telegram. Austria-Hungary has mobilized only against Serbia and only a part of the army. If Russia mobilizes against Austria-Hungary, the part of mediator, with which you have entrusted me in such a friendly manner and which I have accepted at your express desire, is threatened, if not rendered impossible. The entire weight of the decision now rests on your shoulders. You have to bear the responsibility of war or peace." The Emperor Nicholas felt so keenly the gravity of the decision which he had to take that he still shrank from sanctioning a general mobilization. Only after that Sazonoff had assured him that he could do so with a clear conscience, as his Government had not left a stone unturned in their efforts to avert war, did the Emperor finally decide not to leave his country defenceless against the offensive which Germany was already preparing. At four o'clock the same afternoon His Majesty caused the necessary orders to be tele phoned to the Ministry of War.

He had already, earlier in the afternoon of the 30th, telegraphed as follows to the Emperor William: "I am sending Tattischeff with instructions to-night. The military measures now taking form were decided on five days ago for reasons of defence against Austria. I hope with all my heart that these measures will not in any way influence your position as mediator, which I prize very highly. We need your strong pressure on Austria in order that an understanding may be arrived at."

On the following day — the 31st — he telegraphed again: "It is impossible for me, for technical reasons, to suspend my military preparations. But so long as the pourparlers with Austria are not broken off my troops will abstain from any offensive. I give you my word of honour."

The Emperor William replied: "I have gone as far as it is possible for me to go in my efforts to maintain peace. It is not I who will have to bear the responsibility for the horrible disaster that now threatens the whole civilized world. It still rests with you to dispel it. My friendship for you and your Empire, which my grandfather bequeathed me on his deathbed, is always sacred for me. I have been true to Russia when misfortune befell her, especially during the last war. At the present moment you can still save the peace of Europe by stopping your military preparations."

On the same day — the 31st — Sazonoff made a final effort to safeguard peace by modifying, at Sir E. Grey's request, the formula which he had given Count Pourtales so that it should read as follows:

"If Austria consents to stay the march of her troops on Serbian territory, and if, recognizing that the Austro-Serbian conflict has assumed the character of a question of European interest, she admits that the Great Powers may examine the satisfaction which Serbia can accord to the Austro-Hungarian Government, without prejudice to her sovereign rights and to her independence as a State, Russia undertakes to preserve her waiting attitude."

The Emperor, who received the German Ambassador in audience the same afternoon, endeavoured to impress on him the conciliatory spirit in which this formula had been drafted and the prospect which it offered of an honourable settlement of the conflict, but without success.

At eleven o'clock that night Count Pourtales went to the Ministry for Foreign Affairs and informed M. Sazonoff that unless Russia stopped her mobilization before noon the next day, the whole German army would be mobilized. In reply to his passionate appeal for immediate demobilization Sazonoff could but repeat the assurance that so long as the Austro-Russian pourparlers continued, Russia would not take the offensive. There were at that moment signs of a relaxation of the tension between Vienna and St. Petersburg; there had been friendly conversations between their respective Foreign Ministers and Ambassadors, and the Austrian Government seemed even disposed to admit a discussion on the interpretation to be placed on the text of their note to the Serbian Government. But Germany willed it otherwise.

On the morning of August 1 the Emperor Nicholas once more telegraphed to the Emperor William: "I understand that you are forced to mobilize, but I should like to receive from you the same guarantee which I have given you, namely, that these measures do not mean war and that we shall continue to negotiate for the welfare of our two countries and for the universal peace which is so dear to us. With the aid of God it must be possible for our long-tried friendship to prevent the shedding of blood. I expect with full confidence your urgent reply."

To this the Emperor William, after stating that the time limit had expired and that he had been forced to mobilize his army, replied: "An immediate, clear and unmistakable reply of your Government is the sole way to avoid endless misery. Until I receive this reply I am unable, to my great grief, to enter upon the subject of your telegram. I must ask most earnestly that you, without delay, order your troops to commit under no circumstances the slightest violation of our frontiers."

About five o'clock that afternoon I received a telegram from the Foreign Office instructing me to ask for an immediate audience in order to deliver to the Emperor a personal message from King George, in which His Majesty, after referring to the representations which Germany had made on the subject of the Russian mobilization, proceeded to say: "I cannot help thinking that some misunderstanding has produced this deadlock. I am most anxious not to miss any possibility of avoiding the terrible calamity which at present threatens the whole world. I therefore make a personal appeal to you to remove the misapprehension which I feel must have occurred, and to leave still open grounds for negotiation and possible peace. If you think I can in any way contribute to that all-important purpose I will do everything in my power to assist in reopening the interrupted conversations between the Powers concerned. I feel confident that you are as anxious as I am that all that is possible should be done to secure the peace of the world."

About a quarter past seven M. Sazonoff, who had arranged that I should be received by the Emperor at Peterhof at ten o'clock, rang me up on the telephone to tell me that Count Pourtales had just informed him that Germany considered herself in a state of war with Russia. He came to dine with me at eight o'clock, bringing with him a draft reply to the King's telegram for me to submit to the Emperor. I left the Embassy at nine o'clock, but owing to something having gone wrong with the electric lights on my motor, the chauffeur took a wrong turn and I only reached Peterhof at a quarter to eleven. After apologizing to the Emperor for being so late I handed him the King's telegram as well as the draft reply which Sazonoff had drawn up. When His Majesty had finished reading them I ventured to suggest that it would be better were he to answer the King in his own words rather than in the official style of the reply which had been drafted at the Ministry for Foreign Affairs. "I will do so if you will help me," replied the Emperor, "for talking English is a very different thing to writing it correctly." His Majesty then asked me to sit down, and we discussed for more than an hour the situation that had been created by the Austrian ultimatum, the ineffectual efforts that had been made by both the Russian and the British Governments to preserve peace, and the reasons which had forced Russia to mobilize. Mobilization, His Majesty insisted, did not necessarily entail war, and he had given the Emperor William the most categorical assurances in this sense. Then, getting up and going to his writing table, he took some telegraph forms and a pencil and proceeded to write his answer, consulting me from time to time as to how he should turn a phrase if he were at a loss for a word. When he had finished he gave me the autograph telegram to have ciphered on my return to the Embassy. The text was as follows:

"I would gladly have accepted your proposals had not the German Ambassador this afternoon presented a note to my Government declaring war. Ever since presentation of the ultimatum at Belgrade, Russia has devoted all her efforts to finding some pacific solution of the question raised by Austria's action. Object of that action was to crush Serbia and make her a vassal of Austria. Effect of this would have been to upset balance of power in Balkans, which is of such vital interest to my Empire. Every proposal, including that of your Government, was rejected by Germany and Austria, and it was only when favourable moment for bringing pressure to bear on Austria had passed that Germany showed any disposition to mediate. Even then she did not put forward any precise proposal. Austria's declaration of war on Serbia forced me to order a partial mobilization, though in view of threatening situation my military advisers strongly advised a general mobilization owing to quickness with which Germany can mobilize in comparison with Russia. I was eventually compelled to take this course in consequence of complete Austrian mobilization, of the bombardment of Belgrade, of concentration of Austrian troops in Galicia, and of secret military preparations being made in Germany. That I was justified in doing so is proved by Germany's sudden declaration of war, which was quite unexpected by me, as I had given most categorical assurances to the Emperor William that my troops would not move so long as mediation negotiations continued.

"In this solemn hour I wish to assure you once more that I have done all in my power to avert war. Now that it has been forced on me, I trust your country will not fail to support France and Russia. God bless and protect you."

It was past one o'clock when I reached the Embassy to find the door blocked by an enthusiastic crowd eager to know whether Russia could count on England's support.

CHAPTER 16
1914

In the previous chapter I have given what, from personal knowledge, I believe to be a straightforward and accurate account of Russia's attitude during the nine critical days which preceded the war. Nothing that she did, or that she left undone, can possibly be cited against her as evidence of what Baron von Schoen terms her "will for war." In his endeavours to preserve peace, Sazonoff did not reject a single suggestion that was made him. He successively accepted proposals for a conference of four, for mediation by Great Britain and Italy, and for a direct conversation between Austria and Russia. Germany and Austria, on the other hand, either declined these proposals altogether or prevented their materializing by replying in evasive terms. There was one thing that Sazonoff could not do. He could not allow Austria to crush Serbia. Germany and Austria knew this quite well, for they had during the Balkan crisis been given clearly to understand that an Austrian attack on Serbia would bring Russia into the field. Russia, it is true, mobilized, but not until mobilization had been forced upon her by the discovery of Germany's secret military preparations as well as by Austria's threatening attitude. Germany was perfectly aware that the military programme adopted by Russia after the passing of the new German Army Bill in 1913 would not be completed till 1918, and she also knew that the Russian army was inadequately equipped for war on modern scientific lines. It was the psychological moment to strike, and Germany seized it. On the day on which she despatched her final ultimatum to St. Petersburg a high official of the German Foreign Office told the representative of a then neutral Power that the only thing which his Government feared was that Russia would, at the eleventh hour, climb down and accept it. I know this as a fact, as it was told me at the time by the representative of the said neutral Power at St. Petersburg.

As regards our own attitude, I have explained the reasons which prompted the language that I consistently held to Sazonoff. Russia never received from us any promise of armed support or any assurance of a nature to encourage her to push matters to extremes. Up to the very last His Majesty's Government reserved their full freedom of action, though they did, as was but right, warn the German Government not to be misled by our friendly language into thinking that we should stand aside were British interests to become involved.

I am reluctantly compelled to make a personal statement in order to rebut certain charges which have been brought against me. In its issue of April 8, 1922, the *Graphic* published two paragraphs which, after suggesting as an appropriate title for a future book the words, "Someone has blundered," went on to say: "The men of little faith would come badly off. A typical example is afforded in M. Paléologue's new book on Russia in 1914. Sir George Buchanan is said to have said to M. Sazonoff, 'I am afraid our public opinion is far from understanding that our national interest so evidently commands us to' [remain neutral in the Great War]." The words in brackets are the *Graphic's*.

I should not have taken any notice of this silly paragraph had not a friend shortly afterwards told me that people were asking when I was going to answer the charges brought against me by Paléologue. I replied that Paléologue was an old friend, who had been my colleague both at Petrograd and Sofia, and that I was not aware that he had said anything but good of me. I would, however, read his book. On doing so, I found that he makes me say, on July 24, 1914: "*Mais je crains que notre opinion publique ne soit encore tres éloignée de comprendre ce que l'intérêt national nous commande avec tant d'évidence.*" Supposing that I did actually use these words, I would ask whether, on the day following the presentation of the Austrian ultimatum, public opinion in England would have been behind the Government had they, then and there, pledged the country to war on account of what was at that moment regarded as a quarrel between Austria and Serbia. But, quite apart from this question, the *Graphic* has not only mistranslated the passage above quoted, but has, by adding the words "remain neutral in the Great War," read into it, for the benefit of its readers, a meaning which it cannot possibly have. This is quite clear from the context. Sazonoff had, according to Paléologue, said, "*La neutralité de l'Angleterre équivaut à son suicide.*" "C'est ma conviction," I am reported to have answered, while the rest of my reply, if correctly translated, would read as follows: "But I am afraid that our public opinion is still far from understanding what our national interest so clearly commands us to do."

Why, I should like to know, did the *Graphic* have recourse to such deliberate misrepresentation? My personal views with regard to our participation in the war were expressed at the time in my official correspondence with the Foreign Office. In handing me, on the night of August 1-2, his reply to the King's telegram the Emperor begged me to second his appeal for British support, and I did not hesitate to do so. I ventured to tell His Majesty's Government that, were we to stand aside, we should be left without a friend in Europe; that we could not, out of regard for our own safety, allow Germany to crush France; that we should be forced to intervene sooner or later in the war, and that the longer that we postponed intervention the heavier would be the price which we should have to pay.

Owing to the fact that this telegram reached the Foreign Office in a mutilated form, breaking off in the middle of a sentence, it could not be published in the White Book, that, with this one exception, recorded all the communications which passed between me and that department during those critical days.

On the day following Germany's declaration of war a solemn service was held in the Winter Palace, the French Ambassador, as the representative of Russia's ally, being the only foreigner invited. At its close one of the officiating priests read the Imperial war manifesto, in which the Emperor told his people: "We have not only to succour a kindred land that has been unjustly attacked, but to safeguard the honour and dignity of Russia as a great Power. . . .

"In this dread hour of trial may all internal differences be forgotten! May the union of the Tsar and his people become closer and stronger!"

Then, approaching the altar and taking the Gospel in his right hand, the Emperor addressed the officers present as follows: "I salute in you my whole army. I solemnly swear not to make peace so long as there is a single enemy on Russia's soil."

When, a few minutes later, the Sovereigns appeared on the balcony, the huge crowd that filled the square in front of the Winter Palace fell on their knees, singing the National Anthem.

The oath thus taken by the Emperor Nicholas was modelled textually on that sworn by the Emperor Alexander I when the Emperor Napoleon invaded Russia. For the moment, too, the Russian people were animated by the same spirit that had inspired their forefathers in 1812, though this time the sacrifices demanded of them were to prove greater than they could bear.

During the first three days of the war my position was not a pleasant one. Impatient crowds kept demonstrating before the Embassy clamouring for news from London and demanding in no friendly tones whether Russia could count on our support. I pacified them as best I could with vague assurances, but great was my relief when, at five o'clock in the morning of the 5th, one of my secretaries brought me the laconic message from the Foreign Office: "War — Germany — Act," which told me that England had proved true to herself and to her partners in the Triple Entente. I telephoned the good news to the French Embassy, to the Ministry for Foreign Affairs, and to the Emperor at Tsarskoe, and later in the morning attended a solemn Mass in the French Catholic church as the representative of the ally of France and Russia. On my return to the Embassy I found many floral offerings awaiting me which had been sent by Russians of all sorts and conditions as a tribute of gratitude to their new ally.

During those wonderful early August days Russia seemed to have been completely transformed. The German Ambassador had predicted that the declaration of war would provoke a revolution. He had even declined to listen to a friend who had advised him, on the eve of his departure, to send his collection of art treasures to the Hermitage for safe keeping, as the Hermitage would, he foretold, be one of the first buildings to be sacked. Unfortunately for him, the only act of mob violence throughout the whole Russian Empire was the wholesale looting of the German Embassy on August 4. Instead of provoking a revolution, the war forged a new bond between Sovereign and people. The workmen proclaimed a truce to strikes, and the various political parties laid aside their grievances. In the Duma, which the Emperor had convoked for an extraordinary session, the leaders of the different parties vied with each other in supporting the Government whom they had but a few weeks earlier been denouncing. The military credits were voted unanimously, and even the Socialists — who abstained from voting — exhorted the workmen to defend their country against the invader. In thus rallying round the Throne Liberals and progressives were animated by the hope that the war, which had brought the Emperor into such close touch with his people, would inaugurate a new era of constitutional reforms.

But it was at Moscow, where, in accordance with the traditions of his house, the Emperor went to worship at the holy shrines of the Kremlin, that the heart of Russia voiced the feelings of the whole nation. The French Ambassador and I, together with my wife and daughter, had been invited to assist at the coming ceremonies. On the morning of August 6 we proceeded to the Kremlin, and were conducted to the great gallery of the palace, where a crowd of high officials and notables of every kind, as well as representatives of municipal and other institutions, were awaiting the arrival of the Sovereigns. Soon afterwards the Emperor and Empress, followed by the Grand Duchess Elisabeth, the four young Grand Duchesses and the little Tsarevitch (who, having hurt his leg, was carried in the arms of a huge Cossack), made their entrance. Stopping in the middle of the gallery, the Emperor made a short speech in which, after saying that he had come to Moscow to find strength in prayer, he spoke of the splendid spirit with which all classes of his subjects had responded to his call to arms, and concluded by invoking God's blessing on the allied armies.

Then joining the procession that was formed, we followed the Imperial family through a number of rooms and down the famous "Red Staircase" to the Ouspensky Sabor — or Cathedral of the Assumption — where the Emperors were crowned. The appearance of Their Majesties was greeted with a storm of applause, while the bells of all the churches of Moscow rang out a peal of welcome. The service which followed was beautiful and impressive beyond description. The long line of archbishops and bishops, in their vestments of gold brocade, their mitres sparkling with precious stones; the frescoes on the walls, with their golden background; the jewelled icons — all lent colour and brilliancy to the picture presented by the glorious old cathedral.

As soon as we had taken our places behind the Imperial family the deep bass voice of a priest was heard chanting the opening passages of the liturgy, and then the choir, joining in, flooded the church with harmony as it intoned the psalms and hymns of the Orthodox ritual. As the service was nearing its close the Emperor and Empress, followed by the Grand Duchesses, went the round of the church, kneeling in deep devotion before each of its shrines or kissing some specially sacred icon presented them by the Metropolitan. Nor, when the doors were opened, was the scene outside less impressive. Walking along a slightly raised narrow platform to the other wing of the palace, with nothing but a low railing to separate him from the kneeling multitude of his subjects — some of whom even kissed the ground as he passed — the Emperor was acclaimed with one never-ending cheer. Stopping for a moment and inviting the French Ambassador and me to keep near him, His Majesty said, "These acclamations are addressed to you as well as to me."

As I drove away with my French colleague to our hotel I could not help wondering how long this national enthusiasm would last, and what would be the feeling of the people for their "Little Father" were the war to be unduly prolonged.

I do not propose to follow the Russian armies through all the successive phases of the war, as this has already been admirably done by my friend and former military attaché, Major-General Sir Alfred Knox, in his book, "With the Russian Armies, 1914-1917." I shall therefore content myself with a brief sketch of the principal events in the Eastern theatre of war, with reference more especially to their bearing on the general Russian situation.

Yielding to the pressure brought to bear on him by his Ministers, the Emperor had renounced his intention of assuming the command of the armies, and had appointed the Grand Duke Nicolas Nicolaievich commander-in-chief. Though Germany had declared war on Russia on August 1, it was only on the 6th that Austria, who had brought the war about, followed her example and recalled her Ambassador. According to the plan of campaign drawn up by the General Staff, Russia was at once to take the offensive in the south against Austria and to act on the defensive in the north till everything was in order for the far more serious business of an advance against Germany. Had Russia only consulted her own interests this would undoubtedly have been the wisest course for her to follow, but she had also to think of her allies. The advance of the German armies in the west rendered it imperative for her to make a diversion in the east. The original plan of campaign was accordingly changed, and on August 17 — the day following the completion of the mobilization — General Rennenkampf took the offensive and made a raid into East Prussia.

For the first ten days his operations were attended with such complete success that it was even hoped that the whole province would soon be at his mercy. He had, however, advanced farther than was prudent under the circumstances. The German General Staff, alarmed at the number of fugitives who kept streaming into Berlin, caused troops to be transferred from the west, and sent General von Hindenburg to take over the command in the east. At the same time, owing to the forced retirement of the allied armies in the west, the French Ambassador was instructed to urge the Russian Government to press home the offensive in East Prussia. In the opinion of the best Russian generals such an offensive was premature and doomed to failure. The army was not yet thoroughly organized in all its branches. The difficulties of transport were tremendous: the troops were not properly concentrated, and the country, with its forests, lakes and marshes, was not inaptly likened to a sponge that would suck up all who entered it. But Russia could not turn a deaf ear to the appeal of an ally whose capital was threatened by the enemy, and Samsonoff's army was ordered to advance.

The battle of Tannenberg was the result. Owing to tactical errors on the part of the corps commanders on the flanks and to the lack of the necessary means of communication between them and Samsonoff, the two central corps were left without support and had to lay down their arms. The Russians lost all their artillery as well as vast quantities of shells and other war material which they could ill spare. In the course of a few more weeks the Germans, following up their victory, cleared the whole province of the enemy, inflicting on them a total loss of a quarter of a million of men besides striking a serious blow at the *morale* of their army and the prestige of its commanders. Though later in the year the Russians re-entered East Prussia and overran the frontier districts, they had in the following February to evacuate it for good.

This disaster in the north was counterbalanced to some extent by the brilliant victories gained in the south, where General Ivanoff was in command, with General Alexeieff as Chief of the Staff. The Austrians were driven back by the armies under Generals Ruzsky, Brussiloff and Radko Dimitrieff; Lemberg was taken early in September, and in November the great fortress of Przemysl was invested. The Austrians lost in all 1,000 guns and 200,000 prisoners. This rapid advance raised in many quarters exaggerated hopes for the future, and my French colleague was at one moment so optimistic that he even bet me £5 that the war would be over by Christmas. But the Russian "steam roller," in its endeavours to relieve the pressure in the west, had been pushing on at a pace that ill suited its cumbrous mechanism. Russia was heavily handicapped. She had to move troops and supplies enormous distances on bad roads, and in Poland, which the Germans had entered at the beginning of the war, she had to fight in a country flanked on either side by hostile territory. In October the Germans were almost at the gates of Warsaw. The opportune arrival of the Siberian contingent effected a welcome change in the situation. The Russian offensive was resumed, the Germans were driven back and narrowly escaped a crushing defeat at Lodz. They were only saved by the reinforcements which, thanks to their network of strategic railways, they were able to bring up in time. The tables were once more turned in their favour, the Russians had to retire, and by the middle of December their offensive was totally arrested. The curtain had risen on the opening act of the great Russian tragedy.

On September 25 General Joffre had inquired whether Russia's supply of ammunition was sufficient to meet the prevailing high rate of consumption, and had received the comforting assurance that there was no cause for anxiety on that score. Then suddenly, on December 18, the French Ambassador and I were informed by the Chief of the Staff at the Ministry for War that, though Russia had in her depots men enough and to spare to make good her colossal losses in the war, she had no rifles wherewith to arm them and that her reserves of artillery ammunition were exhausted. General Bielaieff added that orders were being placed abroad and that steps were being taken to increase the output of the national factories, but that for the next two or three months the military situation would be not only difficult but dangerous. This announcement came as a bolt from the blue. In that early stage of the war there was little, if any, co-ordination in the plans of the Allied Commanders-in-Chief in their respective theatres of war and they were too much inclined to adhere to the system of watertight compartments. An offensive would be taken in the west when the Russians in the east were obliged to remain on the defensive, and vice versa, with the result that the Germans kept special army corps, which they sent backwards and forwards from the one front to the other, wherever their presence was the most needed.

In protesting at the time against the secrecy that had been observed with regard to Russia's shortage of ammunition, I urged the necessity of closer contact being established between the Allied General Staffs. The Russians had apparently based their calculations on their experiences in the Japanese War, and had not made provision for a war of longer duration. I remember once asking a distinguished member of the Duma who was, during the Balkan crisis, advocating the adoption by the Entente of a firmer policy, whether Russia was ready to face a European war. "No," was his reply; "but she never will be ready." He was right. Her industries were still in a backward state; she had not sufficient factories, and those which she had often lacked the requisite machinery and the necessary number of skilled workmen. The rearmament of Russia was, indeed, soon to become one of the most difficult problems which the Allies had to face. Though I personally did not share the pessimism that had already struck root in Petrograd, as the Russian capital had been rechristened, I felt that there was but little chance of her opening the road to Berlin through Silesia, and that her future role would have to be restricted to wearing out and gradually destroying the enemy forces in a war of attrition.

In addition to the feeling of discouragement occasioned by the military situation, the peace campaign being conducted by Count Witte and his band of Germanophils could not but be regarded as a disquieting sign. Count Witte, as I have already stated in Chapter 14, had always held that Russia's interests dictated a close understanding with Germany, and he was now openly declaring that Russia had nothing to gain by continuing the war and ought to make peace. In one of our conversations with Sazonoff early in November, my French colleague urged that it was time that the Emperor should take some action with regard to a campaign that was assuming dangerous proportions. Sazonoff thereupon suggested that the French

Ambassador should himself bring the matter to the Emperor's notice and promised to arrange an audience for the purpose. In this audience, which took place a week later, the Emperor did not mention Count Witte's name, and Paléologue did not therefore venture to broach the subject himself.

As Count Witte's attacks were mainly directed against Great Britain, I determined to take up his challenge, and I did so in a speech which I made at the English Club on New Year's Eve. "We were," I said, "being accused by certain well-known Germanophils of having pushed Russia into the war for our own selfish ends and of now leaving her to bear the brunt of it. We were constantly being asked by these gentlemen, 'Where is your navy?' 'What is your army doing?' I will tell them," I proceeded to say, "what the British army and navy have done"; and after enumerating all the services which they had rendered the Allied cause, I cited Germany — the special friend of our critics — as a witness to prove the truth of my statement. For it was to England that Germany's poets addressed their hymns of hate, and it was on England that Germany's professors poured the vials of their wrath; and they did so because they knew that the British Empire barred the way to the world dominion of which the Fatherland had dreamed. This speech had an enormous success. Not only was it published *in extenso* in all the leading Russian papers, but it was made the subject of long leading articles, in which I was congratulated on having had the courage to open the sore from which Russia was suffering. The Emperor, whom I saw shortly afterwards, told me that he was very glad that I had been so outspoken.

It also had a sequel. A few days later I received the visit of a well-known journalist, who informed me that he had been sent by Count Witte, who was ill, to inquire whether what I had said in my speech was aimed at him. I replied that this was a question which I must decline to answer as there were so many Germanophils in Petrograd. They might all ask me the same question, and I could not really reply to each one individually. My journalistic friend was not satisfied, saying that Count Witte insisted on receiving an answer. I then said: "You can tell Count Witte from me that when I made my speech I had in my mind all those who had held the language of which I had complained, and that if the cap fits him he can wear it."

CHAPTER 17
1914-15

Almost immediately after the opening of hostilities Sazonoff had made tentative efforts to secure the co-operation of benevolent neutrality of those States which, on account of their geographical position or territorial aspirations, were likely to be drawn into the conflict. Bulgaria was offered certain districts of Serbian Macedonia in the event of a victorious war resulting in Serbia obtaining access to the Adriatic; Roumania was tempted with the promise of the greater part of Transylvania and the northern half of the Bukowina; overtures were made to Italy with regard to Italia Irredenta, while His Majesty's Government were invited to open negotiations with Japan. Japan entered the war on August 22, but Roumania pleaded the close friendship that had so long existed between King Carol and the Emperor Franz Joseph as a reason for not entering the lists. It was only after King Carol's death in the following October that the inter minable negotiations, which ended in Roumania taking the field when it was too late, were opened at Bucharest.

But the one question of paramount importance for Russia, more especially after the passage through the Straits of the *Goeben* and *Breslau*, was the attitude that Turkey would adopt. Negotiations were at once opened at Constantinople with a view to purchasing her neutrality; but Germany's influence, enhanced by the prestige of her victories and by the presence of two of her warships off Constantinople, outweighed that of the Entente Powers and in the end carried the day. Early in October the Straits were closed, and a few weeks later two Turkish torpedo boats entered Odessa harbour and sank a Russian gunboat. The closing of the Straits was a paralysing blow for Russia. With only two ports — Vladivostock in the far east and Archangel in the north, that was ice-bound in winter — she was now virtually shut off from all communication with her allies in the West. The need of free access to the sea was thus brought home to the Russian public, whose eyes turned to Constantinople as the one great prize to be won by the war. Moscow led the movement, and the

Emperor, in the manifesto issued after the recall of the allied Ambassadors from Constantinople, told his people that "Turkey's unwarranted intervention would but prepare the way for the solution of the historic problem bequeathed to us by our fathers on the shores of the Black Sea."

We were at the time engaged in a conversation with Russia on the subject of Persia. While raising no objection to the continued presence of Russian troops in Azerbaijan for the purpose of maintaining order, or to their passage through Persia in the event of a Turkish attack on that country, we did not wish her to act as Germany had acted in the case of Belgium and to violate Persia's neutrality. His Majesty's Government had, however, to take into account the new situation created by Turkey's entrance into the war and to give some satisfaction to the wishes and aspirations of the Russian people. They accordingly instructed me in November to inform the Russian Government that in the event of our defeating Germany the fate of Constantinople and the Straits would have to be decided in conformity with Russia's needs. Though received by Sazonoff with a warm expression of his grateful appreciation, this communication was not quite precise enough to satisfy the Russian Government for long. During the winter months the movement had grown in intensity and, in the Duma, the veiled references of Ministers to the brilliant future opening for Russia on the shores of the Black Sea had been received with acclamation. Early in March Sazonoff spoke to the French Ambassador and me of the emotion which the question of Constantinople was evoking throughout the country and of the necessity of its radical solution. The Emperor, he said, felt that after all the sacrifices which he had imposed on his people he could no longer delay asking his allies for a definite assurance of their consent to the incorporation of Constantinople in the Russian Empire when once the war had been won.

On March 18 I was instructed to inform the Emperor personally that His Majesty's Government were prepared to give this assurance on certain conditions. Though not yet in a position to define all their own *desiderata*, the revision of the Anglo-Russian Agreement of 1907 and the recognition of the neutral zone as a British sphere would have to be conceded by Russia. With regard to Constantinople they would attach the condition that an arrangement should be made for the commercial freedom of the Straits for merchant vessels as well as for a free port for goods in transit from and to non-Russian territory on the Black Sea. They would further expect Russia, among other things, to do everything in her power to facilitate the participation of

Roumania and Bulgaria in the war against Turkey and the Central Powers.

As the Emperor was leaving the next morning for the front, Sazonoff kindly arranged that I should accompany him to Tsarskoe and be received at the same time as himself in an audience which he was to have that evening.

The Emperor received us in his study, and after a few words of friendly greeting said to me: "You have a communication to make?" I replied that I was charged with a message which would, I trusted, give him as much pleasure to receive as it gave me to deliver, namely, that His Majesty's Government consented to the realization of Russia's secular aspirations with regard to Constantinople and the Straits on conditions which he would have no difficulty in accepting. I then enumerated those conditions. After desiring me to convey his warmest thanks to His Majesty's Government the Emperor inquired what was the existing arrangement with regard to the neutral zone. I explained the nature of that arrangement in general terms, adding that its incorporation in the British sphere would put an end to a constant cause of friction between our two Governments and would mark a great step in advance towards a final and friendly settlement of the Persian question. As the Emperor still hesitated, I ventured to say that had I a year ago brought him the offer of Constantinople in exchange for a declaration of Russia's *désinteressement* in the neutral zone, I had no doubt as to what His Majesty's answer would have been.

The Emperor laughed and said I was quite right. On my asking whether I might inform my Government that His Majesty accepted their conditions in principle, Sazonoff intervened with the remark that Russia must in return be allowed complete liberty of action in her own sphere; not, he proceeded to explain, that she had any desire to annex North Persia, but because she wanted an end put to the representations which we were so constantly making about her action there. I replied that we also had not the slightest intention of annexing the neutral zone, and that our object, on the contrary, was to secure the maintenance of Persian integrity. This object was more likely to be attained were ambitious Russian consuls to be precluded, as they would be under the new arrangement, from pursuing a forward policy contrary to the wishes of their Government. At the same time the Russian and British representatives at Tehran might work out an agreement under which Russia could obtain sufficient liberty of action in her own sphere without violating, the principle of Persian independence. Then, turning to the Emperor, I said that after the war Russia and Great Britain would be the two most powerful empires in the world. With the settlement of the Persian question the last cause of friction between them would disappear and the world's peace would then be assured. The Emperor cordially agreed. His Majesty then authorized me to say that he accepted our conditions in principle.

The rest of the audience was occupied with a discussion of Italy's claims to territorial compensation in Dalmatia and on the Adriatic. Taking an atlas, the Emperor followed Sazonoff's report, pointing out the exact position of every town and district mentioned with a promptitude that surprised me. The negotiations with Italy had been complicated by the fact that many of her claims clashed with those of Serbia. It was the old question of Slav interests; and there was a strong party in Russia, including such influential personages as the Grand Duke Nicholas, that was opposed to the acceptance of some of her demands. They contended that Russia could not allow Italy to acquire a position on the Adriatic that would virtually make Serbia her vassal there, and that if Serbia's aspirations were left unsatisfied, we should in no distant future be confronted with fresh troubles if not with another war. In view of the vital importance of securing Italy's co-operation, I had to endeavour to overcome these objections and to induce the Russian Government to make the necessary concessions. Sazonoff, fortunately, was too broadminded to press these views unduly, and subordinating Russia's special interests to the general interests of the Allies, he finally accepted the arrangement under which Italy entered the war on May 23.

Negotiations had at the same time been proceeding with Roumania, Greece and Bulgaria, and from the language originally held by M. Bratiano we had reason to hope that Roumania would at once follow Italy's example. Though aware that Italy was on the point of declaring war on Austria, she let slip the favourable moment in the spring of 1915, when the Russians held the more important of the Carpathian heights, and when her co-operation with the Russian army might have saved the situation. The tide of war had now turned in Germany's favour, and the farther the Russians retired the less disposed was she to throw down the gauntlet to the Central Powers. But, apart from the military question, the negotiations respecting the political agreement that was to record the price to be paid for her intervention dragged on for months. Bratiano demanded the Pruth and the Theiss as her future frontier, a demand that meant the incorporation in Roumania of both the Bukowine and the Banat.

From the point of view of her own national interests Russia was strongly opposed to Roumania's acquiring the whole of the Bukowine, while neither she nor her allies felt justified in extending

Roumania's territory almost to the gates of Belgrade by promising her the whole of the Banat. But necessity is a hard taskmaster, and we could not afford to risk permission being given the Germans to despatch war material to the Turks through Roumania. Sazonoff first made the concession of allowing her to have the major part of the Bukowine, and then, bowing to the wishes of the Allies, he yielded on the question of the Banat. The latter concession was made subject to certain conditions proposed by Sir E. Grey for the safeguard of Serbia's interests and for the protection of her capital as well as on the understanding that the allied Powers would undertake to compensate Serbia by facilitating her union with Croatia if the latter consented. Sazonoff further attached the condition that Roumania should take the field within five weeks. This Bratiano declined to do. He was ready to conclude a political agreement on the above basis, but insisted that the actual date for taking action must depend on the military situation and on conditions to be embodied in a military convention.

The military situation, indeed, at the end of July was such that Bratiano was probably right in saying that for Roumania to march at that moment would be to court certain disaster. It would have been different had we won over Bulgaria to our side, for her intervention would have so improved matters that Roumania could have afforded to run the risk. On the other hand, a definite assurance of Roumania's co-operation would have greatly facilitated our negotiations with Bulgaria. But we had, as Sazonoff remarked to me, been moving in a vicious circle. We had, he said, been trying to please everybody and had signally failed, as it was impossible to satisfy one of the Balkan States without offending the others. We had, therefore, to ask ourselves which of them could render us the most effective assistance and which would prove the most dangerous were it to join our enemies. Greece had had recourse to every pretext in order to evade coming to Serbia's assistance, and it was impossible to count on her co-operation, while, were she to side with Germany, her coasts would be at the mercy of the allied fleets. Serbia, on the other hand, could never make terms with the Central Powers, and it would not be a matter of great moment to us if she did, out of pique, delay taking the offensive against Austria. The one important factor in the situation was Bulgaria. Both for political and national reasons the forcing of the Dardanelles was of vital interest to Russia, and the co-operation of the Bulgarian army would greatly facilitate the accomplishment of that task. We ought, therefore, he maintained, to concentrate all our efforts on securing that co-operation even at the risk of offending other States.

His Majesty's Government had from the very outset realized the importance of Bulgaria's co-operation, but in spite of their untiring efforts they had failed to induce the Governments of Belgrade and Athens to make the sacrifices necessary to secure it. Greece had refused to give up Cavalla, Serbia had declared that she could not cede national territory without the consent of the Great Skuptschina, and that it was impossible to convoke that assembly on account of the war. Roumania, on the other hand, had agreed to the eventual cession of Dobritch and Baltchik. During the course of these negotiations it became clear that the minimum price at which we could purchase Bulgaria's co-operation was the cession of the so-called uncontested zone in Macedonia. That zone had been recognized as hers under the Serbo-Bulgarian Treaty of 1912, but had, after the Second Balkan War, been assigned to Serbia by the Treaty of Bucharest.

At the end of July it was decided, on Sir Edward Grey's suggestion, that the allied representatives at Belgrade should make an urgent appeal to the Serbian Government to consent to its cession on the termination of the war in return for Bulgaria's immediate effective co-operation. The Allies, they were to add, would engage to secure for Serbia such ample compensation as would fully realize the most important of her political and economic aspirations, and would also guarantee that her territorial connexion with Greece should be preserved. In order that this appeal might carry more weight, I was instructed to ask for an audience and to suggest that His Majesty should remind the Prince Regent that he had, at the beginning of the war, placed the fate of Serbia in the Emperor's hands and that the whole course of the war would be imperilled should the Serbian Government refuse to comply with our request.

The Emperor received me in audience on July 28, and after I had explained the situation to him, said that he fully recognized the importance of ensuring the success of our operations in the Dardanelles by securing the co-operation of the Bulgarian army. He could not, however, send such a telegram to the Prince Regent. It was perfectly true that it was on Serbia's account that we had become involved in war; but Serbia was our ally and we had not treated her quite fairly. We had, without consulting her, sacrificed some of her important interests in order to satisfy Italy, and we were now about to give Roumania the Banat. A refusal on the part of the Prince Regent would, the Emperor added, place him in a very awkward position.

I replied that Serbia's heroism had our unstinted admiration and that we fully appreciated the services which she had rendered during the early stages of the war, but that for some months past she had not been in a position to take any action of importance. The Allies, on the other hand, had never ceased making enormous sacrifices, and Serbia could not expect them to do so indefinitely without herself making some counter-sacrifices. However much we might sympathize with her, we were fully justified in asking her to make a concession that would help to shorten the war. At the time of the First Balkan War access to the Adriatic and not Macedonia had been the main object of her ambitions, and that ambition would now be realized in a measure which had never before been contemplated. Macedonia, moreover, had only been Serbia's since the summer of 1913, while previous to that date it had been recognized as Bulgarian by the Emperor Alexander II in 1877, and by Serbia herself in 1912. We were, moreover, only asking her to do what was necessary for her own safety, as, were Bulgaria to join the Central Powers, her very existence as a nation would be at stake.

The Emperor was impressed by what I had said and promised to reconsider the question, adding that it would be easier for him to act as had been suggested were King George, the King of Italy and President Poincare to address similar telegrams to the Prince Regent. Sazonoff, to whom I communicated the substance of this conversation, entirely concurred in the Emperor's suggestion, which was eventually adopted. Sazonoff also remarked that he was very glad that I had spoken as I had done, as all the Emperor's sympathies were on the side of Serbia.

The Serbian reply to the communication eventually made them by the allied Powers was in the nature of a compromise. It was an acceptance in principle, but hedged round with reservations which, as the Bulgars would be content with nothing less than the whole of the uncontested zone, rendered it valueless for our purpose. Under the treaty of alliance which they had concluded in the spring of 1913, Greece and Serbia had agreed not to cede any districts to the west of the Vardar. Greece, who had been careful to evade rendering Serbia the assistance which her treaty obligations prescribed, pressed for the observance of this particular clause. Though the negotiations at Sofia and Belgrade were continued, every day that passed rendered the prospect more hopeless. Russia's attitude during the Second Balkan War had not been forgotten at the former capital, while after the fall of Warsaw and Kovno the cause of the Allies was regarded as lost. King Ferdinand, who had throughout been intriguing with the Central Powers, was not the man to attach himself to the losing side, more especially when Germany was prepared to pay him double the price which the Allies were offering for his co-operation. Our proposals, moreover, were generally regarded as too vague. Nothing, indeed, short of an absolute assurance of Bulgaria's acquisition of the uncontested zone would have stayed the march of events, while the idea of paying off old scores on Serbia was popular with the army.

O'Beirne, who had been with me at Petrograd as Counsellor of Embassy, and who afterwards lost his life when travelling with Lord Kitchener to Russia, had been sent as Minister to Sofia, but unfortunately too late to retrieve the mistakes of his predecessor. He had early in September expressed the opinion that, though Serbia might reject some of our demands, she would acquiesce were they imposed on her, and he was, in my opinion, right. I had myself, in the conversations which I and my French colleague had daily with Sazonoff, spoken in a very similar sense. Paléologue, on the contrary, protested that we could not hold such language or inflict such a humiliation on an ally. The stakes, however, for which we were playing were too high to allow considerations for the feelings of any Government to influence our policy. Could we but have won over Bulgaria to our side, Roumania would almost certainly have cast in her lot with us in the autumn of 1915. Turkey's fate would then have been sealed, and the whole course of the war would have been changed. It was, perhaps, natural that Serbia should hesitate to cede what she regarded as her national territory, but it would have been different had the allied Governments dictated such a course to her. Had they insisted on her allowing Bulgaria to occupy the uncontested zone then and there it is doubtful whether Bulgaria, no matter how far King Ferdinand had committed himself in the negotiations with the Central Powers, would, even at the eleventh hour, have marched against us. She certainly would not have done so had we taken such action earlier in the year. Sazonoff did all that it was possible to do under the circumstances, but he was not empowered to hold the only language that would have turned the scales at Belgrade. Strong pressure would, no doubt, have been required to induce the Emperor, whose sympathies, as was but natural, were all on the side of the Serbs, to consent to the Allies imposing their wishes at Belgrade. But had they done so the war would have been considerably shortened and Russia might have been spared the horrors of the Bolshevik revolution.

With Bulgaria definitely engaged on the side of the Central Powers and with the Russian army exhausted after its long retreat, it was useless to expect Roumania to march. Even before the fall of Warsaw the Emperor had admitted, in the course of my audience recorded above, that it would be a mistake to press her to take the field till the Russian army was in a position to resume the offensive. The Allies had, therefore, to content themselves with the political agreement and to leave the date of her entry into action to be settled later on by a military convention.

CHAPTER 18
1915

Early in 1915 the Russians had taken the great fortress of Przemysl and advanced to within a few miles of Cracau. They had also crossed the Carpathians and made a descent into the Hungarian plain. But, owing to the shortage of shells and rifles, they were unable to follow up these victories; and the Germans, who were aware of this, determined to restore the situation in the eastern theatre of war by the transfer of several army corps from the west. Mackensen, who had been sent to take over the command of the Austro-German forces, commenced operations early in May, and the Russian army — exposed to a terrific bombardment, to which it could make no effective reply, and weakened by the absence of the troops detached for service in the Carpathians — retired all along the line.

One after another of its hard-won conquests had to be abandoned. In June Przemysl and Lemberg fell, and in August Warsaw, Novogeorgievsk, Kovno, Grodno and Brest Litowsk surrendered in rapid succession. During this long and disastrous retreat the losses in killed, wounded and prisoners were colossal. The shortage in rifles was so great that a considerable percentage of the men had to wait unarmed till they could pick up the rifles of their fallen comrades. The only wonder was that the army remained intact. At one time Petrograd itself was in such danger that steps were taken to transfer the archives and gold reserve to Vologda. There had also been a question of removing the art treasures of the Hermitage, but the Emperor had vetoed the proposal for fear that it might create a panic. Happily, the further German advance was stayed, and the arrangements for the evacuation of the capital were suspended. The German offensive in Courland was attended with equal success, and as a precautionary measure the plant of the Riga factories was removed eastwards. For the next nine months the Russian army was virtually immobilized on the line which it had occupied towards the middle of September, though from time to time it achieved a few brilliant local successes.

On September 5, when the military situation was at its worst, the Emperor assumed the supreme command of his armies, with General Alexeieff as chief of the staff, although his Ministers had done their utmost to dissuade him from taking what they regarded as a dangerous step. The allied Governments, who had received the announcement with considerable apprehension, were naturally precluded from expressing their preference for the retention of the Grand Duke Nicholas as commander-in-chief. To have done so would have been to intervene in a purely internal question on which the Emperor had already taken a decision. I had once, indeed — in February, 1915 — been instructed to intercede in favour of a well-known revolutionary (Bourtzeff) who, on returning to Russia for the purpose of inducing his comrades to suspend their subversive activities and to work for the successful prosecution of the war, had been arrested and sentenced to deportation to Siberia. The patriotic letter which Bourtzeff had published before leaving for Russia had, as I told Sazonoff privately, made such a favourable impression in England that it was generally hoped that he would be pardoned.

Sazonoff kindly undertook to plead his cause with the Emperor, and His Majesty, after some hesitation, was pleased to pardon him. But, in discussing the question with Sazonoff, the Emperor had remarked that it was curious what a much greater interest the English and French took in the internal affairs of Russia than the Russians did in those of England and France — a gentle reminder to us that to concern ourselves with questions affecting the Government of Russia was to tread on forbidden ground. I took advantage, nevertheless, of an audience which I had early in September with the Empress to tell Her Majesty that I shared the apprehensions with which the Emperor's decision was viewed by the Council of Ministers. Not only, I said, would His Majesty have to bear the whole responsibility for any fresh disaster that might befall his armies, but he would, by combining the duties of commander-in-chief with those of the autocratic ruler of a great Empire, be undertaking a task beyond the strength of any single man. The Empress at once protested, saying that the Emperor ought to have assumed the command from the very first and that, now that his army had suffered so severely, his proper place was with his troops. "I have no patience," she continued, "with Ministers who try to prevent him doing his duty. The situation requires firmness. The Emperor, unfortunately, is weak; but I am not, and I intend to be firm." Her Majesty kept her word. The Emperor, when in residence at Headquarters, could not keep in constant touch with his Ministers, and was too absorbed by military matters to give that close attention to questions of internal policy which the growing gravity of the situation demanded. The result was that the Empress, more especially after Stürmer became President of the Council in February, 1916, virtually governed Russia.

Among other reasons that had prompted Her Majesty to encourage the Emperor to take over the command was the suspicion that the Grand Duke's prestige as commander-in-chief was gradually eclipsing that of his Sovereign. She was, in fact, jealous of him. On the other hand, the Grand Duke's enemies, of whom Rasputin was one, had done their utmost to discredit him at Court by representing that the reverses of the Russian army were due to his faulty leadership. Rasputin, indeed, had a special reason for hating the Grand Duke, for when, earlier in the war, he had telegraphed for permission to come to the front to bless the troops, the Grand Duke had replied, "Do come! I will hang you."

So much has been written about that ignoble personage that there is little left for me to tell. A story was at one time current at Petrograd that during one of my audiences at Tsarskoe Rasputin suddenly entered the room, and that, on the Emperor naming him to me, I at once took my leave. Needless to say that this, like so many other stories of his sayings and doings, is a pure fable. There were, however, many salons in Petrograd where he was an honoured guest and the centre of an admiring circle of lady devotees — in spite of the fact that he not only dressed like a peasant, but made a point of appearing unwashed and unkempt. My friend Paléologue tells us, in his book on Russia, how he met him in one of these houses, and how Rasputin, at the close of their conversation, "*me serre contre sa poitrine.*" I, personally, never attempted to gratify my curiosity by meeting him in this way, as I did not consider it right to enter into personal contact with him.

The native of a Siberian village and the son of an uneducated moujik, he had been nicknamed "Rasputin," or the Debauchee, on account of his dissolute life. The Russian peasant is a curious combination of good and evil. He is full of contradictions — he can be gentle and brutal, religious and vicious. Rasputin was no exception to this rule. A drunkard and a sensualist, the mysticism latent in his character had in earlier life been awakened by the exhortations of a priest whom he happened to be driving to some distant village. This drive constituted what he himself described as his journey to Damascus, for, as in the case of St. Paul, a voice had spoken to him on the way. Deeply moved, he vowed to lead a new life. Wandering as a pilgrim from village to village, he lived on such alms as he could collect, preaching and effecting cures by his magnetic touch. In one of the monasteries, where he made a prolonged stay, he learned to read and write, and even picked up a smattering of theology. A few years later he went on a pilgrimage to Jerusalem.

He thus gradually acquired the reputation of a holy man, or elder (*staretz*), and was credited with the gifts of healing and prophecy. He experienced, however, many backslidings, and during most of the time he led a double life. He acted up to the doctrine which he preached that repentance can alone bring salvation, but that one cannot repent if one has not sinned. To yield to temptation was, therefore, the first stage on the road to salvation. The sect which he eventually founded was an offshoot of that of the Khlysty, or Flagellants. Its members aspired, in some strange way, to direct communion with God; but their services, which were held at night, savoured rather of the Bacchanalia of ancient Rome than of the rites of a Christian Church. Singing and shouting, they moved round in a circle, quickening the pace at each turn till, after whirling round in a mad dance, they sank exhausted to the ground. There then followed a scene over which it is best to draw a veil. Rasputin was well fitted to be the high priest of such a sect, for he exercised an extraordinary fascination over women. Though as a general rule he behaved abominably to them, his victims put up with every kind of ill-treatment sooner than leave him. Only one woman turned on him and nearly killed him by stabbing him in the abdomen.

Rasputin's reputation for holiness gradually spread to the capital, and in 1905 he was summoned there by a well-known Archimandrite, under whose auspices he made his entrance into St. Petersburg society. He had soon a large circle of admirers, including the two Montenegrin Princesses, the wives of the Grand Dukes Nicholas and Peter, and it was through their good offices that he was, two years later, presented at Court. There he was careful to reveal only the mystic side of his nature. By personal magnetism or by some form of hypnotic suggestion he did undoubtedly relieve the haemophilia from which the Tsarevitch — a charming boy, the idol of both his parents — had long suffered. Believing, as she did, that Rasputin could by his prayers preserve her son's life, the Empress centred all her hopes on him and regarded him with feelings akin to adoration. She absolutely declined to credit the stories of his debauched life, even when one of his drunken orgies had occasioned the intervention of the police. For her he was always blameless — a God-fearing man, reviled and persecuted like the saints of old.

Rasputin had the natural cunning of the Russian peasant, but he was no ordinary impostor. He believed in himself — in his preternatural powers — in his gift of reading the decrees of fate. He warned the Empress that if his enemies succeeded in getting him sent away evil would befall the Tsarevitch, as his presence was indispensable to the latter's well-being. So it turned out. He had to retire to Siberia for a time, and the boy grew worse. On one occasion, in the autumn of 1912, his illness, in consequence of an accident, took such an acute form that his life was in danger. Rasputin, who was at once communicated with, sent a comforting telegram, assuring the Empress that her son would live. An improvement set in, the boy recovered, and the Empress attributed his recovery to Rasputin's intercessions. Still more curious was it that he should have warned her that his own destiny was indissolubly bound up with that of the Imperial family — for he had not been dead three months before the Empire had passed away.

It had been through Madame Wyroubowa, the daughter of Taneiew, the head of the Emperor's chancery, that Rasputin had in the first instance been able to get into such close touch with the Sovereigns. Madame Wyroubowa, who had made an unhappy marriage, had, since her separation from her husband, found consolation in religion, while she had become the inseparable companion and confidante of the Empress, who had taken pity on her when she was in trouble. She was one of the first to profess implicit belief in the *staretz*, and, as he foresaw, she proved an invaluable ally. Acting as intermediary between him and the Empress, consulting him on all questions, corresponding with him during his short visits to Siberia, she consistently encouraged Her Majesty to be guided by his advice. She also made herself useful by reporting to the Empress what people in high positions were saying and thinking, and in order to draw them into an expression of their views on political questions she would give them to understand that she was consulting them on behalf of their Majesties. Too stupid herself to form a clear judgment about men and things, she became the unconscious tool of Rasputin and of those with whom he was acting. I both disliked her and mistrusted her, and saw her seldom.

The rôle actually played by Rasputin at Court is still veiled in a good deal of mystery. His ascendancy over the Emperor was not so absolute as that which he exercised over the Empress, and concerned questions of a religious or ecclesiastical kind rather than of policy. He interested himself chiefly, at first, in securing for his friends and adherents high appointments in the Orthodox Church and in dispossessing any prelate who had ventured to speak disparagingly of him. Thanks to his protection, a most undesirable friend of his boyhood, an uneducated peasant, Varnava by name, was appointed Bishop of Tobolsk, while a little later Pitirim, a man of very doubtful morals, was made Metropolitan of Petrograd.

Gradually, however, he began to take a hand in the political game. He was on intimate terms with several of the more reactionary Ministers, who were at one and the same time his patrons and clients. A few words written on a slip of paper sufficed to secure the granting by these Ministers of the requests of his protégés. He would, on the other hand, in his conversations with the Empress and Madame Wyroubowa, speak in the sense which they desired, or he would advocate the appointment of some reactionary friend of his to a vacant Ministry. He thus indirectly influenced the Emperor in the choice of his Ministers, and consequently in the course of his policy. This was more especially the case when, after the assumption by the Emperor of the supreme command, the Empress became all powerful.

But, while it was Rasputin's influence that was the dominating factor, the political strings were pulled by others whose interests he served and whose intrigues he countenanced. Uneducated, and engrossed by the pursuit of carnal pleasures, he was hardly the man to conceive or formulate any concrete policy. He left that to others, and was content to follow their lead. Self-interest was his guiding principle through life, and no one knew better than he how to turn the tables on those who were rash enough to denounce him to the Emperor. Among others, Kokovtsoff, when President of the Council, had vainly endeavoured to open His Majesty's eyes to Rasputin's true character, with the result that he was eventually dismissed; while Prince Orloff, who had for years been at the head of the Emperor's military cabinet, was, for the same reason, summarily relegated to a post on the Grand Duke Nicholas's staff in the Caucasus.

The internal situation, meanwhile, was going from bad to worse, and the general dissatisfaction with the conduct of the war was venting itself in attacks on the Emperor and Empress. The latter was always spoken of as "The German," in spite of the fact that she had, as she told me herself, broken all the ties that connected her with Germany. Rasputin was at the same time accused of being in German pay — a charge that was not, strictly speaking, correct. He was not in immediate communication with Berlin, and he did not receive money directly from the Germans; but he was largely financed by certain Jewish bankers, who were, to all intents and purposes, German agents. As he was in the habit of repeating to these Jewish friends of his all that he heard at Tsarskoe, and as the Empress consulted him on both military and political questions, much useful information reached the Germans through this indirect channel. Without being their regular agent, he was, moreover, rendering them yeoman service by discrediting the Imperial régime and by thus paving the way for the revolution.

The situation was one which the Germans were not slow to exploit. They had already started their peace propaganda among the troops at the front, and had their spies everywhere. Through one of them — Lieut.-Colonel Miassoyeidow, who was afterwards hanged — they had secured such valuable information about the movements of the Russian troops that they had been able on more than one occasion to counter the latter's projected offensive. Petrograd was throughout the war infested with their secret agents and sympathizers. The atmosphere was generally charged with pessimism, and exaggerated reports were constantly circulated respecting the hopelessness of the military outlook. At Moscow it was different. There the national spirit, instead of being cowed by the disheartening news from the front, was stirred to fresh efforts, and the anti-German feeling was so strong that in June all shops bearing German names or that were suspected of having any German connexions were raided.

By its failure to meet the requirements of the army the administration had forfeited the confidence of the nation, and all parties, with the exception of the extreme right, were agreed that recourse must be had to extraordinary measures for the purpose of intensifying production. Thanks to the initiative taken in the matter by President Rodzianko, the Emperor, early in June, appointed a strong committee, composed of representatives of the army, the Duma and industry, with powers to mobilize Russian industries for war purposes. But this was not sufficient in itself, and Rodzianko at the same time urged His Majesty to convoke the Duma and to purge the Ministry of some of its more reactionary and incompetent members.

His Majesty yielded, and, in spite of the opposition of the Empress's camarilla, Maklakoff, the Minister of the Interior, was replaced by Prince Scherbatoff, a broad-minded man of moderate views. As I happened, a few days later, to meet the Emperor at the launching of a battle cruiser, I endeavoured to encourage him to proceed further in this direction by referring to the recent reconstruction of Mr. Asquith's Cabinet. In England, I told him, all party differences had been forgotten, and Mr. Asquith had now formed a coalition of all the best brains in the country as the surest way of securing a successful prosecution of the war. The Emperor admitted that this was the only course to pursue in a great national crisis like the present, and for a time it almost seemed as if he was going to act up to this principle. Sukholimoff (the Minister of War), Schteglovitoff (the Minister of Justice), Sabler (the Procurator of the Holy Synod) were successively dismissed, and replaced in their respective offices by Polivanoff, Khvostoff and Samarin. It was while he was at Headquarters, and no longer under the Empress's immediate influence, that His Majesty made the above appointments.

One of the first acts of Samarin was to tell the Emperor that he could not be responsible for the administration of the affairs of the Orthodox Church if Rasputin was to be allowed to control them from behind the scenes. Rasputin was in consequence given a hint to absent himself for a few weeks. The convocation of the Duma had also been conceded by the Emperor, and when it met, on July 30, deputy after deputy denounced the incompetence of an administration that had brought such untold disasters on the Russian army. By a large majority the chamber invited the Government to try Sukholimoff, while a Liberal deputy (Maklakoff, the brother of the former Minister of the Interior) declared that what the country required was to have "the right men in the right places."

With the departure of the Emperor for Headquarters to take over the supreme command the reactionaries once more gained the ascendant. On September 26 the Duma was prorogued. Two days later the more liberal-minded members of the Government — Sazonoff, Scherbatoff, Samarin, Krivoshein, Bark and Shahovskoi — addressed a collective letter to the Emperor, beseeching him to change the course of his policy and saying that it was impossible for them any longer to serve under Goremykin. They were summoned by the Emperor to the Stavka and told that he could not tolerate such interference by his Ministers in the choice of his President of the Council. Owing to his having addressed the envelope containing that letter to the Emperor, Sazonoff was regarded by the Empress as the ringleader of this cabal. She never forgave him and never rested till she had secured his dismissal.

About the same time the Union of Zemstvos and the Union of Town Councils had held a meeting at Moscow, in which a resolution was passed demanding the immediate convocation of the Duma and the appointment of a Government that possessed the confidence of the nation. Each union had further deputed three of its members to submit the above demands orally to the Emperor. Acting on the advice tendered by Goremykin, His Majesty refused to receive them, while he commanded Prince Scherbatoff to summon the respective presidents of the two unions — Prince Lvoff and the mayor of Moscow, M. Chelnokoff — to Petrograd, and to read to them the following message: "I place a very high value on the noble work which the zemstvos and town councils have done and are doing for the wounded and refugees (from the provinces in German occupation);

but I do not consider that they have any right to interfere in political matters, which are centred in the Government. I, therefore, command you to say what you have to say to the Minister of the Interior, who has orders to report to me." The two delegates replied that they had been charged by their unions to lay Moscow's representations before the Emperor, and that for His Majesty to refuse to receive them would constitute a break between the Sovereign and his people. Prince Scherbatoff was so impressed by what they said that he finally consented to submit the matter for His Majesty's reconsideration. He did so, and was at once dismissed. Chelnokoff, a man of very moderate views, subsequently summed up the situation by saying that it was intolerable that Russia should be governed by a doting reactionary like Goremykin and by a drunken scoundrel like Rasputin.

Samarin, who was one of the most popular and respected members of the Government, shared Scherbatoff 's fate. It will be remembered that Rasputin had succeeded in getting his friend Varnava appointed Bishop of Tobolsk, and the latter's conduct had since caused such a public scandal that Samarin had had to call him to account. His own dismissal was the result.

Shortly afterwards another excellent Minister — Krivoshein, who had as Minister of Agriculture rendered important services in carrying out Stolypin's agrarian reforms — was forced to resign for no other reason than that he had incurred the displeasure of the reactionary party by his outspoken language on the situation. He was a personal friend of mine, and I had frequently urged on him the necessity of keeping the nation united by timely concessions, as well as the crying need of decentralization in such a vast Empire. A strong nationalist, he was nevertheless liberal-minded, and was in favour of reforming the administration, though he doubted whether it was feasible to introduce far-reaching reforms during the war.

In an audience which I had during a flying visit of the Emperor's to Tsarskoe in November, His Majesty made an earnest appeal to His Majesty's Government to supply the Russian army with rifles. If only they would do so he could, he said, place 800,000 men in his field at once, and strike a crushing blow at the Germans while they were still exhausted after their long campaign. Were the present favourable moment to be allowed to pass, the Germans would have time to fortify their lines, as they had in the west, and any offensive which the Russian army might take later would be doomed to failure. The position of that army was, indeed, a pathetic one, but I could hold out no hope of our being able to supply rifles on so large a scale. I regretted this all the more because, as I told the Emperor, there was a growing feeling of disaffection among the Russian troops, who had been left almost defenceless before the enemy.

I also pointed out that, apart from the question of supply, there was also that of delivery, and that if Russia was ever to receive from abroad the war material in which she was so deficient, drastic steps would have to be taken to expedite the construction of the Murman railway, that was to connect her capital with the only ice-free port — Alexandrovsk. The Emperor agreed that the work of construction ought to be placed under the control of some energetic and competent official, but he did not approve of the candidate whom I had ventured to suggest for the post. He did, however, shortly afterwards appoint a new Minister of Ways and Communications — M. Trepoff — who, though belonging to the extreme right, proved an excellent administrator. It was thanks to his untiring efforts that the railway was completed by the end of 1916.

While the Emperor's internal policy, inspired as it was for the most part by the Empress and those in her immediate entourage, cannot be defended, the two following stories, told me by Sazonoff, will show how irreproachable was his attitude towards Germany.

Early in December Count Frederichs, who had for years past been Minister of the Imperial Court, received a letter from his former friend, Count Eulenburg (the Grand Marshal of the Court at Berlin), suggesting that they ought both to direct their efforts to putting an end to the existing deplorable misunderstanding between their Sovereigns, and to bringing about a *rapprochement* that would enable their Governments to negotiate peace on honourable terms. The Emperor, on being told of this letter, commanded Count Frederichs to read it to him, and the latter proceeded to do so in the original German. His Majesty at once stopped him, saying, "Read it in Russian. I do not understand German." When the Count had finished, the Emperor took the letter and, underlining a passage in which Count Eulenburg had spoken of "their old friendship," wrote in the margin, "That friendship is dead and buried." He then sent for Sazonoff, and told him to prepare a draft reply. When, on the following day, Sazonoff brought him a draft, in which Count Eulenburg was told that if the Emperor William wanted peace he must address a similar proposal to all the Allies, His Majesty said that on reflection he had decided that the letter should be left unanswered, as any reply, however repellent, might be taken as evidence of his desire to enter into negotiations.

A few weeks later further overtures were addressed to His Majesty through another channel. A Mlle. Wassiltchikoff, belonging to an old Russian family, had, when war broke out, been living in her villa on the Semmering, where she had remained ever since. She had recently gone to Darmstadt, on the invitation of the Grand Duke of Hesse, and had been sent by him to Petrograd charged with the mission of inducing the Emperor to conclude peace. She was empowered to say that the Emperor William was prepared to grant Russia most advantageous terms; that England had already made overtures to Germany for a separate peace; and that a reconciliation between Russia and Germany was necessary for dynastic reasons. The Grand Duke gave her a written statement in the above sense for her to give Sazonoff, as well as two open letters for the Emperor and Empress. On arrival at Petrograd she at once went to the Ministry and handed the Grand Duke's statement and letters to Sazonoff. The latter told her that she had acted disgracefully in undertaking such a mission, and the Emperor, to whom he made a report on the subject, was so angry that he gave orders to have her interned in a convent.

Before concluding the story of the year 1915 I may mention that at the end of May I had the personal satisfaction of receiving from Sir Edward Grey a letter in which he said:

I have followed with great appreciation the way in which you have conducted your conversations in Petrograd since the outbreak of the war. All your actions seem to me admirable in substance, form and opportuneness.

I have therefore asked the Prime Minister to recommend you for a G.C.B. in the forthcoming list of Birthday Honours.

Meanwhile I wish you to know that all that you have done is really appreciated by His Majesty's Government, as well as by me.

[End of Volume I]

Sir George and Lady Georgina Buchanan

Tsar Nicholas II and his family, 1913

Crowds at the declaration of war outside the Winter Palace, Petrograd, 1914

Barricades at the Liteyny Prospekt, Petrograd, during the revolution, February 1917

CHAPTER 19
1916

The year 1916 witnessed a distinct improvement in the matter of the delivery of war material from abroad as well as of the output of the factories at home, while, thanks to the initiative taken by the zemstvos and town councils, new munition works were being started in different parts of the country. The military outlook on the whole was more promising. In Armenia the army, under the command of the Grand Duke Nicholas, had advanced in mid-winter over a difficult mountainous country, and by the end of February had occupied Erzeroum. On the Bessarabian front the Russians, ever ready to render what assistance they could to their Allies in the west, had taken the offensive with a view to affording some relief to the gallant defenders of Verdun, who were being so hard pressed by the Germans. Though attended with a certain measure of success, this offensive yielded no concrete results owing to its having been launched without sufficient preparation and to a deficiency of aeroplanes and other engines of war. On the other hand, the offensive begun in June by the army under Brussiloff to relieve the Austrian pressure on the Italian front was completely successful. Before the end of the month the Russians were masters of the Bukowine and, after capturing an enormous number of prisoners, were advancing across the Carpathians.

It was the moment, if ever, for Roumania to march. Her long-expectant attitude had caused a French diplomat to remark that she was but waiting to *voler au secours du vainqueur*; yet, now that the Russians were victorious, she still hesitated. General Alexeieff, therefore, let it be known at Bucharest that, if she allowed the present favourable opportunity to pass, her intervention would leave Russia indifferent. He at the same time made the promised despatch of a Russian detachment to the Dobrudja conditional on her at once attacking Bulgaria. This she refused to do, although, in the opinion of the best military authorities, it was, tactically speaking, the right move for her to make.

The Roumanian Minister, with whom I discussed the question, contended that Transylvania was Roumania's natural objective, as she did not covet any Bulgarian territory. He therefore insisted that it was against Austria that all her efforts must be directed; while I endeavoured to persuade him, but in vain, that the surest way for Roumania to win Transylvania was for her to put the Bulgarian army out of action. Eventually Roumania was allowed to have her way, and at the end of August she declared war on Austria. But it was too late. The Russian offensive was nearly spent; the men were tired out; the artillery ammunition was almost exhausted, and supplies were running short owing to the difficulties of transport. The Roumanian advance into Transylvania, which had proceeded satisfactorily for about a fortnight, was suddenly checked by an Austro-German offensive, and the Roumanian army had to retire precipitately all along the line. In the south, too, they suffered a severe defeat at the hands of the Bulgars, on whose neutrality they had at first been foolish enough to count.

Meanwhile the Emperor at the beginning of February had parted with Goremykin and appointed Stürmer President of the Council. Stürmer's grandfather had been Austrian Commissary at St. Helena during Napoleon's residence on that island, and he had himself successively held the posts of Director of the Ceremonies at the Russian Court and of Governor of Jaroslav. With but a second-rate intelligence, without any experience of affairs, a sycophant, bent solely on the advancement of his own interests and extremely ambitious, he owed his new appointment to the fact that he was a friend of Rasputin and that he was backed by the Empress's camarilla. I shall have more to say about him later on, but I may mention, as showing the sort of man that he was, that he chose as his *chef de cabinet* a former agent of the *okhrana* (secret police), Manouiloff by name, who was a few months afterwards arrested and tried for blackmailing a bank.

The Minister of the Interior, Khvostoff, who had, like Stürmer, risen to power through the camarilla's influence, was dismissed at the same time. The reasons for his disgrace were disclosed by a leading Petrograd journal, and though I cannot vouch for their accuracy, they throw such a light on the situation as to merit reproduction. Khvostoff, it would appear, had quarrelled with his former friends, and being ambitious, had conceived the idea of playing the part of a national benefactor by ridding Russia of Rasputin. He accordingly sent a secret agent, named Rjevsky, to Christlania to confer with the ex-monk Iliodore, who had once been Rasputin's friend but who was now one of his bitterest enemies. After discussing the question in all its bearings, Iliodore and Rjevsky arranged to have Rasputin and some of his intimates assassinated. The assassins, it was further agreed, were to receive 60,000 roubles for their services from the Minister of the Interior. The plot was discovered before it could mature, and Rjevsky, who was arrested at the frontier on his return to Russia, was said to have made a full confession. Whether or not the above story is true in all its details, the fact remains that Rasputin and Khvostoff had engaged in a trial of strength, in which both had done their best to discredit the other with the Emperor. Rasputin in the end gained the day, and Khvostoff was dismissed.

Early in February I had an audience, in which I made my first serious attempt to induce the Emperor to steer a more liberal course. After speaking of the growing feeling of discontent that was finding open expression among all classes of the nation, I told him that officers, and even generals, who had returned from the front were declaring that it was time to make a clean sweep of all those who were responsible for the sufferings of the army. The sacrifices which his people had made in the war merited, I said, some return, and I would appeal to His Majesty to concede, as an act of grace for services rendered, what it might be humiliating to grant as a concession to revolutionary threats. Would he not, I asked, avail himself of the present unique opportunity of drawing closer the bonds which the war had forged between Sovereign and people, by taking some step towards meeting the wishes of his people?

After warning me not to attach exaggerated importance to the stories current in Petrograd, the Emperor went on to say that he fully appreciated the sacrifices which his people had made, but that the time for concessions had not yet come. "You will remember," he continued, "how at the very outset I told the nation that it must concentrate all its efforts on the war and that questions of internal reform must wait till after the conclusion of peace." As I was taking my leave I made a further final appeal, saying: "If Your Majesty is unable to make any fundamental concessions at present, will you not at any rate give your people some sign that will encourage them to hope for better things to come in a not distant future?" The Emperor smiled as he gave me his hand, but did not reply to my question.

Though I cannot take the credit of having suggested the form which it took, His Majesty did, a fortnight later, give such a sign by attending the opening sitting of the Duma and by making a speech in which, after saying how happy he was to find himself in the midst of his people, he invoked God's blessings on its labours. It was, as my friend

Sazonoff said to me at the time, "the happiest day in Russia's history"; but the hopes founded on it were not destined to live. There was to be no break in the reactionary policy of the Government, and it was not long before its relations with the Duma again became strained. In March five Socialist deputies, accused of having organized a revolutionary propaganda in the army, were condemned to deportation for life to Siberia, though, according to Kerensky, who defended them, their action had been confined to trying to counter a movement in favour of an understanding between Russian and German reactionaries. In the following month Polivanoff, the popular War Minister, who had proved himself an honest and capable administrator, was dismissed and replaced by Schouvaleff, a complete nullity. Polivanoff had never been a *persona grata* with the Emperor, and his disgrace was attributed to the fact that he was on intimate terms with the Octobrist leader Guchkoff, who had incurred the Empress's undying hatred for having made a scathing attack on Rasputin in the Duma.

Early in April I went with my wife and daughter to the Crimea for a much-needed holiday, and I never enjoyed anything so much as the fortnight which we spent there. After the ice and snow of Petrograd it was too delightful to see the sunny side of Russia, to revel in the marvellous blue of what is so inaptly termed the Black Sea and in the romantic scenery of its coast. After spending a couple of days at Sebastopol we went to Yalta, and as the Government had kindly placed at our disposal a most comfortable saloon carriage with sleeping compartments for the whole of our trip, as well as motors whenever we wanted them, we were able to make excursions to all the places of interest in the neighbourhood. The only drawback was that the authorities insisted on giving an official character to my visit. Wherever we went we were presented with bread and salt and with addresses of welcome to which I had to reply. At the Yacht Club at Yalta I was received by a guard of honour composed of students of the gymnasium who were training for military service. and by a band playing "God save the King." At Livadia, where we went to assist at the inauguration of a hospital for the wounded, founded by the Empress, the names of the King and Queen were included in the prayers of the Orthodox service that preceded the ceremony, while Their Majesties' healths were enthusiastically drunk at the repast which followed. At one of the many beautiful villas which we visited we were not only presented with bread and salt on a silver platter, but found in our motor, on leaving, a case with a dozen bottles of old Burgundy, whose praises I had sung while drinking it at luncheon.

It is terribly sad to look back on those happy bygone days, and to think of all the misery and misfortunes which have befallen those who showed us such kindness and hospitality.

On our way home we crossed the Aie Petri to Kokos, a Tartar village, where we lunched with Prince Yusupoff in his beautiful villa, built in the Tartar style. On our arrival we were met by the Tartar villagers, who presented us with bread and salt, while the headman made a long speech, which the Prince translated for us, expressing admiration for England and invoking blessings on the King. Then, continuing our journey, we arrived in the evening at Bahtchi Sarai — the former residence of the Khans of the Crimea — close to which there is a ruined town, which was deserted a century ago by its inhabitants, the Karaites, an old Jewish sect whose position is far superior to that of the ordinary Jews in Russia. In 1916 their descendants were still holding their services in the synagogue, the only building left intact, and a special service was held there in our honour in which prayers were said for the King and Queen. After the service we were entertained at a wonderful tea, at which the chief delicacies were roseleaf jam, hot honey-cakes and a kind of Devonshire cream. Then we were given a dinner at the old palace of Bahtchi Sarai — for which we had but little appetite — and after dinner we were taken to a mosque to witness a weird performance by a sect of dancing dervishes. We then drove to the station, where we found our saloon carriage awaiting us, and returned to Petrograd, spending twelve hours at Kieff on our way.

A few days later, on May 5, I had a long audience with the Emperor, in which His Majesty touched on every variety of subject. He began by questioning me about my visit to the Crimea and about the walks which I had taken in the hills, for the Emperor was passionately fond of walking and invariably tired out all who accompanied him. He next spoke of the military situation and of the offensive Brussiloff was about to take. I subsequently started the subject of the railway administration, calling his attention to the congestion existing on the Siberian railway and to the necessity of completing the Murman railway with the least possible delay. His Majesty replied that he fully recognized the importance of relieving the congestion on the former line and that, as regarded the latter, he had told the Minister of Ways and Communications that, if it was not completed by the end of the year, he should entrust the control of its construction to other hands. The Emperor afterwards expressed his admiration of the splendid assistance rendered by our dominions and colonies, and proceeded to question me as to the further steps which we were likely to take in the direction of Imperial Federation. Finally he spoke of the close economic understanding which he hoped to see established between Russia and Great Britain after the war. On my remarking that such an understanding would depend on whether the Russian industrials were prepared to renounce their idea of prohibitive duties on all foreign goods, the Emperor said that, as Russia could not be self-supporting for years to come, she ought to try to develop her industries with the help of British capital and British expert advice.

A few weeks later I again left Petrograd to fulfil a long-standing engagement to dine with the British colony at Moscow, to meet the mayor and the chief civil and military authorities of the town. It was at the close of this dinner that I was informed by M. Chelnokoff of the intention of the municipal Duma to elect me an honorary citizen of Moscow, an honour that had only been conferred on eight Russians and one foreigner before me.

On the following evening I was invited, together with my wife and secretary, "Benjy" Bruce, to attend an extraordinary sitting of the Duma. The council chamber into which we were ushered was a long room with tiers of raised benches at either end, filled on the one side by the deputies and on the other by the invited guests. The mayor and town councillors occupied seats at a table in the centre of the hall, facing the deputies, while we took our places with other notables on specially reserved chairs opposite the mayor. The proceedings opened with a discussion of certain municipal matters, and when these were disposed of I was invited to come and sit next to the mayor. M. Chelnokoff then delivered a speech in Russian, in which he submitted my name for election "as a token of our sympathy for the great and valiant British nation and of the warmth of our feelings of friendship, as well as of our profound respect, for Moscow's honoured guest." The motion was voted by acclamation, and M. Chelnokoff, turning to me, inquired whether I accepted. I thereupon signified my acceptance in the prescribed formula in Russian. After shaking me warmly by the hand M. Chelnokoff presented me with a beautiful fifteenth-century icon of St. George and the Dragon as a gift from the town of Moscow. He concluded his speech by saying that a special chair, with my name inscribed on it, would always be reserved for me in the municipal council chamber as a lasting testimonial of my services and of the good understanding existing between our countries.

I then rose and replied as follows, in French:

C'est du fond du coeur que j'adresse à vous, Monsieur le Maire, et à vous, Messieurs les Conseillers Municipaux, mes plus chaleureux remerciements pour l'honneur insigne que la ville de Moscou vient de m'octroyer. C'est un honneur si inattendu, dont je me sens si peu digne, que je cherche en vain des paroles convenables pour exprimer les sentiments de profonde reconnaissance dont mon âme est remplie. Chaque fois que je m'approche de votre ancienne Capitale, couronnée comme elle l'est de I'auréole d'un si glorieux passé, j'y entre en pélérin se rendant à un lieu saint. Mais aujourd'hui vous me recevez non seulement comme le Représentant de mon Auguste Souverain, l'Ami et l'Allié du Votre, mais en concitoyen. Vous me prenez dans votre sein en inscrivant mon nom au régistre de votre ville, qui compte tant de noms illustres. Et puis vous me comblez en m'offrant cette belle et ancienne Ikône, qui a pour moi un prix tout exceptionnel et personnel. St. Georges, ce Grand Saint, dont je suis fier de porter le nom, est à la fois Patron de Moscou et de I'Angleterre. Je vois dans ce fait un symbole de I'union étroite entre mon pays et Moscou — coeur la Russie.

Quels souvenirs Moscou évoque du premier contacte établi entre la Russie et I'Angleterre! Ce fut vers le milieu du 16me siècle que Richard Chancellor y est venu faire sa cour à votre grand mais terrible Tsar, Jean IV, et c'est de I'audience que Sa Majesté lui a accordée que date le commencement des relations d'amitié et de commerce entre nos deux pays. Moscou a été, pour ainsi dire, le berceau de l'Entente Anglo-Russe. Puis, lorsque deux siècles et demi plus tard la Russie et la Grande Bretagne se trouvaient alliées contre le grand génie, qui a voulu subjuguer le monde, quel sacrifice sublime Moscou a fait pour le vaincre! Ce fut Moscou qui alors lui a crié "Halte!" et qui lui a porté le premier des coups qui ont amené sa chute. Et maintenant que la Grande Bretagne et la Russie sont de nouveau alliées et qu'elles se battent, côte à côte avec la vaillante France, contre un ennemi redoutable, qui n'a rien de commun avec Napoléon sauf une ambition effrénée, Moscou fait preuve du meme esprit de patriotisme que par le passé et ne recule devant aucun sacrifice pour abattre l'Allemagne.

C'est dans un pareil moment que Moscou me donne le droit de cité! Je m'incline, tout confus de l'honneur qu'elle me fait, en réitérant mes remerciements les plus sincères. Je garderai, Messieurs, un souvenir inoubliable de la journée d'aujourd'hui. Je tâcherai de me rendre digne du droit que j'ai de m'appeler citoyen de votre belle et glorieuse ville. C'est un nouveau lien qui m'attache à la Russie et c'est un nouveau et précieux témoignage des sentiments d'amitie et de sympathie envers mon pays, dont Moscou a donné a maintes reprises de si généreuses preuves.

My speech, which was translated into Russian by M. Chelnokoff, was received with loud cheers, and, after being presented to all the members of the Duma, I was conducted to an adjoining room where tea was served at round tables. There another surprise awaited me.

On taking my place at one of them I found a massive Russian drinking bowl, shaped like a helmet, confronting me, and on my admiring it I was told by my neighbour that the members of the Duma hoped that I would accept it as a personal gift from themselves, after they had had their names engraved on it. It was hardly to be wondered at that, after all these manifestations of friendship and sympathy for our country, I should have felt, as I told Chelnokoff when I took leave of him at the station, that my life's work had been crowned and that Anglo-Russian friendship was secured for all time.

This impression was confirmed by the many congratulatory telegrams which I received after my return to Petrograd. The Emperor, in a telegram addressed to Chelnokoff, ratified my election in the following words: "Moscow, always correctly interpreting the feelings of the Russian people, has rightly appraised the services of Sir George Buchanan in promoting a *rapprochement* between the British and Russian peoples, a *rapprochement* which to-day has been completed by a brotherhood of arms on the field of battle. I welcome the resolution of the Moscow municipal Duma electing the British Ambassador, Sir George Buchanan, a citizen of the city of Moscow."

The rector of the university telegraphed expressing his pleasure at my election, and saying that it formed a new link in the chain of friendship forged between Great Britain and Russia on the battlefield. He further announced my election as an honorary member of the University of Moscow.

Among others, Count Serge Cheremeteff telegraphed as follows:

Maladie m'ayant empêché d'acclamer Votre Excellence à Moscou vous prie, comme Moscovite d'ancienne rôche, d'accepter l'expression de vive joie et de vraie satisfaction à tout Russe de pouvoir saluer en vous le citoyen honoraire de notre antique capitale.

The above telegrams will, I think, furnish a conclusive reply to those kind friends who, on my return to England in 1918, circulated a report to the effect that the Freedom of Moscow was the price paid me for the part which I had played in starting the Russian Revolution.

On November 25 a delegation from Moscow brought to the Embassy my charter of citizenship — a beautifully illuminated scroll recording the Duma's resolution, as well as the Emperor's telegram confirming my election — together with the silver goblet on which the names of the donors had been inscribed. In presenting them to me, M. Chelnokoff said:

Moscow has authorized me, dear Sir George, to convey to you her greetings and to say that her feelings of sympathy, respect and friendship for you have only grown and strengthened since our last sitting in the hall of the municipal Duma.

The political situation, unfortunately, had undergone such a change for the worse during the intervening months that I could no longer look forward to the future with the same confidence as at the time of my election.

CHAPTER 20
1916

Almost immediately after the opening of hostilities in August, 1914, the Emperor had recognized the expediency of considering the question of the reconstitution of Poland and of taking steps to secure the loyal co-operation of its inhabitants in the war, of which their country was about to become the theatre. With this object in view the Grand Duke Nicholas had, by His Majesty's orders, issued a manifesto to the Poles, foreshadowing the grant of a large measure of autonomy. This manifesto made an excellent impression, and the Russian troops, on first entering Galicia, met with a friendly reception on the part of the population. Unfortunately, the conciliatory policy thus initiated by the Emperor was not put into practice by those who were entrusted with the provincial administration of Galicia, and the sympathies of the Poles were alienated by their attempts to Russify everything Polish, as well as by the persistent efforts of Orthodox bishops to proselytize the population.

Sazonoff, who had from the first championed their cause, realized that it was to Russia's interest to satisfy their aspirations by proclaiming at once an autonomous constitution for a reconstructed Poland. In July, 1916, he succeeded, in spite of the opposition of his reactionary colleagues, headed by Stürmer, in obtaining the Emperor's support for such a policy. According to the scheme submitted by Sazonoff, the future Polish Government was to consist of a viceroy, a council of Ministers and two chambers, with full administrative powers in all matters save the army, diplomacy, customs, strategic railways and common finance, which were to remain under the control of the Imperial Government. Stürmer, who was at Headquarters, fearing that he would be outvoted in the Council of Ministers summoned by the Emperor to examine the question, absented himself on the ground that he had to return to Petrograd. On July 13, as Paleologue and I were in conference with Neratoff, the Assistant Minister for Foreign Affairs, Sazonoff suddenly appeared, having just returned from Headquarters. He was triumphant: he had carried the day, and been charged by the Emperor with the task of drafting a manifesto proclaiming Polish autonomy. He was, he told us, leaving at once for Finland on a short holiday. Stürmer, however, had but *reculé pour mieux sauter*. He knew that he had a better chance of talking over the Emperor when he was alone with him than in the Council of Ministers, and he had returned to the Stavka for this purpose. He had also, in the meanwhile, secured the support of the Empress, who had never forgiven Sazonoff for having tried to prevent the Emperor assuming the supreme command, for having written the letter asking His Majesty to dismiss Goremykin, and for his well-known dislike of Rasputin.

On returning from a drive on the islands about ten o'clock on the evening of July 19, I found the Assistant Foreign Minister waiting to see me at the Embassy. He had, he said, come to tell me that an Imperial ukase announcing Sazonoff 's resignation was to be sent to the Stavka on the following day for the Emperor's signature, and that unless someone intervened the consequences might be very serious for the Allies, as Stürmer was certain to take his place. I asked Neratoff whether the object of his visit was to get me to intervene, adding that as it was too late to ask for an audience I did not quite see what I could do. Neratoff replied that my intervention in such a question as that of the Emperor's choice of his Foreign Minister might no doubt compromise my position, but that, if nothing was done, Stürmer's appointment would be an accomplished fact within twenty-four hours. He then left me.

After thinking the matter over I telephoned for my secretaries and addressed the following telegram to the Emperor, which I sent in cipher through General Hanbury Williams, our military representative at Headquarters:

Your Majesty has always allowed me to speak so frankly on all questions that either directly or indirectly affect the successful issue of the war and the conclusion of a treaty of peace that will guarantee the world against its renewal for years to come, that I venture humbly to approach Your Majesty on a matter which may, I fear, at a moment like the present, seriously increase the difficulties of the Allied Governments. In so doing I am acting entirely on my own initiative and responsibility, and I must crave Your Majesty's forgiveness for taking a step which is, I know, contrary to all diplomatic etiquette.

Persistent rumours have reached me that it is Your Majesty's intention to relieve M. Sazonoff of his duties as Your Majesty's Minister for Foreign Affairs, and, as it is impossible for me to ask for an audience, I venture to appeal to Your Majesty to consider, before taking your final decision, the serious consequences which M. Sazonoff's retirement may have on the important negotiations at present proceeding with Roumania and on the still more urgent ones that are bound to arise as the war progresses.

M. Sazonoff and I have worked together for nearly six years to bring our two countries into closer contact, and I had always counted on his support to convert the alliance which had been cemented by this war into a lasting one. I cannot exaggerate the services which he has rendered the cause of the Allied Government by the tact and ability that he has shown in the very difficult negotiations which we have conducted since the war began. Nor can I conceal from Your Majesty the apprehensions which I feel at losing him as a collaborator in the work that still lies before us. Of course, I may be altogether mistaken, and it may be on account of ill-health that M. Sazonoff is about to retire, in which case I shall regret the cause of his departure all the more.

I would once again pray Your Majesty to forgive me for sending this personal message.

On the following day Hanbury Williams, who had often on previous occasions rendered me valuable assistance by his tactful treatment of the many delicate questions which he had to discuss at Headquarters, telegraphed to say that my message had been delivered to the Emperor and that he was hopeful of the results. Unfortunately the Empress had in the meanwhile arrived at the Stavka, and Sazonoff's fate was sealed. He was still in Finland when he received an autograph letter from the Emperor thanking him for his services and saying that, as their respective views differed on so many questions, it was better that they should part.

On the 22nd Sir E. Grey telegraphed to me as follows: "Your action entirely approved. I am grateful to Your Excellency for having so promptly undertaken this responsibility." Two days later, in reply to a telegram which I had sent requesting permission to go to Finland for a few days' rest, and suggesting that I might at the same time inform Sazonoff that the King had been pleased to confer on him the G.C.B. in recognition of his services to the allied cause, he again telegraphed: "I entirely approve and trust you will take sufficient rest to re-establish your health completely, as your services are invaluable. I much appreciate the work you have done and are doing."

I had been careful to keep the fact of my having telegraphed to the Emperor a profound secret; but one of our postal bags, containing a private letter from Lord Hardinge, in which reference was made to this telegram, was subsequently seized by the Germans. I do not know whether it was in consequence of this discovery, or of my having been granted the Freedom of Moscow, but it was about this time that the

Germans paid me the compliment of dubbing me "the uncrowned king of Russia."

It was Stürmer's appointment that first caused me to take a really serious view of the internal situation. Writing to the Foreign Office on August 18 I said:

I can never hope to have confidential relations with a man on whose word no reliance can be placed, and whose only idea is to further his own ambitious ends. Though self-interest compels him to continue the foreign policy of his predecessor, he is, according to all accounts, a Germanophil at heart. As a pronounced reactionary, he is, moreover, at one with the Empress in wishing to maintain the autocracy intact. . . .

... If the Emperor continues to uphold his present reactionary advisers a revolution is, I fear, inevitable. The civil population has had enough of an administrative system which, in a country so rich as Russia is in natural resources, has, thanks to incompetence and bad organization, rendered it difficult for them to procure many of the first necessaries of life even at famine prices. The army, on the other hand, is not likely to forget or to forgive all it has suffered at the hands of the existing administration. Sazonoff's dismissal and Stürmer's appointment have made an immense impression on the country and on the army.

As a reactionary with pro-German sympathies, Stürmer had never viewed with favour the idea of an alliance with the democratic Governments of the West, for fear that it might serve as a channel through which liberal ideas might penetrate into Russia. He was, however, far too astute to advocate a separate peace with Germany. Such a suggestion would, he knew, never have been tolerated by either the Emperor or Empress, and would almost certainly have cost him his place. The same may be said of General Woyeikoff, the Prefect of the Imperial Palaces, whose special duty it was to see that the necessary measures were taken for the Emperor's protection. As he was in constant touch with His Majesty, he was used by the Empress as her mouthpiece, and in his conversations with the Emperor he always expressed her views with regard to Ministerial appointments and other questions of internal policy. But neither he nor any of the German clique at Court ever risked saying anything that was likely to be resented by Their Majesties. What they would have done, had they had the opportunity, was to work for a peace as favourable as possible to Germany, with a view to re-establishing the closest possible understanding with that country. There were others who, like Woyeikoff's father-in-law, Count Frederichs, the Minister of the

Court, and Count Benckendorff, the Grand Chamberlain, whose brother was so long Ambassador in London, were not pro-German.

In spite of his intimate relations with the German Court before the war. Count Frederichs, like Count Benckendorff, was a strong pro-Ally. A typical Russian grand seigneur of the old school, devoted to his Sovereign and having the good of his country at heart, he realized the danger of the course which the Emperor was steering and more than once tendered moderating counsels. Stürmer, on the other hand, in his frequent audiences with the Empress, knew that he was on safe ground when he opposed all concessions; but he was, at the same time, careful to veil his pro-German sympathies. Inordinately ambitious, his one idea was to retain office. He even seems to have hoped to play the role of a Nesselrode or a Gortchakoff, as, in one of our conversations, he suggested quite seriously that the future peace conference should be held at Moscow so that he might be called on to preside over its deliberations.

In his dealings with me Stürmer was always courteous and correct; but the fact that we both mistrusted each other made our relations somewhat strained. Some three weeks after he assumed charge of the Foreign Office I had a serious passage of arms with him. A reactionary journal, which I had reason to believe was inspired by those in his *entourage*, had published an outrageous attack on the British army, declaring, among other things, that it had only advanced two hundred yards in the course of two years. I protested to Stürmer that it was monstrous that such an article should have been passed by the censor, and demanded a public retraction and apology on the part of the writer — a certain Boulatzel. Stürmer demurred, saying that he was powerless in the matter. I insisted, and he eventually said that he would send Boulatzel to see me. I told the latter, when he called, what I thought of him and his paper; but it took me over an hour to force him to publish a refutation which I had prepared for communication to the Press. Later in the day Stürmer telephoned asking me to tone down this statement, but I only consented to omit one phrase which might, I feared, have wounded the feelings of our friends in the Russian army.

In October I paid my one and only visit to the Emperor's Headquarters at Mohileff. I had a few weeks previously been instructed to inform the Minister of Marine that the King desired to confer the G.C.B. on the admiral in command of the Baltic fleet as a compliment to the Russian navy. Admiral Grigorowitch had objected that the commander-in-chief of the Baltic fleet was on a par with the commander-in-chief of the Black Sea fleet, and that to confer a decoration on the one without conferring it on the other would create an invidious distinction. I had therefore suggested that the Emperor, as commander-in-chief of all Russia's land and sea forces, should be asked to accept the G.C.B. as a mark of the King's appreciation of the services rendered by his navy. This suggestion was adopted, and the Emperor, on being sounded, sent me a warm message of acceptance inviting me to come to the Stavka with as many of my staff as I liked to bring as soon as I received the insignia. A second and still more pressing message reached me a few days later. As soon, therefore, as the insignia arrived, I requested Stürmer to ascertain which day it would suit His Majesty to receive me. Stürmer, who did not relish the idea of my seeing the Emperor alone, at once said that, as he was himself going to the Stavka in a few days' time, he would arrange that we should go there together. I replied that I should have liked nothing better, but that, as the Emperor had given me to understand that I was to come at once, I must ask him to take His Majesty's orders without further delay. The reply was as I had forecasted, and as he could not himself be present at my audience, Stürmer took other steps to put spokes in my wheel.

I went to Mohileff on October 18, accompanied by General Knox and Captain Grenfell, our military and naval attaches, and by Bruce, the head of the chancellery. The Emperor received us at once in a short private audience, and after I had in an appropriate speech presented him with the insignia of a Knight Grand Cross of the Military Division of the Bath, His Majesty kept us talking for about ten minutes. The Empress, who had arrived with her daughters a few days previously, did not attend the luncheon that followed our audience. Instead of sitting next the Emperor, as was usual on such an official occasion, I was placed between the Grand Duchess Olga and one of her sisters, so that I could not possibly talk to His Majesty. After luncheon an informal circle was held, but as General Hanbury Williams had told me that the Emperor would be sure to ask me to come and talk to him in his study, I did not try to approach him. After conversing with several of his other guests, His Majesty came up to me and thanked me warmly for having come.

When he was on the point of bidding me good-bye I ventured to interrupt him by saying that there were one or two things about which I wished to speak to him. On receiving permission to do so, I said that His Majesty would shortly be receiving the Japanese Ambassador in farewell audience on his appointment as Minister for Foreign Affairs at Tokio. Viscount Motono was very well disposed towards Russia, and His Majesty might with advantage try to enlist his powerful influence on Russia's behalf. Japan had already furnished the Russian army with guns and munitions, and it was just possible that she might be induced to send a contingent of troops to the Russian front were she to be offered some substantial compensation. While approving this idea in principle, the Emperor asked whether I had any suggestion to make with regard to the nature of the compensation. I replied that I had no definite proposal to make, but that I rather gathered from a remark which Viscount Motono had made in one of our recent conversations that the cession of the Russian or northern half of Saghalien would be very acceptable to his Government. The Emperor at once said that this was quite out of the question, as he could not cede a foot of Russian territory. I ventured to remind His 'Majesty of Henri IV's famous saying — "*Paris vaut bien une messe*" — but without success. As I saw that the Emperor was not quite at his ease, I did not try to prolong the conversation, and concluded by inquiring whether His Majesty proposed returning shortly to Tsarskoe. "Yes," replied the Emperor. "I hope to be there in a few weeks' time, and I shall be very glad to see you. We can then have a long talk."

Stürmer and his powerful friends at Court, who suspected me of working against them, had been careful to arrange matters so that I should have no private conversation with the Emperor. But what surprised me most, after His Majesty's warm messages of appreciation of the compliment paid his navy, was the fact that he did not, as was customary, either propose the King's health or wear the Star of the Bath at luncheon.

That Stürmer was afraid of my using such influence as I possessed with the Emperor in a sense hostile to himself was evidenced by his change of tactics when I applied a few weeks later for my promised audience. I happened to be dining with him to meet Viscount Motono, the retiring Japanese Ambassador, on the evening of the day on which I had written to tell him that the Emperor had expressed a wish to see me on his return to Tsarskoe. Much to my surprise, I was on this occasion accorded, for the first time, a most flattering reception both by my host and hostess. On my admiring the flowers on the dinner table the Empress asked me which of them I liked best, and the two plants which I had innocently selected were sent the next morning to the Embassy. After dinner Stürmer came up to me and said: "*Vous voyez, Monsieur l'Ambassadeur, que vos appréhensions au sujet de la nomination de Monsieur B.*" — a pronounced Germanophil against whose appointment to a high post in the Foreign Office I had recently protested — "*n'étaient pas fondeées.*" "I should," he proceeded to say, "deeply regret were anything that I did not to meet with your approval. My one great wish is that we should always work together on the most intimate and confidential terms, and that you should for many years to come continue to represent your Sovereign at Petrograd."

I had, as a matter of fact, been asked by two members of the Imperial family to try to induce the Emperor to part with Stürmer on the ground that he did not command the confidence of the Allied Governments and to sound His Majesty as to the possibility of Sazonoff's return. It had been my intention to do this; but I had been warned by Neratoff, the Assistant Foreign Minister, that it would be premature to raise the question. I confined myself, therefore, in my audience to dwelling on the increase of German influence, on the anti-British campaign, and on the gravity of the internal situation. If, I told the Emperor, I had taken such strong action with regard to Boulatzel's attack on the British army, it was because I knew that his paper was subsidized by a powerful anti-British clique. It was not only in Petrograd, but in Moscow and in other towns, that this campaign was being carried on, and I had reason to believe that German sympathizers in Russia were working for a peace that would be favourable to Germany, and trying to persuade the public that Russia had nothing to gain by continuing the war. The Emperor replied that people who held such language when several Russian provinces were still in enemy occupation were traitors. After reminding me that he had at the beginning of the war declared that he would never make peace so long as there was a single enemy soldier on Russian soil, he said that nothing would make him spare Germany when the time for peace negotiations came. Moscow, he added, had given a signal proof of Russia's feelings for Great Britain by electing me an honorary citizen, and I need not be anxious.

On my asking whether he had ever considered the question of the rectification of Russia's frontiers on the side of Germany, His Majesty replied that he was afraid that he would have to be content with his present frontier, bad as it was. The Germans would have to be driven out of Poland, but a Russian advance into Germany would entail too heavy sacrifices. His idea had always been to create a united Poland, under Russia's protection, as a buffer state between Germany and Russia ; but he saw no prospect at present of including Posen in it. I next ventured to ask whether it was true that, in the interview which Protopopoff had had with a German agent at Stockholm, the latter had stated that, if Russia would make peace, Germany would evacuate Poland and raise no objection to Russia's acquisition of Constantinople. The Emperor replied that he could not quite remember whether the above statement had been made to Protopopoff or not, but that he had certainly read it in a report from one of his agents. I might, he added, rest assured that such an offer would carry no weight with him.

I then proceeded to speak of the profound discontent prevailing all over the country owing to the shortage of food supplies, and of the disturbances that had already taken place in Petrograd. The Minister of Ways and Communications had, I said, recently told me that the parties of the Left were trying to exploit the situation in order to squeeze political concessions out of the Government; but much as I liked and respected M. Trepoff, I could not agree with the view which he took of this question. It was not a political one in the strict sense of that word, nor was it a movement in favour of constitutional reform. I trusted that the authorities would not have recourse to repressive measures, as the discontent was caused by the knowledge that, in a country so rich as Russia, the working classes could not obtain the first necessaries of life in consequence of the incompetence of the administration. I could not, either, conceal from His Majesty the fact that, according to reports which I had received from our consuls, the peasantry, who had always regarded their Emperor as infallible, were beginning to lose faith in him and that the autocracy was losing ground, thanks to his Ministers' shortcomings.

The Emperor, who looked somewhat embarrassed while I was speaking, questioned me about the Petrograd strikes; but I was not in a position to give him any precise data as to what had actually happened when the troops had been called out. The food question, he admitted, was becoming very serious, but the Ministers of the Interior, of Agriculture, and of Ways and Communications, who were taking the matter in hand, would, he believed, be able to cope with it. He passed over in silence my allusions to the incompetence of the administration and, after keeping me for an hour and a half, bade me good-bye in his usual friendly manner.

CHAPTER 21
1916

The following extract from a letter which I wrote to the Foreign Office on October 18 will show how German influence was spreading:

I do not wish to be ultra-pessimistic, but never since the war began have I felt so depressed about the situation here, more especially with regard to the future of Anglo-Russian relations. German influence has been making headway ever since Sazonoff left the Foreign Office. The Germans, who during the early stages of the war, and even up to a quite recent date, were proclaiming through their agents that we were making Russia bear all the brunt of the fighting, have changed their tactics. They are now representing Great Britain, with her navy and her new armies, as the future world power, bent on prolonging the war for her own inordinate ambitions.

"It is Great Britain," they keep on repeating, "that is forcing Russia to continue the war and forbidding her to accept the favourable peace terms which Germany is ready to offer, and it is Great Britain, therefore, that is responsible for the privations and sufferings of her people." . . .

The losses which Russia has suffered are so colossal that the whole country is in mourning. So many lives have been uselessly sacrificed in the recent unsuccessful attacks against Kovel and other places, that the impression is gaining ground that it is useless continuing the struggle, and that Russia, unlike Great Britain, has nothing to gain by prolonging the war. This insidious campaign is much more difficult to meet than the old lies about our former inaction.

Hugh Walpole, who is, as you know, doing such excellent work at our information bureau, is greatly preoccupied by all that he hears, and has asked me to publish some statement to counteract the effect of this German propaganda.

Early in November the Anglo-Russian Society, which had just been reconstituted, held its inaugural meeting under the presidency of M. Rodzianko at the municipal Duma. As I had to speak I took the opportunity of showing how the German party in Russia was endeavouring to poison the mind of the public against Great Britain; how they were representing us as having dragged Russia into the war; how they were accusing us of prolonging it in order that we might dominate the world and exploit Russia; and, after pointing out that all these lies were being circulated for the purpose of undermining our alliance and of paving the way for a premature peace, I concluded by saying: "It is not only on the battlefields of Europe that the war must be fought out to a victorious end. The final victory must also be won over the more insidious enemy within our gates."

The Duma met a few days later and Miliukoff, in an historic speech, denounced Stürmer as a traitor, while Puriskevitch, who but two years before had been an ultra-reactionary, called on Ministers in impassioned language to throw themselves on their knees before the Emperor, to tell him that things could not go on as they were, and to beseech him to liberate Russia from Rasputin and from all the occult influences which were governing and betraying her. In a letter which I wrote to the Foreign Office on November 16 I said:

The inaugural meeting of our new Anglo-Russian Society last week was a great success, and my speech has had a very good Press both here and at Moscow. At the Duma yesterday Great Britain was specially signalled out for applause, and, as someone remarked, it was "an English day." This morning, when we were discussing the question of the publication of our Constantinople agreement, Stürmer said to Paleologue, who had received no instructions on the subject: "You saw what a *chaleureuse ovation* your British colleague had in the Duma yesterday! It was probably owing to their having heard that His Majesty's Government have agreed to Russia having Constantinople." I cannot imagine why he said this, as he knows quite well that the reason of the demonstration in our favour was the fact that we have been made the subject of attack by the pro-German party in this country.

When Paléologue and I got up to go, Stürmer asked me to remain. After telling me that he proposed taking legal proceedings against Miliukoff for the speech in which the latter had accused him of treason, he called my attention to the two following passages in that speech:

"In order to disclose all the ways and means of the German propaganda, about which we were recently told in such outspoken language by Sir G. Buchanan, we should have to have a legal investigation. . . .

... "That is why I was not surprised to hear from the lips of the British Ambassador a weighty accusation against that coterie of persons of wishing to prepare the way for a separate peace."

He then inquired whether Miliukoff had said this with my permission, as otherwise he had had no business to name me. I replied that I had not spoken to Miliukoff since I made my speech, but that I could not take exception to his referring to what I had said at a meeting at which he had been present. I had been obliged to reply in that speech to attacks made on my country, and I had but repeated textually what was being said about Great Britain both in Petrograd and Moscow. Stürmer pretended that he had not seen my speech, and asked who were the leaders of the anti-British campaign. On my saying that this was exactly what I was trying to ascertain, he begged me to let him know if I discovered anything about them. . . .

If there is trouble, the troops, I am told, will refuse to fire. The trouble, if it comes, will be due to economic rather than to political causes, and it will begin, not with the workmen in the factories, but with the crowds waiting in the cold and snow outside the provision shops.

Stürmer fell before the storm — which he had raised — broke. During a short visit which the Emperor had paid her at Kieff, the Empress Marie had spoken to him so seriously about the political outlook that, on returning to the Stavka at the end of November, His Majesty decided to part with him. The Empress Alexandra, whose intervention Stürmer had invoked, tried but failed to save him. She succeeded, nevertheless, in stopping any radical change of policy. Her Majesty, unfortunately, was under the impression that it was her mission to save Russia. She believed — and, in principle, as subsequent events have shown, she was not altogether wrong — that the autocracy was the only regime that could hold the Empire together. The Emperor, she knew, was weak, and she therefore preached firmness. He must, she repeatedly told him, be an autocrat in deed as well as in name. In her desire to help him and to relieve him of some of the burden of his double role of autocrat and commander-in-chief, she assumed an active part in the government of the country, and in advocating, as she did, a policy of "Thorough," she was honestly convinced that she was acting in Russia's interests. She was so obsessed with the idea that there must be no weakening of the autocracy that she was opposed to all concessions, while she encouraged the Emperor to choose his Ministers more out of regard for their political opinions than for their qualifications for office.

The weaker will yielded to the stronger, and the Emperor was entirely under her influence. But woefully mistaken as she was, the Empress was throughout inspired by the best of motives — love of her husband and love of her adopted country. The same cannot, however, be said of the little band of unscrupulous and self-seeking adventurers who, in their turn, influenced Her Majesty, using her as their unconscious agent to further their own political ends and ambitions. It was to Rasputin more especially that she looked for guidance before tending advice to the Emperor; and as her health failed her — for, what with the strain of the war, anxiety about her son, and the overtaxing of her strength in hospital work, she had fallen into a nervous neurotic state — she came more and more under his baneful influence.

Stürmer was succeeded as President of the Council by Trepoff, the Minister of Ways and Communications, who, though a reactionary, was in favour of reasonable reforms, while Pokrowski was appointed Minister for Foreign Affairs. The latter, a broadminded, honourable, intelligent man of moderate views and a recognized authority on financial and economic questions, proved himself an excellent Minister. But, satisfactory as were these and one or two other minor appointments, no Government of which Protopopoff was a member could hope to work in harmony with the Duma. Belonging to the Octobrist, or moderate Liberal party, Protopopoff had been Vice-President of the Duma and had headed the delegation from that chamber and the Council of Empire which had visited France and England earlier in the year. On his return journey he had had an interview with a German financier named Warburg, at Stockholm, that had seriously compromised him. His explanations failed to satisfy the Duma, and finding that he had lost all hold on that chamber, he determined to throw in his lot with the Court party. He made friends with Rasputin and Pitirim, and as in an audience, which he had had to report on the delegation's visit to London and Paris, his ingratiating manners had made a favourable impression on the Emperor and Empress, he was through their influence appointed Minister of the Interior. Never altogether normal, his unbalanced mind had been turned by his sudden rise to power, and he embarked on an ultra-reactionary policy which, coupled with the fact of his being a political renegade, made him the bête noire of the Duma. Trepoff, who was aware of this, had, on his appointment to the Presidency of the Council, tried to persuade the Emperor to dismiss Protopopoff, and would have succeeded had not the Empress intervened. He then tendered his resignation, but His Majesty declined to accept it.

On December 2 — the eve of the sitting of the Duma at which Trepoff was to make his declaration of policy —Protopopoff came to see me. He began by complaining of the way in which his former friends, and more especially Rodzianko, were giving him the cold shoulder without, however, ever telling him what he had done to merit such treatment. The Emperor, he proceeded to say, had expressed the wish that he should remain, and it was his duty to obey His Majesty's commands. He would, he knew, be attacked in the Duma, but he was not afraid. He would answer his accusers. It was, nevertheless, a great pity that, at a moment like the present, the members of the Duma should be quarrelling among themselves. Could I not, he asked, use my influence with Rodzianko to induce him to discourage personal attacks on him? I replied that as the Duma was meeting on the following day I should have no opportunity of seeing Rodzianko. I could tell him, however, that I had quite recently, in conversation both with members of the Government and with members of the Duma, emphasized the necessity of their laying aside party and personal differences and of all working together for the common good.

The opening sitting of the Duma was a very stormy one, and Trepoff, who was received with hoots and hisses, had to leave the tribune three times before he could obtain a hearing. I was much struck by his patience and forbearance, and felt that the Duma was making a great mistake and putting itself in the wrong. His declaration of policy was most satisfactory, and he was emphatic as to the necessity of fighting out the war to victory and of defeating the Germans at home as well as in the field. The chamber, however, continued hostile, and even the announcement, which the Allied Governments had authorized him to make with regard to the Constantinople Agreement, fell perfectly flat. The Duma and the public were so engrossed by the internal crisis that they could think of nothing else. The name of Trepoff was, moreover, so associated with the events of 1905 that the left regarded his appointment merely as a change of persons and not of systems, and would accept nothing at his hands. Protopopoff, who was made the subject of violent attacks, had not, after all, the courage to face the music. He retired instead to Headquarters, and on his return took to his bed and announced that he was seriously ill. He did, however, write a letter to the *Novoe Vremja* explaining that it was at the special request of the Russian Minister that the Stockholm interview had taken place — a statement that was proved to be a pure invention on his part.

Even the reactionary Council of Empire was almost as outspoken as the Duma in protesting against the occult influences at work in high places. The same note was struck at the Congress of the United Nobility, one of the most Conservative bodies in Russia, while in all parts of the Empire voices were raised in condemnation of the dark forces behind the throne which made and unmade Ministers. With the exception of the extremists Russia was once more united; but whereas at the beginning of the war she had rallied round the

Emperor, an insuperable barrier had now arisen between Sovereign and people.

In December several members of the Imperial family tried to open the Empress's eyes to the true character of Rasputin and to the gravity of the situation. Among these was Her Majesty's elder sister, the Grand Duchess Elisabeth, who, ever since the assassination of her husband, the Grand Duke Serge, had lived retired from the world as the Superior of a little sisterhood which she had founded at Moscow, devoting her life to relieving the sufferings of the poor. Beautiful in person as in character, a ministering angel to all who were in distress, she came to Tsarskoe, determined to make a last effort to save the sister whom she loved. But the Empress's faith in the man whom she regarded as God's chosen instrument was not to be shaken, and after listening impatiently to what the Grand Duchess had to say, she cut short the conversation. The two sisters parted to meet no more.

A little later the Grand Duchess Victoria, the wife of the Grand Duke Cyril, made another attempt. She did not mention Rasputin by name, but after speaking very openly about the general situation, she appealed to the Empress to change her attitude for the sake both of the Emperor and the dynasty. Her Majesty was quite nice to the Grand Duchess, but told her that the situation required firmness and that she was not going to let the Emperor yield any more. It was to the interest of the dynasty that she should be firm, and nothing would induce her to sacrifice Protopopoff. The army, she maintained, was not disaffected, but was, on the contrary, loyal to the Emperor. She then made a violent attack on Sazonoff, whose Polish policy she severely criticized, and concluded by saying that he was no friend to the Emperor. One of the reasons why the Empress believed to the last that the army and the peasantry were on her side, and that she could count on their support, was that Protopopoff was in the habit of having bogus telegrams despatched to her from all parts of the Empire, signed by fictitious persons, assuring her of their love and support.

After so many unsuccessful attempts to deliver Russia from the man who was generally regarded as her evil genius, Rasputin's position seemed unassailable. It was from an unexpected quarter that deliverance eventually came, and on the morning of December 30 Petrograd was roused by the news of his assassination. The three chief actors in this historic drama were Prince Felix Yusupoff, Puriskevitch (the former reactionary who had led the attack on Rasputin at the opening sitting of the Duma), and the Grand Duke Dmitri. The latter's role was a purely passive one, his presence signifying apparently his approval of what they all three regarded as a judicial execution.

Rasputin, who had been placed under special police protection, seems to have had a premonition of his danger, and it was with some difficulty that Prince Felix, who went to fetch him in his motor, persuaded him to come to supper at the Yusupoff Palace. There a Borgia-like repast, with poisoned cakes and poisoned wine, awaited him. Rasputin partook of both but was none the worse. After vainly waiting for the poison to work the Prince rose and, making some excuse, went up a little winding staircase to a room on the floor above, where the Grand Duke, Puriskevitch and a doctor were waiting. Borrowing the Grand Duke's revolver, he rejoined Rasputin and, as the latter was looking at an old crystal crucifix on one of the walls, shot him behind the left shoulder. Hearing the shot, the other three came down, and the doctor pronounced the death agony to have begun. They then went out to make arrangements for removing the body. But Rasputin was not dead. Raising himself up and throwing himself on Prince Felix as the latter, on returning to the dining-room, was bending over him, he managed to make his way through an adjoining passage to an outer court. Here he was shot dead by Puriskevitch. The body was then taken in a motor to the Kristovski island and dropped into the Neva through a hole in the ice. Owing to tracks of blood left in the snow it was recovered the following morning. A few days later Rasputin was buried at night at Tsarskoe in the presence of the Emperor and Empress, of the Metropolitan Pitirim and Protopopoff.

Rasputin's death was a terrible blow to the Empress. All the hopes which she had centred on him were shattered, while the disasters which he had foretold would befall the dynasty should he be removed might, she feared, at any moment supervene. By her orders the Grand Duke Dmitri and Prince Felix were placed under arrest, though immunity from arrest was a recognized prerogative of all members of the Imperial family. The Emperor had returned at once from the Stavka and had told the Grand Duke Paul, who had asked that his son might be allowed to come to his palace at Tsarskoe, that "the Empress cannot allow it at present." A few days later the Grand Duke Dmitri was deported to Persia, while Prince Felix Yusupoff was ordered to retire to his estates near Moscow. On .January 11 the members of the Imperial family met at the palace of the Grand Duchess Marie Pawlovna and signed a collective letter in which they petitioned the Emperor to pardon the Grand Duke Dmitri. They at the same time represented in respectful language the dangers with which His Majesty's internal policy was fraught both for Russia and the dynasty. They received the following crushing reply: "It is given to nobody to occupy himself with murder. I know that the conscience of many gives them no rest, as it is not only Dmitri Pavlovitch who is implicated. I am astonished that you should address yourselves to me."

Rasputin's assassination, though prompted by patriotic motives, was a fatal mistake. It made the Empress more determined than ever to be firm, and it set a dangerous example, for it prompted people to translate their thoughts into action. It rendered it, besides, more difficult for the Emperor to make concessions even had he been disposed to do so, as he would in that case have exposed himself to the suspicion of having yielded out of fear of assassination. According to Rodzianko and others, His Majesty was really much relieved to be rid of Rasputin, but I cannot say whether or not this was the case. At the end of the year the internal situation was about as bad as it could be, as the prevailing discontent had been increased by the prohibition of the meeting of the Union of Zemstvos at Moscow and by the adjournment of the Duma in order to prevent any further discussion of that prohibition.

The change of Government which had recently taken place in England had not made a favourable impression in Petrograd, and the Empress, as one of the Grand Duchesses told me, had spoken very disparagingly of some of its members. I tried to correct this impression in a speech which I made at the British Club on New Year's Eve, pointing out that when a country is engaged in a life and death struggle it must entrust its destinies to men who have the necessary brain power and energy to prosecute it with vigour and success, though I had but little hope of this lesson being taken to heart by the rulers of Russia. Of the Ministerial changes in England the one that most interested political and official circles in Petrograd was the retirement of Viscount Grey, as Sir Edward had now become. During his long term of office he had done so much to promote and maintain a close understanding with Russia; he had rendered her so many services during the critical years that preceded the war, and during the war itself he had shown such readiness to meet her wishes, that his departure from the Foreign Office meant for Russia the loss of a friend. He had, moreover, won for himself such a commanding position among the statesmen of Europe; his word carried such weight; his strong and upright character, as well as his able conduct of affairs, inspired such confidence, that it was generally felt that the Entente was losing in him one of its most valued assets. No one felt his loss more than I did, who had served under him for over ten years. He was an ideal chief, taking one completely into his confidence, listening to one's suggestions, showing consideration for one's difficulties and encouraging one to persevere by his kindly appreciation of one's work. In his last letter to me, written on December 24, 1916, he wrote:

I had not time to write private letters while I was in office, but I do not want to quit it without telling you how much I appreciated and admired the way in which you have handled the relations with Russia. It has been an immense help to the public service. I think even the public realizes something of it from the demonstrations there have been in Russia. But only those who have been behind the scenes here and at Petrograd know how much you have done and what the difficulties have been. When the war ends well I hope that it will be possible to tell the country more of this and to get fuller recognition for it.

CHAPTER 22
1917

At the beginning of January, Trepoff, finding that it was impossible to carry on the Government so long as Protopopoff remained Minister of the Interior, tendered his resignation, which was accepted by the Emperor. The Duma was adjourned till the end of February, and Prince Golitzin, a member of the Extreme Right, was appointed President of the Council. Honest and well-meaning, but without any administrative experience and out of touch with the Duma, he had not the necessary energy or strength of character to cope with a situation that was every day becoming more threatening. Revolution was in the air, and the only moot point was whether it would come from above or from below. A Palace revolution was openly spoken of, and at a dinner at the Embassy a Russian friend of mine, who had occupied a high position in the Government, declared that it was a mere question whether both the Emperor and Empress or only the latter would be killed. On the other hand, a popular outbreak, provoked by the prevailing food shortage, might occur at any moment.

I had no excuse for asking for an audience, but I did not like to await the development of events without making one last effort to save the Emperor, in spite of himself. In order to give greater weight to the language which I proposed to hold, I asked for permission to speak in the name of the King and His Majesty's Government, instead of making, as on former occasions, purely personal representations. I was informed, in reply, that owing to the King being absent from London, His Majesty's orders could not be taken, and that, as the Emperor was as well acquainted with the state of affairs in his country as I was, no good could come from such action on my part. I did not share this view, as the Emperor and Empress were, unfortunately, kept in ignorance of the true feelings of their people. I therefore replied that the crisis through which Russia was passing was fraught with such untold dangers that I must ask His Majesty's Government to reconsider their decision. We owed it, I said, to the Emperor, who had always been such a loyal friend and ally; we owed it to Russia, who had made such sacrifices in the common cause; and we owed it to ourselves, who were so directly interested, to endeavour to avert those dangers. If His Majesty's Government would not authorize me to speak in their name, I was prepared, with their permission, to speak in my own name and to assume all the responsibility for doing so. This permission was eventually given me.

While awaiting a reply to my request for an audience I called on the President of the Duma, in order to ascertain what concessions would really satisfy that chamber. Rodzianko assured me that all that the Duma asked for was the appointment as President of the Council of a man who commanded the confidence both of the Emperor and of the nation, with a free hand to choose his colleagues in the Government.

On January 12 — the day eventually fixed — I proceeded to Tsarskoe in a special train, accompanied by one of the Imperial chamberlains, and was on arrival shown into one of the large reception rooms, where I remained some little time in conversation with several of the high officers of the Court. As I was looking out of one of the windows I saw the Emperor leaving the palace and taking a brisk walk in the snow, as was often his habit between audiences. On his return, some ten minutes later, I was conducted to his presence. On all previous occasions His Majesty had received me informally in his study, and, after asking me to sit down, had produced his cigarette case and asked me to smoke. I was, therefore, disagreeably surprised at being ushered this time into the audience chamber and at finding His Majesty awaiting me there, standing in the middle of the room. I at once realized that he had divined the object of my audience, and that he was purposely giving it a strictly official character as a hint to me not to touch on matters outside an Ambassador's province. My heart, I confess, sank within me, and for a moment I seriously contemplated renouncing my original purpose. In these democratic days, when Emperors and Kings are at a discount, such nervousness on my part may seem out of place. But the Emperor of all the Russias was then an autocrat, whose slightest wish was law; and I was about not only to disregard the hint which he had so plainly given me, but to put myself in the wrong by overstepping the bounds of an Ambassador's sphere of action.

His Majesty began the conversation by expressing the deep regret with which he had that morning received the news of the death of Count Benckendorff, who had done so much to promote Anglo-Russian friendship. He would, he said, be very difficult to replace; but he mentioned Sazonoff, whose appointment was announced a few weeks later, as an Ambassador likely to prove agreeable to His

Majesty's Government. Speaking next of the importance of the Allied Conference that was about to meet at Petrograd, His Majesty expressed the hope that it would be the last one which we should have to hold before the final peace conference. I replied that I saw but little chance of its proving to be the precursor of the peace conference, as the political situation in Russia did not encourage me to expect any great results from its deliberations. I could not, indeed, help asking myself whether, under present circumstances, it was worth while exposing the lives of so many distinguished men to the fate that had befallen Lord Kitchener on his ill-starred journey to Russia.

On His Majesty asking why I took so pessimistic a view of the conference's prospects, I said that, even if it succeeded in establishing closer co-ordination between the Allied Governments, we had no guarantee that the present Russian Government would remain in office or that the decisions of the conference would be respected by their successors. As His Majesty protested that such apprehensions were unfounded, I explained that co-ordination of our efforts would not suffice unless there was in each of the Allied countries complete solidarity between all classes of the population. We had recognized this fact in England, and it was to secure the collaboration of the working classes that Mr. Lloyd George had included a representative of Labour in his small War Cabinet. In Russia it was very different, and His Majesty, I feared, did not realize how important it was that we should present a united front to the enemy, not only collectively as allies, but individually as nations. "But I and my people," interjected the Emperor, "are united in our determination to win the war." "But not," I replied, "as regards the competence of the men whom Your Majesty has entrusted with the conduct of the war. Does Your Majesty," I asked, "wish me to speak with my usual frankness?"

On the Emperor signifying his assent, I went on to say that there was now a barrier between him and his people, and that if Russia was still united as a nation it was in opposing his present policy. The people, who had rallied so splendidly round their Sovereign on the outbreak of war, had seen how hundreds of thousands of lives had been sacrificed on account of the lack of rifles and munitions; how, owing to the incompetence of the administration, there had been a severe food crisis, and — much to my surprise, the Emperor himself added, "a breakdown of the railways." All that they wanted, I continued, was a Government that would carry on the war to a victorious finish. The Duma, I had reason to know, would be satisfied if His Majesty would but appoint as President of the Council a man in whom both he and the nation could have confidence, and would allow him to choose his own colleagues. The Emperor, while passing over this suggestion, referred by way of justification to certain changes which he had recently made in the Ministry. I therefore ventured to observe that His Majesty had of late changed his Ministers so often that Ambassadors never knew whether the Ministers of to-day with whom they were treating would still be Ministers on the morrow.

"Your Majesty, if I may be permitted to say so, has but one safe course open to you — namely, to break down the barrier that separates you from your people and to regain their confidence." Drawing himself up and looking hard at me, the Emperor asked: "Do you mean that *I* am to regain the confidence of my people or that they are to regain *my* confidence?" "Both, sir," I replied, "for without such mutual confidence Russia will never win this war. Your Majesty was admirably inspired when you went to the Duma last February. Will you not go there again? Will you not speak to your people? Will you not tell them that Your Majesty, who is the father of your people, wishes to work with them to win the war? You have, sir, but to lift up your little finger, and they will once more kneel at your feet as I saw them kneel, after the outbreak of war, at Moscow."

I had in the course of our conversation referred to the necessity of having a strong man at the head of the Government, and the Emperor now seized on this remark, saying that the situation undoubtedly required firmness and a strong man to deal with it. I told His Majesty that I entirely agreed, provided always that that firmness was not applied to enforce repressive measures or to obstruct the admirable work being done by the Zemstvos. While expressing his appreciation of the services rendered by the Zemstvos during the war, the Emperor said that he disapproved of the attitude and political speeches of some of their leaders. I tried to defend them on the ground that if they had erred it was through excess of patriotism, but without much success.

I next called His Majesty's attention to the attempts being made by the Germans, not only to create dissension between the Allies, but to estrange him from his people. Their agents, I said, were everywhere at work. They were pulling the strings, and were using as their unconscious tools those who were in the habit of advising His Majesty as to the choice of his Ministers. They indirectly influenced the Empress through those in her *entourage* with the result that, instead of being loved, as she ought to be, Her Majesty was discredited and accused of working in German interests. The Emperor once more drew himself up and said: "I choose my Ministers myself, and do not allow anyone to influence my choice." "How, then," I ventured to ask, "does Your Majesty select them?" "By making inquiries," His Majesty replied, "as to the qualifications of those whom I consider most fitted to conduct the affairs of the different Ministries." "Your Majesty's inquiries," I rejoined, "are not, I fear, always attended with success. There is, for example, M. Protopopoff, who, if Your Majesty will forgive my saying so, is bringing Russia to the verge of ruin. So long as he remains Minister of the Interior there cannot be that collaboration between the Government and the Duma which is an essential condition of victory."

"I chose M. Protopopoff," the Emperor here interposed, "from the ranks of the Duma in order to be agreeable to them — and this is my reward!" "But sir," I said, "the Duma can hardly place confidence in a man who has betrayed his party for office, who has had an interview with a German agent at Stockholm, and who is suspected of working for a reconciliation with Germany." "M. Protopopoff," His Majesty declared, "is not a pro-German, and the reports circulated about his Stockholm interview have been grossly exaggerated." "I was not," I replied, "acquainted with what had passed in that interview. But, even admitting that the charges brought against him on that count had been exaggerated, he had told a deliberate falsehood in announcing in the Press that it was at the special request of the Russian Minister at Stockholm that he had seen the German in question." The Emperor did not attempt to deny this.

Did His Majesty, I then asked, realize the dangers of the situation, and was he aware that revolutionary language was being held, not only in Petrograd, but throughout Russia? On the Emperor saying that he was quite aware that people were indulging in such talk, but that I made a mistake in taking it too seriously, I told him that a week before Rasputin's assassination I had heard that an attempt was about to be made on his life. I had treated this report as idle gossip, but it had, after all, proved true. I could not, therefore, now turn a deaf ear to the reports which had reached me of assassinations, said to be contemplated of certain exalted personages. If such assassinations once began, there was no saying where they would stop. Repressive measures would, no doubt, be taken, and the Duma would be dissolved. Were that to happen, I should abandon all hope of Russia.

"Your Majesty," I concluded, "must remember that the people and the army are but one, and that in the event of revolution only a small portion of the army can be counted on to defend the dynasty. An Ambassador, I am well aware, has no right to hold the language which I have held to Your Majesty, and I had to take my courage in both hands before speaking as I have done. I can but plead as my excuse the fact that I have throughout been inspired by my feelings of devotion for Your Majesty and the Empress. If I were to see a friend walking through a wood on a dark night along a path which I knew ended in a precipice, would it not be my duty, sir, to warn him of his danger? And is it not equally my duty to warn Your Majesty of the abyss that lies ahead of you? You have, sir, come to the parting of the ways, and you have now to choose between two paths. The one will lead you to victory and a glorious peace — the other to revolution and disaster. Let me implore Your Majesty to choose the former. By following it you will, sir, secure for your country the realization of its secular ambitions and for yourself the position of the most powerful Sovereign in Europe. But above all else. Your Majesty will assure the safety of those who are so dear to you and be free from all anxiety on their account."

The Emperor was visibly moved by the warmth which I had put into this appeal, and, pressing my hand as he bade me good-bye, said, "I thank you, Sir George."

M. Bark, the Minister of Finance, who had an audience immediately afterwards, asked me the next day what I had said to the Emperor, as he had never seen him so nervous and agitated. His Excellency had handed His Majesty a letter tendering his resignation, and the Emperor had torn it up, saying, "This is no time for Ministers to abandon their posts." But whatever momentary impression I may have made was not strong enough to counterbalance the adverse influence of the Empress, whose displeasure I had already incurred on account of the language which I had held in previous audiences. So much was this the case that, according to a current report, the question of asking for my recall was seriously considered. That the Empress did not forgive those, who tried to dissuade the Emperor from giving effect to her policy, was evidenced by the case of my friend, the Grand Duke Nicholas Michaelowich. We had frequently exchanged views on the internal situation, in the hope that by our concerted action we might induce the Emperor to change his attitude. His Imperial Highness had, early in January, both by letter and by word of mouth, warned the Emperor of the dangers of the present course. Two days after my audience I received the following letter from him:

Ce 1/14. 1, 1917.

Pour vous seul.

BIEN CHER AMBASSADEUR, — J'ai reçu I'ordre de S. M. l'Empereur de m'en aller pour deux mois dans ma propriété de Grouchevka (près de Khersov).

Au revoir et bonne chance.

Vive I'Angleterre et vive la Russie.

Cordialement à vous,

NICHOLAS M.

His brother, the Grand Duke Serge, whom I met at a dinner shortly afterwards, remarked that had I been a Russian subject I should have been sent to Siberia. Without being seriously preoccupied, I was nevertheless relieved to find, at the Russian New Year's reception a few days after my audience, the Emperor as friendly disposed as ever. In the short conversation which I had with him no reference was made by either of us to my recent audience. I said nothing more about the internal situation; but having heard that His Majesty suspected a young Englishman, who had been a college friend of Prince Felix Yusupoff, of having been concerned in Rasputin's murder, I took the opportunity of assuring him that the suspicion was absolutely groundless. His Majesty thanked me and said that he was very glad to hear this.

About a week later a Russian friend of mine, who was afterwards a member of the Provisional Government, sent me a message through Colonel Thornhill, our assistant military attaché, to say that there would be a revolution before Easter, but that I need not be alarmed, as it would not last more than a fortnight. I have reason to believe that this message was founded on fact, and that a military *coup d'état* was then being prepared, not for the purpose of deposing the Emperor, but of forcing him to grant a Constitution. Its promoters were, unfortunately, forestalled by the popular rising which carried through the March revolution. I say "unfortunately," because it would have been better, both for Russia and the dynasty, had the long-expected revolution come from above instead of from below.

The publication on January 20 of an Imperial rescript, directing the President of the Council to devote special attention to the food and transport questions and to work in harmony with the Duma and the Zemstvos, aroused hopes that were not destined to materialize. Protopopoff, on whose shoulders Rasputin's mantle had fallen, was now more powerful than ever. Mentally deranged, he would, in his audiences with the Empress, repeat warnings and messages which he had received in his imaginary converse with Rasputin's spirit. He had completely won Her Majesty's confidence, and having convinced her that, with the measures which he was taking to reorganize the police, he was equal to dealing with any situation that might arise, he was given a free hand to continue his insane policy.

On January 29 the Allied delegates arrived, and a preliminary meeting of the conference was held in the afternoon under the presidency of the Foreign Minister, Pokrowski. Great Britain was represented by Lord Milner, Lord Revelstoke, General Sir Henry Wilson and myself; France, by M. Doumergue, General Castelnau and Paleologue; and Italy, by Signor Scialoja, General Ruggieri and Carlotti, the Italian Ambassador. On the 31st the delegates were received by the Emperor, and on February 3 we were all invited to a gala dinner at the palace at Tsarskoe. As doyen of the diplomatic body, I had the honour of being placed on the Emperor's right, and His Majesty talked to me during the greater part of the dinner. The only questions, to which I called his attention, were the food crisis and Russia's man power. As regarded the first, I told him that, according to my reports, there was such a scarcity of foodstuffs in some provinces that the supplies were not expected to last more than a fortnight. This shortage seemed to be due to lack of co-ordination between the Ministries of Agriculture and Transport and to the absence of any organized system of distribution. The latter duty, I suggested, might with advantage be entrusted to the Zemstvos. The Emperor agreed that the Minister of Agriculture ought to avail himself of the services of the latter, adding that, if workmen ran short of food, strikes were certain to follow.

With regard to the second question, I observed that Russia was not making the most of her vast man power, and that, though she badly needed certain metals, her mineral wealth was not properly exploited. Had His Majesty, I asked, ever contemplated following Germany's example, and instituting some form of obligatory auxiliary service for all? The Emperor replied that he had already had this question under his consideration, and that he hoped that it might be possible to take some step in the direction which I had indicated. It was, he added, but right that in times of national crises everybody should serve the State to the best of his abilities. The rest of our conversation was of a non-political character. For myself, personally, a melancholy interest attaches to this dinner, for it was the last occasion on which I ever saw the Emperor. At the same time it is some satisfaction to me to remember his marked friendliness at what, unsuspected by either of us, was to be our last interview. It was as if His Majesty wished to show me that not only he did not resent my outspoken language at my recent audience, but that he appreciated the motives which prompted me to speak so frankly to him.

With a view to expediting matters, the conference had been split up into three commissions — political, military, and technical. It was the last named, dealing as it did with the all-important questions of transport and munitions, that accomplished the most useful work. In his speech at the opening of the conference, General Gourko stated that Russia had mobilized fourteen million men, had lost two millions in killed and wounded, as well as two million prisoners, and had at present seven and a half millions under arms and two and a half millions in her reserve depots. He did not hold out any hope of her army being able to take an offensive on a large scale till the new divisions, about to be formed, had been finally constituted, trained and equipped with the necessary guns, rifles and munitions. All that it could do meanwhile was to hold the enemy by actions of secondary importance. The outcome of the conference was a series of recommendations with regard to the war material and credits which it was proposed that the Allied Governments should place at Russia's disposal.

The conference separated on February 21, 1917.

CHAPTER 23
1917

The session of the conference had synchronized with a temporary improvement in the internal situation, and there had been but few outward or visible signs of political unrest. It is hardly, therefore, to be wondered at that the Allied delegates, on returning to their respective countries, should have expressed themselves somewhat too optimistically with regard to the Russian outlook. My own views had undergone but little change. I had been instructed to report, for the information of the Imperial conference that was about to meet in London, as to the prospects of Russia continuing in the war; and, after consultation with Lord Milner, with whom it had been my privilege to work during his stay in Petrograd, I telegraphed to the Foreign Office on February 18 as follows:

Though attacks are occasionally made on us in the reactionary gutter Press, the anti-British campaign has died out and Anglo-Russian relations were never better than at present. The Emperor, most of his Ministers and the bulk of the nation are all firm supporters of the Anglo-Russian Alliance. It may, indeed, be safely said that the mass of the people fully appreciate the enormous services which Great Britain is rendering with her fleet, her armies and her purse, and that it is to her that they look for the realization of their hopes of final victory.

It is more difficult to speak with precision on the question of Russia continuing in the war. The majority of the nation, including the Government and the army, are at one in their determination to fight it out to a victorious finish; but there the national unity ends. The Emperor, the supreme factor, is deplorably weak; but the one point on which we can count on his remaining firm is the war, more especially as the Empress, who virtually governs Russia, is herself sound on this question. She is not, as is so often asserted, a German working in Germany's interests, but a reactionary, who wishes to hand down the autocracy intact to her son. It is for this reason that she prompts the Emperor to choose, as his Ministers, men on whom she can rely to carry out a firm policy quite regardless of their qualifications; but in so doing she is acting as the unconscious tool of others, who really are German agents. While the latter are doing all they can to press on the Emperor a policy of reaction and repression, they are at the same time preaching revolution to his subjects in the hope that Russia, rent by internal dissensions, will be forced to make peace. The Emperor, by allowing Protopopoff to take measures directly calculated to provoke disturbances, has played into their hands. Protopopoff, as Minister of the Interior, has appointed to posts in his own and other Government departments reactionaries who are as corrupt as they are incompetent; he has virtually vetoed all public meetings, notably those of the Union of Zemstvos, and has tried but failed to dissolve the latter altogether; he is working for the dissolution of the Duma, restricting the liberty of the Press and re-establishing the preliminary censorship. His latest move has been to arrest a dozen of the workmen's representatives in the industrial war committees. There would already have been an explosion were it not for the fact that the Duma is so conscious of the gravity of the situation that it will do nothing to compromise the success of the war. Though the workmen are greatly incensed at the arrest of their representatives, high wages, combined with patriotism, have so far averted strikes.

Should there be a shortage of food supplies, strikes will inevitably follow; and it is the economic rather than the political situation that causes me anxiety. If only it was a question of the latter, the final settlement might be postponed till after the war; but the former is an ever-present danger. It may at any moment fan the smouldering political discontent into a flame, with results that will seriously prejudice the cause of the war. On the railways the reserve stock of fuel has fallen so low that on one line there is said to be only enough for a few days, and many people fear that, even if the reserve stocks are temporarily replenished, the shortage will again make itself felt when once the regular traffic, which is at present reduced to a minimum, is resumed. Many munition factories have already been temporarily closed owing to want of fuel and raw materials, and the danger of a shortage of supplies, both for the army and the towns, cannot be altogether excluded.

I would sum up the situation as follows: Although the Emperor and the majority of his subjects are bent on fighting out the war to a finish, Russia will not, in my opinion, be able to face a fourth winter campaign if the present situation is indefinitely prolonged. On the other hand, Russia is so rich in natural resources that there would be no cause for anxiety were the Emperor to entrust the conduct of the war to really capable Ministers. As it is, the future is a sealed book. The political or the economic situation may have some disagreeable surprise in store for us, while the financial situation may be compromised by repeated issues of paper money. Russia, however, is a country that has a happy knack of muddling through, and my only hope is that she will be able to hold out to the end if we continue to give her the necessary assistance.

On February 27 the Duma met, and the opening sitting, which I attended, passed off so quietly that I thought I could safely take a short holiday in Finland. During the ten days which I spent there no rumours reached me of the coming storm. It was only as my wife and I were returning on Sunday, March 11, by the last train which got into Petrograd, that my servant brought us news, as we were nearing the capital, of a tramway and isvostchick (cab) strike. The part of the town through which we passed on our short drive to the Embassy was perfectly quiet, and, except for a few; patrols of soldiers on the quays and the absence of trams and isvostchicks, there was nothing very unusual about its general aspect.

The situation, nevertheless, was already very serious. Owing to the coal shortage referred to in my telegram quoted above, some of the factories had to close down, and there were consequently several thousand workmen unemployed. This fact, taken by itself, would not have been very alarming, as they had been paid and were not out to make trouble. But they wanted bread, and many of them, after waiting for hours in the queues outside the bakers' shops, had been unable to get any. On Thursday, March 8, there had been a stormy sitting in the Duma, in which the Government had been violently attacked on account of its failure to revictual Petrograd; and it was the bread shortage that was at the root of the agitation which began on the same day to manifest itself among the workmen. In the evening several of the bread shops in the poorer quarters of the town were looted, and a patrol of Cossacks was for the first time seen galloping down the Nevski.

On the following day the agitation increased. The people wanted an assurance that something would be done to relieve the food crisis, but none was forthcoming. Groups of workmen and students paraded the streets, followed by a crowd of men, women and children who had come out of curiosity to see what was going to happen. But for the most part it was a good-humoured crowd that made way for the Cossacks when the latter were ordered to clear some street, and even occasionally cheered them as they passed. The Cossacks, on their side, were careful not to hurt anybody and — what was of bad omen for the Government — laughed and talked with those near them. It was only towards the police, with whom they had several collisions in the course of the day, that the crowd adopted a hostile attitude. In some of the streets also tramcars were broken and overturned.

Meanwhile the Socialist leaders, who had for months past been carrying on an active propaganda in the factories and barracks, had not been idle, and on Saturday — the 10th — the town assumed a more serious aspect. There was what almost amounted to a general strike, and the crowd of workmen who surged up and down the Nevski presented a more organized appearance. Nobody quite knew what was going to happen, but there was a general feeling that the opportunity was too favourable to be allowed to pass without something being done. On the whole, however, the attitude of the people was still peaceful. In the evening there was a little shooting, for which the policemen, whom Protopopoff had had dressed up in soldiers' uniforms, were held responsible.

It was now that the Government determined to have recourse to stern repressive measures. On the Sunday morning (March 11) General Khabaloff, military governor, had had notices posted up all over the town warning the workmen that those who did not return to work on the following day would be sent to the front, and announcing that the police and military had orders to disperse any crowd that collected in the streets with all the forces at their command. This warning was disregarded, the crowds were as great as ever, and, in the course of the day, some two hundred were killed by the fire of the troops. In the afternoon, however, a company of the Pavlovsk Regiment mutinied on receiving the order to fire, and had to be disarmed by the Preobrazhenski Regiment. By the evening all resistance had been overcome, the crowds had been dispersed and order temporarily restored. But the movement, whose original object had been to secure the immediate adoption of measures for remedying the shortage of provisions, now assumed a political character and aimed at the overthrow of a Government that was responsible for the shooting as well as for the food crisis.

With the fatality that dogged his footsteps the Emperor, who had spent the months of January and February at Tsarskoe, feeling that he could no longer absent himself from Headquarters, had returned to Mohileff — more than twenty hours distant by train — on Thursday, March 8. Had he remained at Tsarskoe a few days longer, within reach of those who could have kept him accurately informed of the development of events in the capital, he would have been better able to appreciate the extreme gravity of the situation. On the Saturday General Alexeieff had advised him to lose no time in making the necessary concessions, and on the Sunday Rodzianko had telegraphed to him, saying that anarchy prevailed in the capital and that it was absolutely necessary for him to entrust someone, who enjoyed the confidence of the nation, with power to form a new Government. "I pray God," Rodzianko concluded, "that at this hour the responsibility may not fall on the wearer of the Crown." Rodzianko at the same time communicated this telegram to the generals in command of the various fronts with a request for their support, and soon afterwards received replies from General Ruszki and General Brussiloff , saying that they had carried out his wish. Whether Rodzianko's telegram ever reached the Emperor, or whether it was purposely kept back from him. General Voyeikoff, the prefect of the Imperial palaces, did, in his conversations with His Majesty, undoubtedly misrepresent the true state of affairs and scout the idea of a revolution. The Government, meanwhile, could think of nothing better to do than to prorogue the Duma.

During the night of Sunday there was violent agitation in the barracks, where the soldiers had met to consider what was to be their attitude on the following day. Were they to shoot down their own kith and kin if the order to fire was given? That was the question which they were asking one another. The answer to that question was given on Monday morning, when the soldiers of one of the Guard regiments — the Preobrazhenski — on being ordered to fire, turned and shot their officers. The Volynski Regiment, that was sent to coerce them, followed their example. Other regiments did the same, and by midday some 25,000 troops had made common cause with the people. In the course of the morning the arsenal was stormed and its store of rifles, guns and ammunition seized. Then followed in rapid succession the burning of the law courts, the raiding of the central office of the secret police and the destruction of all its compromising archives, the release of both the political and criminal prisoners in the three principal prisons, and the surrender of the fortress of SS. Peter and Paul.

The Government, supine and incapable, had mismanaged matters from the first. A strong energetic Minister like Stolypin could, with tact and firmness, have kept the movement within bounds; but the Government failed altogether to reassure the people with regard to the food crisis, while they adopted ineffective measures to restore order that did but serve to exasperate the masses and to play into the hands of the real revolutionaries. Finally, by ordering the troops to fire on the people, they fanned the prevailing discontent into a blaze that spread with lightning speed over the whole town. But the initial mistake lay with the military authorities, who ought, had they not been altogether lacking in foresight, to have left a small body of well disciplined and reliable troops to maintain order in the capital. As it was, the garrison — some 150,000 in all — was composed solely of depot troops. They were all young soldiers, fresh from their villages, and undergoing training prior to being sent to fill up the gaps made in their regiments at the front. The corps of officers entrusted with their training was far too small to handle so large a body of men. It consisted of men who had been invalided home on account of their wounds, and of inexperienced boys from the military schools who were quite incapable of maintaining discipline when the crisis came.

The mistake thus committed was the more inexplicable as Petrograd, from the revolutionary point of view, had always been the danger spot. It was the centre of the Socialist propaganda that was making headway both in the barracks and the factories. It was full of German agents, working for the overthrow of the Empire as the surest stepping stone to the eventual elimination of Russia from the war. Its atmosphere, moreover, was so charged with pessimism that the Emperor more than once told me how glad he was to shake off its depressing influence and to return to the more bracing air of the front.

I had, as already stated, only got back to Petrograd on the Sunday evening, and on Monday at noon I went, as usual, with my French colleague to the Ministry for Foreign Affairs. While I was there General Knox telephoned to tell me that a large part of the garrison had mutinied and was in undisputed control of the Liteini Prospekt. I repeated this message to Pokrowski, saying that Protopopoff might congratulate himself on having brought Russia face to face with revolution by his provocative policy. Pokrowski agreed, but contended that order and discipline must be restored. A military dictator, he said, would be appointed, troops would be sent from the front to quell the mutiny, and the Duma would be prorogued till April 25. I replied that it was madness to prorogue the Duma, and that the only result would be that the insurrectionary movement, which was at present confined to Petrograd, would spread to Moscow and other towns. It was too late now to repress the movement by force, and the only remedy lay in a policy of concession and conciliations. Pokrowski dissented, saying that had it been merely a rising of the civil population the Government might have tried to come to terms with them; but in the case of soldiers who had broken their military oath to the Emperor, military discipline must first of all be re-established.

In spite of the order for the prorogation of the Duma, the committee of that chamber remained in session; while Rodzianko had despatched a second telegram to the Emperor, telling him that the last hour had come in which to decide the fate of the country and dynasty, and that His Majesty must take immediate steps or to-morrow would be too late. Shortly afterwards the Duma learnt that the Minister of War, General Belaieff, had received a telegram from the Emperor, stating that he was returning to Petrograd, and that General Ivanoff — whom he had appointed dictator — would shortly arrive with a large body of troops. This telegram repeated the views, expressed to me by Pokrowski, with regard to the action to be taken against soldiers who had broken their military oath.

At half-past one, delegates from the troops on the north side of the river came to inquire what directions the Duma had to give them. Rodzianko, who received them, said that the watchword of the Duma was the abolition of the present Government. He said nothing about the Emperor, for the Duma, like most people, had been so taken by surprise by the rapid march of events that it was at a loss what to do. A little later a detachment of insurgent troops arrived, and were harangued by Kerensky and Cheidze, who told them that they must maintain order, prevent excesses, and stand firm for the cause of freedom. They were asked by Kerensky to furnish a guard for the Duma, and, in order to avoid trouble, Rodzianko consented to the removal of the old guard. Kerensky, a young lawyer — the son of a former director of the Tashkent High School and of a Jewish mother — had already made his mark by the fiery speeches, which he had delivered in the Duma as leader of the Social Revolutionary Party. I shall have much to say about him later on, but for the moment it is sufficient to record the fact that during these critical days he acted, when due allowance is made for his Socialist convictions, loyally with the Duma committee. Cheidze, on the contrary, who represented the Social Democrats, worked solely in the interest of his party. About three o'clock, after a sitting held with closed doors, the Duma appointed an executive committee for the preservation of order, representative of all parties except the extreme right. It was to be presided over by Rodzianko, and included two Conservatives, three Moderates, five Cadets and Progressists, and two Socialists — Kerensky and Cheidze.

The executive committee of the council of workmen's delegates at the same time summoned a meeting of their representatives in the palace of the Duma for the same evening. The soldiers, who had passed over to the people, were invited to send one delegate for each company and the factories one for each thousand workmen.

All through the afternoon troops kept arriving at the Duma, which gradually became crowded with a mob of soldiers, workmen and students. In the evening Schteglovitoff, the president of the Council of Empire, formerly Minister of Justice, and an ultra-reactionary, was brought in under arrest, while towards midnight a shabby-looking man, in a soiled fur coat, appeared, saying: "I am the late Minister of the Interior, Protopopoff. I desire the welfare of our country, and so I surrender myself voluntarily."

Thanks to the efforts of the executive committee, the situation in the town showed signs of improvement on Tuesday (March 13). The two principal events were the surrender of the Admiralty, after a threat that otherwise it would be destroyed by artillery fire from the fortress, and the attack on the Hotel Astoria in consequence of shots having been fired from it at a company of soldiers that was marching past with the Red Flag at its head. Though shooting continued the whole day, it was for the most part confined to the firing by the police of the machine guns, which Protopopoff had had placed on the roofs of the houses, and to the attempts made by the soldiers to dislodge the police by rifle fire. I was able to walk to the Ministry of Foreign Affairs in the morning to pay my farewell visit to Pokrowski, and on my way home with my French colleague we were, on being recognized, cheered by the crowds gathered on the quay. In the afternoon I again went out with Bruce to call on Sazonoff, who was staying in an hotel on the Nevski; and, though the rattle of the machine guns overhead was not a pleasant accompaniment, we got there and returned without any incident.

The old Government had by this time ceased to exist, and all its members, with the exception of Pokrowski and of the Minister of Marine, Admiral Grigorowich, had been arrested, together with Stürmer, the Metropolitan Pitirim, and a few other reactionaries. By the evening the whole garrison, as well as all the troops which had arrived from Tsarskoe and the neighbouring districts, had gone over to the Duma, while many officers had also offered their services. So far as Petrograd was concerned, the revolution was already an accomplished fact; but the situation was beset with colossal difficulties. The workmen were armed, numbers of released criminals were at large, in many regiments the soldiers were without officers, while in the Duma a sharp struggle was proceeding between the executive committee and the newly formed Soviet.

The Duma had been the rallying point of the troops who had achieved the revolution. Its leaders were for the most part Monarchists and advocates of a war to a victorious finish. But at the critical moment they failed to assert themselves, and allowed the Democrats, who were pronounced Republicans, with a large percentage of pacifists, to forestall them and to assume control over the troops. They had further tolerated the session in one of their own assembly rooms of a rival body, the Soviet, that, without any legal status, had constituted itself the representative council of the workmen and soldiers. If only there had been among its members a real leader of men, capable of profiting by the first natural move of the insurgent troops towards the Duma, to rally them round that assembly as the only legally constituted organ in the country, the Russian revolution might have had a happier sequel. But no such leader arose, and, while the Duma was still deliberating and seeking for a policy, the Democrats, who knew their own minds, acted. Once assured of the support of the troops, Cheidze, their leader, was, as he told a British officer, master of the situation.

Meanwhile the Emperor had left the Stavka for Tsarskoe on the night of the 12/13th; but finding on arriving at Bologoi that the rails in front of the train had been pulled up by workmen, His Majesty had proceeded to Pskoff, the headquarters of General Ruszki, the commander-in-chief of the northern front. On Wednesday, the 14th, the Grand Duke Michael, who was stopping in a private house near the Embassy, asked me to come and see him. He told me that, in spite of what had happened at Bologoi, he still expected the Emperor to arrive at Tsarskoe about six that evening; that Rodzianko was to submit for His Majesty's signature a manifesto granting a constitution and empowering Rodzianko to select the members of the new Government; and that he himself, as well as the Grand Duke Cyril, had appended their signatures to the draft of this manifesto in order to strengthen Rodzianko's hands.

His Imperial Highness added that he hoped to see the Emperor in the evening, and inquired whether there was anything special that I would like him to say. I replied that I would only ask him to beseech the Emperor, in the name of King George, who had such a warm affection for His Majesty, to sign the manifesto, to show himself to his people, and to effect a complete reconciliation with them. But while I was talking with the Grand Duke the proposed manifesto was vetoed by the Soviet, and the abdication of the Emperor decided. Almost at the same time the Emperor, on being informed by General Ruszki of the state of affairs at Petrograd, had telegraphed saying that he was ready to make all the concessions desired by the Duma if the latter thought that they would restore order in the country; but, as Rodzianko telegraphed back, it was "Too late." As the only other alternative was civil war, the Emperor on the following morning (the 15th) handed General Ruszki a telegram for despatch to Petrograd announcing his abdication in favour of his son. A few hours later — as M. Gilliard tells us in his sad but very interesting story of the Emperor Nicholas's tragic destiny — His Majesty sent for the Court physician, Professor Feodoroff, and asked him to tell him the truth about the Tsarevitch's health. On being told that, as the illness was an incurable one, his son's life might be cut short at any moment, the Emperor said, "Since Alexis cannot serve his country as I would have wished him to, we have the right to keep him." When, therefore, in the evening, the two Duma delegates, Guchkoff and Schulgin, arrived, charged with the mission of demanding the abdication of the

Emperor in favour of his son, under the regency of the Grand Duke Michael, the Emperor handed them the following ukase, in which he renounced the throne in favour of his brother:

The destiny of Russia, the honour of our heroic army, the good of the people, the future of our beloved Motherland, demand the prosecution of the war at all costs until a victorious end. . . . In these days, that are supremely decisive for Russia, we have considered it as a duty, laid on our conscience, to facilitate for our people the close union and rallying of all popular forces for the purpose of a speedy achievement of victory, and, in concert with the Duma, we have deemed it good to abdicate from the throne of the Russian Empire and to divest ourselves of the supreme power. Not wishing to part with our beloved son, we transmit our inheritance to our brother, the Grand Duke Michael Alexandrovich, and give him our blessing on his ascending the Throne of the Russian Empire.

The Emperor's last official act was to appoint the Grand Duke Nicholas Nicholaievich commander-in-chief and Prince Lvoff (the popular leader of the Zemstvos) as the new President of the Council. For, as the result of a compromise between the Duma committee and the Soviet, a Provisional Government had been formed to carry on the administration of the country till a constituent assembly had decided whether Russia was to be a Republic or a Monarchy. The principal members of this Government belonged to the Cadet and Octobrist parties. Miliukoff, the leader of the former, was appointed Minister for Foreign Affairs, and Guchkoff, the leader of the latter, Minister of War. Kerensky, who was made Minister of Justice, served as a link between the Soviet and the Government, and it had been mainly thanks to him that the opposition of the former had been overcome. During the heated discussion that had taken place on the question of the regency he had, in announcing his appointment as Minister of Justice, said in the Soviet: "No one is a more ardent Republican than I; but we must bide our time. Nothing can come to its full height at once. We shall have our Republic, but we must win the war; then we can do what we will." With the constitution of the Provisional Government Rodzianko, who had played such a prominent part during the early days of the revolution, retired into the background; and the Duma, which had fought so hard and so long to secure the appointment of a Ministry responsible to itself, now gradually came to be regarded as an archaic institution, till it finally disappeared from the scene.

The question of the Grand Duke Michael's claim to the throne had still to be decided, and during the whole of Thursday (the 16th) the members of the Provisional Government were in consultation with him on the subject. Miliukoff and Guchkoff alone supported his claim, contending that it was necessary that someone should be appointed head of the State. The others held that the fact that the Emperor had confirmed Prince Lvoff's appointment as head of the Provisional Government sufficed. Finally, the Grand Duke, who personally had no ambition to assume the burden of Empire, yielded to Kerensky's passionate appeal and signed a manifesto, declaring that he could only accept the supreme power should such be the desire of the nation, clearly expressed in a constituent assembly elected for the purpose of definitely deciding the form of government to be adopted. He further called on all citizens to obey the Provisional Government. The new Government of Russia was thus not, strictly speaking, a Republican Government; and, on my once referring to it as such, Miliukoff caught me up, saying that it was only a Provisional Government pending the decision of the future constituent assembly.

As regarded the conduct of the war, its task had been rendered extremely difficult, if not impossible, by the publication by the Soviet, on March 14, of the famous Prikas No. 1. By forbidding soldiers to salute their officers, by transferring the disciplinary powers of the latter to committees of soldiers, and by decreeing that in all their political actions the troops were to obey the orders of the Soviet, it directly undermined the discipline of the army. Nor did the announcement, contained in the Government's first published declaration, that the military units which had taken part in the revolutionary movement were neither to be disarmed nor transferred from Petrograd, help to improve matters.

CHAPTER 24
1917

The Emperor — who after his abdication had returned to his former headquarters at Mohileff— was now styled "Colonel" Romanoff, according to his official rank in the army. On March 22 he was brought to Tsarskoe, where he and the Empress were placed under arrest. When the news of his abdication had first reached the palace the Empress had refused to credit it, and she was almost stunned on being told by the Grand Duke Paul that it was an accomplished fact. But, when the first shock was over, she behaved with wonderful dignity and courage. "I am now only a nursing sister," she said; and on one occasion, when a conflict seemed imminent between the insurgent troops and the palace guard, she went out with one of her daughters and implored the officers to arrange terms with the latter so that no blood should be shed. Her children had all fallen ill with the measles, which, in the case of the Tsarevitch and the Grand Duchess Marie, had taken a somewhat serious turn, so that all her time was spent in going from one sick-room to the other.

Though, during their stay at Tsarskoe, Their Majesties were under constant guard, and could not even walk in their private garden without being stared at by a little crowd of curious spectators who watched them through the park railings, they were spared any ill-treatment. Special measures for their protection were taken by Kerensky, as at one moment the extremists, who clamoured for their punishment, had threatened to seize them and to imprison them in the fortress. In the first speech which he delivered at Moscow, Kerensky had declared that he would not allow more blood to be shed, and that he was not going to be the Marat of the Russian revolution. One of his reasons for abolishing the death penalty was to forestall a possible demand for the Emperor's execution. His Majesty, on being informed of this, exclaimed, "It is a mistake. The abolition of the death penalty will ruin the discipline of the army. If he is abolishing it to save me from danger, tell him that I am ready to give my life for the good of my country." The removal of Their Majesties to Tobolsk in August was also mainly prompted by the desire to guard them against the dangers to which they would have been exposed in the event of a successful Bolshevik rising; and there can be but little doubt that, had they remained at Tsarskoe, they would not long have outlived the November revolution. Their children, who were offered the choice of residing with the Empress Marie in the Crimea or accompanying their parents to Tobolsk, chose the latter course, though warned that they would have to submit to the same regulations as the Emperor and Empress.

At the end of September I had a conversation with the Government commissary, who accompanied the Imperial family to Tobolsk, which I recorded in the following letter to Lord Stamfordham:

Makharoff, who is a moderate Socialist, spoke very nicely of the Emperor, and seems to have done all he could to meet His Majesty's wishes. He said that the departure from Tsarskoe was very painful to witness, as nearly all members of the Imperial family were in tears, but that, with the exception of the Empress, they very soon recovered their spirits, and were laughing and talking an hour later. The railway journey lasted three or four days, and the train stopped for an hour every day, in order to let the Emperor and his children take a walk. The journey on the steamer took another four days; but, as certain alterations had to be made in the house at Tobolsk, the Emperor and his family remained a few days longer on board the steamer. Makharoff admitted that the house was not a large one, especially in the eyes of those accustomed to live in palaces, and that it was not luxuriously furnished. He had since endeavoured to remedy this latter defect by forwarding carpets, family pictures, wine, etc., from the Palace at Tsarskoe. The worst feature of the house was that it was situated in the lower part of the town, and consequently rather damp, and that it had but a small garden. It had, however, a largish park just opposite it, where the members of the Imperial family had now permission to walk. They were also allowed to attend divine service in the church, instead of in the house as had been arranged at first. The Emperor had also permission to go shooting if he wished.

Tobolsk, he said, was a small town of some 27,000 inhabitants, and was at such a distance from any railway station that the Emperor was in perfect safety there. The land all round it was owned by large Tartar peasant proprietors, who cordially disliked the revolution, as they were afraid of being expropriated, should there be a redistribution of land among the peasants. Many peasants, he added, came on pilgrimage to Tobolsk to see the house where the Emperor lived.

As regarded the climate, he said that, though damp at certain seasons, it was healthy, and that the winter was really more tolerable than at

Petrograd, as it was not accompanied by the same biting winds to which we are subjected here.

He had begged the Emperor, when he took leave of His Majesty, not to hesitate to tell him if he had any complaints to make; but the Emperor had assured him that he was quite satisfied. Both the Emperor and the Empress had bid him good-bye in a friendly way. The Emperor had spoken to him more than once of the political situation, and had said that he was quite ready to die for Russia. Makharoff added that he was sure that His Majesty was quite sincere in saying this.

For the story of all that they suffered during the latter part of their stay at Tobolsk, I must refer my readers to the graphic pages of M. Gilliard's "Le Tragique Destin de Nicholas II," while I devote the rest of this chapter to a short review of the Emperor's reign.

The Emperor Nicholas II is one of the most pathetic figures in history. He loved his country. He had its welfare and greatness at heart. Yet it was he who was to precipitate the catastrophe, which has brought it to utter ruin and misery. Had he lived in classic times, the story of his life and death would have been made the subject of some great tragedy by the poets of ancient Greece. They would have represented him as a predestined victim pursued, in each successive act, by some relentless fate, till the curtain fell on that heartrending scene in the basement of the house at Ekaterinburg, where, with his only son by his side, with his wife and daughters looking on, awaiting the same doom, he was brutally murdered by the Bolsheviks. The only ray of light in the dark picture is the fact that, united as they had been in their lives, they remained so till the end, and that in death they were not divided.

The Emperor's marriage with Princess Alix of Hesse had not been prompted by reasons of State. They had from the first been drawn together by feelings of mutual affection, and their love for each other had grown stronger with every passing year. Ideally happy though they .were in their married life, the Emperor's choice was nevertheless an unfortunate one. Despite her many good qualities — her warm heart, her devotion to husband and children, her well-meant but ill-advised endeavours to inspire him with the firmness and decision which his character lacked — the Empress Alexandra was not a fitting helpmate for a Sovereign in his difficult position. Of a shy and retiring disposition, though a born autocrat, she failed to win the affection of her subjects. She misjudged the situation from the first, encouraging him, when the political waters were already running dangerously high, to steer a course fraught with danger to the ship of State. The tragic element is already discernible in the first act of the drama. A good woman, bent on serving her husband's interests, she is to prove the chosen instrument of his ruin. Diffident and irresolute, the Emperor was bound to fall under the influence of a will stronger than his. It was her blind faith in an unbridled autocracy that was to be his undoing. Had he had as his consort a woman with broader views and better insight, who would have grasped the fact that such a regime was an anachronism in the twentieth century, the history of his reign would have been different and he might still be Emperor of Russia.

But, baneful as was her influence over her husband in matters of internal policy, the Empress must be acquitted of the charge, so often brought against her, of having worked in Germany's interest. Kerensky himself once told me that not a single compromising document had been found to show that either she or the Emperor had ever contemplated making a separate peace with Germany. He had, he said, had a long private conversation with the Empress after the revolution, in which Her Majesty had indignantly protested against the idea that she was pro-German. "I am English," she had declared, "and not German, and I have always been true to Russia." She was, he was convinced, speaking the truth, and though she unconsciously played the German game by inducing the Emperor to pursue a reactionary policy, she aimed solely at maintaining the autocracy intact, and not at bringing about a closer understanding with Germany. There were, however, he added, German agents in Rasputin's entourage.

Possessed of many gifts that would have fitted him to play the part of a constitutional Sovereign — a quick intelligence, a cultivated mind, method and industry in his work, and an extraordinary natural charm that attracted all who came near him — the Emperor Nicholas had not inherited his father's commanding personality nor the strong character and prompt decision which are so essential to an autocratic ruler. Alexander III had, on the advice of Pobiedonostseff , the Procurator of the Holy Synod, dropped the scheme of reforms which Alexander II was on the point of signing when his life was cut short by a Nihilist bomb. He had throughout his reign pursued a reactionary policy based on bureaucratic centralization. On his death the hopes of the nation were centred on his son. These hopes were reflected in many of the loyal addresses presented by the Zemstvos on his accession to the throne. In one of them — that of Tver — the desire for some form of constitutional government was definitely formulated.

The occasion was, indeed, one that afforded a young Sovereign a golden opportunity of winning over his people by some timely concession; but the Emperor Nicholas let it slip, as he was to let other similar occasions slip during the course of his reign. A devoted and admiring son, and a pupil of that arch reactionary, Pobiedonostseff, he had been brought up in the strictest school of orthodox autocracy without ever acquiring the habit of himself taking the initiative. He had assimilated his tutor's doctrines, and he regarded the autocracy as a sort of sacred heritage which he was bound to preserve intact in the form in which it had been bequeathed to him. His one idea on succeeding to the throne was to follow in his father's footsteps and to leave things as his father had left them. Such reverence had he for his father's memory that he even refused to assume a higher rank in the army, of which he was commander-in-chief, than that of colonel, which his father had conferred on him. The representatives of the Zemstvos were therefore dismissed with the chilling response that they must abandon all such "insensate dreams," as it was his firm intention to continue his father's policy. It seems, however, from what M. Isvolsky tells us in his "Souvenirs de mon Ministère," that the Emperor's original intention had been to hold less uncompromising language, but that he had been persuaded that it was his duty to uphold the traditions of his father's reign. It was only at the last moment that Pobiedonostseff handed him the reply, drafted by himself, which the Emperor read to the representatives of the Zemstvos without having fully grasped its purport. He was so wanting in self-reliance that he allowed himself in this, as well as on many subsequent occasions, to be influenced against his better judgment by persons possessed of stronger wills than his own.

Such an inauspicious opening of the new reign created a feeling of despondency in the minds of all thinking Russians, while the terrible disaster that marred the Coronation festivities in May, 1896, was interpreted by a superstitious people as of evil augury for the future. Owing to faulty arrangements on the part of the responsible authorities, the huge crowd which had forgathered in the enclosure set apart for the distribution of the customary gifts was seized with panic, and in the crush which ensued some three or four thousand were trampled to death. A further incident, trivial in itself, produced, according to M. Isvolsky, a profound impression on His Majesty. As the Emperor, wearing the Imperial crown and mantle, was approaching the altar to receive the consecrating unction, the collar of the Order of St. André became detached and fell at his feet. Naturally prone to fatalism and superstition. His Majesty regarded this as a Divine warning of misfortune to come.

His initial and fundamental mistake was in failing to comprehend that the Russia of his day could not be governed on the same lines as the Russia which Peter the Great had known. The Empire had in the interim undergone a vast territorial expansion. Its population had risen to over 160 millions; it had witnessed the liberation of the serfs, the birth of industries in the great towns, the consequent increase in the numbers of the proletariat, and the growing influence of the intelligentsia. There were new forces at work, and the nation's aspirations had grown with its growth. The old policy of centralization was no longer workable, and devolution was the only effective remedy. But to entrust the Zemstvos with a direct share in the administration of their respective provinces would have been resisted by the bureaucracy, which had succeeded in monopolizing all the functions of the administration. It was not, moreover, in the Emperor's character to initiate such a policy nor to face the opposition of those who would regard it as an encroachment on their prerogatives. Impossible as it was for him personally to control the administrative machinery of his vast Empire, he had to bear the responsibility for the sins of omission and commission of the bureaucracy that governed Russia in his name. Even when, after the revolutionary movement that followed the disastrous war with Japan the principle of national representation was conceded, the administration of the country remained as centralized as before.

Nor did the reformed Ministry that was constituted at the same time greatly advance matters. It was not a Cabinet in the ordinary sense. It had no collective responsibility and it worked in water-tight compartments. Each of its members was directly responsible to the Emperor for the conduct of the affairs of his own department without being under any obligation to consult the President of the Council with regard to them. It was, moreover, like all its successors, composed of heterogeneous elements. Witte, the first President, was a progressist, while the Minister of the Interior (Dumovo) was an extreme reactionary. The natural consequence was that owing to divided counsels it could never take any concerted action. Though I, personally, mistrusted Count Witte on account of his pronounced pro-German views, I fully recognize his merits as an able and far-seeing statesman who rendered his country invaluable services. He introduced the gold currency, he negotiated the Treaty of Portsmouth that re-established peace with Japan, and he induced the Emperor to publish the October manifesto of 1905 that called the Duma into existence. In his most interesting and instructive book, "The Eclipse of Russia," Dr. Dillon has ably played the part of an admiring Boswell and done full justice to his memory; but, in his devotion to his idol. Dr. Dillon is inclined to see things too much through Witte's spectacles. Now, the Emperor and Witte were mutually antipathetic, and the latter's dislike of his Sovereign so biased his judgment that, in his eyes, His Majesty could do nothing right. Dr. Dillon, taking his cue from Witte, has not a good word to say for the Emperor — he applies to him every sort of injurious epithet, attributes to him unworthy motives, and accuses him of falseness. His initiative in convoking the Hague Peace Conference in 1898 is represented as having been prompted by the desire to hoodwink the Austrian Government and to enable the Russian Minister of War to steal a march on his colleague in the Austrian capital. Again, while admitting that the Emperor did not wittingly lead Russia into the disastrous war with Japan, Dr. Dillon hints that he was financially interested in Bezobrazoff's schemes for Russia's political and economic expansion in the Far East. Inexplicable as it is that the Emperor should have allowed himself to be guided by the advice of such men as Bezobrazoff and Abaza, and should even have permitted them to direct the course of the negotiations, with regard to the question of the forest concessions on the Yahi that was the immediate cause of the final rupture, his tastes were so simple that he would never have been tempted to supplement his enormous revenues by speculating in such an enterprise. What it is difficult to explain is his misplaced confidence in unscrupulous adventurers who persuaded him that a firm, uncompromising attitude was necessary if he wished to avert war.

In order to show how false the Emperor was, both Count Witte and Dr. Dillon have cited the secret treaty signed by him and the Emperor William at Bjorkoe in July, 1905, as an act of treason directed against France. Under the terms of that treaty the two Emperors were to come to each other's assistance with all their land and sea forces in the event of either of them being attacked by another European Power. It was to come into force on the conclusion of peace between Russia and Japan, and the Emperor Nicholas was then to invite France to associate herself in its provisions by becoming a signatory. This last clause is sufficient in itself to show that the treaty was not directed against France. It was, as M. Isvolsky has conclusively proved in his memoirs, directed against Great Britain. The Emperor William had for months past been trying to persuade the Tsar to join a Continental league against us, but the latter had already (in November, 1904) objected that any treaty of this kind must be submitted to France before he could sign it. The Emperor William had thereupon contended that France would do nothing to constrain Great Britain to maintain peace unless she was confronted with the *fait accompli* of a signed treaty. As these arguments failed to overcome the Emperor Nicholas's objections, the question was for a time left in abeyance. In the following summer, however, the Kaiser determined to see what a little personal persuasion would accomplish.

As the Emperor Nicholas was cruising with his family on the *Polar Star* in Finnish waters, the Emperor William suggested joining him on his own yacht and paying him what was to be treated as a surprise visit. He insisted on nobody being told about his intended visit, as he was most anxious that Count Lamsdorf, the Minister for Foreign Affairs, should not be summoned from St. Petersburg to assist at the meeting. The Emperor William arrived at Bjorkoe on July 23 with the text of the treaty in his pocket, to which he succeeded in getting the Emperor Nicholas to attach his signature, after a luncheon on board the Hohenzollern, only a few minutes before his departure at the end of his three days' stay. He further insisted on the treaty being countersigned by Herr von Tchirsky, a high official in the German Foreign Office, who was German Ambassador at Vienna at the outbreak of war, and by Admiral Birileff, the Russian Minister of Marine, who happened to be on board the Polar Star, but who was kept in ignorance of the nature of the document which he was to countersign. As M. Isvolsky points out, at the time the treaty was signed Great Britain and Russia were almost open enemies, and it was a perfectly legitimate act on the part of the Emperor to conclude an alliance directed against Japan's ally. On the other hand, he never contemplated being false to France. He had from the .first desired to consult her before definitely committing himself, but the dominating personality of the Kaiser overcame his resistance and made him, against his own better judgment, sign the treaty without having first secured her adhesion. He had fallen into the trap laid for him by the Emperor William. The latter, while professing to be our friend, was, with his usual falseness, endeavouring to form a coalition against us — a coalition into which he hoped to force France by confronting her with the spectre of a Russo-German alliance.

Already realizing the mistake which he had committed, the Emperor Nicholas on his return to St. Petersburg consulted Count Lamsdorf. The latter had no difficulty in convincing him of the necessity of taking immediate steps for the annulment of the treaty, and representations were accordingly made in Berlin to the effect that the treaty, not having been countersigned by the Russian Minister for Foreign Affairs, must be considered invalid. As these representations were unsuccessful, the Emperor Nicholas subsequently addressed a letter to the Emperor William, explaining that it was impossible to carry out its provisions owing to the adhesion of France being unobtainable. Though the Kaiser seems never to have admitted the invalidity of the treaty, the incident was finally closed in 1907, when Isvolsky, on the eve of the meeting of the two Emperors at Swinemünde, informed the German Chancellor that the Emperor Nicholas considered the Bjorkoe Treaty definitely abrogated and could not listen to any further arguments in favour of its revival.

The fact that the Emperor Nicholas sometimes allowed Ministers, whom he was about to dismiss, to believe up to the very last that they still enjoyed his confidence, is also cited by His Majesty's critics as a proof of his falseness. He would, when receiving them in what, unknown to them, was to be their final audience, give them no hint that he was about to part with them. They would leave his presence and return to their Ministries without the least suspicion that they would, in the course of the next twenty-four hours, receive a letter from His Majesty dispensing with their services. Most of us dislike giving our servants notice, and so did the Emperor. He was not wittingly false, but he preferred to convey to them in a letter what he had not the moral courage to tell them to their faces, more especially when, in cases like that of Sazonoff, he was but acting under pressure from the Empress.

It was this besetting sin of weakness, combined with a lack of confidence in his own judgment, that made him the easy prey of those evil counsellors whom the Empress chose for the carrying out of her policy. He had many faults, but the charge of falsehood is non-proven. When I returned from Russia at the beginning of 1918 he was accused of having been on the point of betraying the Allies by making a separate peace with Germany. I refuted that infamous charge at the time, and I have, I trust, in the present work established the fact that we never had a more loyal friend and ally than the Emperor Nicholas. He was true to us till the very last, for there is reason to believe that, had he been prepared to purchase his life and liberty by recognizing and confirming the Treaty of Brest Litovsk, the Germans would have saved him.

It was his misfortune to have been born an autocrat, when he was by nature so unfitted for the role. He never really governed Russia, and by allowing the ruling bureaucracy to disregard his promises of freedom of speech, meeting, etc., made in the October manifesto of 1905, he forfeited to a great extent the confidence of his people. The burden of his inheritance grew heavier as his reign progressed. A vast Empire, in which some seventy-five per cent, of the population were illiterate, in which the revolutionary spirit of 1905 had never been laid, in which the Church, that had since the abolition of the Patriarchate by Peter the Great become a department of State, was rapidly losing its hold on the people owing to the scandalous appointments made through Rasputin's influence, in which justice was ill-administered, and in which nearly every branch of the administration was as incompetent as it was corrupt; and then, on the top of all this, a world war! The whole system was out of joint, and he, poor Emperor, was certainly not born to set it right.

It was no wonder that the fall of the old régime was welcomed with a sigh of relief, that the revolution spread from Petrograd to Moscow, from Moscow to Kieff, and thence all over the Empire. But it was not so much the Emperor as the regime of which the nation as a whole was weary. As a soldier remarked during the first days of the revolution: "Oh, yes, we must have a Republic, but we must have a good Tsar at the head." The Emperor and the Orthodox Church, of which he was the head, still represented the two great symbols of the political and spiritual creed of the mass of the Russian peasants. It was the Little Father who personated Russia in their eyes and who formed the only link between the peasants of Siberia and the Ukraine and of the Caucasus and the northern provinces. It was an evil day for Russia when that link was broken, for it left a void that has never been filled. Could it have been averted? I believe that it could, had the Emperor been at Tsarskoe when the revolution broke out, or had he at once returned there. Even on the Monday (March 12) he might have saved the situation by going to the Duma and proclaiming a constitution. Mistrust of the Empress would have been the chief obstacle in the way of a settlement, and the Duma might have insisted on a separation — a condition to which the Emperor would never have consented. As it was, he only left the Stavka on the Monday night. When, on the Wednesday, he telegraphed from Pskoff offering a constitution, the Duma had lost control of the situation and it was too late. After that, he had only two courses open to him — either to abdicate or to go to the front and, after granting a constitution, to make a personal appeal to his troops. Those at the front were not nearly so disaffected as those in the rear, and the Emperor's prestige still counted for much. But such an appeal, if successful, would have meant civil war in the face of the enemy, and the Emperor therefore preferred to abdicate — a decision which, M. Gilliard tells us, he regretted when he heard at Tobolsk of the state of demoralization to which the army had been brought by Bolshevik propaganda.

In the farewell Order of the Day which he addressed to the army before finally leaving the Stavka — the publication of which was vetoed by the Provisional Government — the Emperor is seen at his best. All personal considerations are cast aside, and all his thoughts are centred on his country, his allies, and on fighting out the war to a victorious finish.

These are his words:

This is the last time that I shall address you, my well-loved troops. Since I renounced the throne for myself and my son, the supreme power has, on the initiative of the Duma, passed into the hands of the Provisional Government. May God aid it to lead Russia along the path of glory and prosperity! May God also aid you, my valiant troops, to defend our country against its stubborn enemy.

For two years and a half you have fought incessantly; you have endured hardships; you have shed your blood; you have made great efforts; and now the hour approaches when Russia, united to her valiant Allies by the common desire for victory, will triumph over the resistance of the enemy. This war, unparalleled in history, must be fought out to a final and complete victory. Whoever thinks of peace at a moment like the present, whoever desires peace is a traitor to his country. I know that every true soldier thinks as I do.

Do your duty then — defend your country valorously — obey the Provisional Government — obey your officers — remember that any slackening of discipline is to render a service to the enemy. I firmly believe that unbounded love for your great Fatherland still lives in your hearts.

May God bless you and may the Great Martyr, St. George, lead you to victory.

Can anyone after reading the above appeal, written as it was at a moment when, having fallen from his high estate, he was being placed under arrest, believe, as his detractors would have us believe, that the Emperor was false?

Whether or not he had, as some pretend, a premonition of coming troubles, he bore his misfortunes and sufferings with wonderful resignation and courage. A firm believer and a fatalist, he was always ready to accept anything that God might send him. As illustrating his general frame of mind, I may quote a story which Isvolsky tells in his "Souvenirs de mon Ministère." It was during the summer of 1906, and Isvolsky, who was then Minister for Foreign Affairs, had gone to Peterhof, where the Court was in residence, to make his usual weekly report to the Emperor. A serious mutiny had just broken out at Cronstadt, as a protest against the recent dissolution of the Duma, and the fortress was being bombarded by the fleet. Though the cannonade continued during the whole of the audience, the Emperor followed his report with the greatest attention, as if nothing unusual was happening, discussing all the more important points with him. When, at its close, the Emperor got up and looked out of the window towards Cronstadt, some ten miles distant on the other side of the gulf, Isvolsky could not resist asking him how he could remain so calm at a moment when the fate of his dynasty hung in the balance. The Emperor, turning to him, said — I give His Majesty's reply in Isvolsky's own words, and it forms a fitting ending to this review of his reign:

Si vous me voyez si peu troublé, c'est que j'ai la ferme, I'absolue croyance, que le sort de la Russie — que mon propre sort et celui de ma famille — est entre]es mains de Dieu, qui m'a placé là ou je suis. Quoi qu'il arrive, je m'inclinerai devant sa volonté, avec la conscience de n'avoir jamais eu d'autre pensée que celle de servir le pays qu'il m'a confié.

CHAPTER 25
1917

WHILE there was still a chance of the Grand Duke Michael being accepted either as Regent or Emperor, I had asked for and received permission to recognize any Government that might be established *de facto*, in order that it might be the better able to assert its authority. I had also, in my conversations with Miliukoff — who had assumed charge of the Ministry for Foreign Affairs — strongly advocated the retention of the services of the Grand Duke Nicholas as the commander-in-chief best qualified to keep the army in hand. After the Grand Duke Michael's renunciation of the crown our only possible policy was to strengthen the hands of the Provisional Government in their struggle with the Soviet. The latter was ruining the army with its Socialist propaganda, and though the majority of its members professed themselves in favour of continuing the war, those on the extreme left advocated peace at any price. The speedy recognition of the Provisional Government was therefore, in my opinion, necessary; but when, on March 18, Miliukoff broached the subject to me, I told him that before acting on the authorization already given me I must have an assurance that the new Government was prepared to fight the war out to a finish and to restore discipline in the army. Miliukoff gave me this assurance, but said that they were obliged to proceed cautiously on account of the extremists, and that his own position was a very difficult one. He was regarded with suspicion for having supported the Grand Duke Michael's claim to the throne, and he must either make some concessions or resign. Which course, he asked, would I prefer him to take? The former, I unhesitatingly replied.

The United States Ambassador was the first to recognize the Provisional Government officially on March 22, an achievement of which he was always very proud. I had, unfortunately, been laid up for a few days with a bad chill, and it was only on the afternoon of the 24th that I was allowed to get up and go with my French and Italian colleagues to the Ministry, where Prince Lvoff and all the members of his Government were waiting to receive us. As doyen, I had to make the first speech. After expressing my pleasure at entering into relations with them and assuring them of my support in all matters touching the strengthening of our alliance and the conduct of the war, I proceeded to say:

A cette heure solennelle où une nouvelle ère de progrès et de gloire s'ouvre devant la Russie, il est plus que jamais nécessaire de ne pas laisser detourner les yeux de I'Allemagne. Car le triomphe de I'Allemagne aura pour suite l'écroulement de ce beau monument, que le peuple Russe vient d'élever à la Liberté. La Grande Bretagne tend la main au Gouvernement Provisoire, persuadée que ce dernier, fidele aux engagements pris par ses prédécesseurs, fera tout son possible pour mener la guerre à une fin victorieuse, en veillant surtout au maintien de I'ordre et de I'unite nationale, à la reprise du travail normal dans les usines et a I'enseignement et à la discipline de I'armée. Oui, Messieurs les Ministres, si aujourd'hui j'ai I'honneur de vous apporter les salutations d'une nation amie et alliee, c'est parceque mon Gouvernement aime à croire que, sous votre haute direction, la Nouvelle Russie ne reculera devant aucun sacrifice at que, solidaire avec ses Alliés, elle ne deposera pas les armes avant que ces grands principes de droit et de justice, de liberté et de nationalité, dont nous avons pris la défense, soient fermement soutenus et établis.

After the other two Ambassadors had also spoken, Miliukoff , in the name of his colleagues, assured us that the Provisional Government were determined to uphold the agreements and alliances concluded with their predecessors and to continue the war to a victorious finish.

My speech was, on the whole, well received, though one journal warned me that I could not hold the same language to the representatives of free Russia as I had to "the minions of the Tsar."

Those of my readers who have had the patience to follow me through the successive stages of the Russian revolution down to our official recognition of the Provisional Government will, I trust, acquit me of the charge of having had any hand in bringing it about. Many people, nevertheless, still believe that I was the prime mover who pulled the strings and started it on its course. Ever since my return to England, at the beginning of 1918, this charge has fastened on me, and I have never been able to shake it off. Some of my former Russian friends still regard me with suspicion, and some have even turned their backs on me, as being indirectly responsible for the misfortunes that have befallen their country and their late Emperor.

The stories of my revolutionary activities are as numerous as they are ridiculous. The two following will suffice as typical examples:

One day in the spring of 1919 I had gone to Marlborough House to see Arthur Davidson, one of my oldest and dearest friends, whose death so many of us deplore. He was telling me that certain exalted personages were inclined to credit some of these stories, when a Russian friend of mine, who was in attendance on the Empress Marie, came into the room. After exchanging greetings, I asked if he also suspected me of having been a revolutionary. "Well," he replied, "it is difficult not to believe it after what one has read in the papers." On my inquiring what the papers had been good enough to say about me, he continued: "I read in one paper that, when the victims of the revolution were buried in the Champ de Mars, you attended the funeral, accompanied by all your staff, in full uniform, that you made a speech belauding the revolution, and that you concluded by expressing the hope that England would at no distant date follow Russia's example and get rid of her King." "That," I replied, "is really the limit. If you Russians believe such a story, you will believe anything. Do you suppose that if I had made such a speech I should have been kept on at Petrograd as Ambassador, and should, on my return to London, have met with a most gracious reception on the part of my Sovereign?" He could not deny the force of this argument, and withdrew the charge.

The other story is still more humorous. It was told quite seriously at a luncheon party in London in 1918 by an ex-diplomat who is now dead, and was repeated to me by a lady who had been present. "Buchanan," the ex-diplomat said, "had found that German influence so dominated the Russian Court that the only hope of keeping Russia in the war and preventing a separate peace was to start a revolution. He accordingly got into touch with the extreme Socialists, and attended revolutionary meetings with a false nose and a false beard." As I could not speak Russian, such a disguise would hardly have proved effective.

Stories such as these do not call for further comment, but I cannot pass over in silence the more serious and specific charges brought against me in articles and letters which have been published in the Press of various countries. It will be sufficient for my purpose to take as my text one of the more recent of such articles, which, owing to the world-ide repute of the review in which it appeared, has attracted more general notice. My attention was first called to it by a gentleman who at one time held a high position in the French diplomatic service. He kindly came to ask me to tell him the truth about the part which I had played in the revolution, in order that he might be in a position to correct the unfavourable impression which the article in question had created in certain circles in Paris with regard to His Majesty's Government's Russian policy.

In June of last year the *Revue de Paris* published the first of a series of articles by Princess Paley, the widow of the Grand Duke Paul, entitled, "Mes Souvenirs de Russie." In it she makes the following statement:

L'Ambassade d'Angleterre, sur des ordres de Lloyd George, était devenue un foyer de propagande. Les Libéraux, Prince Lvoff, Miliukoff, Rodzianko, Maklakoff, Guchkoff, etc., s'y retrouvaient constamment. C'est à l'Ambassade d'Angleterre qu'il fût decidé d'abandonner les voies légales et de s'engager dans le chemin de la Révolution. II faut dire que, dans tout cela, Sir George Buchanan, Ambassadeur d'Angleterre à Péétrograd assouvissait des rancunes personelles. L'Empereur ne I'aimait pas et il etait avec lui de plus en plus froid, surtout depuis que I'Ambassadeur d'Angleterre frayait avec ses ennemis personnels. La dernière fois que Sir George demanda une Audience, l'Empereur le reçut debout, sans le prier de s'asseoir. Buchanan jura de se venger, et comme il était très lié avec un jeune couple grand-ducal, il cut un instant l'idée de faire une Révolution de Palais. Mais les événements dépasserènt ses prévisions et lui et Lady Georgina se détournèrent de leurs amis déchus sans ia moindre pudeur. On racontait a Petersbourg, au debut de la Révolution, que Lloyd George, apprenant la chute de Tsarisme en Russie, se frotta les mains en disant: "Un des buts de guerre de I'Angleterre est atteint."

That Princess Paley is gifted with a vivid imagination is no secret to me, and I can but congratulate her on this *chef-d'oeuvre*. As I was looking over some old letters a few months ago I came across one which I had written to Lord Carnock in December, 1914, when he was Under-Secretary of State for Foreign Affairs, with regard to the military situation on the Russian front. In it I spoke of the pessimism prevailing in certain quarters, and cited as an example a story to the effect that the Grand Duke Nicholas was in such a state of depression that he spent most of his time on his knees before his icons, declaring that God had abandoned him. I added that this story was a pure invention, and that it had been told me by Paléologue, who had been dining with Countess Hohenfelsen (as Princess Paley then was) in her palace at Tsarskoe, which was generally reputed to be a hotbed of gossip. I am not therefore surprised that she should have so entirely misrepresented my conduct.

As I have no intention of sheltering myself behind any imaginary instructions from home, I may at once state that I accept the full responsibility for our attitude towards the revolution. It was on my advice that His Majesty's Government consistently acted. Needless to say, I never engaged in any revolutionary propaganda, and Mr. Lloyd George had our national interests far too much at heart ever to have authorized me to promote a revolution in Russia in the middle of a world war. It is perfectly true that I did receive at the Embassy the Liberal leaders named by Princess Paley, for it was my duty as Ambassador to keep in touch with the leaders of all parties. I was, moreover, in sympathy with their aims, and, as already stated, I consulted Rodzianko on the subject of those aims before my final audience with the Emperor. They did not want to provoke a revolution so long as the war lasted. On the contrary, they practised such patience and restraint that the Government regarded the Duma as a negligible quantity and imagined that they could go all lengths. When the revolution came, the Duma sought to control it by giving it the sanction of the only legally constituted organ in the country. The majority of its leaders were Monarchists. Rodzianko, up to the last, had hoped to save the Emperor by drafting a manifesto for him to sign granting a constitution. Guchkoff and Miliukoff had both supported the Grand Duke Michael's claim to the succession.

Maklakoff — one of the most brilliant of its orators — was also a Monarchist. I remember how, at a luncheon given later on by Tereschenko (the then Foreign Minister) to Kerensky, he roused the latter's wrath by saying, "I have always been a Monarchist." *"Et maintenant?"* exclaimed Kerensky, pointing an indignant finger at him. Instead of replying, Maklakoff proceeded to denounce those who had cringed to the Emperor when he was all-powerful and who had declared themselves ardent Republicans when his star had set. I have nothing to reproach myself with for having cultivated the friendship of these men. They disappointed me, it is true, by failing, when the crisis came, to keep control of the situation; but they were, I must admit, confronted with colossal difficulties, and, unfortunately, they were none of them supermen. I would further remind Princess Paley that the real promoters of the revolution were people like Rasputin, Stürmer, Protopopoff, and Mme. Wyrobouwa. I was careful to keep them at a distance, while Mme. Wyrobouwa, who was directly responsible for the influence gained by Rasputin over the Empress, was, as well as, if I mistake not, other disciples of the saint, an honoured guest in her house. I have even been told that the Princess herself had at least one interview with Rasputin.

I will leave Princess Paley for a moment and briefly explain my attitude throughout the crisis. I had been at one with the Duma leaders in holding that the course of the military operations must not be compromised by any grave internal crisis; and it was in order to avert such a catastrophe that I repeatedly warned the Emperor of his danger. Apart, moreover, from purely military considerations, I believed that it was by a process of gradual evolution, and not by revolution, that Russia would find salvation. With her millions of uneducated peasants she was not ripe for a sudden plunge into a parliamentary regime such as ours. Nor was I one of those who looked on a Republic as a panacea for all the ills from which she was suffering. Till education has permeated the Russian masses they will not be able to dispense with a strong ruler any more than their Slav ancestors, who, in the ninth century, invited the northern vikings to come and rule them, as their land lacked order. I was rather, as I once told the Emperor, in favour of what I termed a benevolent autocracy, combined with a policy of decentralization and devolution of authority. Self-government, in my opinion, had to begin at the bottom, and not at the top; and it was by learning to manage their provincial affairs that Russians would best qualify themselves for the task of administering the affairs of the Empire.

When once the revolution had swept away the whole Imperial edifice beyond all hope of reconstruction, when the Emperor, abandoned by all but a faithful few, had been forced to abdicate, when none of his countless subjects had raised a finger in his defence — what could an Allied Ambassador do but support the only Government capable of combating the subversive tendencies of the Soviet and of fighting out the war to a finish? It was in the Provisional Government that the Emperor himself had seen the only hope for Russia, and, inspired by a pure and unselfish love of his country, he had, in his last Order of the Day, called on his troops to yield it implicit obedience. I gave it from the outset my loyal support; but my position was a difficult one, as I was regarded with some suspicion by the public on account of my former relations with the Imperial family. It was Hugh Walpole, the head of our propaganda bureau, who, in calling my attention to this fact, begged me to show by the warmth of my language at some public meetings where I had to speak that I was wholeheartedly on the side of the revolution. I accordingly did so. But if I spoke with emotion about Russia's new-won liberty, that was already degenerating into licence, it was to render more palatable my subsequent appeal for the maintenance of discipline in the army, and for fighting, instead of fraternizing with, the Germans. My only thought was how to keep Russia in the war.

If, as my critics would have people believe, I really was responsible for the revolution, I can only say that my services were very ill-requited, for only a couple of months after its consummation I was categorically disavowed by the official organ of the Council of Workmen's and Soldiers' Delegates. In an article published on May 26, 1917, that journal stated:

In the early days of the Revolution the great change was regarded by many as the triumph of the War Party. From this point of view the Russian Revolution was said to be due to the intrigues of England, and the British Ambassador was named as the source of its inspiration. But neither by sentiment nor inclination is Sir George Buchanan guilty of the triumph of freedom in Russia.

Princess Paley, unlike my other critics, has rendered me one service for which I am grateful. I have often wondered what was the motive that prompted me to start the Russian revolution, and she is good enough to tell me. The Emperor did not like me — he had received me at my last audience standing — he had never offered me a chair. What more natural than that after such treatment I should, *pour assouvir mes rancunes personelles*, try to bring about a palace revolution with the object of placing the Grand Duke Cyril on the throne, and that, on finding this impracticable, I should have *lâché* the Grand Duke and gone in for a revolution from below? I had hitherto been under the impression that, in spite of my outspoken language, the Emperor rather liked me — but I was evidently mistaken. Princess Paley was on such intimate terms with him that His Majesty would doubtless have confided to her his likes and dislikes as regarded the Ambassadors accredited to him. But what the Princess does not know is that, no matter what the Emperor may have thought of me, I was personally devoted to him, and it was the fear of the consequences of a possible palace revolution that made me warn him of the danger in which he stood of assassination.

I can forgive much to a lady who has suffered so cruelly — who has lost a husband and a most brilliant and attractive son through the Bolshevik revolution. She has my fullest sympathy. But I also have had my sorrows, and what I cannot pardon is her lack of feeling in accusing my dead wife of having *sans la moindre pudeur* turned her back on her fallen friends. My wife never turned her back on anyone who stood in need of help or sympathy. She might be alive to-day had she not, from the beginning of the war down to her last fatal illness, overtaxed her strength by ministering to the needs of Russians of every class of society, whether they were wounded soldiers or indigent refugees.

But as Princess Paley has cited a specific case and has accused my wife and me of having abandoned our former friends, the Grand Duke and Grand Duchess Cyril, I will tell her what we really did. In one of the first conversations, which the French Ambassador and I had with him after the revolution, Miliukoff expressed the hope that we would refrain from seeing members of the Imperial family. I at once told him that I could not comply with this request. Many members of that family had shown me great kindness when they were all-powerful, and now that they were down I was not going to turn my back on them. I further warned him that the Grand Duchess Victoria (the wife of the Grand Duke Cyril) was a British Princess, and that, if necessary, I should take her under my protection. As it happened, she never stood in need of it, as the Grand Duke Cyril had been one of the first to recognize the revolution and to hoist the red flag. I subsequently went to see the Grand Duchess Xenia and my friend the Grand Duke Nicholas Michaelovich. I also, as well as my wife, paid several visits to the Grand Duchess Victoria, and my wife once took her out driving. After a few weeks the fact that I was in the habit of visiting members of the Imperial family became known, and, as the Press took up the question, I was given to understand that I must either renounce these visits or go. My wife, therefore, wrote to the Grand Duchess explaining that in my official capacity I had no choice but to comply with the wishes of the Provisional Government. Her Imperial Highness replied in a charming note, in which she said that she perfectly understood, and that she hoped that we might meet again under happier circumstances. I do not know who had in the meanwhile made mischief between us, but a year later, in an interview which he gave a British journalist in Finland, the Grand Duke reproached me with having, after the revolution, given him and the Grand Duchess the cold shoulder — which, he was good enough to add, "was neither very nice nor brave of him." We were then in England, and, in spite of this utterly false and unfriendly statement, my wife, hearing that their children could not get proper food, sent out some cases of provisions. The only thanks which she got was the acknowledgment of their receipt by the nurse.

In a subsequent number of the same review Princess Paley makes the following statement:

Le Roi d'Angleterre, inquiet pour son Cousin Germain — l'Empereur — et pour sa famille, télégraphia aux Souverains par l'entremise de Buchanan, de partir au plus vite pour l'Angleterre, où la Famille trouverait un asile tranquille et sûr. Il ajoutait même que l'Empereur d'Allemagne faisait serment de ne pas faire attaquer par ses sous-marins le navire qui transporterait la Famille Impériale. Que fait Buchanan au reçu de la dépêche, qui était un ordre? Au lieu de la remettre au destinataire — comme c'était son devoir — il va consulter Milioukoff, qui lui conseille de ne pas donner suite à ce télégramme. La plus élémentaire honnêteté, surtout dans un "pays libre" était de remettre la dépêche a qui elle était destinée. Dans son journal 'Les dernières Nouvelles,' Miliukoff a avoué que tout cela était exact et que Sir George Buchanan I'avait fait sur sa demande "et par égard pour le Gouvernement provisoire."

Carried away by her feelings of personal animosity, Princess Paley has made a deliberate misstatement. I was never charged by the King to deliver to the Emperor a telegram urging him to leave at once for England. The only telegram which His Majesty addressed to the Emperor after his abdication was one sent through General Hanbury Williams, our military representative at headquarters, in which not a word was said about his coming to England. As the Emperor had already left for Tsarskoe when this telegram reached Mohileff, General Hanbury Williams forwarded it to me, with the request that I would have it delivered to His Majesty. Now, the Emperor was virtually a prisoner in his palace, and I and my colleagues were debarred from holding any communication with him. The only course, therefore, open to me was to ask Miliukoff to have it at once handed to His Majesty. After consulting Prince Lvoff, Miliukoff agreed to do so. On the following day (March 25) he told me that, much to his regret, he was unable to give effect to his promise. The extremists, he said, were strongly opposed to the idea of the Emperor leaving Russia, and the Government, were afraid that the King's words might be misinterpreted and used as an argument in favour of his detention. I objected that no political meaning could be read into the King's telegram. It was but natural that His Majesty should wish the Emperor to know that his thoughts were with him, and that the misfortunes which had befallen him would in no way alter the King's feelings of friendship and affection. Miliukoff said that he, personally, quite understood this, but that, as others might place a different construction on it, the telegram had better not be delivered at present.

I was subsequently instructed to take no further action in the matter.

As others besides Princess Paley have intimated that neither I nor His Majesty's Government did all that we might have done to get the Emperor out of Russia, I will briefly state what we actually did do.

On March 21, while His Majesty was still at the Stavka, I asked Miliukoff whether it was true, as had been stated in the Press, that the Emperor had been arrested. He replied that this was not quite correct. His Majesty had been deprived of his liberty — a pretty euphemism — and would be brought to Tsarskoe under an escort furnished by

General Alexeieff. I therefore reminded him that the Emperor was the King's near relative and intimate friend, adding that I should be glad to receive an assurance that every precaution would be taken for his safety. Miliukoff gave me this assurance. He was not, he said, in favour of the Emperor proceeding to the Crimea, as His Majesty had originally suggested, and would prefer that he should remain at Tsarskoe till his children had sufficiently recovered from the measles for the Imperial family to travel to England. He then asked whether we were making any arrangements for their reception. On my replying in the negative, he said that he was most anxious that the Emperor should leave Russia at once. He would, therefore, be grateful if His Majesty's Government would offer him an asylum in England, and if they would accompany this offer with an assurance that the Emperor would not be allowed to leave England during the war. I at once telegraphed to the Foreign Office for the necessary authorization. On March 23 I informed Miliukoff that the King and His Majesty's Government were happy to accede to the request of the Provisional Government, and to offer the Emperor and his family a refuge in England, of which they hoped that Their Majesties would avail themselves for the duration of the war. In the event of this offer being accepted, the Russian Government would naturally, I added, have to make suitable provision for their maintenance. While assuring me that a liberal allowance would be made them, Miliukoff begged that the fact that the Provisional Government had taken the initiative in the matter should not be published. I subsequently expressed the hope that no time would be lost in arranging for Their Majesties' journey to Port Romanoff. We relied, I said, on the Provisional Government taking all the necessary measures for their protection, and I warned him that, if any mischance befell them, that Government would be discredited in the eyes of the civilized world. On March 26 Miliukoff told me that they had not yet broached the subject of this projected journey to the Emperor, as before doing so they wanted to overcome the opposition of the Soviet, and that Their Majesties could not in any case start till their children got better.

I more than once received assurances that there was no cause for anxiety on the Emperor's account, and there was nothing more that we could do. We had offered the Emperor an asylum, in compliance with the request of the Provisional Government; but as the opposition of the Soviet, which they were vainly hoping to overcome, grew stronger, they did not venture to assume the responsibility for the Emperor's departure, and receded from their original position. We also had our extremists to count with, and it was impossible for us to take the initiative without being suspected of ulterior motives. It would, moreover, have been useless for us to insist on the Emperor being allowed to come to England, seeing that the workmen had threatened to pull up the rails in front of his train. We could take no steps to protect him on his journey to Port Romanoff. This duty devolved on the Provisional Government. But, as they were not masters in their own house, the whole project eventually fell through.

Since the publication of this chapter in the *Révue de Paris* on March 15, M. Miliukoff has entered a protest against the statement made in its concluding paragraph.

While adhering to all that I said in that statement, I would point out [*Added to Chapter, April 25, 1923*] that I did not call in question the good faith of the Provisional Government, nor suggest that they intentionally placed impediments in the way of the Emperor's departure. On the contrary, I made it clear that it was they who took the initiative in the matter by asking us to offer the Emperor and his family an asylum in England. We, on our part, at once complied with their request, and at the same time pressed them to make the necessary arrangements for the journey to Port Romanoff. More than this we could not do. Our offer remained open and was never withdrawn. If advantage was not taken of it, it was because the Provisional Government failed to overcome the opposition of the Soviet. They were not, as I asserted and as I repeat, masters in their own house.

The genesis and objects of Mr. Henderson's Mission, which M. Miliukoff cites as an indication of our changed attitude, are explained in Chapter 28.

CHAPTER 26
1917

It is difficult to say how many lives were lost in the "bloodless" revolution, but according to most accounts they were under a thousand. It was at Viborg and Cronstadt where the worst scenes were enacted. In both these places a number of officers of the army and of the fleet were either subjected to the most brutal treatment or massacred by the insurgents. In Petrograd, thanks to the measures taken by the Government, the town rapidly resumed its normal aspect and, in spite of the absence of any police force, order generally prevailed. This was especially noticeable on the occasion of the burial of the victims of the revolution in the Champ de Mars on April 5, when a never-ending procession filed past in the most perfect order from ten in the morning till late in the evening. There were in all but some two hundred coffins, and as each one was lowered into the grave a salute was fired from the fortress; but no priests officiated at the ceremony, which was divested of any religious character. Though the Government had, on assuming office, issued a proclamation calling on citizens and soldiers alike to present a united front to the enemy, and telling the latter that they must obey their officers, their efforts to ensure an energetic prosecution of the war were paralysed by the action of the Soviet. A well-disciplined army was regarded by the majority of its members as a dangerous weapon that might be one day turned against the revolution, while the Bolsheviks foresaw that the break-up of the army would place at their disposal a mass of armed peasants and workmen who would help them to rise to power.

The impression which the new Ministers made on me when I went to convey to them our official recognition was not such as to inspire me with great confidence for the future. Most of them already showed signs of strain and struck me as having undertaken a task beyond their strength. Prince Lvoff had, as leader of the Zemstvos, done invaluable work in organizing subsidiary services for supplying the army with warm clothing and other things of which it stood in urgent need, and both he and his colleagues would have made excellent

Ministers in more normal times. But the situation was the very reverse of normal, and in the impending struggle with the Soviet what was required was a man of action, prompt to seize the first favourable opportunity for suppressing that rival and illegally constituted assembly. There was no such man in the Government. Guchkoff, the Minister of War, was capable and energetic and fully alive to the necessity of restoring discipline in the army. But he could not carry his colleagues with him, and eventually resigned as a protest against their weakness. Miliukoff , staunch friend as he was of the Allies, advocated the strict observance of the treaties and agreements which the Imperial Government had concluded with them. He held that the acquisition of Constantinople was a matter of vital moment for Russia; but on this question he was almost in a minority of one in the Government.

As regarded the propaganda which the Socialists were carrying on at the front, Miliukoff was deplorably weak, contending that nothing could be done but to meet it with counter-propaganda. Kerensky was the only Minister whose personality, if not altogether sympathetic, had something arresting about it that did not fail to impress one. As an orator he possessed the magnetic touch which holds an audience spellbound, and in the earlier days of the revolution he unceasingly strove to instil into the workmen and soldiers some of his own patriotic fervour. But, while advocating fighting out the war to a finish, he deprecated any idea of conquest, and when Miliukoff spoke of the acquisition of Constantinople as one of Russia's war aims, he promptly disavowed him. With his hold on the masses, with his personal ascendancy over his colleagues, and in the absence of any qualified rival, Kerensky was the only man to whom we could look to keep Russia in the war. Tereschenko, the Minister of Finance, who subsequently became Minister for Foreign Affairs, was one of the most promising members of the new Government. Very young, an ardent patriot, brilliantly clever, and possessed of an unbounded faith in Kerensky, he was inclined to be too optimistic. I had a great personal regard for him, and we soon became friends. His mother was very rich, and he was supposed — though without cause — to have financed the revolution. An amusing story is told to the effect that when, after the Bolshevik revolution, Tereschenko, together with his colleagues, was imprisoned in the fortress, Schteglovitoff, the reactionary Minister of Justice, and a fellow-prisoner, meeting him in the exercising yard, remarked, "You paid five million roubles to come here. I would have sent you here for nothing."

Having now introduced my readers to the more important members of the Provisional Government, I propose, in order to make them better acquainted with these gentlemen as well as with my personal impressions of an ever fluctuating situation, to give extracts from some of my private letters to the Foreign Office:

April 2.

"There has been a cleavage in the Soviet, and the Socialist-pacifist elements are losing ground. The troops as a whole are said to be in favour of continuing the war, and even the Socialists declare that they will only fraternize with the German Socialists if the latter dethrone the Hohenzollerns. Work is being resumed in the factories, but, owing to many engineers and foremen having been dismissed, the output is much less than it was. The most striking feature of the situation is the perfect order that reigns in the town. It is only in the trams and in the railway trains, where the soldiers force their way into the best seats without paying for them, that there is any real disorder. In certain country districts, however, the peasants have been cutting down the woods of the landed proprietors and are talking of dividing up their lands. But, so far as I am aware, there has been no incendiarism nor anything in the shape of an organized *Jacquerie*."

April 9.

"The Socialistic propaganda in the army continues, and though I miss no opportunity of impressing on Ministers the disastrous consequences of this subversion of discipline, they appear to be powerless to prevent it. Not only are the relations of officers and men most unsatisfactory, but numbers of the latter are returning home without leave. In some cases they have been prompted to do so by reports of an approaching division of the land and by the desire to be on the spot to secure their share of the spoils. I do not wish to be pessimistic, but unless matters improve we shall probably hear of some serious disaster as soon as the Germans decide to take the offensive.

"The Russian idea of liberty is to take things easily, to claim double wages, to demonstrate in the streets, and to waste time in talking and in passing resolutions at public meetings. Ministers are working themselves to death, and have the best intentions; but, though I am always being told that their position is becoming stronger, I see no signs of their asserting their authority. The Soviet continues to act as if it were the Government and has been trying to force Ministers to approach the Allied Governments on the subject of peace.

"Kerensky, with whom I had a long conversation yesterday, does not favour the idea of taking strong measures at present, either against the Soviet or the Socialist propaganda in the army. On my telling him that the Government would never be masters of the situation so long as they allowed themselves to be dictated to by a rival organization, he said that the Soviet would die a natural death, that the present agitation in the army would pass, and that the army would then be in a better position to help the Allies to win the war than it would have been under the old regime.

"Russia, he declared, was in favour of what he termed a war of defence, as opposed to a war of aggression, though a military offensive might be necessary to secure the objects of such a war. The presence of two great democracies in the war might eventually cause the Allies to modify their ideas about the terms of peace, and he spoke of an ideal peace as one 'that would secure to every nation the right to determine its own destiny.' I told him that the reply which we had returned to President Wilson's note showed that we were not fighting for conquest, but for principles which ought to appeal to Russian democracy. The question as to whether effect was to be given to the Constantinople agreement — about which he and Miliukoff held such opposite views — was a question for Russia to decide. Kerensky next spoke of the hopes which he entertained of influencing the German Social Democrats through the Russian Socialists, contending that Russia had brought a new force into the war which, by reacting on the internal situation in Germany, might bring about a durable peace. He admitted, however, that if these hopes proved fallacious we should have to fight on till Germany yielded to the will of Europe.

"It is a misfortune that Petrograd is the seat of Government, as at Moscow and in the provinces the situation is more encouraging, and I fancy that the majority of the nation is as sick of their present capital as I am. It is only here in Petrograd, where there are any number of German agents, that attacks have been made on us in the Press of the extreme Labour party. Otherwise, the general feeling of the country towards us is excellent. There was a great demonstration of some four thousand Cossacks before the Embassy a few days ago. The general in command of these regiments had originally asked me to come and review them on the Champ de Mars, and had kindly offered to place a 'quiet' horse at my disposal. I had to tell him that this was an honour which I, as Ambassador, could not accept, so it was arranged that the regiments should march past the Embassy instead, while I watched them from the balcony. After the march past the commander, with a delegation of some fifty Cossacks, came up to my study and made a patriotic speech in favour of continuing the war.

"Last Saturday I and my French and Italian colleagues were invited to attend a performance at the Opera House that had been organized by the regiment which is credited with having made the revolution, on account of its having been the first to side with the people. We sat in one of the Imperial boxes on the grand tier, while the Government were in a box just opposite us. The central box was occupied by revolutionaries who had returned, after long years of exile, from Siberia. They included Vera Figner, who was sentenced as an accomplice in the assassination of Alexander II, and Vera Zasoulich, who made an attempt on Trepoff's life in 1877. After paying a visit, in one of the *entr'actes*, to the Ministers, we were taken to the central box and introduced to its occupants. No one would have conceived such a thing possible a couple of months ago."

April 10. (To LORD MILNER.)
"What a transformation scene we have witnessed here since you left! Though I was prepared for something unexpected happening, I never imagined that the Empire would crumble to pieces in a few days at the first breath of revolution. . . .

"The military outlook is most discouraging, and I, personally, have abandoned all hope of a successful Russian offensive in the spring. Nor do I take an optimistic view of the immediate future of this country. Russia is not ripe for a purely democratic form of government, and for the next few years we shall probably see a series of revolutions and counter-revolutions, as in the 'troublous times' nearly five hundred years ago. As an old literary lady wrote me the other day, 'Russia is like a Slav woman who loves the man in whom she finds a master and who, in the words of an old peasant song, asks her husband if he does not love her any more when he no longer beats her out of jealousy.' The Emperor was too weak to be respected as a master, while he was blind to the fact that the time for concessions had come. A vast Empire like this, with all its different races, will not long hold together under a Republic. Disintegration will, in my opinion, sooner or later set in, even under a federal system. The Russian people are very religious, but their religion is one of symbols and ceremonies, and in their political life they look for symbols also. They must have as chief of the State some figurehead whom they can look up to with feelings of reverence as the personification of their national ideals."

April 16.
"I yesterday went to see Prince Lvoff, whom I found in a very optimistic mood. On my calling his serious attention to the state of the army, he asked me the reasons for my pessimism. I told him that while Ministers were constantly assuring me that the army would now render us far greater services than it had under the Empire, our

military attachés, who had visited the Petrograd regiments and talked to officers returned from the front, took the contrary view. From what they told me I feared that, unless steps were at once taken to stop the visits of Socialist agitators to the front, the army would never be able to play an effective part in the war. I was also much preoccupied by the fact that the Government seemed powerless to shake off the control of the Committee of Workmen's and Soldiers' Deputies. Lvoff reassured me by declaring that the only two weak points on the front were Dvinsk and Riga. The army as a whole was sound, and any attempts made by agitators to subvert its discipline would meet with no success. The Government could count on the support of the army, and even the Petrograd garrison had, like the troops at the front, offered to suppress the Workmen's Council. This, he added, was an offer which the Government could not accept without exposing themselves to the charge of planning a counter-revolution.

"I cannot share the optimism with which Prince Lvoff and his colleagues regard the situation. The revolution has put the machinery of government temporarily out of gear, and disorganization reigns in many of the administrative services. There is but little enthusiasm for the war, and the Socialist propaganda is being reinforced by the arrival of fresh Anarchists from abroad. I am only speaking of Petrograd, but Petrograd at present rules Russia and is likely to do so for some time to come.

"Referring to the phrase, 'Peace without annexation,' in the resolution passed by the Workmen's Congress, Lvoff remarked that it was open to any interpretation which we liked to put on it, such as liberation from the enemy's yoke.

"I had a long conversation with O'Grady and Thorne — our two Labour delegates — on Saturday. They made an excellent impression on me, and I hope that they may be able to do some good. The extreme Socialists, however, are not very amenable to foreign influence."

Among the recently arrived Anarchists to whom reference is made in the above letter was Lenin, who had travelled in a sealed carriage through Germany. He made his first public appearance at a meeting of the Social Democratic party, and was badly received. He installed himself, without permission and without the Government taking any steps to prevent him, in the palace of the well-known danseuse, Kchessinskaia, and as we drove to the islands in the afternoon we sometimes saw him or one of his followers addressing a crowd from the balcony.

April 23.

"On several points on the front the German soldiers are fraternizing with the Russians, and trying to complete the work begun by the Socialists by urging them to kill their officers. But, disquieting as is the state of the army, I fear that, were we to take collective action here and to threaten to stop the despatch of all war material unless the subversive propaganda is at once suppressed, we should only be playing into the hands of the Socialists, who would contend that Russia, being left without munitions by the Allies, had no choice but to make peace.

"Kerensky dined at the Embassy last night to meet Thorne and O'Grady, and in a long conversation I told him quite frankly why my confidence in the army, and even in the Provisional Government, was shaken. He admitted the accuracy of the facts which I cited, but said that he knew his people and that he only hoped that the Germans would not delay taking the offensive, as, when once the fighting began, the army would pull itself together. He wanted, he said, to make the war a national one, as it was in England and France. He saw no danger of the Provisional Government being overthrown, as only a small minority of the troops were on the side of the Soviet. He added that the Communistic doctrines preached by Lenin have made the Socialists lose ground.

"It will be best for us, at present, to confine our action to individual representations on the part of the Allied Ambassadors. If the results of the fighting should show that the army has been demoralized, we must then have recourse to some collective action.

"Tereschenko told me this morning that the Soviet has been so frightened by Lenin's anarchist speeches that they are becoming more amenable.

"I had some conversation with him about Constantinople. He had, he said, never been a partisan of its permanent occupation by Russia, as it would prove a white elephant and have to be held by a large garrison. He would like to see it made an open port, over which Russia should be given some controlling power. He told me that I was wrong in supposing that Prince Lvoff, like Miliukoff, favoured annexation, but added — to my surprise — that the present Government was in some respects quite as nationalist as the late Imperial Government. There were, he then said, other Turkish provinces, like Armenia and Kurdistan, which were of vital interest to Russia. He evidently shares Kerensky's view that our agreements about Asia Minor ought to be considerably modified, and that the end and aim of all our arrangements about Asia Minor ought to be to bar all possibility of future German penetration. On my remarking that if Russia did not want Constantinople the sooner that she said so the better, he replied that it was not within the competence of the Provisional Government to abandon what Russia had been promised until they had ascertained the washes of the people on the subject.

"Tereschenko is very intelligent and anxious to help us as regards the despatch of the wheat and timber promised. I am on the best of terms with him, and am gradually also making friends with Kerensky, who was at first rather suspicious of my real sentiments about the revolution. Unfortunately, he can talk but little French, but when he dined at the Embassy, Lockhart (our consul-general at Moscow), who talks Russian fluently, acted as our interpreter, and we had a long and straight talk. He told me on leaving that our conversation would bear fruit. I was rather amused at his coming to dinner accompanied by his *officier d'ordonnance*, whom I had not invited. It was a curious proceeding on the part of a Socialist Minister who never wears anything but an ordinary workman's black jacket."

April 30.

"A battle royal is being fought between Kerensky and Miliukoff on the famous formula, 'Peace without annexations,' and as the majority of the Ministers are on Kerensky's side, I should not be surprised if Miliukoff has to go. He would be a loss in many ways, as he represents the moderate element in the Cabinet and is quite sound on the subject of the war, but he has so little influence with his colleagues that one never knows whether he will be able to give effect to what he says.

"The Government is still playing a waiting game, and prefers that the initiative in dealing with Lenin should come from the people. Miliukoff, with whom I discussed the question the other day, said that the popular feeling against Lenin was growing, that the troops were ready to arrest him whenever the Government gave the word, but that the latter did not wish to precipitate matters for fear of provoking civil strife. I told him that the time had come for the Government to act, and that Russia would never win the war if Lenin was allowed to go on inciting soldiers to desert, to seize the land, and to murder. He replied that the Government were but waiting for the psychological moment, which was not, he thought, far distant. Miliukoff also spoke more hopefully of the relative positions of the Provisional Government and the Soviet. The latter is being completely reorganized. Its members have been reduced to six hundred, and a new executive committee has been appointed. The effect of this reorganization will be to render it a more moderate, but at the same time a stronger, body. It is not therefore likely to renounce its claim to control and direct the policy of the Government.

"In view of the military situation on the front and of the new moral element brought into the field by the revolution, I, personally, think that we shall have to consent to the revision of some of our agreements. I am anxious to conciliate the Labour party and the Socialists, who are constantly attacking us for wishing to continue the war for imperialistic ends. I have in my speeches tried to disillusion them of this idea, but without much success. I have also endeavoured to explain that it was not on account of their political opinions, but on account of the want of transport, that some of the Russian political refugees have been prevented returning to Russia. My statements have but exposed me to fresh attacks, while the Socialist Press is accusing our Labour delegates of being the paid emissaries of our Government and not the real representatives of British Labour."

I must supplement what I said at the end of this letter by a short explanatory statement. The attacks made against us in the Press on account of our detention of Russian political refugees had taken such a serious turn that they were even endangering the lives of some of the British factory owners, whose position was already anything but secure owing to the uncertain attitude of the workmen. I had, therefore, to speak seriously to Miliukoff and to request him to take steps to put an end to this Press campaign. On his replying that the Russian Government was being similarly attacked, I said that that was not my concern, and that I could not allow my Government to be used as a lightning conductor to divert the attacks made on his Government. I then reminded him that I had, early in April, informed him that Trotzky and other Russian political refugees were being detained at Halifax until the wishes of the Provisional Government with regard to them had been ascertained. On April 8 I had, at his request, asked my Government to release them and to allow them to proceed on their journey to Russia. Two days later he had begged me to cancel this request and to say that the Provisional Government hoped they would be detained at Halifax until further information had been obtained about them. It was the Provisional Government, therefore, that was responsible for their further detention till April 21, and I should have to make this fact public unless a statement was published to the effect that we had not refused visas to the passports of any Russians presented by the Russian consular authorities. This he consented to do.

The attacks on our Labour delegates had been inspired by a message sent to a Russian Socialist by a member of the Independent Labour Party in London. The matter was eventually put right by Mr.

Hyndman, who requested Kerensky by telegraph to "contradict most emphatically lying statement of the I.L.P."

CHAPTER 27
1917

I will begin the present chapter with a few further extracts from my letters to the Foreign Office.

May 7.
"Since I last wrote we have passed through another crisis, provoked by Miliukoff's note to the Allied Governments on the subject of the war. That note was the result of a compromise between Kerensky's and Miliukoff's supporters. It was accepted and approved by the former in return for the consent of the latter to the communication to the Allies of the Government's proclamation disavowing all ideas of the acquisition of territory by force. Miliukoff has throughout contended that Russia must acquire possession both of Constantinople and the Straits, and for this reason, as well as out of regard for the engagements already entered into by Russia with the Allies, has persistently refused to suggest a revision of existing agreements. He held that to communicate to the Allied Governments the proclamation addressed to the Russian people was an indirect way of inviting them to reconsider their agreements. There was a regular duel between him and Kerensky, and at one moment his position was so shaken that it almost looked as if he would have to go. The Cadet party, of which he is the leader, came to the rescue and brought pressure to bear on the Government by threatening that Miliukoff 's resignation would be followed by that of all the other members of the Government who belong to that party.

"In the end Miliukoff agreed to communicate the proclamation, while the Government approved his covering note. The latter was couched in language which, if it did not actually contravene the letter of the proclamation, was an unquestionable contravention of its spirit. It raised a perfect storm in the Council of Workmen's and Soldiers' Deputies, where it was regarded as a revocation of all that had been said in the proclamation. Thursday was a very critical day. In the afternoon a number of regiments marched to the space in front of the Palais Marie, where the Council of Ministers sits, and joined the crowd that had already assembled there to demonstrate against the Government. Cries of 'Down with the Government,' 'Down with Miliukoff,' were raised, but eventually the troops were persuaded to return to their barracks.

"Later in the evening there were counter-demonstrations directed chiefly against Lenin and his adherents, and after several Ministers had addressed the crowd from the balcony of the palace the tide turned in their favour. The Government remained firm, declaring its complete solidarity on the subject of the note; and the threat that they would resign *en bloc* and that, if they did so, a new Provisional Government would be formed at Moscow, caused the council to pour water into their wine. The council, moreover, were aware, as they subsequently admitted, that they were not themselves strong enough to form an administration, and, on the Government consenting to publish an explanatory *communiqué* on the subject of the note, they declared the incident closed. This agreement was only reached on Friday evening, and during the whole of that afternoon the Nevski and adjoining streets were the scenes of demonstrations and counter-demonstrations. A collision took place on the Nevski between a pro-Lenin and an anti-Lenin crowd, in which several persons were killed and wounded. Between 9 and 10.30 P.M. I had to go out three times on the balcony of the Embassy to receive ovations and to address crowds who were demonstrating for the Government and the Allies. During one of them a free fight took place between the supporters of the Government and the Leninites.

"All is quiet again now and demonstrations have been forbidden for a couple of days. Miliukoff is naturally much elated at what he terms a great victory for the Government; but though the Government is no doubt to be congratulated on the result of its conflict with the council, the latter continues to act as if it were master of the situation.

"Since writing the above I have had a conversation with Tereschenko. In reply to a question of mine, he said that he did not share Miliukoff 's view that the result of the recent conflict between the council and the Government was a great victory for the latter. It had been a moral victory, and fortunately it was the opponents and not the supporters of the Government who were responsible for the bloodshed. It had also demonstrated the numerical superiority of those who had sided with the Government. Against this must be set off the vindication by the council of its exclusive right to give orders to the troops. The Government, he told me, were taking steps to counteract this by increasing the powers of General Korniloff, who is in command of the Petrograd garrison, and he was confident that they would eventually become masters of the situation, though they might have to admit into their ranks one or two Socialists. The workmen were getting disgusted with Lenin, and the latter would, he hoped, be arrested at no distant date.

"He was, he said, most anxious to see peace negotiations opened with Turkey, and, if Constantinople was the only bar to such a peace, he thought that His Majesty's Government might approach the Russian Government with a proposal for its neutralization. I said that were we to do so we should lay ourselves open to the charge of ill-faith, and under present conditions it would be difficult for either Russia or the Allies to propose a revision of their respective agreements. He admitted this, but contended that, with the exercise of a little tact, an exchange of views on the subject of Constantinople might be invited."

May 7.

"I told Kerensky, who came to see me to-day, how discouraged I was by the attacks of the Press that kept on accusing us of waging a capitalist or imperialistic war. Kerensky admitted that some of these attacks had gone too far, but contended that the Government could not violate the principle of freedom of the Press. The extreme left, he said, believed that the German Social Democrats were on the point of revolt, and though, after Scheidemann's recent declaration, he did not personally think this likely, the Germans might, nevertheless, make overtures of peace at any moment. The Allies ought, therefore, to enter into an exchange of views so as to be in a position to state their terms when the time came. If only, he continued, they would make some gesture indicative of their readiness to follow the example set by Russia's renunciation of Constantinople, all these Press attacks would at once cease. On my remarking that Miliukoff had given me to understand that he was determined to keep Constantinople, Kerensky remarked that Miliukoff would not have the deciding voice in the matter."

The Government took a step in the right direction on May 9 by announcing that the right to dispose of the troops was vested exclusively in the military governor of the town. On the same day the Foreign Office handed the Russian *chargé d'affaires* in London our reply to Miliukoff's famous note that had been the cause of the recent crisis. We welcomed that note as showing that Russia would not relax her glorious efforts to defend, with her allies, the cause of justice and humanity. We further noted with satisfaction that the Provisional

Government, while safeguarding Russia's rights, would strictly respect their engagements towards their allies.

On *May* 21 I wrote as follows to the Foreign Office:

"The last two weeks have been very anxious ones, as the victory which the Government had won over the Soviet in the matter of the note to the Powers was not nearly so complete as Miliukoff had imagined. So long as the Soviet maintained its exclusive right to dispose of the troops, the Government, as Prince Lvoff remarked, was 'an authority without power,' while the Workmen's Council was 'a power without authority.' Under such conditions it was impossible for Guchkoff, as Minister of War, and for Korniloff, as military governor of Petrograd, to accept responsibility for the maintenance of discipline in the army. They both, consequently, resigned, while the former declared that if things were to continue as they were the army would cease to exist as a fighting force in three weeks' time. Guchkoff's resignation precipitated matters, and Lvoff, Kerensky and Tereschenko came to the conclusion that, as the Soviet was too powerful a factor to be either suppressed or disregarded, the only way of putting an end to the anomaly of a dual Government was to form a Coalition. Though this idea did not at first find favour with the Soviet, it was eventually agreed that the latter should be represented in the Government by three delegates — Tseretelli, Chernoff and Scobeleff. Miliukoff was at headquarters when the crisis broke out, and he had on his return to choose between accepting the post of Minister of Education or leaving the Cabinet. After a vain struggle to retain charge of the Foreign Office he tendered his resignation.

"Though the more moderate section of the Government, with which I am naturally in sympathy, will be weakened by Miliukoff's and Guchkoff's departure, their loss will, I think, be compensated by gains in other directions. The former is so obsessed by one idea — Constantinople, which to the Socialists represents the imperialistic policy of the old regime — that he has never voiced the views of the Government as a whole; and I personally prefer to deal with someone who, even if he does not see eye to eye with us, can speak with authority as the exponent of the Government's policy. Guchkoff, on the other hand, suffers from a weak heart and is hardly up to his work. His views with regard to discipline in the army are very sound, but he has been unable to impose them on his colleagues. He has not, moreover, any hold on the masses — the principal factor — as he lacks Kerensky's gift of personal magnetism. The new Coalition Government, as I have already telegraphed, offers us the last and almost forlorn hope of saving the military situation on this front. Kerensky, who assumes charge of both the War Office and the Admiralty, is not an ideal War Minister, but he hopes, by going to the front and making passionate appeals to the patriotism of the soldiers, to be able to galvanize the army into new life. He is the only man who can do it if it can be done, but his task will be a very difficult one. The Russian soldier of to-day does not understand for what or for whom he is fighting. He was ready formerly to lay down his life for the Tsar, who in his eyes impersonated Russia; but now that the Tsar has gone Russia means nothing to him beyond his own village. Kerensky has begun by telling the army that he is going to re-establish the strictest discipline, to insist on his orders being obeyed, and to punish all recalcitrants. He has been going round the barracks to-day, and to-morrow he leaves for the front to prepare for the coming offensive.

"Tereschenko, who has succeeded Miliukoff at the Foreign Office, has made a good start by his tactful treatment of the delicate question of our agreements in his statement to the Press. He serves as a link between the bourgeoisie and the democracy, though he is not liked by the extremists. If our reply to Miliukoff's note is published in its present form there is certain to be friction, and the Soviet will try to force his hands. After discussing the question with Albert Thomas, I think that we ought to forestall any action of this kind by ourselves making some conciliatory but non-committal statement on the subject. We have got to face the fact that Socialism is now dominant and that, if we are to enlist its support in favour of a fight to a finish, we must try to win its sympathies. The new Socialist Ministers will naturally be apprised of the contents of Russia's secret agreements, and if the Russian soldiers are told that they must go on fighting till the objects of those agreements have been realized they will demand a separate peace. I would therefore suggest the addition of a paragraph in our reply explaining that our agreements with regard to Asia Minor were inspired by the idea of barring the road to German penetration, but that, if this object can be attained by other means, we would be prepared to re-examine the question as soon as an opportune moment arrived for an exchange of views on the eventual conditions of peace.

"Prince Lvoff is unwell, but as soon as he can see me I propose to call his attention to the disgraceful treatment to which the Empress Marie has been subjected in the Crimea. From a message which Her Majesty sent me through the Swiss tutor of the Grand Duchess Xenia's children, it seems that, about ten days ago, two Roumanian men-of-war, manned by Russian sailors, arrived at Yalta about three o'clock in the morning. After visiting and making perquisitions in several houses, they went to the Grand Duchess Xenia's villa, where the Empress is staying, between five and six o'clock. They entered Her Majesty's bedroom, told her to get up, refused to let her send for her maid, saying that the woman whom they had brought with them to search her would help her to dress. When the Empress had put on a dressing-gown they proceeded to search her bed and mattress, while she sat in an armchair. They ransacked the whole house, taking away all her private correspondence as well as a Danish Gospel. They treated the Grand Duchess and her children in much the same way and stole some of her rings and silver. They also perquisitioned the villa of the Grand Duke Nicholas. I have not yet been able to ascertain whether these perquisitions were made by anyone in authority or whether the sailors, who had been led to believe that there was a wireless telegraphic station in one of these villas and that arms were concealed in them for a counter-revolution, had taken the law into their own hands."

I subsequently made strong representations to several members of the Government on the subject of this outrage, and a special commissary was sent to Yalta to inquire into and report on the whole matter. But anxious as they really were to provide for her protection, the situation in many of the provinces had already got beyond their control, and in the distant Crimea their writ did not run. During the remainder of her stay there the Empress's life was in constant jeopardy, more especially after the November revolution. But Her Majesty's extraordinary courage and self-possession never failed her, as the following incident will show. In order to maintain a strict control over the movements of all the inhabitants of the villa, the Bolsheviks had instituted a roll-call, which the former were obliged to attend every evening. The Empress's name was the last on the roll, and on Her Majesty answering "Present," the commissary remarked, "That's the last of them?" The Empress at once corrected him. "No. I am not the last. You have forgotten my little dog."

One unfortunate result of the reconstruction of the Government was the cancelling of Sazonoff's appointment as Ambassador in London. Sazonoff was so identified with the policy of the Imperial Government, more especially as regarded the question of Constantinople, that he was no longer considered a suitable representative of the new Russia. In telling me this, Tereschenko explained that, as he hoped to retain his services for the final peace negotiations, he was anxious that Sazonoff should not undertake a mission that might sooner or later discredit him in the eyes of the Russian public. He was to have left for London on May 16 together with our Labour delegates and Paléologue, who was being replaced at the French Embassy by Noulens, and it was only on arriving at the station that he was handed a letter from Prince Lvoff requesting him to postpone his departure. Though several names were subsequently submitted to our Government, no Ambassador was ever appointed, and during the rest of the war M. Nabokoff continued to act as *chargé d'affaires*.

In Paléologue, I lost an old friend and colleague with whom, during three critical years, I had been closely associated and on whose loyal collaboration in furthering the common interests, which we both had so much at heart, I could always count. I was also very sorry to say good-bye to my new friends Will Thorne and James O'Grady. They were such splendid types of the British working man that I had hoped that they would have impressed the workmen's delegates in the Soviet and made them understand that we were not fighting the Germans for imperialistic or capitalist aims. But those delegates were not real working men. They were only demagogues. As O'Grady said to Thorne on their first visit to the Soviet: "Look at their hands! Not one of them has done an honest day's work in his life!" They left Petrograd much depressed by their experiences both at the front and in the rear. We had seen a great deal of them during their stay, and I shall never forget the charming little speech which Will Thorne made the last night they dined with us as he drank to our healths after dinner in the drawing-room in his favourite whisky-and-water.

On going one afternoon towards the end of the month to call on Tereschenko, I found him in conference with the three new Socialist Ministers — Tseretelli, Chernoff and Scobeleff — who had later in the day to attend a meeting of the Soviet to give an account of their stewardship. Hearing that I was there, they expressed the wish to see me, and I was accordingly invited to join them. After I had been introduced by Tereschenko, Tseretelli, who acted throughout as spokesman, proceeded to catechize me for nearly two hours on various matters connected with the revolution, the war and our agreements. Had the revolution, he asked, had any repercussion in England; was it likely to bring the views of the British and Russian democracies into harmony, more especially as regarded the war; and did His Majesty's Government really represent British public opinion? I replied that a great revolution like that through which Russia had just passed could not fail to react on all countries to a greater or less extent, and that, as it would certainly exercise a democratizing influence on British public opinion, it would tend to bring our views into closer touch with those of the Russian people. Though we had retained the monarchical system, we were the freest people in the world, and we had long since adopted the maxim, "*Vox populi suprema lex.*" I could assure him that no British Government could retain office that did not represent public opinion.

Turning next to the question of our agreements, he inquired whether, if Russia were to renounce any of the advantages which would accrue to her under them. His Majesty's Government would be prepared to do the same.

In reply to this question I cited the revised text of our above-mentioned note, which I had been authorized to hand Tereschenko only two days previously, stating that, though we considered that there was nothing in those agreements that was opposed to the principles proclaimed by the Russian democracy, we were prepared to re-examine them in concert with our Allies and, if necessary, to revise them. This statement caused him the greatest satisfaction.

The Allied democracies, he then proceeded to say, ought to come to a complete agreement on the subject of their war aims and of their eventual peace terms. Would His Majesty's Government consent to a conference for this purpose?

This, I replied, was a question which I could not answer without consulting my Government, and, on his then pressing me for my personal views, I said that the statement which I had just made to him showed that we were prepared to take a considerable step in the direction which he had indicated. Such a re-examination of our agreements would necessarily entail an exchange of views, but my Government might prefer to conduct the negotiations through its Ambassadors in the Allied capitals instead of at a conference.

Tseretelli next spoke of the necessity of maintaining the closest contact between our two democracies by means of an exchange of visits between the representatives of the various Labour and Socialist groups in each country.

This wish, I assured him, was cordially shared by His Majesty's Government, and I could tell him that Mr. Henderson, who represented our Labour party in the Cabinet, was already on his way to Petrograd on a special mission. That, he replied, was quite satisfactory; but it was generally believed here that His Majesty's Government would not allow representatives of other groups like Mr. Ramsay Macdonald to come. Would I authorize him to tell the Soviet that this was not the case, and that His Majesty's Government would, on the contrary, give Mr. Macdonald every facility? I could not, I said, give him such an assurance, but I would report what he had said to my Government. I would be quite frank with him. When the question of Mr. Macdonald's coming to Petrograd had been first raised by the Soviet I had opposed it, as I was afraid that his visit might encourage the Pacifist movement. From what M, Yandervelde and Mr. O'Grady had since told me about Mr. Macdonald's views, I had changed my opinion and, as I now believed that his visit might do good, I would give his proposal my support.

The last question raised by Tseretelli was that of detaching the German Socialists from their Government. I told him at once that this was, in my opinion, a Utopian idea. The German people had so identified themselves with their Government, both as regarded the latter's annexation policy and its ruthless methods of warfare, that it was only by military pressure or by the blockade that we should ever make them rise against their Government. Chernoff here intervened with the remark that the revolution had at one time been regarded as a Utopian idea and that it had, nevertheless, been realized. I disputed the correctness of this assertion, saying that it had only come sooner than had been expected. Tseretelli then said that the reason why he wanted the Allied and Russian Socialists to go to Stockholm was in order that they might tell the Germans to their faces that if they did not make civil war on their Government we should discard them altogether. On my asking him, as I was leaving, whether the Government could count on the Soviet's support for the prosecution of the war, he replied in the affirmative. The Soviet, he said, wanted the democratization, not the demoralization, of the army.

A few days later I received the following telegram from Lord Robert Cecil, who was then in charge of the Foreign Office, with reference to the above conversation: "Your Excellency spoke with great courage and discretion under very difficult circumstances. I desire to express my warm approval."

Of the three Socialist Ministers Tseretelli, who was Minister for Posts and Telegraphs, alone impressed me favourably. A Georgian, of a princely family, and the leader of the Social Democrats, he had, under the Empire, spent several years in Siberia under a sentence of hard labour. With a refined and sympathetic personality, he attracted me by his transparent honesty of purpose and his straightforward manner. He was, like so many other Russian Socialists, an Idealist; but, though I do not reproach him with this, he made the mistake of approaching grave problems of practical politics from a purely theoretical standpoint. There was nothing of the Idealist about his two colleagues. Scobeleff, the Minister of Labour, was also a Social Democrat, who held very advanced views as to the rights of workmen in the factories. Of a nervous, excitable temperament and not overburdened with brains, he was rather insignificant in appearance and did not strike me as a man who would ever make his mark. Tchernoff, the Minister of Agriculture, had, on the other hand, the appearance of a man of strong character and considerable ability. He belonged to the advanced wing of the Social Revolutionary party, and advocated the immediate nationalization of the land and its division among the peasants without awaiting the decision of the Constituent Assembly. He was generally regarded as dangerous and untrustworthy, and I found him the reverse of sympathetic. He had been among the Russian refugees detained at Halifax — a fact of which he was careful to remind me.

Before proceeding farther, I had better perhaps say a few words respecting the views and aims of the different political groups. The so-called *bourgeois* party was represented, in the main, by the Cadets and, in a lesser degree, by certain Moscow industrial groups. They advocated an energetic prosecution of the war and the restoration of discipline in the army, while they were in favour of leaving the solution of the various social and constitutional questions raised by the revolution to the final decision of the Constituent Assembly. They did not, however, wish that assembly to meet till after the local elections for the newly organized Zemstvos and town councils had provided the necessary machinery for organizing and controlling the general elections.

Of the Socialist groups, the Social Revolutionaries, of whom Kerensky was the leader, were agrarian, in contradistinction to the Social Democrats, who, under the leadership of Tseretelli, represented the interests of the proletariats of the towns. Their watchword had always been, "Land and Liberty." During the latter part of the last and the commencement of the present century they had adopted terrorism as a weapon for attaining their ends. After the murder of the Grand Duke Serge in 1905 terroristic methods had been suspended, and political assassinations, such as that of Stolypin in 1911, had been the exception rather than the rule. The Social Democrats, on the other hand, had, after the conference held in London in 1903 — at which the Leninites outvoted their opponents on the question of the party organization — been split up into Mensheviks and Bolsheviks, or Minority and Majority Socialists, though moderates and extremists would have been a more appropriate term. The former, like most of the Social Revolutionaries, had advocated collaboration with the advanced Liberals for the overthrow of the Empire, and, now that this had been done, they aimed at the establishment of a Republic on democratic lines. The Bolsheviks, on the contrary, would have nothing to do with any *bourgeois* group, no matter how advanced it might be. With them it was the masses which alone counted, and it was to the workmen and to the peasants that they turned for the support necessary to enable them to carry out their programme — the establishment of the dictatorship of the proletariat and the transformation of the whole social system. Their battle-cry had from the outset been, "All power to the Soviet." Neither the Mensheviks nor the Social Revolutionaries were prepared to rally to this call, but those of their members who took office did, nevertheless, recognize their responsibilities to that assembly and did invariably render an account to it of all their official acts. The moderates of both Socialist groups never, indeed, forgot that, in spite of the differences which separated them from the Bolsheviks, they had been and remained "Comrades," and they were thus in closer touch with them than with their Liberal collaborators. Though they were in agreement with the latter on the question of leaving to the Constituent Assembly the decision on all fundamental questions, they were led by the march of events to anticipate several of its decisions.

As regarded the war, both Mensheviks and Social Revolutionaries advocated the speedy conclusion of peace without annexations or contributions. There was, however, a small Menshevik group, led by Plekhanoff, that called on the working classes to co-operate for the purpose of securing the victory over Germany, which would alone guarantee Russia's new-won freedom. The Bolsheviks, on the other hand, were out and out "Defeatists." The war, as Lenin had contended at the Keinthal Conference in 1916, had to be brought to an end by any means and at any cost. The soldiers had to be induced by an organized propaganda to turn their arms, not against their brothers in the enemy ranks, but against the reactionary bourgeois Governments of their own and other countries. For a Bolshevik there was no such thing as country or patriotism, and Russia was but a pawn in Lenin's game. If his dream of a world revolution was ever to be realized, the war being raged by Russia against the Germans had to be converted into a civil war at home — and this was now the end and aim of his policy.

CHAPTER 28
1917

After having been accused by Princess Paley of having made the Embassy *a foyer de propagande révolutionnaire*, it was really hard that I should, shortly after my conversation with the Socialist Ministers, have been attacked by the Bolsheviks on the charge of its being the centre of the counter-revolutionary movement. Tseretelli's name — and this, considering his antecedents, was rather surprising — was also coupled with mine, and we were represented as being the chief promoters of the aforesaid movement. This charge, no doubt, owed its origin to the fact that we were conducting an active Allied propaganda in favour of the war and for the purpose of exposing German misrepresentations. The Germans had for some time past been paying me the most flattering attentions. In April the *Hamburger Nachrichten* had published an article — of which the writer, fortunately for my reputation, had never witnessed my exploits on the links — attributing my success as a diplomatist to my passion for golf. "The conditions," it went on to say, "in which this tiresome game is played do really produce the qualities necessary for any statesmanlike or diplomatic work. Silent, tough, resigned — the good golfer goes round the field, keeping his eye on his ball and steers for his goal. Sir George Buchanan walked round the golf links of Europe for years, until at last he was able to hole out in Petrograd."

The article in the *Hamburger Nachrichten* furnished Mr. Punch with the subject of some verses on "A School for Statesmen," which, I trust, he will not object to my reproducing here:

Oft have I wondered, as my weapon's edge
  Disintegrated solid chunks of greenery,
Or as my pilule flew the bounding hedge
  Into outlying sections of the scenery.
      What moral value might accrue
      From billiards played beneath the blue.

Little I fancied, when I topped the sphere,
  And on its candour left a coarse impression,

Or in the bed of some revolting mere
  Mislaid three virgin globes in swift succession.
    That I was learning how to grip
    The rudiments of statesmanship.

Yet so it was. I schooled myself to gaze
  Upon the object with a firmly glued eye.
And, though I moved by strange and devious ways.
  To keep in view the goal or *finis ludi*,
    And ever let my language be
    The language of diplomacy.

Thus Balfour learned the politician's game.
  And thus Lloyd George was trained to be a premier;
Thence many a leader, who has leapt to fame.
  Got self-control, grew harder, tougher, phlegmier,
    Reared in the virtues, which prevail
    At Walton Heath and Sunningdale.

Golf being thus the source of so much good,
  I own my conscience suffers certain wrenches.
Recalling how the Links at Chorley Wood
  Have seen me on the Sabbath carving trenches,
    Where Tommies might be put to pitch
    The deadly bomb from ditch to ditch.

For I reflect that my intruding spade,
  That blocked the foursome and debarred the single,
May well have checked some statesman yet unmade,
  Some budding Hogge, some mute inglorious Pringle;
    And that is why my shovel shrinks
    From excavating other links.

O. S.

The Germans now paid me a still greater compliment, as our legation at Stockholm reported that a German agent there was trying to induce a Russian, whose name I have forgotten, to assassinate me; but I was somewhat humiliated on hearing that the price set on my head was only three hundred roubles. The local Bolshevik organ at Riga at the same time published an article stating that Russia was now governed by the all-powerful and autocratic Tsar Buchanan the First — that the Ministers did whatever he told them, and that it was at his orders that

Kerensky was re-establishing discipline in the army and preparing an offensive.

It would have been well, both for themselves and Russia, had Ministers heeded my advice and taken effective measures for restoring discipline, instead of relying solely on the effect of patriotic speeches.

On May 24 I received a telegram from Lord Robert Cecil, who was then in charge of the Foreign Office, informing me that the War Cabinet were impressed with the necessity of creating a more favourable attitude among Russian Socialists and workmen towards the war, and of rectifying the false impressions that were being circulated in Russia about our aims. Feeling that this could be done with better chance of success by a Labour leader than by anyone else, they had decided to send out Mr. Henderson on a special mission. After kindly expressing warm appreciation of my work. Lord Robert went on to say that they felt sure that Mr. Henderson could count on my cordial co-operation, and suggested that, if I saw no objection, it might be well were I, a few weeks after Mr. Henderson's arrival, to come to London to give the Government the benefit of my personal advice.

While I quite appreciated the reasons that had prompted the War Cabinet to send out Mr. Henderson, I failed to understand why they were so anxious that I should come home. "If," as I afterwards wrote to Lord Hardinge, "it was because they were afraid that, were I to remain, Mr. Henderson would not have a free hand to deal with the situation, and that I might not work in line with him, I can only say that such lack of confidence greatly distresses me. When Lord Milner came out to the conference last winter, I was only too ready to efface myself, and it was a real pleasure for me to work under him. I should have been glad to do the same again and to serve under Henderson, who is a Cabinet Minister. His mission will be one of extraordinary difficulty, and, as I understand the Russians better than most people, I might have been able to help him in many ways."

As, however, there was no question of my remaining on, I was determined, at any rate, to have my own position cleared up. I accordingly sent the following reply to Lord Robert's telegram:

> Please assure Mr. Henderson that he can count on my most cordial co-operation and support. As regards question of my going on leave, I am entirely at your orders. I should like to know the approximate date at which you would wish me to start on leave, and whether I am to consider that leave as my definite recall.

On May 29 I received the following reply:

It is difficult to give you even an approximate date for coming on leave until we see how things shape after Henderson's arrival. In any case, I think it very desirable that you should not start until he has got thoroughly into touch with the Russian Government and the Socialist leaders.

There is no question of your being *recalled*. Your services have been and remain most highly valued by His Majesty's Government, and, so far as can be seen at present, we shall most certainly wish to have you back in Petrograd in due course.

What I appreciated much more than the soothing syrup thus dispensed by the Foreign Office were the many proofs of sympathy and attachment given me by the members of my staff. While some took upon themselves to telegraph to their friends at the Foreign Office and the War Office, protesting against the idea of my going, others declared that they would send in their resignations if I went. Henderson arrived on June 2, with George Young, afterwards first secretary at Vienna, who proved most helpful in many ways. In my first conversation with Henderson I expressed my feelings and wishes in the frankest language; but, though quite friendly, he gave me clearly to understand that I should have to go. As regarded the genesis of his mission, he told me that he had one day been asked to come to the War Cabinet half an hour after his colleagues, and that when he got there he had been informed by the Prime Minister that the Cabinet had decided that he was to go to Petrograd on a special mission, and that they wished him to start on the following day. It had subsequently been suggested to him that he should, in a few weeks' time, intimate to me that I had better go home on leave. He had refused to do this, and had told the Foreign Office that they ought to tell me so themselves — and to tell me at once.

Henderson dined with us next night to meet Prince Lvoff and Tereschenko. Among our other guests were Vandervelde, the Belgian Socialist Minister, and Albert Thomas, the French Minister of Munitions, who had taken over charge of the Embassy when Paléologue left. During the two months which he had spent in Russia Thomas had not only tried to bring home to Ministers the need of firmness in dealing with the internal situation, but had endeavoured to rouse with his fiery eloquence the fighting spirit of the people. At Petrograd, at Moscow and at the front he had addressed numberless meetings of soldiers and workmen, and it was not his fault if the seed which he sowed fell on barren soil. We were always delighted to see him, as his whole personality radiated cheerfulness and prevented our feeling depressed. Talking to me after dinner, he asked: "What would you have said had you been told five years ago that I and two other Socialists would one day be guests at your table?" "The very idea of such a thing would," I replied, "have appalled me." But now *la guerre a changé tout cela* — and we are all "comrades." A fortnight later, when he was dining with us on the night before his return to France, he told me that as soon as he had heard that I was going home he had telegraphed to the Prime Minister, saying that if I went there would, after his own departure, be no one left who understood the situation. He hoped that it would now be all right, as Henderson had, in the course of his last conversation with him, said, "I have decided to leave Buchanan."

I afterwards heard from another source that Henderson had consulted Prince Lvoff as to whether it was better that I should remain in charge of the Embassy or that he should replace me. Lvoff had replied that I had rendered great services under the Empire, and that, though my close relations with the Court had, after the revolution, made me an object of suspicion, I had adapted myself loyally to the new situation. I had, it was true, been attacked by the Bolsheviks, but I enjoyed the confidence of the Government and the Moderates. He would, he added, consult his colleagues. On his doing so, I received a vote of confidence from all, even including the Socialist Ministers. I am glad to have this opportunity of rendering justice to Henderson, who behaved in the most gentlemanly and straightforward manner. He weighed the evidence — pro and con — quite impartially, and finally wrote a very nice letter to the Prime Minister recommending my remaining on. Mr. Lloyd George agreed, and Henderson returned home early in July. During the six weeks that he was at Petrograd we worked together on the most cordial terms. We held the same views on many questions, and particularly with regard to Ramsay Macdonald's suggested visit to Petrograd, as his visit could not possibly do any harm, while the proceedings of the Russian extremists might, we hoped, serve as an object-lesson to him. In consequence of our representations passports were granted him, but owing to the action of the Seamen's Union he never started. The following little story will serve to show what a good fellow Henderson really was. He was talking to my wife after dining at the Embassy the night before he was leaving when he suddenly burst out laughing, and on my wife asking what had amused him, he said, "It's all so funny! It's you, not I, who ought to be going" I was really grateful to him for the line which he had taken, for my fate was entirely in his hands. But, after having been officially told that there was no question of my recall, it was rather a shock to me to discover that he had full powers to replace me should he think it desirable. As it turned out, the result of his mission was most satisfactory to me personally.

The internal situation, meanwhile, had undergone but little change. The Government had dealt firmly with an attempt made by the sailors at Cronstadt to set up an independent Republic of their own, and had also scored a certain success by stopping an armed demonstration that had been organized by the Bolsheviks. In a conversation which I had with him on June 27, Prince Lvoff assured me that my fears as to Russia being unable to continue the war were groundless, and that, now that the Government had the requisite forces at their disposal, they were determined to maintain order. These assurances were discounted by the fact that on the very next day they failed to enforce compliance with the orders which they had given for the evacuation of two villas which had been occupied and held by the Bolsheviks, a failure which, as I told Tereschenko, was tantamount to an abdication of their authority.

The Soviet, on the other hand, had not been idle. They had already, in May, addressed an appeal to the Socialists of all countries to send representatives to an international conference at Stockholm for the purpose of securing a general peace, on principles acceptable to the proletariat, in accordance with the prescribed formula, "without annexations or contributions." In June a new factor was introduced into the situation by the convocation of an all-Russian congress of delegates from the workmen's councils throughout Russia. The idea of its promoters had been to transform the local Petrograd council into a national one, that would be invested with greater authority and influence, while the admission of workmen's and soldiers' deputies from the provinces would, it was thought, act in a moderating sense and establish closer co-operation with the Government. It had also been their intention to include in it representatives of the peasants, but as the latter demanded representation on a proportional basis — namely, about 80 per cent. — the proposal fell through, and the peasants, who had already an independent council of their own, took no part in it. At the opening sitting of the congress Lenin made a violent speech denouncing the war aims of the Allies, which, as Kerensky showed, was taken word for word from the latest German wireless. The only outcome of the sitting was an invitation to all citizens to take part in an unarmed and peaceful demonstration on July 1 in support of the Government before the burial place of the victims of the revolution on the Champ de Mars. Owing to the Bolsheviks having threatened to come out armed, most of the moderates remained at home, and the few who did participate in it were roughly handled. As the Embassy almost adjoins the Champ de Mars, we were, as usual, the centre of the demonstration; but with the exception of a few free fights, which we watched from our windows, and some muttered Bolshevist threats that our house was the next that they would burn, nothing unpleasant occurred.

On the following day telegrams were received from Kerensky from the front announcing a brilliant commencement of the long-projected offensive. In the evening there were several patriotic demonstrations in front of the Embassy, and at the head of one of them came Miliukoff, who made me a speech from his automobile, to which I replied from the balcony. It was, however, rather a case of "save me from my friends," as the sight of Miliukoff caused a group of soldiers of the Pavlovski Regiment to start a counter-demonstration. Some of them were even heard to say, "Let's go for that house and kill them all" — but nothing came of it. The hopes inspired by Kerensky's optimistic telegrams were not destined to be long-lived. He had done all that a man could do who relied on speeches and on speeches alone to produce a sustained offensive in a war-weary army whose discipline had already been undermined. The main offensive was launched on the south-western front, and was to have been followed by minor offensives on other fronts, and as the Russians had a superiority both of guns and bayonets, there was no reason why, had it been vigorously pushed, it should not have been successful. It began with an initial success, and on July 8 the army under General Korniloff broke the Austrian front and occupied Halicz and Kaluscz. But while at various points along the line Kerensky had been preaching discipline and a fight to the death, he had allowed Bolshevik agitators at other points to preach peace and fraternization with the Germans. Instead, moreover, of restoring the disciplinary powers of the officers, he had sent commissaries to assist in the maintenance of discipline in the different armies. While some of the regiments fought gallantly, and while the officers sacrificed their lives heroically in what was too often but a vain attempt to induce their men to follow their example, no reliance could be placed on troops that had acquired the habit of debating whether the orders to attack should be obeyed or not. It was hardly surprising, therefore, that when, on July 19, the enemy attacked, one of the regiments engaged beat a precipitate retreat and the front was broken. In the course of a few days the rout became general, and in addition to the places occupied during the offensive, Tarnopol and Stanislau were abandoned.

I must now, once more, draw on my letters to the Foreign Office for an account of the crisis and of what was meanwhile taking place at Petrograd.

July 12.

"Kerensky 's work among the troops at the front has throughout been hampered by the anti-war propaganda of the agitators, whom the Bolsheviks are constantly sending there to dissuade the men from joining in the offensive. The political atmosphere is such that he does not venture to appeal to the troops to fight for victory, but for the speedy conclusion of peace. For peace is the universal desideratum. It is this fact that renders it essential for us to do nothing to give the pacifists here a pretext for contending that the Allies are prolonging the war for imperialistic aims. A refusal of the proposal for a conference, which Tereschenko submitted to Albert Thomas about a month ago, would certainly be interpreted in this sense; and, great as will be the difficulties with which we shall be confronted at such a conference, they will have to be faced sooner or later. To postpone the discussion of our war aims will but discourage Russia from continuing her active participation in the war.

"From what Tereschenko has said to me about the proposed conference, I do not think that he wants to bind us down to any definite peace terms. Those terms would, as he remarked to me one day, depend on the course of the military operations, and it would, therefore, be difficult to define them with precision so long as the war was in progress. On another occasion he spoke of the elaboration of a minimum and maximum peace programme as being worth considering. He is not an idealist, as are most of his Socialist colleagues, and we can, I think, count on his doing his best to induce them to take a practical view of things."

July 23.

"The events of the past week have, once more, proved the truth of the saying that Russia is a country of surprises. Early on Monday morning I received a telephone message telling me that the four Cadet members of the Government had resigned during the night. Tereschenko and Tseretelli had just returned from Kieff with a draft agreement, which they had negotiated with the Rada for the settlement of the Ukrainian question. The Cadets took exception to it on the ground that the Government would, if they ratified it, be usurping the functions of the Constitutional Assembly. It was not, however, so much considerations of this kind as the fact that they had throughout been in a minority of four that decided them to refuse to assume any further responsibility for measures of which they disapproved.

"Tereschenko, whom I saw in the evening, severely criticized their action. They had, he said, put an end to the existence of the Coalition Government at a moment when Russia was faced with dangers, both from within and from without, while they had not sufficient backing in the country to replace that Government themselves. Tereschenko, nevertheless, spoke with confidence about the internal situation, and when I left him at six o'clock had not the slightest suspicion of the storm that was brewing.

"The first signs which we saw of it were the reappearance of motor lorries and cars filled with armed soldiers and machine guns as we were about to drive to the islands after dinner. We had only got half-way across the bridge when, finding the road blocked, we turned back and took a short drive along the quay and through the town. On our return to the Embassy at a quarter-past nine we found groups of soldiers in excited conversation, and shortly afterwards a long procession crossed the bridge. It was composed of workmen and of three regiments, all fully armed, with banners bearing the usual inscriptions: 'Down with the Capitalist Ministers,' 'Down with the War,' 'Give us Bread.' Soon afterwards we heard shots at the back of the Embassy, and saw people bolting for safety down the quay.

"As Kerensky was leaving that evening for the front, some of the soldiers drove in motors to the Warsaw station with the intention of arresting him, but arrived there after his train had left. Others went to the Palais Marie to arrest Prince Lvoff and his colleagues, who were holding a Cabinet Council there. On being invited to enter and to talk to the Ministers, they thought better of it, fearing that a trap was being laid for them, and contented themselves with requisitioning the Ministers' motors. On Tuesday things looked very black, as several thousand sailors had arrived from Cronstadt. In the afternoon another monster procession crossed the bridge by the Embassy, and rifle and machine gun firing went on in many parts of the town during the rest of the day. About luncheon time Tereschenko telephoned to say that as soon as troops arrived from the front the disorders would be put down with a firm hand, and that as most of the fighting would probably take place near the Embassy, he would feel happier if we were to go away for a few days. This, however, I declined to do.

"The position of the Government on that afternoon was a very critical one, and had not the Cossacks and a few loyal regiments come out in time to save them they would have had to capitulate. While we were at dinner the Cossacks charged the Cronstadt sailors, who had gathered in the square adjoining the Embassy, and sent them flying for their lives. The Cossacks then rode back along the quay, but a little higher up they got caught in a cross-fire. We saw, several riderless horses returning at full gallop, and two Cossacks who were bringing back a prisoner were attacked by some soldiers and all but murdered under our windows. On Tuesday night an order was issued forbidding anyone to go out in the streets after noon on the following day, and all the bridges were either opened or strongly guarded so as to prevent the Bolsheviks crossing over from the other side. A guard, consisting of an officer and ten men, had been placed in the Embassy, and General Knox and Colonel Thornhill also slept in the house.

"Wednesday was a more or less quiet day, but at six o'clock on Thursday morning we were woke up by our officer, who begged us to retire to the back of the house. The Government troops, he told us, had been ordered to seize the fortress, which had been occupied by the insurgents, as well as Lenin's headquarters on the other side of the river; and, were the guns of the fortress to be turned on the troops stationed on this side, we should be in the line of fire. A little later Tereschenko telephoned, placing an apartment in the Ministry at our disposal; but I did not like to leave the Embassy, while my wife and daughter would not leave me. We spent an exciting morning watching the movements of the troops. A strong guard of soldiers and sailors, with several armoured cars, were stationed by the bridge, while artillery was held in reserve behind the Embassy. An alarm was occasionally sounded, and then a few troops would dash half-way across the bridge, kneeling down and taking such cover as they could find. By one o'clock both the fortress and the villa where Lenin had established his headquarters had surrendered, and, though on Friday night there was again a good deal of firing with machine guns from some river barges, we have had since then a comparatively quiet time.

"In the course of conversations which I had with him on Thursday and Friday, Tereschenko told me that Kerensky had telegraphed from the front, saying that he could not continue to work with colleagues, who were constantly temporizing with the extremists instead of putting them down. I said that I quite sympathized with him. The Government had been too weak. The loyal troops, after occupying the offices of the Bolshevist organ, the Pravda, and seizing compromising documents, had been ordered to evacuate the premises and to restore the documents; the Cronstadt sailors had been disarmed, but had not been punished; and two of Lenin's lieutenants who had been arrested had been released. I did not know which of the Ministers were opposed to the adoption of stern measures against the promoters of the disorders which had resulted in five hundred casualties, but I was afraid that the Prime Minister was not strong enough to take advantage of this unique opportunity of suppressing anarchy once for all. Tereschenko replied that the opposition had come from the Soviet, but that their eyes had now been opened to the gravity of the situation. There had, he added, been a moment during the recent disorders when many of them might have lost their lives at the hands of the insurgents had not the Government sent troops for their protection."

CHAPTER 29
1917

Owing to the loss of heavy artillery, guns and military supplies, the situation at the front was becoming desperate, while the economic and financial position was almost as serious. But, black as was the outlook, I was nevertheless inclined to take a more hopeful view of things. The Government had suppressed the Bolshevik rising and seemed at last determined to act with firmness. So long as anarchy reigned supreme there could be no real or lasting improvement, but the restoration of order would, I trusted, react favourably on all branches of the national life. Kerensky had returned from the front on the evening of July 19, and had at once demanded, as a condition of his retaining office, that the Government should have complete executive control over the army without any interference on the part of soldiers' committees, that an end should be put to all Bolshevik agitation, and that Lenin and his associates should be arrested. The public and the majority of the troops were on the side of the Government, as their indignation had been aroused by the publication of documents proving that the Bolshevik leaders were in German pay. The psychological moment had come for the Government to deal a final and crushing blow at the enemy .within the gates. But the Soviet raised objections. They had no wish to see the charges brought against the Bolsheviks investigated for fear that some of their own members might be compromised, and they declined to invest the Government with the powers demanded by Kerensky unless it took its stand on a thoroughly democratic platform. The conditions on which they insisted were the immediate proclamation of a Republic and the adoption of Chernoff's scheme for the settlement of the land question, without awaiting the decision of the Constituent Assembly. These conditions gave rise to a stormy discussion in the Cabinet, the Socialist Ministers siding with the Soviet, while Prince Lvoff threatened to resign, declaring that, were the Government to accept them, they would be acting beyond their powers and usurping those of the Constituent Assembly. Tereschenko vainly tried to play the part of mediator and to evolve some compromise that would reconcile these conflicting views. While the discussion was still proceeding Kerensky was called away to fulfil an engagement to address a hussar regiment. On his return he was handed a telegram which brought the first news of the Germans having broken through the Russian front. On his reading it to his colleagues, Prince Lvoff expressed the wish to resign the premiership in Kerensky 's favour, as being a younger and more active man and in closer touch with the democracy. This was agreed to, and Kerensky was at the same time accorded all the powers which he had asked for. As he was to retain the post of Minister of War, it was further decided that Nekrassoff should be appointed Vice-President of the Council, and that he should replace Kerensky during the latter's absence at the front. Nekrassoff, who belonged to the left wing of the Cadet party, was a strong and capable man, who was credited with the ambition of becoming Prime Minister. He did not, however, inspire confidence, as he was too much of an opportunist and had changed parties more than once in order to advance his own interests.

On my calling on him a few days later, Tereschenko assured me that the Government was now completely master of the situation and would act independently of the Soviet. Taking me to the window, he showed me the disarmed men of the machine gun regiment drawn up in the Winter Palace square, and said that they were about to be entrained for work on the Murman railway. The committee of the All Russian Workmen's and of the All Russian Peasants' Councils had, he further told me, given the Government full powers to deal with the army, as well as with the Anarchists in the rear, and Kerensky had already, in compliance with Korniloff's request, empowered the army commanders to shoot without trial all men who disobeyed orders. But, though he now possessed all the powers necessary for dealing with the situation, Kerensky completely failed to turn them to proper account. He made no attempt to find and arrest Lenin; he countermanded the order for the arrest of Trotzky and another leading Bolshevik on account of their being members of the executive committee of the Soviet, and he contented himself with issuing proclamations ordering the workmen to deliver up their arms, instead of allowing the military authorities to disarm them by force. In fact, I doubt very much if any of the organizers of the Bolshevik rising or any of the men who took part in it were ever really punished. I was anything but satisfied with the attitude of the Government, and in my conversation with Tereschenko I endeavoured to impress on him the necessity of applying the same disciplinary measures in the rear as had been sanctioned at the front, and of reorganizing the defective transport system that was at the root of most of Russia's economic troubles. I further suggested that the troops at the front should be reduced to the minimum necessary for holding the Germans, and that the rest should be brought back to work in the rear under a system of national obligatory service.

Kerensky, meanwhile, was endeavouring to reconstruct his Government with a view to giving it a more national character. The Cadets, with whom he had entered into negotiations, attached as conditions to their participation the resignation of Tchernoff, the active prosecution of the war, and the independence of the Government from the Soviet — with all of which, as I told Tereschenko, I heartily sympathized. The first condition proved unacceptable, as Kerensky was afraid that Tchernoff's enforced resignation would lose him the support of the Social Revolutionaries.

I will now once more quote from my correspondence with the Foreign Office and from a diary which I had begun to keep after the revolution.

August 2.

"Tereschenko told me this morning that both he and Kerensky had tendered their resignations, but had withdrawn them at the request of their colleagues. Tchernoff had also resigned and had, on going to the Soviet, received a great ovation. Tereschenko then proceeded to say that if the Government did not now apply stringent measures they would have to give up their places to men of the counter-revolution. His country had the first place in his eyes, and the situation brooked no delay. He had told Kerensky that unless the latter acted with vigour he would resign. It was necessary, in his opinion, to militarize the whole country, to repress all disorders, and to admit Komiloff into the Government. Kerensky shared these views, but his hands were tied, while the Socialist Ministers did not wish to assume responsibility for the measures necessary to save the country. Tseretelli, he said, would prefer to leave the Government and to act as an independent member of the Soviet, while the Cadets wanted a complete party triumph and to replace the Government.

"The situation is so obscure that I personally see no daylight. The carrying out of Tereschenko's policy can only be undertaken by a Government in which the Socialists are strongly represented, otherwise it will be accused of paving the way for a counter-revolution, with the result that there will be another Bolshevik rising and a lapse into anarchy. The Cadets have not got the army with them, and it is premature for them to assume office with any prospect of success."

August 2.
"I have reason to believe that the non-Socialist members of the Government would much prefer that the Stockholm conference should not take place for fear that peace talk might have a bad influence on the army. They will not, however, place any obstacles in the way of the attendance of Russian Socialists, but they will not consider themselves bound by the decisions which the conference may take. They are anxious that it should be attended by Socialists of other allied countries so that Russia should not be left *tête-à-tête* with Germany.

"My personal opinion is that it would be a mistake to leave the Germans a clear field at Stockholm, more especially as it would render our attitude open to misconstruction here. As we have no intention of being bound by the conference's decisions, I do not see how the attendance of British Socialists can prejudice our interests."

August 4.
"I would venture to submit that the time has come for us, in reply to Russia's appeal for our co-operation, to tell her Government frankly that, while we will continue to do all that is possible to relieve the pressure on her front by pushing our offensive, we expect her in return to concentrate all her energies on the reorganization of her armies and to re-establish discipline both at the front and in the rear. It would be well were the Allied Ambassadors to be instructed to speak in the above sense to the president of the council as soon as the new Government is formed."

As a result of the above telegram the representatives of the Allied Governments, assembled in conference in London, sent Kerensky, through their Ambassadors at Petrograd, a message which, though intended as a protest, did but express a pious wish for the reestablishment of discipline in the army. I was, however, authorized, if I thought it advisable, to speak to him privately, in the name of His Majesty's Government, on the lines which I had suggested.

August 6.
"Kerensky has formed a Government composed of six Socialist and eight non-Socialist members. Five of the latter belong to the Cadet party. Aksentieff, the president of the Council of Peasants, becomes Minister of the Interior, and Savenkoff, the former Terrorist, vice-Minister of War. Korniloff is appointed Commander-in-Chief.

August 11.
"I met Kerensky to-day at a luncheon given by Tereschenko. In the course of our conversation I said that I was much depressed by the fact that everybody seemed to regard the situation entirely from the party point of view, and that political considerations had precedence over military exigencies. Referring next to a request which Korniloff had addressed to us for more guns, I remarked that we had seen the initial success of the July offensive converted into a rout owing to lack of discipline, and that our military authorities were hardly likely to accede to the above request unless assured that Korniloff would be given full powers to restore discipline. It would, I added, help to reassure my Government could I inform them that Petrograd had been included in the front zone and placed under martial law. Kerensky, after declaring that the Government were determined to maintain order, said, somewhat huffily, that if we were going to haggle about guns and would not help Russia, we had better say so at once. I told him that he had misunderstood me, that we had had every desire to help Russia, but that it was no good our sending guns to her front if they were to be captured by the Germans. We had need of every gun we could get on our own front, and by using them there we were rendering her effective assistance."

A week later I received a reply to the above telegram instructing me to assure Kerensky of the earnest desire of His Majesty's Government to assist Russia, and to tell him that, though the British army was engaged in the heaviest offensive it had yet undertaken, they had given orders to resume the despatch of heavy guns to Russia.

August 13.
"The publication of the correspondence between the Prime Minister and Mr. Henderson respecting the latter's attitude towards the Stockholm conference has caused the Russian Government much embarrassment and exposed it to attacks on the part of the Soviet. In speaking to me on the subject, Tereschenko said that he had instructed the Russian *chargé d'affaires* to inform His Majesty's Government that the Russian Government regarded the Stockholm conference as a party conference, whose decisions would not in any way bind them, but that Nabokoff's covering note to Mr. Balfour, on which the Prime Minister had laid stress, had been written without his instructions. He had never intended him to say that the Russian Government were opposed to the conference. (Mr. Nabokoff had in his note to Mr. Balfour used words that had been interpreted in this sense.)

"While both Tereschenko and Kerensky have admitted to me that they would prefer that the conference should not take place, they never intended that we should state publicly that they were opposed to it. Kerensky begged me this morning to urge His Majesty's Government not to refuse passports to our Socialists."

August 15.

"I have kept you fully informed by telegraph of the various stages of the recent ministerial crisis and of the final reconstruction of the Government. It is an improvement on the old one, and some of the new Ministers are good men. Plekhanoff, who has done excellent work, was to have entered the Government, but the Soviet would not allow it, as they have never forgiven him for saying that he was a patriot before he was a Socialist.

"We have come to a curious pass in this country when one welcomes the appointment of a terrorist, who was one of the chief organizers of the murders of the Grand Duke Serge and Plehve, in the hope that his energy and strength of character may yet save the army. Savenkoff is an ardent advocate of stringent measures, both for the restoration of discipline and for the repression of anarchy, and he is credited with having asked Kerensky's permission to go with a couple of regiments to the Tauride Palace to arrest the Soviet. Needless to say that this permission was not given. On the other hand, he is unfortunately against re-investing the officers with their former disciplinary powers, and prefers to confer those powers on the Government's commissaries at the front as a safeguard against a possible counter-revolution.

"Though the news from the army is better and though everything is quiet at Petrograd, I cannot look upon the situation as satisfactory. The Government lost a unique opportunity of putting down the Bolsheviks once and for all after the disturbances of last month. On my reproaching Tereschenko with this, he said that Kerensky was unfortunately at the front when those disturbances broke out. He had, on his return, remarked that it would have been better had Prince Lvoff delayed for a couple of hours the despatch of troops and guns to protect the members of the Soviet, who on the Monday evening were in danger of being arrested or murdered by the insurgent troops. The Government as a whole does not inspire much confidence. Guchkoff takes the gloomiest view of the situation and declares that not only will the army soon be confronted with famine, but that, if the war has to be continued through the winter, it will dissolve and melt away. He told me the other day that the present Government was hopeless and could never save the country. He would, of course, like to get rid of the Socialists and replace them with men from the parties of the right. I replied that no Government could do anything unless it could count on the support of the Petrograd garrison, which as at present disposed was more likely to obey the orders of the Soviet than those of the Government.

"I had a long conversation with Prince Kropotkin the other day. He takes a very similar view to what I do of the situation, though he is rather more pessimistic than I am about the future, I still hope that Russia will pull through, though the obstacles in her path — whether they be of a military, industrial or financial character — are appalling. How she is going to find the money to continue the war and to pay the interest on her national debt beats me altogether, and we and the Americans will soon have to face the fact that we shall have to finance her to a very considerable extent if we want to see her carry on through the winter. We cannot, however, be expected to do this till we have proof of her determination to put her house in order by restoring strict discipline in the army and repressing anarchy in the rear. General Korniloff is the only man strong enough to do this, and he has given the Government clearly to understand that unless they comply with his demands and give him the powers which he considers necessary he will resign his command. The danger is that, if he succeeds and acquires a predominant influence with the army, he may become an object of suspicion to the Soviet, whose policy of undermining discipline was originally dictated by the fear of seeing the army become the dominant factor in the country."

August 24.

"I returned last night from a week's holiday in Finland and saw Tereschenko this morning. I told him that I was greatly disappointed to find that the situation had, if anything, changed for the worse, that hardly any of the disciplinary measures contemplated had been applied, and that the Government seemed to me weaker than ever. On my inquiring whether Kerensky was in agreement with the commander-in-chief on the question of the death penalty in the rear, he said that it was only during the past few weeks that it had been possible even to moot this question and that the Government had been obliged to move very cautiously. Kerensky, he told me, had, in the Council of Ministers advocated its application to certain offences committed against the State by soldiers and civilians alike, but the Cadets had objected to its being applied to the latter for fear that it might be used against persons suspected of promoting a counter-revolution. I replied that, whatever reasons the Government may have had for caution in the past, they had now no time to lose, as, apart from the military outlook, the economic situation was so serious that unless drastic measures were at once taken there would be serious trouble in the winter. I had once warned the Emperor that hunger and cold would bring revolution in their train, and if the Government did not act with promptitude the same causes would provoke a counter-revolution. Tereschenko admitted that the Government was not as strong as he could wish, but said that General Korniloff would, at the Moscow conference, which opens to-morrow, submit his programme and explain the measures which he considers it necessary to take. The conference will constitute the first great national gathering since the revolution, and will be attended by all the Ministers as well as by representatives of the Soviet and of other institutions."

August 29.
"Though, with the exception of the extremists, all parties were agreed not to cause the Government embarrassments, the conference, so far from securing national unity, has rather accentuated the differences existing between the different parties, and we shall probably be faced with another crisis before many weeks are passed."

August 30.
"Tereschenko, with whom I had a conversation on his return from Moscow, considers that the conference has strengthened the hands of the Government. The commander-in-chief, he said, had now full powers to deal with the army at the front, but had not asked for the immediate application of the death penalty everywhere in the rear. Martial law had been proclaimed at Kazan, but it would be risky to proclaim it at Petrograd. Other measures would, however, be taken to deal with the situation here, which he admitted was very unsatisfactory."

August 31.
"I saw Kerensky this morning and, on my questioning him about the conference, he expressed himself as satisfied with its results. I told him that, though I was one of the few who had not abandoned all hope of Russia being able to pull herself together, I could not assume the responsibility of sending favourable reports to my Government unless he could give me satisfactory assurances as regarded the maintenance of order in the rear as well as on the food and transport questions. Korniloff had spoken at Moscow of the danger of a breakdown of the railways and of the army being faced with famine,

and were this to happen there would be a general collapse, for which I must prepare my Government.

"Kerensky could not deny that the situation was very serious. He could, he said, make no prophecies or give any absolute guarantees as regarded the future. At Moscow the representatives of the Soviet and of the industrial organizations had promised the Government their support. Tseretelli had declared that the war must be continued until the enemy had been expelled from Russian territory, and that it was only over the body of the revolution that a separate peace would ever be made. He could but reaffirm this declaration and assure me that Russia would never withdraw from the war unless she was materially incapable of continuing it. The death penalty, he added, would be applied in the rear in the case of all persons guilty of high treason. I told him that what preoccupied me most was the fact that the Socialist members of the Government were afraid of making the army a really efficient fighting force lest it might one day be used against the revolution. This was a fatal mistake, and if there ever was a counter-revolution it would be due to the failure of the Government to take the necessary measures to save the country. If the Government did their duty they had nothing to fear. Kerensky said that I was mistaken, that the danger already existed, and that he could never lend a hand to forge a weapon that might be delivered over to those who would use it against the revolution. On his appealing to me to give the Provisional Government my active support and to discourage all talk of reaction, I said that I had in two interviews, which I had recently given the Press, called on all parties and on all classes to sink their differences and to rally round the Government in defence of their country. I could not, however, conceal from him how painful it was to me to watch what was going on in Petrograd. While British soldiers were shedding their blood for Russia, Russian soldiers were loafing in the streets, fishing in the river and riding on the trams, and German agents were everywhere. He could not deny this, but said that measures would be taken promptly to remedy these abuses."

September 3.

"The fears expressed by Kerensky of a counter-revolution are to a certain extent justified, as I have since been told that a group of persons, who are said to have the support of prominent financiers and industrials as well as of certain regiments, contemplate arresting the Government and dissolving the Soviet. Though discontent is growing in consequence of the fall of Riga and the serious situation at Dvinsk, such an attempt has no chance of success."

September 3.

"Since I last wrote public interest has centred round the Moscow conference and the influence it is likely to exercise on the political situation. The only concrete results, so far as I can judge, are that, after the very outspoken language of Ministers, the nation knows the truth about the desperate state of the country, while the Government has learnt the views of the various parties and industrial organizations. So far from contributing to establish national unity, the conference has but served to accentuate party differences, and though all the speeches, with the exception of those pronounced by the Bolsheviks, were surcharged with patriotic sentiments, no attempt was made to bridge the gulf that separates the right and the left. Kerensky indulged in generalities. He neither told his audience what he had done in the past nor what he proposed doing in the future. Neither he nor any of the party leaders, with the exception of Cheidze, the president of the Soviet, submitted any concrete proposals.

"While expressing their readiness to support the Government, they did so conditionally and under reserve, and showed not the slightest disposition to sink their differences or to sacrifice their class interests. The curious thing is that they all seem to think that they scored a success at the conference, but nobody is agreed as to what the conference actually accomplished. On the whole, however, the Government as a body has strengthened its position, as, though no resolution was passed, it has now virtually full powers to deal with the situation if it will only use them.

"Kerensky, on the other hand, has personally lost ground, and he made a distinctly bad impression by the way in which he presided over the conference and by the autocratic tone of his speeches. According to all accounts, he was very nervous; but whether this was due to overstrain or to the rivalry which undoubtedly exists between him and Korniloff it is difficult to say. Korniloff is a much stronger man than Kerensky, and were he to assert his influence over the army and were the latter to become a strong fighting force he would be master of the situation. I hear from several sources that Kerensky did his best to prevent Korniloff addressing the conference, and though he has been obliged by the force of circumstances to accede to all the General's demands, he evidently regards him as a dangerous rival. Rodzianko and his friends on the right went out of their way to compromise Korniloff by putting him forward as their champion, while the Socialists, in consequence, adopted a hostile attitude and acclaimed Kerensky.

"Korniloff's conduct, moreover, was hardly calculated to lull the suspicions with which he was regarded by Kerensky. He made a dramatic entry into Moscow, surrounded by his Turcoman guard, and before proceeding to the conference visited the sacred shrine, where the Emperor always went to pray whenever he came to Moscow. Kerensky, whose head has been somewhat turned of late and who has been nicknamed 'the little Napoleon,' did his best to act up to this new role by posing in several of Napoleon's favourite attitudes and by making his two *aides-de-camp* stand behind him during the whole of the proceedings. There is little love, I imagine, lost between the two men, but our chief safeguard lies in the fact that, for the moment at any rate, neither can get on without the other. Kerensky cannot hope to retrieve the military situation without Korniloff, who is the only man capable of controlling the army; while Korniloff cannot dispense with Kerensky, who, in spite of his waning popularity, is the man best fitted to appeal to the masses and to secure their acceptance of the drastic measures which must be taken in the rear if the army is to face a fourth winter campaign.

"Rodzianko and others have been talking far too much about a counter-revolution and have been saying that a military *coup d'état* is the only thing that can save Russia. The Cadets, too, though they have been more prudent in their language, are determined to try to overthrow the Government, and have by their tactics inspired the belief that they also are working for a counter-revolution. In a telegram which General Barter sent me on his return to headquarters from Moscow, he spoke as if some sort of *coup d'état* might be attempted at any moment. I have told him that anything of the kind would be fatal at present, and would inevitably lead to civil war and entail irreparable disaster. I do not regard Kerensky as an ideal Prime Minister, and, in spite of the services which he has rendered in the past, he has almost played his part. But I do not see who is to replace him with advantage, nor do I believe that a purely Cadet and Octobrist Government would do any better than the present one, though certain changes ought certainly to be made in its composition and Tchernoff ought more especially to be dismissed.

"The long conversation which I had with Kerensky a few days ago rather depressed me, as he could not deny that there might be an eventual collapse owing to the breakdown of the railways and the scarcity of supplies, while the fear of the army being one day used to carry out a counter-revolution makes him hesitate to go all lengths to restore its discipline and efficiency. He more than once spoke of the necessity of our all doing our utmost to shorten the duration of the war, as if he feared that Russia could not hold out indefinitely. I told him that it was with this object that all the Allies were pushing their offensives on the various fronts and that, if he wished the war shortened, he must help us by restoring the combative power of the Russian army by restoring order in the interior and by applying to the troops in the rear the disciplinary measures in force at the front. He gave me positive assurances on all these points, but whether he will give effect to them I will not venture to predict."

CHAPTER 30
1917

The Moscow conference had hardly separated when the rumours of a projected *coup d'état* began to take a more material shape. Journalists and others who were in touch with its promoters even told me that its success was assured, and that the Government and Soviet would capitulate without a struggle. On Wednesday, September 5, a Russian friend of mine, who was the director of one of the principal Petrograd banks, came to see me and said that he found himself in rather an embarrassing position, as he had been charged by certain persons, whose names he mentioned, with a message which he felt that it was hardly proper for him to deliver. These persons, he then proceeded to say, wished me to know that their organization was backed by several important financiers and industrials, that it could count on the support of Korniloff and an army corps, that it would begin operations on the following Saturday, September 8, and that the Government would then be arrested and the Soviet dissolved. They hoped that I would assist them by placing the British armoured cars at their disposal and by helping them to escape should their enterprise fail.

I replied that it was a very naïve proceeding on the part of those gentlemen to ask an Ambassador to conspire against the Government to which he was accredited and that if I did my duty I ought to denounce their plot. Though I would not betray their confidence, I would not give them either my countenance or support. I would, on the contrary, urge them to renounce an enterprise that was not only foredoomed to failure, but that would at once be exploited by the Bolsheviks. If General Korniloff were wise he would wait for the Bolsheviks to make the first move and then come and put them down.

The fall of Riga and the retreat of the Russian army had created a panic in the town, and everybody who could was preparing to leave. Steps had already been taken to remove the State archives to Moscow, and the Government were seriously considering the question of transferring their headquarters there. In a conversation, which I had with him on the 6th, Tereschenko informed me that three cavalry divisions had been summoned from the front to guard against the danger of a Bolshevik rising, and I rather hoped from what he told me about the political situation that Kerensky and Korniloff were, after all, working together for the maintenance of order. I had spent Sunday, the 9th, at Mourina, a village some fifteen miles from Petrograd, where the British colony had laid out a rough golf course, and on returning in the evening I found a telephone message from Tereschenko asking me to come to the Ministry with the French Ambassador, M. Noulens, immediately after dinner. He then told us of the complete breach which had just taken place between Kerensky and Korniloff.

So many different accounts have been published of the genesis of their quarrel that it is still difficult to apportion the share of blame attaching to each or even to state correctly what actually happened. The person, whether wittingly or not, responsible for bringing matters to a head was the former Procurator of the Holy Synod, Vladimir Lvoff. He had a conversation with Kerensky on the 4th, and immediately afterwards proceeded to headquarters, apparently with the object of arranging for the formation of a stronger Government. According to a statement subsequently published by Savinkoff, he gave Korniloff the choice between three possible courses, and he did so in such a way that Korniloff was under the impression that he was speaking in Kerensky's name: —

1. Korniloff to form a Government, with Kerensky and Savinkoff respectively Ministers of Justice and War.
2. A triumvirate, with dictatorial powers, composed of Kerensky, Korniloff and Savinkoff.
3. Korniloff to declare himself dictator.

On returning to Petrograd on Saturday, the 8th, Lvoff told Kerensky that Korniloff had decided to declare himself dictator, and that he wished Kerensky and Savinkoff to come to the Stavka on the following Monday and to act under him as Ministers of Justice and of War. After asking Lvoff to give him this message in writing, Kerensky had a conversation with Korniloff by direct wire in which he asked him whether he confirmed the message which Lvoff had brought. He received a reply in the affirmative. Tereschenko afterwards told me that the above account was more or less correct, but that Kerensky had made the great mistake of promising Korniloff in the course of their conversation to come to the Stavka in a couple of days. It was only after consulting Nekrassoff that Kerensky, in accordance with the latter's advice, decided to denounce Korniloff as a traitor and to demand his resignation. According to Savinkoff, Lvoff had, whether intentionally or not, misrepresented Korniloff's attitude by giving to his message the form of an ultimatum instead of presenting it as the expression of his views. Nekrassoff, on the other hand, declared that Lvoff had saved the revolution by discovering and disclosing the plot before it could be put into execution. Tereschenko, unfortunately, at the critical moment was half-way between Petrograd and the Stavka, when he received a telegram from Kerensky telling him to return at once. Had he been at Petrograd he would have prevented Kerensky pushing matters to a complete rupture, while had he been at the Stavka he would have exercised a restraining influence on Korniloff.

In a conversation which I had with him in London in 1918, Kerensky, in reply to a question of mine as to his relations with Korniloff, said that he had always looked on him as a patriot and an honest man, but as a very bad politician. He had acceded to all Korniloff's demands with regard to the death penalty and to the extension of the front as far as Petrograd, but he could not allow the seat of Government to be placed under his orders, as in that case the Ministers would all have been at his mercy. He had also sent Savinkoff to the Stavka to try to effect a working arrangement with him. He was aware that a counter-revolutionary plot, having for its object the overthrow of the Government, was being organized by Zavoiko, Aladin and others in his entourage, and some ten days before the final rupture he had warned Korniloff that he must not be in too great a hurry, but must give the Government time to promulgate gradually the disciplinary measures on which he was insisting. He had even asked him if he contemplated establishing a military dictatorship, and Korniloff had replied: "Yes, if God wills." He (Kerensky) had expressly stipulated that the Caucasian Division, known by the name of the "Division Sauvage," was not to be included among the troops to be sent to Petrograd and that those troops were not to be placed under the orders of General Krimoff; but in spite of this Korniloff had placed Krimoff in command and was sending the "Division Sauvage" with him. Though he had had a conversation with Lvoff before the latter started for the Stavka, he had not charged him with any mission; and in the telegraphic conversation, which he had had with Korniloff after Lvoff 's return, he had put the question quite clearly to the former, in terms which could not be misunderstood, and had received an affirmative answer. As he knew that Krimoff's troops had already reached Luga and that a rising was being organized at Petrograd that was to take effect as soon as he left for the Stavka, he had no alternative but to declare Korniloff a traitor. In two orders of the day to the army, published September 10 and 11, Korniloff gave his version of the story, which puts his conduct in a very different light.

On September 7 the former Procurator of the Holy Synod, M. Vladimir Lvoff, came to the Stavka and, speaking on behalf and in the name of M. Kerensky, asked me to state my views regarding three different ways of organizing a new Government, suggested by M. Kerensky himself: 1 — The withdrawal of Kerensky from all part in the Government; 2 — the participation of Kerensky in the Government; and 3 — a proposal to me to assume the dictatorship, which was to be proclaimed by the existing Provisional Government.

I replied that the only solution lay in the establishment of a dictatorship and the proclamation of martial law throughout the country.

Under the dictatorship I understood not a one-man dictatorship, inasmuch as I had pointed out the necessity of Kerensky and Savinkoff participating in the Government.

I have always held and still consider any return to the old regime to be an utter impossibility; and the task of the new Government should be exclusively devoted to saving the country and the civic liberties won by the revolution.

On the evening of September 8 I exchanged telegrams with Kerensky, who asked me if I would confirm what I said to Lvoff.

As I could not believe that the emissary, sent to me by the Provisional Government, could distort the sense of my conversation with him, I replied that I did confirm my words fully, and I again invited Kerensky and Savinkoff to come to the Stavka, as I could not answer for their safety if they remained in Petrograd.

In reply, the Minister President stated that he would start on the 9th.

From the foregoing it is clear that, up to the evening of the 8th, my actions and decisions were proceeding in full accord with the Provisional Government.

On the morning of the 9th I received a telegram from the Minister President, intimating that I must immediately hand over the office of supreme commander-in-chief to my chief of the staff and leave at once for Petrograd.

The chief of the staff declined to take over the post, and I considered it impossible to hand it over till the situation had been fully cleared up. . . .

There could not be the slightest doubt in my mind that irresponsible influences had got the upper hand in Petrograd, and that our country was being led to the edge of the grave.

At such moments one cannot discuss, one must act. And I took the decision, which you know of, to save my country, or to die at my post.

On receiving Kerensky's telegram calling on him to resign Korniloff had to choose between absolute submission or open revolt, and he opted for the latter in the honest conviction that a continuance of the Government's undecided policy would spell disaster for Russia. The following extract from my diary and from my telegraphic reports to the Foreign Office will show how grave was the situation during the critical days which followed.

September 10.

"On my calling on Tereschenko this morning I found him much preoccupied by the turn which events have taken. General Alexeieff, he told me, had arrived at midnight and had urged the adoption of a policy of conciliation. The Government were considering the question when they received the news that Korniloff had proclaimed himself dictator and that he had, in the manifesto which he had issued, accused them of having provoked the crisis by sending Lvoff to the Stavka as an agent provocateur. He had further instructed General Krimoff to advance on Petrograd with a cavalry corps and artillery, which were at Luga at a couple of days' march from the capital. This meant the beginning of civil war, and it was, therefore, impossible for the Government to have any further dealings with him. The advance on Petrograd would be resisted by force, but he was afraid that the consequent cutting off of supplies would provoke a Bolshevik rising that would end in a Commune. He would therefore advise the diplomatic body to leave at once for Moscow or Finland, and on hearing from me he would make the necessary arrangements for their doing so. I told him that I could not possibly run away and leave the British colony unprotected, and that there was not sufficient time to arrange for the evacuation of all the Allied colonies. I would call a meeting of the heads of missions and let him know their wishes, but I would, at the same time, urge on the Government the necessity of a reconciliation with the commander-in-chief and of sending General Alexeieff as an intermediary to arrange terms with him. As he held out no hope of any such step being taken, there is nothing to be done but to await events and to trust that Korniloff will be strong enough to overcome all resistance in the course of a few days.

"On returning home I endeavoured to persuade my wife and daughter to go to Finland, but, with characteristic courage, they absolutely refused to leave me. At the meeting of the heads of missions, held at the Embassy in the afternoon, it was decided that we should remain at Petrograd in order to ensure protection for our nationals; while the Allied representatives subsequently passed a resolution tendering their good offices, as mediators, in the conflict that had arisen between the Provisional Government and the commander-in-chief, with the sole object of averting civil war and of serving the interests of Russia and her allies."

September 10.
"In handing to Tereschenko this evening the resolution passed by the Allied representatives, I told him that, while we had no wish to intervene in Russian internal affairs, we desired, as Russia's friends and allies, to place our services at the Government's disposal could we in any way help to avert what might prove an irreparable disaster.

"After expressing his thanks and saying that he would at once inform the Prime Minister of the action we had taken, he told me that, in his opinion, a conflict was now inevitable. The social revolutionaries, together with Kerensky, held that there was nothing to do but to fight it out, as matters had gone too far to admit of any compromise. The Cadets, on the other hand, were in favour of the Government giving in and of allowing Korniloff to form a Ministry. Tereschenko had himself always been a warm admirer of the commander-in-chief and would be prepared to go very far to save the country from civil war. He could not, however, regard without serious apprehension the idea of entrusting Russia's destinies to the group of men by whom Korniloff was surrounded. His chief adviser, Zavoiko, was designated for the post of Minister of Finance, but his past record was such that no confidence could be placed in him; while his future colleagues, including Aladin, who was to be Minister for Foreign Affairs, were not much better. Tereschenko added that he was personally still working for a reconciliation, and was urging that both Kerensky and Korniloff should retire, and that a new Government should be formed of representatives of the Moderate parties to the exclusion of the Soviet."

September 11.
"Minister for Foreign Affairs informed me this morning that the Prime Minister had charged him to thank the Allied Ambassadors for their action, which had greatly touched him, and to express regret that the commander-in-chief's attitude made it impossible for the Government to try to make terms with him.

"Tereschenko tells me that the Petrograd garrison has declared for the Government, and that the only troops on whom Korniloff can rely are the three cavalry divisions under Krimoff. All the Ministers have resigned, though continuing to act as heads of their respective departments, and Kerensky is virtually dictator."

September 12.
"In consequence of the slowness of Korniloff's advance the Government has had time to organize the garrison, to bring up soldiers and sailors from Cronstadt, to arm thousands of workmen, and to arrest many of his supporters."

September 12.
"Tereschenko tells me that Korniloff has definitely resigned, that Kerensky will assume the supreme command of the army, with General Alexieff as chief of the general staff, and that General Verkhovski, the commander-in-chief of the Moscow district, will become Minister of War."

Korniloff 's venture had from the outset been marked by the almost childish incapacity of its organizers, and ended in a complete fiasco. On arriving at a station some seventeen miles distant from Petrograd his troops were met by Tchernoff and, as they had been kept in ignorance of the object of their expedition, were persuaded by him to declare for Kerensky. Krimoff, their commander, was brought to Petrograd in a motor, and after an interview with Kerensky shot himself. Korniloff was placed under arrest while awaiting his trial for high treason, but succeeded in escaping after the Bolshevik revolution.

Although all my sympathies were with Korniloff, I had always done my best to discourage the idea of a military *coup d'état*, as Russia's best hope of salvation lay in a close co-operation between him and Kerensky. Korniloff, who was not a reactionary, honestly believed that Lvoff had been sent by Kerensky to ascertain his views on the political situation; and he expressed them with his usual frankness, without giving them the form of an ultimatum. The role played by Lvoff in the affair is quite impossible to explain. He misrepresented Kerensky to Korniloff and Korniloff to Kerensky; but whether he was a knave or a fool I cannot say. He was in any case an arch mischief-maker. It was only after being called on by Kerensky to resign his command that Korniloff decided to act, and in doing so he was prompted solely by patriotic motives. But while he personally would have been ready to work with Kerensky, there were men behind him who had for weeks past been plotting to overthrow the Government and who were bent on using him as their instrument and on forcing his hand.

There were so many persons in the secret of this counter-revolutionary movement that it was a secret no longer. Kerensky knew it, so that when Lvoff brought him what purported — though quite incorrectly — to be an ultimatum from Korniloff, he was already suspicious of and predisposed against him. Though Kerensky undoubtedly regarded him as a dangerous rival, who if he once got control of the army might use it against the Government, I do not believe that he purposely laid a trap for Korniloff in order to get him out of the way. But, like the latter, he had evil counsellors behind him who, for personal or party reasons, encouraged him to remove the commander-in-chief. That he was still hesitating to do so is shown by the fact that he had, in his telegraphic conversation with Korniloff, promised to come to the Stavka; and it was Nekrassoff who finally persuaded him to denounce the latter as a traitor. His policy throughout had been weak and vacillating; fear of the Soviet seemed to paralyse his every action; he had the chance after the July rising of suppressing the Bolsheviks once and for all — and he refused to use it; and now, instead of endeavouring to come to an understanding with him, he dismissed the one strong man capable of restoring discipline in the army. By way, moreover, of defending the revolution, which ever had the first place in his thoughts, he made the further mistake of arming the workmen, and thus played directly into the hands of the Bolsheviks. Writing to the Foreign Office on September 21, I said: "As a well-known foreign statesman remarked to me yesterday, Kerensky has two souls — one as head of the Government and a patriot and the other as a Socialist and Idealist. So long as the former is in the ascendant he issues orders for strong measures and talks of establishing an iron discipline; but, as soon as he listens to the promptings of the latter, he relapses into inaction and allows his orders to remain a dead letter. I fear, moreover, that, like the Soviet, he has never wished to create a really strong army, and that, as he once remarked to me, he will never lend a hand to forge a weapon one day to be used against the revolution."

CHAPTER 31
1917

The failure of Korniloff's attempted *coup d'état* had, as I told Tereschenko, destroyed my last hopes of an improvement in the situation either at the front or in the rear, as it had deprived officers of the little authority which they previously possessed, while it had restored the waning influence of the Soviet. The latter had passed resolutions abolishing the death penalty, declaring all existing secret treaties invalid, and demanding the immediate conclusion of a universal democratic peace. They were, I said, the masters, and the Government only existed on sufferance till such time as they should decide to take the reins into their own hands. Tereschenko tried to reassure me by saying that he had told the Socialist Ministers that strong disciplinary measures must be adopted at once and that any Bolshevik rising must be sternly suppressed.

The next step taken by the Soviet was to decline to recognize Kerensky's newly formed Coalition Government, and to convoke a democratic congress for the purpose of determining the composition of a Government capable of realizing the programme of revolutionary democracy. Pending the meeting of this congress, the administration of the country was entrusted to a council of five, of whom Kerensky, Tereschenko and the Minister of War (Verkhovski) were the principal members, on the understanding that it was to maintain close contact with the Soviet; while on September 15 the Republic was proclaimed, in order to show that the revolution had come to stay.

Kerensky had originally intended to confront the congress, that met on the 27th, with an accomplished fact, but his courage failed him, and on October 3 he submitted to its directorate the names of those whom he proposed to include in his Cabinet. He at the same time delivered a speech in which, after depicting the situation in the blackest colours, he insisted that it was only by a Coalition Government, representative of all parties, that Russia could be saved. The congress, nevertheless, proceeded to pass a series of contradictory resolutions for and against a Coalition Government, which virtually vetoed the participation of the Cadets in any Ministry, and it was only on October 9, after prolonged negotiations between Kerensky and the directorate of the congress, that a Coalition Government, which included half a dozen Cadets and Industrials, was constituted. The Petrograd Soviet, whose executive committee had been reconstituted on a Bolshevik basis under the presidency of Trotzky, at once recorded its vote against it.

Writing to the Foreign Office on the subject of the congress, I said:

"The original idea of its promoters was to give the democracy an opportunity of presenting a united front to the non-Socialist parties; but the only result has been to split up the democracy into an infinite number of small groups, and to undermine the authority of its recognized leaders. The Bolsheviks, who form a compact minority, have alone a definite political programme. They are more active and better organized than any other group, and until they and the ideas which they represent are finally squashed, the country will remain a prey to anarchy and disorder. Unfortunately the more moderate Socialist leaders, like Tseretelli and Scobeleff, whose mission it is to combat their extreme doctrines in the Soviet, can never quite forget that, however wide the gulf that separates the Bolsheviks from themselves, they are nevertheless comrades and fellow-fighters in the Socialist cause. They will, therefore, never sanction the adoption of strong measures against the Bolsheviks as a party, that has brought Russia to the verge of ruin, but only against individual members of it, who are proved guilty of treasonable conduct. If the Government are not strong enough to put down the Bolsheviks by force, at the risk of breaking altogether with the Soviet, the only alternative will be a Bolshevik Government.

"Ministers are anxious to put off the Korniloff trial as long as possible, so as to allow public excitement to calm down. In defending himself in the Democratic Congress against the charge of having, to a certain extent, acted in collusion with Korniloff, Kerensky threw no new light on what actually occurred. On the other hand, he went out of his way to explain that all the extraordinary military measures adopted by the Government were taken under pressure of the ultimatums which Korniloff had addressed to them."

Though Tereschenko had consented to retain the post of Minister for Foreign Affairs in Kerensky's reconstructed Government, he had done so under protest. He had had a serious disagreement with the Minister of War of which I had been the involuntary cause. I had complained to Tereschenko of a statement published in a Moscow

Socialist paper to the effect that British armoured cars had taken part in Korniloff's ill-starred adventure, and orders had, in consequence, been given by Kerensky for the suppression of the paper. Instead of carrying out these orders, Verkhovski had contented himself with causing legal proceedings to be taken against the editor, and the paragraph of which I had complained had been reproduced. Verkhovski was young and intelligent, and had done well when in command of the Moscow district. He had in 1903 been expelled from the Corps des Pages, in which he was a Cadet, for having, during some civil disturbances, harangued the men of a lancer regiment and told them not to fire on the people. His programme for the reorganization of the army by demobilizing as many men as could be spared and by forming a smaller and more efficient force out of its better elements was sensible enough, but he was too much of an enthusiast to make a really practical War Minister.

In a conversation which I had with him on October 8, Tereschenko said that, while remaining at the Foreign Office, he had refused to act as Vice-President of the Council or to take part in any Cabinet councils, except on questions of foreign policy or on matters on which his colleagues especially desired his advice, until the Government had elaborated a definite programme. He read to me a letter which he had addressed to Kerensky tendering his resignation — a letter that constituted a scathing criticism both of the Government and the Soviet. They had, he wrote, during the six tragic months through which Russia had passed since the revolution learnt nothing and forgotten nothing. Instead of trying to save Russia, demagogues had but thought of their own party interests and of how to control and impede the Government's action. A counter-revolution, though not necessarily a monarchical one, offered, he concluded, the only hope of saving the country. The reading of this letter, which he threatened to publish, produced a tremendous impression on his colleagues. The Cadets, who formerly had been his bitterest opponents, declared that they would not enter the Government if he left it, and he eventually withdrew his resignation. I had, immediately after the Korniloff affair, discussed with my French, Italian and United States colleagues the question of making collective representations to the Russian Government on the subject of both the military and internal situations. At a meeting which I had convoked for the purpose we had drafted the text of a note, and had agreed to obtain from our respective Governments authorization to present it when we considered the moment opportune for doing so. In that note, after expressing the hope that, now that the danger of civil war had been averted, the Government would be able to concentrate all its energies on the prosecution of the war, we emphasized the necessity of their reorganizing all Russia's military and economic forces by the adoption of rigorous measures for the maintenance of internal order, for increasing the output of the factories, for improving the transport services, and for re-establishing strict discipline in the army. As the United States Ambassador had not, for some unexplained reason, received any instructions from his Government, my French and Italian colleagues and I decided to act without him, and on October 9 we were received by Kerensky, Tereschenko and Konovaloff (the Vice-President of the Council). I began by explaining that we had some weeks ago been instructed to ask for an interview in order to discuss the situation with him, but that we had deferred doing so on account of the recent Ministerial crisis. Now, however, that a new Government had been formed under his presidency, we considered the moment opportune for acting on our instructions, more especially as it afforded us the occasion for saluting him as head of the Republican Government and offering him our sincere congratulations. I then, as doyen, read him our collective note.

Kerensky replied in Russian, Tereschenko translating what he said into French, sentence by sentence. He commenced by telling us that he would do all he could to prevent a false interpretation being placed by others on the communication which we had just made to him. The war, he then proceeded to say, was a war of nations, and not of Governments, and the Russian people had in the course of it made untold sacrifices. The Imperial régime had left the country in a deplorable state of disorganization, and it would have been better had the Allies shown less consideration for the feelings of the Emperor's Government and had called it oftener to account for its shortcomings. They had also been ill advised in hesitating, after the revolution, to continue the despatch of war material to Russia. There must, he continued, be complete union between the Allies — their interests were the same, and the defection of one would be fatal to all alike. There must also be continuity of policy, and, in spite of all her difficulties, Russia was determined on carrying on the war to the end. He was leaving in the afternoon for the front in order to set the work of army reorganization in motion at once. He concluded by reminding us that Russia was still a great Power.

Tereschenko had hardly finished translating the last sentence when Kerensky got up, and with a wave of his hand signified that our interview was at an end. After hurriedly shaking hands with us, he made for the door. As I had some documents to give him, I followed him, and when I had explained their contents I said that I wished him to understand that our action had been inspired solely by the desire to strengthen his hands. Kerensky was always fond of theatrical effects and evidently wished to mark his displeasure by the Napoleonic touch which he gave to our dismissal. On my remarking to Tereschenko afterwards that Kerensky had no business to treat Allied Ambassadors so cavalierly, he said that Kerensky had been annoyed at our making such representations at a moment when he was doing all he could to act as we wished. He further told me that Kerensky, immediately after our interview, had called on the United States Ambassador to thank him for not having accompanied us. M. Nabokoff was subsequently instructed to read to Mr. Balfour a formal protest on the subject of our collective note, while a letter which Kerensky had addressed to Mr. Lloyd George on the military situation was held back. On Tereschenko telling me this, I remarked that, if his idea was to punish our Prime Minister for a step which the gravity of the situation fully justified, it was a very childish proceeding on his part. Mr. Lloyd George, I added, would no doubt get over his disappointment. The letter was despatched a few days afterwards.

The Germans had towards the middle of October made a naval demonstration off the Dago and Osel Islands and landed some 12,000 men on the latter, and the Russian Government had, in consequence, appealed to us to send our fleet into the Baltic — a request with which we could not, for obvious reasons, comply. The following extract from my diary records the substance of the conversations which I had had on the subject with Tereschenko and Kerensky:

October 25.

"After observing that a naval demonstration in the Skagerak was more likely to create a diversion than any steps that we might take in the North Sea, Tereschenko said that he had felt considerable diffidence about appealing to us for assistance so long as Russia made no effort to save herself. He had, indeed, only been emboldened to do so by the gallant stand which the Russian fleet had made against a vastly superior foe.

"I replied that, while I fully recognized the gallantry displayed by the ships engaged in the recent fighting, Russia could hardly expect us to risk sacrificing our fleet, while her army, that was numerically stronger than the forces opposed to it, did but little to stem the German advance.

"In the course of our conversation Tereschenko said that in the speech which he was about to make in the Provisional Council he proposed to review the part which Russia had played in the war. In doing so he would venture to add that France, he was sure, would never forget that Russia had sacrificed 300,000 men to save Paris, and that Italy would remember with gratitude how the pressure on her front had been relieved by Brussiloff's great offensive. He had hoped to have been able to add that Russia also would never forget the assistance rendered by the British fleet when her own fleet was threatened with destruction.

"I told Kerensky, whom I saw later in the day, that were our fleet, as Admiral Stanley had already explained to the chief of the naval general staff, to enter the Baltic, the German fleet would at once retire into the Kiel Canal, and, as our exit could be blocked by their sinking a few ships, we should be caught in a trap.

"While expressing satisfaction at our projected diversion in the North Sea, Kerensky did not conceal his disappointment. He personally, he said, understood our position, but it was difficult to explain it to the growing number of persons who were constantly complaining that the Allies were giving Russia the cold shoulder. It was even feared in certain quarters that they contemplated making peace at Russia's expense. I replied that we had already categorically denied this charge, and that he might rest assured that we would never abandon Russia if she did not first abandon herself. To make peace at her expense would be suicidal on our part. We could, however, hardly be expected to furnish her with large quantities of war material till we had some guarantee that her army would use it to good purpose. On his expressing the fear that there was a strong anti-Russian feeling both in England and France, I said that though the British public was ready to make allowances for her difficulties, it was but natural that they should, after the fall of Riga, have abandoned all hope of her continuing to take an active part in the war. Any resentment, moreover, that they might feel was due to the fact that her army had been wantonly destroyed as a fighting force by those who were afraid of its being used against the revolution. Kerensky replied that, had it not been for the Korniloff affair, discipline would already have been to a great extent restored, but that now the work of reconstruction had to be begun all over again. We had, I rejoined, greatly appreciated the efforts which he had made to galvanize the army into life, and I believed that he could still do this. There was, however, no longer any time for half measures, and the iron discipline of which he had so often spoken must be introduced at any cost. Bolshevism was at the root of all the evils from which Russia was suffering, and if he would but eradicate it he would go down to history, not only as the leading figure of the revolution, but as the saviour of his country. Kerensky admitted the truth of what I had said, but contended that he could not do this unless the Bolsheviks themselves provoked the intervention of the Government by an armed rising. As he added that they would probably rise in the course of the next few weeks, I expressed the hope that he would not this time let the opportunity slip, as he had in July."

I must now go back a little and resume the story of the conflict of parties that was proceeding in the political arena at Petrograd. Kerensky's Government had for some time past been considering the expediency of calling into existence a consultative chamber that might afford them moral support and act at the same time as a buffer between them and the Soviet. The Moscow conference had proved a failure on account of its composition, while the democratic conference had been the offspring of the Soviet; but a pre-parliament or provisional council, summoned by themselves as the precursor of the Constituent Assembly, would, the Government thought, strengthen their position. This idea, which had been mooted while the democratic conference was still in session, took shape, and before that conference separated the nucleus of such a council was formed by the election of three hundred of its delegates as the representatives of the different democratic groups, while a hundred and fifty representatives of the so-called bourgeois parties were subsequently added. Its functions were never very clearly defined, but the Government made it quite clear that they did not consider themselves in any way responsible for what was intended to be a purely consultative chamber.

On October 21 the Provisional Council was opened by Kerensky with a speech in which he dwelt mainly on the necessity of convoking the Constituent Assembly in the course of the next month, of restoring the fighting spirit of the army, and of putting down anarchy. After the election of Aksentiev, a moderate Socialist — who had been Minister of the Interior in one of Kerensky's Cabinets — as president, Trotzky made a violent attack on the Government and declared that the Maximalists would work neither with them nor with the council. He then left the chamber, accompanied by his thirty irreconcilable followers. The first question discussed by the council was that of the evacuation of Petrograd; and at first there seemed a fair prospect of the bourgeois and moderate Socialist groups working together and forming a solid *bloc* against the Bolsheviks. The constitution of such a *bloc* afforded, indeed, the one and only hope of escape from the dangers which loomed ahead. The one crucial question, however, around which all interest centred, was the representation of Russia at the Allied Conference that was to meet at Paris in November. In its declaration of policy, published early in October, the Government had announced its intention of participating in that conference, and of including among Russia's representatives a delegate possessing the special confidence of the democratic organizations of the country. Those representatives, they further stated, would not only discuss with the representatives of the Allied Governments the military questions raised at the conference, but would also endeavour to negotiate an agreement based on the principles proclaimed by the Russian revolution. In making this declaration the Government had wished to placate the Soviet, who had not only demanded assurances as to the subjects to be discussed at the conference, but had also claimed the right to be represented at it. Tereschenko had always admitted that the first task of the conference was to consider how the war could be brought to a speedy and victorious end, but he had also held that a discussion of the means must necessarily entail a consideration of the ends. He had also recognized that Russia could not speak with two voices, and that he, as head of the Russian Government, must be the sole mouthpiece of the Russian Government and people.

The democratic representative, therefore, would, as Tereschenko told the Socialists, have to play but a passive role as a delegate appointed by the Government, and, though free to express to him personally the views of the Russian democracy, would not be at liberty to voice them at the conference. The Soviet, who took a very different view of the matter, had already chosen Scobeleff, the former Minister of Labour, as their representative, and had furnished him with instructions which reflected their own ultra-pacifist sentiments. The Allied Governments, on the other hand, while ready to discuss the situation with the Russian delegates in an informal manner, had no wish to see the question of peace terms raised at a regular conference. They did not, moreover, relish the idea of the presence at such a conference of a representative of the Soviet. I, personally, thought that it would be a mistake on our part either to veto the discussion of peace terms or to raise difficulties about Scobeleff attending it. Such a discussion, as I pointed out, need not commit us in any way, while we could count on Tereschenko keeping the latter in his place. I had a twofold reason for wishing to humour the Socialists. In the first place, though Russia could not be expected to play more than a passive role, it was incumbent on us to try and keep her in the war so that her vast resources should not be exploited by Germany, and, in the second, I was afraid that if we drove the more moderate Socialists into opposition we should promote the triumph of Bolshevism.

On October 31 Tereschenko delivered a speech in the Provisional Council in which he not only made a firm stand against the Soviet's claim to any separate representation at the conference, but also denounced in no measured language the instructions which they had given to Scobeleff. While his speech did not go far enough to satisfy the right, the Socialists complained that his uncompromising attitude on the subject of their instructions had rendered co-operation between the Government and the democracy almost impossible. In the discussion which followed Tereschenko was bitterly attacked, and on the following day Scobeleff told Kerensky that, unless the Government sent someone else to Paris, revolutionary democracy would give up all idea of being represented at the conference. The leaders of the different democratic groups, whom Kerensky consulted, all supported Scobeleff, and warned Kerensky that if Tereschenko went to the conference the Government would find its relations with the left wing of the Provisional Council seriously compromised.

CHAPTER 32
1917

Rumours of a Bolshevik rising had been circulating for some weeks past, and it was generally expected that it would take place a few days before the meeting of the all-Russian congress of Soviets. Tereschenko had even admitted that most of the troops of the garrison had been won over by the Bolsheviks, but Kerensky was more optimistic. He had in my recent conversations with him more than once exclaimed, "I only wish that they would come out, and I will then put them down." It had been arranged that Tereschenko was to leave for London on November 8 on his way to the Paris conference, and that we were to accompany him, as the Government wished to consult me with regard to the situation in Russia.

It will, I think, help my readers to follow the development of events during the last two months which I spent in Russia if I record them in the form of extracts from my diary:

November 2.

"Tereschenko, whom I met this afternoon at the Provisional Council, told me that Scobeleff had to-day held more conciliatory language and had spoken of the instructions which he had received as representing, not the demands, but the wishes of the Russian democracy as to the attitude to be adopted by their delegate should the subjects touched on come up for discussion at the conference. The question as to whether Scobeleff would accompany him to Paris would not, he added, be settled till the close of the debate on Monday, the 5th. Tereschenko is much perturbed by the statement recently made in the House of Commons that the conference will deal exclusively with the conduct of the war. It had, he said, greatly added to his difficulties, as, though the conduct of the war must naturally form the main object of discussion, it was unnecessary to tell the Russian democracy at such a critical moment as the present that all discussion of our war aims would be barred."

November 3.
"Verkhovski, the Minister of War, has resigned. He had always contended that if the troops were to be kept in the trenches they must be told what they were fighting for, and that we ought, therefore, to publish our peace terms and to throw the responsibility for the continuance of the war on the Germans. At last night's meeting of the committee of the Provisional Council he seems to have completely lost his head, declaring that Russia must make peace at once, and that, when once peace had been concluded, a military dictator must be appointed to ensure the maintenance of order. On Tereschenko, who was supported by all the other members of the committee, demanding the withdrawal of this declaration, he tendered his resignation, which was accepted."

November 3.
"The arrival this afternoon of a guard of cadets of the military school for the protection of the Embassy indicates the approach of a storm."

November 5.
"I heard this morning that the executive committee of the Soviet had decided to form a Government, and at half-past twelve one of the cadets sent me a message to say that the Bolsheviks would oust the Ministers from their respective departments in the course of the next few days.

"At one o'clock the three Ministers — Tereschenko, Konovaloff and Tetriakoff — whom I had asked to luncheon arrived quite unmoved. On my remarking that after the reports which had reached me that morning I had hardly expected to see them, they said that those reports, to say the least, were premature. Tereschenko then told me that he had, on the preceding evening, gone to Kerensky and had persuaded him to issue an order for the arrest of the executive committee of the Soviet, but that after he had left that order had been cancelled on the advice of a third person. They all three assured me that the Government had sufficient force behind them to deal with the situation, though Tetriakoff spoke very disparagingly of Kerensky, saying that he was too much of a Socialist to be relied on to put down anarchy. I told him that I could not understand how a Government that respected itself could allow Trotzky to go on inciting the masses to murder and pillage without arresting him, and Konovaloff said that he quite agreed. The Russian revolution, he remarked, had passed through several phases and we had now arrived at the last. He trusted that I would, before leaving for England, see a great change in the situation. Turning to Tereschenko, I said: 'I shan't believe that we are really going till we are in the train.' 'And I,' he replied, 'not till we have crossed the Swedish frontier.'

"Unless Kerensky is prepared to throw in his lot unreservedly with those of his colleagues who advocate a firm, continuous policy, the sooner he goes the better. The Government is but a Government in name and things cannot be much worse than they are at present. Even if they have to make way for the Bolsheviks, the latter would not be able to hold out for long, and would sooner or later provoke a counter-revolution.

"Tereschenko spoke again this afternoon in the Provisional Council, but on the question being put to the vote there was a majority against the Government. The resolution eventually adopted, while condemning the contemplated Bolshevik rising, threw the responsibility for the crisis on the Government. The situation, it affirmed, could only be saved by transferring the control of the land to the land committees and by inducing the Allies to publish their conditions and to commence negotiations for peace. In order, moreover, to cope with any counter-revolutionary or subversive movement it advocated the formation of a committee of public safety, composed of representatives of the organs of revolutionary democracy, that was to act in concert with the Provisional Government."

November 6.

"Tereschenko tells me that there were troubles last night in the suburbs and other quarters of the town; that the Bolsheviks had intended organizing an armed demonstration; that their courage failed them at the last moment and that it had been countermanded. They had, moreover, formed a revolutionary military committee, which has issued an injunction to the troops forbidding them to obey any orders which are not countersigned by themselves.

"At three o'clock this morning the printing presses of several Bolshevik papers, which the Government had decided to suppress, were seized, and Tereschenko expects that this will provoke a Bolshevik rising. He is urging Kerensky to arrest the members of the revolutionary military committee, and will not in any case leave for London till the situation has been cleared up."

November 7.

"Yesterday evening the executive committee of the Soviet decided to arrest the Ministers and to form a Government themselves. On telephoning this morning to the Ministry I was informed that Tereschenko had given up all idea of going to London and that he could not see me. A little later I heard that all the troops of the garrison had obeyed the summons of the Bolsheviks and that the whole town, including the State Bank, stations, post and telegraph offices, were in their hands.

"All the Ministers are in the Winter Palace, and their motors, which had been left unguarded in the adjoining square, have been either damaged or seized by the soldiers. About ten in the morning Kerensky sent out an officer to try to get him another motor. The officer found Whitehouse, one the secretaries of the United States Embassy, and persuaded him to lend Kerensky his car with the American flag. They drove back together to the Winter Palace. After telling Whitehouse that he proposed driving to Luga to join the troops which had been summoned from the front, he begged him to ask the Allied Ambassadors not to recognize the Bolshevik Government, as he hoped to return on the 12th with sufficient troops to re-establish the situation.

"At 4 A.M. this morning the Provisional Government called out the Cossacks, but the latter refused to act alone, as they had never forgiven Kerensky for having, after the July rising in which some of their comrades had been killed, prevented them putting down the Bolsheviks, as well as for having proclaimed their chosen leader, Korniloff, a traitor. About 8 a.m. the cruiser Aurora and three other ships arrived from Cronstadt and landed sailors, while sections of the armoured car detachments, which had originally declared for the Government, now joined the Bolsheviks. Though a certain amount of firing went on during the day, the Bolsheviks practically met with no resistance, as the Government had neglected to organize any force for their own protection. In the afternoon I walked down the quay to the Winter Palace Square and watched from a distance the troops surrounding one of the Government buildings, whose evacuation had been demanded. The aspect of the quay itself was more or less normal except for the groups of armed soldiers stationed near the bridges."

November 8.

"At six o'clock yesterday evening armoured cars took up positions at all points commanding the approaches to the Winter Palace, and shortly afterwards delegates from the revolutionary committee came and demanded its unconditional surrender. As no answer was returned the signal for attack was given by the firing at 9 P.M. of a few blank rounds by the guns of the fortress and of the cruiser *Aurora*. The bombardment which followed was kept up continually till ten o'clock, when there was a lull for about an hour. At eleven o'clock it began again, while all the time, as we watched it from the Embassy windows, the trams were running as usual over the Troitski Bridge. The garrison of the palace consisted mainly of cadets from the military school and of a company of the women's battalion — for Russian women had been fighting at the front, and had by their courage and patriotism set a bright example that ought to have shamed the men. There was, however, no organized defence, and the casualties on either side were but few in number. The Ministers meanwhile must have passed through a terrible ordeal as they moved about from room to room, not knowing what fate was in store for them. By half-past two in the morning parties of the attacking force had penetrated into the palace by side entrances and disarmed the garrison. The Ministers were then arrested and marched off through hostile crowds to the fortress. They seem to have been well treated by the commandant, who apparently thought it prudent to make friends with the mammon of unrighteousness for fear, as he remarked to someone, that the tables might be one day turned and that he might find himself an occupant of one of their cells.

"I walked out this afternoon to see the damage that had been done to the Winter Palace by the prolonged bombardment of the previous evening, and to my surprise found that, in spite of the near range, there were on the river side but three marks where the shrapnel had struck. On the town side the walls were riddled with thousands of bullets from machine guns, but not one shot from a field gun that had been fired from the opposite side of the Palace Square had struck the building. In the interior very considerable damage was done by the soldiers and workmen, who looted or smashed whatever they could lay hands on.

"In the evening two officer instructors of the women's battalion came to my wife and beseeched her to try and save the women defenders of the Winter Palace, who, after they had surrendered, had been sent to one of the barracks, where they were being most brutally treated by the soldiers. General Knox at once drove to the Bolshevik headquarters at the Smolny Institute. His demands for their immediate release were at first refused on the ground that they had resisted desperately, fighting to the last with bombs and revolvers. Thanks, however, to his firmness and persistency, the order for their release was eventually signed, and the women were saved from the fate that would inevitably have befallen them had they spent the night in the barracks."

November 9.

"Aksentieff, the president of the Provisional Council, who came to see me to-day, assured me that, though the Bolsheviks had succeeded in overthrowing the Government owing to the latter's criminal want of foresight, they would not hold out many days. At last night's meeting of the Congress of All Russian Soviets they had found themselves completely isolated, as all the other Socialist groups had denounced their methods and had refused to take any further part in the proceedings. The Council of Peasants had also pronounced against them. The Municipal Council, he went on to say, was forming a Committee of Public Safety composed of representatives of the Provisional Council, the Central Committee of the Soviet, the Peasants' Council, and the Committee of Delegates from the front ; while the troops, which were expected from Pskov, would probably arrive in a couple of days. I told him that I did not share his confidence.

"I received to-day the following reply from Mr. Balfour to my telegram informing him that I was remaining on at Petrograd:

I appreciate your intention to remain at your post, and wish to give you once more an assurance of the sympathy of His Majesty's Government and of their complete confidence in your discretion and judgment. You have, of course, full discretion to leave for Moscow or any other place, should you think it desirable to do so, and you should pay special attention to your own personal safety."

November 10.

"The Bolsheviks have formed a Government, with Lenin as First Commissary and Trotzky as Commissary for Foreign Affairs. It is to be called 'The Council of the People's Commissaries,' and is to act under the immediate control of the Central Committee of the All Russian Congress of Soviets. Trotzky went this afternoon to the Ministry and sent for the members of the staff, and expressed the hope that he could count on their collaboration. They all refused, and some of the lady clerks even told him that he was a German. He asked Tattischef, Tereschenko's *Chef de Cabinet*, whether the Ambassadors would call on him or whether he ought to pay them the first visit. On being told that the usual procedure was for a new Minister to inform them by letter of his assumption of office, he said that such a procedure was all very well under the old regime but hardly suited present conditions. One paper announced that he had called on me but had not got further than the doormat; and I, quite undeservedly, received in the afternoon a bouquet of flowers from some 'Young Russians,' with 'Bravo! Thank you!' written on a card. The example set by the staff of the Ministry for Foreign Affairs has been followed in most of the other Ministries, and the machinery of government is consequently at a standstill.

"The All Russian Congress of Soviets yesterday published a decree, appealing to the democracies of all belligerent Powers to assist them in relieving humanity from the horrors of war, and proposing an immediate armistice of three months to allow time for the conclusion of a democratic peace without annexations or contributions. The term 'annexations,' it was explained, referred to the forcible retention of any foreign territory irrespective of the date of its occupation. The Congress further decreed the nationalization of the land.

"The Committee of Public Safety appears to favour the formation of a purely Socialist Government, exclusive of, but relying on, the support of the Cadets. They are united in their wish to suppress the Bolsheviks, but there their union ends, some being in favour of adopting the Bolshevist programme with regard to peace and the land, while the others are strongly opposed to such a course.

"Paget telegraphs from Copenhagen that our Military Attaché had been informed by an escaped Russian prisoner that he had been engaged by the Germans as an agent for anti-British propaganda in Petrograd. He had, he said, been instructed to get into touch with the Bolsheviks and to arrange, among other things, for my assassination. I have also received a copy of a leaflet, which the Germans have recently been dropping from aeroplanes among the Russian troops on the southern front, telling them that though they had got rid of Tsar Nicholas, the British Ambassador was still enthroned as Tsar at Petrograd, that he imposed his wishes on the Russian Government, and that so long as he remained reigning in Russia and drinking Russian blood they would never have peace or liberty.

"Korniloff has succeeded in escaping and has joined Kaledin in the south. They are believed to be masters of the Donetz basin. Kerensky is utterly discredited with all parties, and the troops, if they do come to Petrograd, will not fight to restore his Government, but to support the Socialist groups who have turned against the revolution."

November 11.

"The last two days have passed without disturbance, and yesterday it was generally believed that Kerensky's troops would be here by now and that the situation would be liquidated. Acting under this belief, the Committee of Public Safety encouraged the cadets of the military schools to occupy the Central Telephone Office and to act on the offensive in other parts of the town. The situation has in consequence once more become acute, and there is firing all over the town.

"Our guard of eight cadets distinguished themselves the other day by appropriating a case of whisky and a case of claret belonging to the secretaries. Most of them were ill the next day, and some were sick in the hall. So far from their protecting us, it is rather we who are protecting them. Luckily an extra guard of Polish soldiers with an officer was given us on Friday, and we have managed to send the cadets safely home dressed up as civilians."

November 12.

"The telephone station was recaptured yesterday by a combined force of soldiers, sailors and workmen, but not without casualties on both sides. Detachments of troops with field guns then surrounded the different military schools and demanded their unconditional surrender. At one of them, where serious resistance was offered, it is said that the casualties exceeded two hundred and that several cadets were thrown out from the windows on the top story. By 10 p.m. the Bolsheviks were once more in possession of the whole town."

November 13.

"Kerensky has again failed us, as he did at the time of the July rising and of the Korniloff affair. His only chance of success was to make a dash for Petrograd with such troops as he could get hold of; but he wasted time in parleying, issued orders and counter-orders which indisposed the troops, and only moved when it was too late. The Bolsheviks have reoccupied Tsarskoe and are now confident of victory. In Petrograd they are supported by the ships which they have brought up from Cronstadt, one of which is anchored close to the Embassy. Were the Cossacks now to try to effect an entry the town would probably be bombarded. We are so entirely cut off from the outside world that we know but little of what is passing in the Provinces; but at Moscow, where a regular battle has been going on for the last few days, the Bolsheviks are regaining the upper hand. The number of killed is said to be about a couple of thousand, and the town appears to be given over to pillage at the hands of a drunken mob that had seized the spirit stores.

"Nobody at the Embassy or in the colony has so far suffered, but we are still having a very anxious time. Yesterday a report reached us from two sources that an attack was to be made on the Embassy in the course of the night. In addition to our Polish guard we have six British officers sleeping in the house, and Knox, who acts as commander-in-chief, is a tower of strength in these troublous times. Though the Bolsheviks, who want to stand well with the Allies, are hardly likely to encourage such an attack, there is always the danger that German agents may incite the Red Guard to raid the Embassy in order to cause friction between Great Britain and Russia. In spite of the measures taken for the maintenance of order, life is not very secure at present, and this morning a Russian petty officer was shot dead in front of our windows for refusing to give up his sword to some armed workmen."

November 14.

"Verkhovski came to see me to-day. He said that Kerensky had not wanted the Cossacks to suppress the rising by themselves, as that would have meant the end of the revolution. He declared that the moderate Socialists still had a chance of forming a Government, and said that if he were authorized to tell the troops that the Allies would discuss and draw up their peace terms for presentation to the Germans he would be able to detach many of them from the Bolsheviks."

November 17.

"The Cossacks under Krasnov, who were to have come to Petrograd, have made terms with the Bolsheviks, and Kerensky has escaped dressed as a sailor.

"The situation is now hopeless, as the Bolsheviks are masters in the north and at Moscow and though Kaledin holds the south, there is no chance of his making headway in the north."

CHAPTER 33
1917

Kerensky's Government had fallen, as the Empire had fallen, without a struggle. Both the Emperor and he had been wilfully blind to the dangers which threatened them, and both had allowed the situation to get beyond their control before taking any measures for their own protection. It was only when his hour had already struck and when, as Rodzianko telegraphed, it was too late that the Emperor consented to grant a constitution. It was the same with Kerensky. He waited and procrastinated. When at last he made up his mind to act, he found that the Bolsheviks had secured the support of the garrison and that it was he, and not they, who was to be suppressed. If I had to write the epitaphs of the Empire and the Provisional Government, I would do so in two words — lost opportunities.

From the very first Kerensky had been the central figure of the revolutionary drama and had, alone among his colleagues, acquired a sensible hold on the masses. An ardent patriot, he desired to see Russia carry on the war till a democratic peace had been won; while he wanted to combat the forces of disorder so that his country should not fall a prey to anarchy. In the early days of the revolution he displayed an energy and courage which marked him out as the one man capable of securing the attainment of these ends. But he did not act up to his professions, and every time that a crisis came he failed to rise to the occasion. He was, as subsequent events proved, a man of words and not of action; he had his chances and he never seized them; he was always going to strike and he never struck; he thought more of saving the revolution than of saving his country, and he ended by losing both. But while, as head of the Government, invested with full powers, of which he had made but a sorry use, he must bear the chief responsibility for Russia's surrender to the Bolsheviks, the other party leaders cannot be acquitted of all blame. The moderate Socialists, the Cadets and the other non-Socialist groups all contributed their share to the final catastrophe. For in a crisis which called for their close collaboration they failed to sink their party differences and to work whole-heartedly together for the salvation of their country.

The Socialists, obsessed by the fear of a counter-revolution, shrank from the adoption of measures that alone could make the army an effective fighting force. The Cadets, on the other hand, insisted, and rightly, on the restoration of discipline in the army and on the maintenance of order in the rear. But instead of trying to convince the Socialists by the correctness of their attitude that they had nothing to fear from a well-disciplined army, they went out of their way to create the impression that they were secretly working for a counter-revolution, in which the army was to be the dominant factor. Party spirit, unfortunately, ran too high to admit of any sustained collective effort against the common enemy. The inability of Russians to work cordially together, even when the fate of their country is at stake, amounts almost to a national defect. Whenever, as one of their own statesmen once said to me, a dozen or more Russians meet round a table to discuss some important question, they will talk for hours without coming to a decision and end by quarrelling among themselves. The one member of the Government who tried throughout, but failed, to keep his colleagues in line and to induce them to pursue a firm, consistent policy was Tereschenko. Belonging to no party, he thought only of his country; but, owing to his misplaced confidence in Kerensky, he took, and sometimes induced me to take, a too optimistic view of the situation. He only realized when it was too late how weak a reed to lean on was his chosen leader.

The Bolsheviks, on the other hand, constituted a compact minority of determined men, who knew what they wanted and how to get it. They had, moreover, all the best brains on their side and, with the help of their German patrons, they developed a talent for organization with which no one had at first credited them. Much as I detest their terroristic methods and much as I deplore the ruin and misery which they have brought on their country, I readily admit that Lenin and Trotzky are both extraordinary men. The Ministers, in whose hands Russia had placed her destinies, had all proved to be weak and incapable, and now by some cruel turn of fate the only two really strong men whom she had produced during the war were destined to consummate her ruin. On their advent to power, however, they were still an unknown quantity, and nobody expected that they would have a long tenure of office. The outlook, indeed, was so obscure that one could but grope in the dark. I gave my general impressions of the present without attempting to forecast the future, and, as will be seen from the following extracts from my diary, those impressions were not always right.

November 18.
"The Bolsheviks are gaining more adherents at the front, and the Ukrainian party has made common cause with them. They have distributed arms among the workmen."

November 19.
"There is no progress to report as regards the formation of a Coalition Socialist Government. On the other hand, there has been a serious split in the ranks of the Bolsheviks, and eight of the fourteen commissaries have tendered their resignation as a protest against such arbitrary measures as the suppression of liberty of the Press, etc. The Government is now in the hands of a small clique of extremists, who are bent on imposing their will on the country by terroristic methods. There are signs of growing dissatisfaction at the prolongation of the crisis, both among the troops and the workmen, and several factories have sent delegates to the Smolni Institute to tell the Bolsheviks that they must come to an agreement with the other Socialist organizations. Some of them held very outspoken language, saying that all that Lenin and Trotzky wanted was to sleep, as Kerensky had done, in Nicholas's bed. It was hoped at first that the secession of so many of their leaders would bring the more moderate members of their party into line with the representatives of the other Socialistic groups, and that a Government would be formed from which Lenin and Trotzky would be excluded. This hope has not been realized, and the extremists are now making great efforts to win over the left wing of the Social Revolutionary party and to induce the seceding members of their own party to return. If they succeed in this they will consolidate their position for the time being; but if the peace which they have promised is long delayed and if the supply of bread, which is getting scarcer every day, fails, the masses may rise and overthrow them. Except in the Ministry of War, the majority of the departmental staffs are still on strike. The supply of coal on the railways is getting dangerously short; the army and the large towns are threatened with famine; and, sooner or later, the whole machinery of government must break down altogether. What will happen then it is impossible to say. Some people declare that we shall have a monarchy in a couple of months. But, though a large section of the population is disenchanted with the revolution, I do not see how such a change is to be effected, unless Kaledin succeeds in rallying the army round him — and there is but little likelihood of his doing so. At the present moment force alone counts, and as the bourgeois parties have neglected to organize themselves for defensive

purposes, the Bolsheviks have it all their own way. During the recent fighting at Petrograd and Moscow the cadets of the military schools alone sided with the Government, and, being without officers and hopelessly outnumbered, sacrificed their lives in vain. At Moscow there are said to have been as many as five thousand casualties, as owing to the haphazard firing of the Red Guard the civil population lost heavily.

"Here everything is quiet for the moment, but if food supplies fail we shall be faced with a very serious situation. As a precautionary measure we are having stores brought into the Embassy and arranging to house all the staff, as well as the officers belonging to the various military missions, so as to form, if necessary, a strong garrison for its defence."

November 20.

"It would not do for me to leave Petrograd, as my presence here reassures the colony, and it is better that I should remain and await events. My Allied colleagues, with whom I have discussed the question of the attitude which we should adopt towards the new Government when it is formed, all agree that we cannot recognize it officially, but differ as to whether we should or should not enter into unofficial relations with it. I personally am of opinion that we must establish some sort of contact with it for the conduct of certain current affairs.

"Mr. Balfour agreed that this was essential in the interests of the Allied Colonies, and it was decided that our Consuls should, when necessary, serve as the channel of communication between us and the Government."

November 20.

"Scobeleff, the ex-Minister of Labour, and Chaikovsky, the president of the Provisional Council, representing, as they said, the working classes and the peasantry, came to see me to-day. They told me that a Socialist Government, exclusive of the Bolsheviks, was about to be formed, that it would include representatives of the Cossack democracy, and that it would be supported by the Cadets. On my asking how they proposed to put down the Bolsheviks, they replied — by force. They could, they asserted, count on certain troops, sufficient for the purpose, as the army cared nothing for the Bolsheviks and only wanted peace. Russia was worn out and could not fight any more; but if they were to succeed they must be authorized to tell the army that the Allies were prepared to discuss peace terms with a view to bringing the war to a speedy conclusion. Such an assurance would, they said, give them a great advantage over the Bolsheviks, with whom the Allied Governments would not treat.

"I replied that, though the Allied Governments might consent to discuss peace terms with such a Government were it once constituted, they could give no assurance as regarded the early termination of the war, for they could not, after all their sacrifices, accept a premature peace that offered no guarantee for the future. Russia could only purchase peace on terms disastrous to herself, and it was surely to her interest to make an effort to hold out, without trying to take the offensive, till we had defeated Germany. After consulting together they said that, if they received an assurance that the Allies would hold a conference for the discussion of peace terms and would endeavour to arrive at an agreement with regard to those terms, they might be able to form a small army for defensive purposes. Scobeleff, who was to leave in the evening for the Stavka to meet other Socialist leaders, asked whether he might give a provisional assurance to the above effect in my name; but I told him that all that I could do was to submit this proposal to my Government."

November 21.

"A meeting of compositors was held this afternoon to protest against the suppression of so many newspapers. On their threatening to strike they were told that, if they carried out this threat, they would be made to work twenty-four hours a day with soldiers standing behind them to prod them in the back with their bayonets if they slacked their work.

"The following story is worth recording as illustrating the curious mentality of the Russian peasant. It was told me by a friend, who vouched for its truth. A landlord was recently condemned to death by the Bolsheviks, and his peasants were told to carry out the sentence. They went to him one morning, fell on their knees, kissed his hand, and thanked him for having been such a good master. They had, however, received orders which they were bound to obey, and they must ask him to accompany them. They then took him to a neighbouring wood and killed him in the most cold-blooded way.

"On the night of the 20th Ensign Krilenko, who was in charge of the Ministry of War, acting under Lenin's instructions, sent a wireless message to General Dukhonin, the commander-in-chief, ordering him to propose an armistice to the German commanders, with a view to the commencement of peace negotiations. The Allied representatives in Petrograd had, the message added, already been told of the step which the Government was about to take. This latter statement was not correct, as it was only late in the evening of the 21st that I received a note from Trotzky informing me of the constitution of the Government and submitting a proposal for an armistice and for the immediate opening of peace negotiations. Trotzky had further, on the same day, announced his intention of publishing all the secret agreements. In telegraphing the above to the Foreign Office, I suggested that no reply should be returned to Trotzky 's note, but that His Majesty's Government should make a statement in the House of Commons to the effect that, while ready to discuss peace terms with a legally constituted Government, they could not do so with one that had broken the engagements taken by one of its predecessors under the agreement of September 5, 1914.

"General Dukhonin has replied that, while agreeing that peace is necessary in Russia's interests, he considers that negotiations for peace can only be advantageously conducted by a Government that is recognized by the country as a whole. He has in consequence been superseded by Ensign Krilenko. The latter has issued a proclamation calling on all the different army committees to elect their representatives and to open negotiations for an armistice at once.

"Chaikovsky came to see me again to-day before proceeding to the front, where, as he told me, some twenty representative men had already gone, for the purpose of forming a new Government and of organizing a force strong enough to suppress the Bolsheviks. He spoke with great confidence of the approaching fall of the latter. On my telling him that I did not share his confidence, he had to admit that the Bolsheviks, by proposing an armistice, had stolen a march on him and his friends."

November 24.

"The Mayor of Petrograd called to-day to assure me that Russian democracy strongly condemned the opening of negotiations for a separate armistice and the publication of our secret agreements. He takes far too optimistic a view of the political outlook. In the course of our conversation he remarked that were the Allied representatives to leave Russia it would be a severe blow to true democracy and to all classes in the country except the Bolsheviks."

November 25.

"The Allied military representatives at headquarters have protested officially to Dukhonin against the infraction of the agreement of September, 1914, and told him that it might have the most serious consequences. The veiled threat contained in the last words has been interpreted to mean that we are about to call on Japan to attack Russia. It was an ill-advised step that has done us any amount of harm. Trotzky has in consequence issued a fiery appeal to the soldiers, peasants and workmen against our interference in Russian affairs. He told them that our imperialistic Governments were trying to whip them back to the trenches and to make cannon fodder of them. He urged the soldiers to elect their representatives and to open negotiations at once with the Germans.

"The elections for the Constituent Assembly commenced to-day. At yesterday's meeting of the garrison, which was attended by representatives of all the political groups, the Bolsheviks obtained what virtually amounted to a vote of confidence."

November 27.
"Trotzky has communicated to the Allied military attachés a note asserting that his Government never desired a separate but a general peace, but that it was determined to have peace. It will, the note concluded, be the fault of the Allied Governments if Russia has after all to make a separate peace."

November 27.
"I have come to the conclusion that the only thing for us to do is to *faire bonne mine à mauvais jeu*. Acting on an idea originally suggested by Knox, I have telegraphed to the Foreign Office as follows:

I share the view, already expressed by General Knox, that the situation here has become so desperate that we must reconsider our attitude. In my opinion, the only safe course left to us is to give Russia back her word and to tell her people that, realizing how worn out they are by the war and the disorganization inseparable from a great revolution, we leave it to them to decide whether they will purchase peace on Germany's terms or fight on with the Allies, who are determined not to lay down their arms till binding guarantees for the world's peace have been secured.

It has always been my one aim and object to keep Russia in the war, but one cannot force an exhausted nation to fight against its will. If anything could tempt Russia to make one more effort, it would be the knowledge that she was perfectly free to act as she pleased, without any pressure from the Allies.

There is evidence to show that Germany is trying to make an irreparable breach between us and Russia, so as to pave the way for the German protectorate which she hopes eventually to establish over the latter. For us to hold to our pound of flesh and to insist on Russia fulfilling her obligations, under the 1914 Agreement, is to play Germany's game. Every day that we keep Russia in the war against her will does but embitter her people against us. If we release her from those obligations, the national resentment will turn against Germany if peace is delayed or purchased on too onerous terms. For us it is a matter of life and death to checkmate this latest German move, for a Russo-German Alliance after the war would constitute a perpetual menace to Europe, and more especially to Great Britain.

I am not advocating any transaction with the Bolshevik Government. On the contrary, I believe that the adoption of the course which I have suggested will take the wind out of their sails, as they will no longer be able to reproach the Allies with driving Russian soldiers to the slaughter for their Imperialistic aims."

November 28.

"I have received a note from Trotzky demanding the release of two Russians — Chicherin and Petroff — who have been interned in England for the anti-war propaganda which they have apparently been making among our workmen. Russian democracy would not, the note went on to say, tolerate the imprisonment of two innocent fellow countrymen and allow British subjects who were carrying on an active propaganda in favour of a counter-revolution to go unpunished."

December 3.

"Trotzky, I hear, is very angry with me for not answering his note. On my sending Consul Woodhouse to endeavour to obtain the necessary permission for some of our subjects to go home, he said that it had been decided that no British subjects would be allowed to leave Russia till the question of the two interned Russians had been satisfactorily settled. He added that Chicherin was a personal friend of his, and he was particularly anxious to secure his release as he proposed appointing him his diplomatic representative in one of the Allied capitals. In the event of our Government refusing to release him he threatened to arrest certain British subjects whom he knew to be counter-revolutionaries.

"About half-past nine the same evening General Niessel, the French military representative, came to see me. Trotzky, he said, had told a French officer, who was a Socialist and in close touch with the Bolsheviks, that he had a special grudge against me, not because I was indisposing my Government against him, but because I had, ever since the overthrow of the late Government, not only been in constant touch with Kaledin and the committee of public safety, but had even supplied the latter with funds. He was therefore contemplating arresting me, and should this lead to a rupture of relations between our two Governments he would keep a certain number of British subjects as hostages. General Niessel did not think that Trotzky would dare arrest me in the Embassy, but as he knows that I am in the habit of taking a daily walk he might do so when I was out of doors. By way of cheering me, the General added that, from inquiries which he had made, he believed that the most comfortable cells in the fortress were between the Numbers 30 and 86 and that should the worst happen I had better bear this in mind."

I did not take Trotzky's threat too seriously and continued my walks as usual without any unpleasant consequences. Only once, as I was turning into a side street off the quay, I nearly got into the middle of a fight that was going on at the other end. I was fortunately stopped in time by a friend of ours. Princess Marie Troubetzkoi, who happened to be passing. She assured me that she had saved my life, and insisted on seeing me safe home to the Embassy, as no one would, she said, attack me if I was with a lady.

December 4.

"Our position is becoming very difficult as, while it is impossible for our Government to yield to threats, it is very hard on our subjects, who have come here from the provinces on their way home, to be put to the expense of remaining on indefinitely. I do not, moreover, at all want to see the members of our propaganda bureau arrested. There is, after all, something in Trotzky's argument that, if we claim the right to arrest Russians for making a pacifist propaganda in a country bent on continuing the war, he has an equal right to arrest British subjects who are conducting a war propaganda in a country bent on peace. He has further got it in his power to prevent our couriers coming or going and even to stop us leaving if we are recalled. Noulens hears from the French Consul at Helsingfors that there is an idea of arresting us should we pass through Finland on our way home. Our Consul in that town has also been informed by a Finnish banker that a German agent, who has an expert knowledge of bombs, has recently arrived there, charged, among other things, with the mission of blowing up our train on its way through Finland.

"In order to put an end to the uncertainty prevailing as to our attitude, I have, in a *communiqué* to the Press, explained that we cannot recognize the present Government, and that I have been instructed to abstain from any step that might imply recognition. Trotzky's note proposing a general armistice had, I pointed out, been only delivered at the Embassy nineteen hours after General Dukhonin had received the order to open pourparlers with the enemy. The Allies had thus been confronted with an accomplished fact on which they had not been consulted. Although I had telegraphed to the Foreign Office the substance of all the notes which Trotzky had addressed to me, I could not reply to the notes of a Government which my own Government did not recognize. A Government, moreover, which, like mine, derived its powers direct from the people could not take a decision on a matter of such grave importance without first assuring itself that that decision would meet with the approval and sanction of the people."

December 6.
"Trotzky has published a reply to the effect that the Allied Governments had been made aware of his intention to propose a general armistice by the appeal, which the Soviet had addressed to the democracies of the world on November 8. If his note had reached the Embassy rather late, this was entirely due to secondary causes of a technical character. I hear that the Soviet disapproves of Trotzky's recent attitude towards me."

December 7.
"Opinions are so divided as to the strength of the Bolsheviks that it is very difficult to see clearly ahead. While the pessimists predict massacres, the optimists assert that their reign is drawing to a close, that they will not dare to dissolve the Constituent Assembly should it declare against them, and that if we only hold out till that assembly meets the situation will change to our advantage. I rather doubt this, as a good many Bolsheviks have been returned in the provinces, and, as they are the only party with any real force behind them, they will probably be the ruling power for some time to come. During the past few days there have been signs of a desire on their part to establish better relations with the Allies, and certain recommendations respecting the terms of the armistice which the Serbian Minister communicated privately to Trotzky were well received by the latter.

"I sent Captain Smith (the Embassy translator) yesterday to Trotzky to see if it was possible to come to some understanding with him with regard to the British subjects who want to leave Russia. I told him to explain that, while I could not advise my Government to yield to threats, I would ask them to reconsider the case of the two interned Russian citizens if he, on his part, would rescind the order forbidding the departure of our subjects. Trotzky replied that in the note which he had addressed to me he had not intended to convey a threat and that I must make allowance for his ignorance of diplomatic language. He had only wished to make it clear that the same treatment must be meted out to Russians in England as to Englishmen in Russia. It was only four days later, after receiving no reply to his note and after reading in the Press that I had declined to forward his note to my Government (the statement that had appeared in the Press to the above effect was false), that he had issued the order in question. He had also thought it well to warn me that he knew as a fact that I was in touch with some of Kaledin's agents, though he would not mention their names. He could not, he said, act on my suggestion by taking the first step; but he would engage to allow British subjects to leave at once as soon as I published a statement in the Petrograd Press to the effect that His Majesty's Government were prepared to reconsider the cases of all interned Russians and to allow those who were not proved guilty of any illegal acts to return to Russia. He added that he quite understood the difficulties of my position. I had, as he was aware, been on intimate terms with many members of the Imperial family; but I had since the revolution been ill-advised and ill-informed, especially by Kerensky. I gather that he was referring to the fact that I had under-estimated the strength of the Bolshevik movement — and in this he was right. Kerensky, Tereschenko and some of the other Ministers had all misled me on this point, and had repeatedly assured me that the Government would be able to suppress them."

The above question was finally settled by His Majesty's Government consenting to repatriate the interned Russians, provided that freedom of movement was restored to British subjects in Russia.

December 7.

"Ever since the Bolshevik rising there have been persistent rumours that their operations were being conducted by German staff officers in disguise. Information has now reached me, though I am unable to vouch for its accuracy, to the effect that there are six of their officers attached to Lenin's staff in the Smolny Institute.

"Lenin has issued a proclamation to all Mussulmans of the East, and in particular to those of India, calling on them to rise and free themselves from the hated yoke of alien capitalists."

CHAPTER 34
1917-1918

My diary continues to be a useful reminder of events:

December 8.
"I received a few days ago a telegram from Mr. Balfour giving a statement of our views with regard to the opening of armistice negotiations. It was based on a decision taken by the Paris conference that the Allied Ambassadors should be instructed to make it generally known that their Governments would be prepared to examine their war aims, as well as the possible conditions of a just and enduring peace, as soon as Russia had a stable Government recognized by the nation. I have embodied this telegram in a somewhat modified form in the first three paragraphs of the following statement, which I propose giving representatives of the Press this afternoon. In the other five paragraphs I reply to the attacks made on me by Lenin and other Bolshevik leaders:

Judging by recent practice, secret diplomacy will soon be a thing of the past and diplomatists must therefore more than ever have recourse to the Press as a channel of communication with the people. It is for this reason that I welcome your visit in order that through your kind offices I may appeal to the Russian democracy against those who wilfully misrepresent the policy of my Government.

What, you ask me, is our attitude towards Russia, and how do we view the negotiations for an armistice that have been opened on the Russian front? As regards the first of these questions, I can assure you that our attitude is one of sympathy for the Russian people, worn out as they are by their heavy sacrifices in this war, and by the general disorganization that is the inevitable consequence of any great political upheaval such as that of your revolution. We bear them no grudge, nor is there a word of truth in the reports that have been circulated to the effect that we are contemplating any coercive or punitive measures, in the event of their making a separate peace. With regard to the second question, the Council of the People's Commissaries, in opening negotiations with the enemy without previous consultation with the Allies, committed a breach of the agreement of August 23 — September 5, 1914, of which we had a right to complain.

We cannot for a moment admit the validity of their contention that a Treaty, concluded with an autocratic Government, can have no binding force on the democracy, by which that Government has been replaced, as such a principle, if once accepted, would undermine the stability of all international agreements. But, while we repudiate this new doctrine, we do not desire to induce an unwilling ally to continue to contribute her share to the common effort by an appeal to our treaty rights. There are still higher principles to which we might, if we so desired it, appeal — principles, moreover, that are fully recognized by the Council of the People's Commissaries. They are those of a democratic peace; of a peace which accords with the wishes of the smaller and weaker nationalities; that repudiates the idea of extracting plunder out of conquered enemies under the name of war indemnities, or of incorporating in great Empires the territories of reluctant populations. Such, broadly speaking, is the peace which my Government, equally with the Russian democracy, desires to see secured to the world.

The Council of the People's Commissaries is, however, mistaken in thinking that they can secure this peace by asking for an immediate armistice, to be followed by an agreement. They are, if I may use a homely expression, putting the cart before the horse. The Allies, on the contrary, desire to arrive first at a general agreement, in harmony with their declared aims, and then to secure an armistice. So far, not a word has been said by any German statesman to show that the ideals of Russian democracy are shared by the German Emperor or his Government, and it is with the German autocracy and not with the German people that negotiations for an armistice are being conducted. Is it likely that the Emperor William, when once he knows that the Russian army has ceased to exist as a fighting force, will be disposed to subscribe to a democratic and durable peace, such as the Russian people desire? No. The peace which he contemplates is a German and Imperialistic one. Though the Allies cannot send representatives to take part in the armistice negotiations, they are ready, so soon as a stable Government has been constituted that is recognized by the Russian people as a whole, to examine with that Government the aims of the war and the possible conditions of a just and durable peace. Meanwhile, they are rendering Russia the most effective assistance by holding up the bulk of the German armies on their respective fronts. The important victories recently achieved by the British troops near Cambrai are of good augury for the future, for the democratic peace which we all so ardently desire will never be attained till the military power of the Kaiser has been broken.

I have, I hope, shown how friendly are our feelings, and how sincerely we desire to stand by Russia in this hour of crisis. Can, I venture to ask, the same be said of Russia's feelings to us? Is it not a fact that hardly a day passes without some bitter attack being made on my country by what are now the official organs of the Press? To read them one would think that Great Britain provoked the war for her own imperialistic and capitalist aims, and that she is responsible for all the blood that is being shed. I am not going to repeat the oft-told tale of the origin of the war. I should only like to ask what would be Russia's position to-day had we not intervened when Belgium's neutrality was violated by Germany. Without the British Fleet and our newly formed armies, in which three million volunteers had enlisted, Russia would to-day be Germany's vassal, and autocracy would reign supreme in Europe. Had we stood aside there would have been no revolution and no liberty for the people. The German army would have seen to that, and without our co-operation in the war Russia would have never won her freedom.

Are we not therefore entitled to claim that we should be treated as friends, instead of being made the object of scurrilous attacks? In his appeal to the Moslems of the East, Mr. Lenin spoke of us as rapacious extortioners and plunderers, while he incited our Indian subjects to rebellion. He placed us on a somewhat lower level than the Turks, to whom he would hand over Armenia, forgetful of the awful massacres already perpetrated there. It is an unheard-of thing for a man who claims to direct Russian policy to use such language of a friendly and Allied country. How does he think that the British tyrant enforces his will on India, with its 300 million inhabitants? Is he aware that the British garrison, which before the war amounted to 75,000 men, has since been reduced to 15,000 owing to the loyal support of the native races? Is he aware that one of our chief aims is to prepare the diverse and often hostile races for self-government, and that our Government encourages the formation of Indian societies and committees for this very purpose? Hardly any of them are anti-British, and none approach the Soviet in character.

The position of Englishmen in this country is not an enviable one at the present moment. They are singled out for attacks, or regarded with suspicion. Our propaganda bureau, which was started with the object of making our two countries better known to each other, is even accused of being in league with counter-revolutionaries. There is not the slightest foundation for such a charge, unless it is a crime to defend one's country against the calumnies and misrepresentations of German agents. So long as Russia was taking an active part in the war our bureau, as was but natural, also conducted a war propaganda, but it no longer does so.

I wish the Russian people to know that neither I myself nor any agency under my control have any wish to interfere in the internal affairs of their country. During the seven years that I have been Ambassador here I have worked heart and soul to bring about the closest understanding between Russia and Great Britain ; but, though I have associated, as it is my duty, with members of all parties, I have ever since the February revolution maintained a strictly neutral attitude. Prior to that date I did, it is true, endeavour to use all my influence with the ex-Emperor in favour of some form of Constitutional Government, and I repeatedly urged him to concede the legitimate wishes of the people. Now that his sovereign rights are vested in the Russian people, the latter will, I trust, pardon my transgression of the strict rules of diplomatic etiquette.

I would, in conclusion, venture to address one word of warning to the Russian democracy. Their leaders are, I know, animated by the sincere desire of creating a brotherhood of the proletariats of the world, in order to secure universal peace. I fully sympathize with the object which they have in view, but I would ask them to consider whether their present methods are likely to appeal to the democracies of Allied countries, and more especially to my own. They are creating, no doubt unintentionally, the impression that they set more store by the German than by the British proletariat. Their attitude towards us is more calculated to estrange than to attract the sympathies of the British working classes. During the great war that followed the French Revolution, the speeches delivered against Great Britain and the attempts made to provoke a revolution in our country did but steel the resolve of the British people to fight out the war to the end, and rallied them round the Government of the day. History will, if I mistake not, repeat itself in this twentieth century."

December 10.

"More than twenty-five journalists, representing papers of every shade of opinion save the Bolsheviks, attended the interview to which I had invited the Press. It was rather a trying ordeal, as, after Harold Williams had read my statement in Russian and after copies had been handed round, the representatives of the *bourgeois* Press asked me a number of unnecessary and compromising questions which I could not answer without exposing myself to still more embarrassing questions from the Socialists. Then the correspondent of the *Novaya Jizn*, Gorki's paper, wanted to know what was meant by 'a Government recognized by the people,' and whether, when such a Government had been constituted, the Allies would at once open peace negotiations. I replied that a legally constituted Government ought, strictly speaking, to derive its powers from the Constituent Assembly, but that Russia was a country of such surprises that we would not consider ourselves bound by this definition. We were prepared to discuss peace negotiations with such a Government, but before negotiations could be opened with the enemy the Allies must first come to an agreement between themselves, as till such an agreement had been reached they could not treat with Germany with any hope of success. This reply has been severely criticized by the *Novaya Jizn* and by some of the Bolshevik papers as showing that we will not meet the wishes of the Russian democracy. My statement, on the other hand, has met with warm approval in diplomatic circles and has evoked a cordial expression of thanks from the Russian colony in London. Trotzky alluded to it in a speech which he delivered yesterday. I had, he said, expressed my affection for Russia in five columns of the Press, and the warmth of my sentiments had gladdened him. He would, however, prefer deeds to words."

December 18.

"I had a bad breakdown a week ago. On getting up in the morning I found I could not walk straight, but lurched about the room as if I were on board ship. Vertigo was, I gather, the cause. I have had to lie up ever since, and my doctor tells me that I am at the end of my tether. I, therefore, telegraphed for leave to come home and have now been authorized to start whenever I like. I am feeling better to-day and propose remaining on till the Constituent has either met or been sent about its business. The latter seems the more likely, as the Bolsheviks have issued a proclamation ordering the arrest of the Cadet leaders and declaring that the enemies of the people, the landlords and the capitalists, must have no place in that assembly. They have already arrested six Cadets who had been elected.

"On December 1 the Stavka was occupied by the Bolsheviks without any fighting, as General Dukhonin had not allowed the Death Battalion, who had placed themselves at his disposal, to offer any resistance. As Dukhonin was about to leave Mohileff by train he was dragged from his carriage and brutally murdered. On the 3rd the Bolshevik delegation, under Joffe, arrived at Brest Litovsk and commenced negotiations. As the Germans declined to accept their first proposals they returned to Petrograd on the 5th to consult the Government. They left again for Brest Litovsk on the 11th, and an armistice that was to continue till January 14 was signed on the 15th. The Germans accepted the clause in which the Bolsheviks had insisted that during the armistice there was to be no transfer of troops to other fronts; but, as they attached the condition that the clause was not to apply to transfers which had already commenced, they have been able to move as many troops as they wished to our front. There was also a dangerous clause about the exchange of commodities. Peace negotiations are to begin to-day.

"Meanwhile the situation at Petrograd is getting worse and worse. There has lately been a perfect orgy of drunkenness. On the 7th a band of soldiers and sailors broke into the Winter Palace and pillaged the cellars, while five successive guards sent to arrest them did but follow their example and get hopelessly drunk. There was much shooting, but only a few soldiers were wounded. Eventually someone had the happy thought of ending the debauch by flooding the cellars, and in the process several drunken men were drowned. The soldiers have since been turning their attention to the cellars of private persons, and last night some friends of ours came to take refuge in the Embassy, as their cellars had been occupied by soldiers who were indulging in promiscuous firing. Robbery and murder are becoming common everyday proceedings, and at night people are stopped in the streets and stripped of all their clothes and valuables. Not a night passes without the constant firing of rifles and machine-guns, but nobody can ever tell me what it's all about. One night there was so much firing on the bridge, close to the Embassy, that my wife, whose bed is in a line with the windows of the room, slept on a mattress on the floor for greater security. One never knows what a day or night may bring forth."

December 19.

"Trotzky called this afternoon on the French Ambassador and said that the Allies had always refused to revise their war aims, and that, as he did not wish to be repeatedly put off as his predecessors in office had been, he had decided to open peace negotiations. They would, however, be suspended for a week so as to give the Allies the opportunity of participating in them. He was quite correct and civil. He has not honoured me with a visit for fear that I should decline to receive him.

"About a week ago Trotzky raised the question of diplomatic visas for his couriers' passports and threatened that, unless we accorded him full reciprocity, he would prevent the King's Messengers either entering or leaving Russia. In conversation with Captain Smith he said that he was perfectly entitled to do this, as I was accredited by a Government which did not recognize the present Russian Government, to one which no longer existed. I was, therefore, technically only a private individual. As I pointed out to the Foreign Office, we are quite at his mercy, and unless we come to an amicable arrangement we shall not only be deprived of our messenger service, but exposed to other reprisals, such as a refusal to pass our cyphered telegrams or to recognize our diplomatic status. Should that happen the Allied Governments would have to recall their Ambassadors."

December 22.

"I was instructed two days ago to inform Trotzky that we would grant visas, but that, as his Government had no accredited representative in London, he would have no occasion to send a courier there. This made him perfectly furious, and he at once telegraphed to Tornea to stop our messenger crossing the frontier. This telegram fortunately arrived too late, and, as he had forgotten to telegraph to the Finnish frontier at Beliostroff, the messenger arrived in due course at Petrograd."

December 23.

"Roudneff, the Mayor of Moscow, Goltz, who belongs to the left wing of the social revolutionaries, and the Mayor of Petrograd, sent me a message the other day saying that they wanted to see me and suggesting that I should meet them in the Summer Garden so as not to attract attention. I declined to give them a clandestine meeting of this kind, but said that if they would come to the Embassy I should be happy to see them. Roudneff and Goltz came late this evening, having apparently taken every precaution not to be followed. It is symptomatic of the times we live in that a Socialist of Goltz' extreme views has to come to the Embassy secretly for fear of being arrested as a counter-revolutionary. They had, they said, come to ask me what would be our attitude were the Constituent Assembly to appeal to us to convert the present negotiations for a separate peace into negotiations for a general one. They next inquired whether, if Russia, who could not go on with the war, were to conclude a separate peace, we could do anything to help her from being forced to accept terms prejudicial to the interests of the Allies. Finally they wanted to know whether Mr. Lloyd George's statement that we were going to fight out the war to a finish was meant seriously or intended as a bluff for the Germans. I returned non-committal answers to all their questions, and, on my explaining the reasons which forced us to go on with the war, they assured me that the social revolutionaries did not hold us, but the Germans, responsible for its continuation. As they were leaving, Roudneff told me that my chair in the municipal council chamber was always at my disposal as the Moscow Duma was not Bolshevik. I am not, however, tempted to occupy it in present circumstances."

December 28.

"On Christmas night we gave what will be our last entertainment at the Embassy to over a hundred members of our staff and of the various military missions. We began with a concert and variety entertainment, arranged by Colonel Thornhill, and ended up with a sit-down supper. In spite of the prevailing scarcity of provisions, my cook gave us a most sumptuous repast.

"In consequence of the reprisals with which Trotzky threatened British subjects, if his couriers were not at once accorded diplomatic passports, we have had to acquiesce, and I have been authorized to give the necessary visas unconditionally. In informing him of this. Captain Smith expressed, in my name, the hope that he would in the future try to seek an amicable adjustment of any debatable question that might arise before having recourse to arbitrary measures. Trotzky replied that he was always ready to adopt a conciliatory attitude, but that he had found by experience that such a policy did not pay and only led to protracted discussions.

"I have had a relapse, and my doctor insists on my going home without awaiting the meeting of the Constituent. I have, therefore, decided to start on January 7. Lindley, who, ever since he was appointed Counsellor in 1915, has rendered me such valuable assistance, will remain in charge of the Embassy. In accordance, however, with the decision taken by the Paris Conference that the Allied Governments, while not condoning Russia's treason, are to enter into unofficial relations with the Petrograd Government, Lockhart, who had done such excellent work at Moscow, will act as our unofficial agent with them."

December 30.

"Trotzky has addressed a message to the people and Governments of all Allied countries. The Russian Revolution has, he declares, opened the door for an immediate general peace, and if only the Allied Governments will avail themselves of the present favourable opportunity, general negotiations may be commenced at once. If, on the other hand, they refuse to participate in the negotiations, the labouring classes in their respective countries must rise against those who refuse to give the people peace. He concluded by promising the former his full support."

December 31.

"The first detachment of the German Peace Delegation has arrived. They are, it is said, astounded at the state of anarchy prevailing here, and declare that Russia's financial and industrial ruin is so complete that no one country could by itself restore normal conditions."

January 2, 1918.
"The Germans have subscribed to the formula of a peace without annexations or contributions on the condition that the Allies will do the same ; but there has been a hitch in the self determination clause. Trotzky affirms that the German delegates at Brest agreed to evacuate the occupied territory in order to leave the population free to take a decision without pressure. The Germans, on the other hand, have refused to withdraw their troops from Poland, Courland and the Baltic Provinces, on the ground that all these provinces wish to remain within the sphere of the Central Powers. On the Russian delegates asking for instructions they were told to give the Germans a "slap in the face." They have apparently done so metaphorically, and have warned them that, if they come to Petrograd, both they and the population will starve. Trotzky has declared the German conditions unacceptable, and in a speech which he delivered on New Year's Day, said:

We will make no more concessions. Let the German soldiers know that there exists a new army that has no chiefs, no penal code, and that is not driven into battle with sticks. Let them know that there is a front, where each citizen soldier is animated with the spirit of the revolution, and let them take into account what such an army is capable of.

"In spite of this bombastic language, Trotzky knows perfectly well that the Russian army is incapable of fighting. The adoption of the system of election of officers by the men has, as someone remarked, had the result that cooks have been made colonels and colonels cooks. Even in some military hospitals a committee of soldiers decides which of the wounded is to be operated. One regiment at the front is said to have sold to the Germans a battery and all the artillery horses."

January 5.
"Trotzky has raised another awkward question by proposing to appoint a Russian Representative in London. It is very difficult for us to consent to this, while, if we refuse, he may retaliate by divesting the Allied Embassies of their diplomatic immunities. I have pointed out to the Foreign Office that we shall have to choose between coming to some working arrangement with the Bolsheviks or breaking with them altogether. A complete rupture would leave the Germans a clear field in Russia and would deprive our vested interests of such protection as the Embassy can give them. We should, therefore, in my opinion, only have recourse to it in the last resort.

"Trotzky, who is leaving for Brest Litovsk to renew the peace negotiations, is now accusing us of intending to make a peace *sur le dos de la Russie*. He told a friend of mine yesterday that it is clear from what Mr. Lloyd George said in a recent speech that the Allies would like to see Germany make a peace "with annexations" with Russia, in the hope that she would, after gorging herself in the east, be more disposed to make concessions in the west. It seems pretty clear from this that he is preparing to beat a retreat and to accept Germany's terms. It is not easy to understand what he is really driving at. Even if he does take money from the Germans for his own purposes he is not their paid agent, though he could not serve them better if he were. Both he and Lenin are out to overthrow all the so-called imperialistic governments, but it is against Great Britain rather than against Germany that their main offensive will be directed. The situation is quite hopeless, as the Bolsheviks have monopolized all the energies and organizing power of the nation. Even were the social revolutionaries to form a Government, with a majority in the Constituent Assembly, they are incapable of making a stand either against the Bolsheviks or the Germans."

January 6.

"Our last day in Petrograd! — and yet, in spite of all that we have gone through, we are sad at the thought. Why is it that Russia casts over all who know her such an indefinable mystic spell that, even when her wayward children have turned their capital into a pandemonium, we are sorry to leave it? I cannot explain the reason, but we *are* sorry. This afternoon I paid a sorrowful farewell visit to my friend, the Grand Duke Nicholas Michailovich. Though he faces the future with his usual courage, and though he was as witty and charming as ever, he has, I think, the presentiment that sooner or later his fate will be sealed. We both, indeed, felt that we should never meet again, and as I bade him good-bye he embraced me in the old Russian fashion, kissing me on both cheeks and on the forehead. (The Grand Duke Nicholas, his two brothers, and the Grand Duke Paul were shot by the Bolsheviks in the following summer.) Then, when I got back to the Embassy, I wrote a farewell minute thanking the members of my staff from my heart for their many services during those strenuous years of war and revolution, and telling them how warmly I appreciated the loyal support and the many proofs of personal attachment which they had given me. I have just received a charming note in reply which touched me very deeply, written by Lindley on their behalf. To-night we dine with Benjy Bruce, who, as head of the Chancery, has had to bear the burden and heat of the day. He had been my right-hand man throughout, always trying to spare me and to relieve me of as much work as possible, a true and devoted friend for whom I have a sincere affection."

CHAPTER 35
1918-1922

The start from the Embassy in the early hours of that mid-winter morning was not calculated to cheer us. There was no electric light, and the candles placed here and there on the staircase and in the corridors did but serve to accentuate the prevailing darkness. Then, when, after a slow motor drive through the deep snow, we reached the Finnish station, the way that the evil-looking Red Guards on duty there scowled on us as we passed made me wonder whether we should get through our journey unmolested. Trotzky had made no difficulties about my leaving, and had granted me the usual customs facilities. He had, however, refused to extend this privilege as an act of courtesy to General Knox, Admiral Stanley and the five other officers who were travelling with us unless I guaranteed that similar facilities would be accorded any military attachés or officers whom he might wish to send to England. I told him that I could not do this. Our officers, I pointed out, were returning home after having served several years in Russia, and as he had no Russian officers in England who wished to return to Russia, there could be no question of reciprocity. The Commissariat for Foreign Affairs had also declined to take any steps to reserve special accommodation for us on the train; but having won the station-master's heart by the present of two bottles of old brandy, we succeeded in getting a whole sleeping-car placed at the disposal of our party. In spite of the early hour and of the bitter cold, most of my colleagues, as well as the members of my staff and several friends from the British colony, came to see us off and to bid us God-speed.

We had, on the whole, a very comfortable journey, and having brought food and wine with us, we had very cheery picnic meals in our carriage. The first day passed without any incident; but in the middle of the night we were woken up by some half-dozen armed soldiers who demanded our passports. After examining them and finding that they were in order, they left us in peace and we went to sleep again. The next day (January 8) was rather a trying one, as the farther north we got the deeper was the snow and the slower our progress. We were timed to arrive at Tornea, on the Finnish side of the frontier, at midday; but on reaching Uleaborg late in the afternoon, we were met by the British consul at Tornea, who told us that there was no chance of our catching the Swedish train. He accordingly arranged that we should sleep in our carriage and that the engine should be left on the train and shunt us about during the night in order to keep it heated.

We had a long wait the next morning at the Tornea station, where the customs officials made difficulties about passing our luggage. As we had been warned to take as few things as possible with us, we had only brought the canvases of six or seven of our best pictures as well as a few valuable pieces of plate, leaving most of our wearing apparel and other possessions in the Embassy. When, thanks to a judicious distribution of roubles, these difficulties were at last overcome, we drove in open sledges for some twenty minutes, crossing a frozen river, to an hotel on the Swedish side of the frontier at Haparanda. I had woken up in the morning with a bad sore throat and was afraid that I was in for an attack of influenza; but whether it was the intense cold — 80 degrees of frost Fahrenheit — that killed the germs, or relief at having got safely through to a civilized country, I enjoyed an excellent luncheon and felt quite myself again.

After an early dinner we had once more to face the cold and to drive to the station, where the Swedish authorities had kindly reserved a most comfortable sleeping-car for us. We reached Stockholm about six o'clock on the evening of Friday, the 11th, after a journey of forty hours, and were met by Esme Howard and by Colebrooke, who had been honorary attaché at Petrograd. On the next day we lunched with the Howards at the Legation and had tea with the Crown Prince and Princess in their palace, and left in the evening for Christiania, which we reached on the afternoon of the 13th. On arriving there I was handed the following very flattering telegram from Mr. Balfour, which had, as I subsequently learned, been published in the London press:

I am very sorry to learn that your health is still so unsatisfactory.

The War Cabinet desires me to express to you their warmest thanks for all the eminent services which you have rendered your country. They hope that, by a much-needed rest, your health may soon be restored, and that you may long be spared to continue your career of public usefulness.

May I be permitted to add my own cordial acknowledgments for all you have done for us ? If I may be permitted to say so, your courage, resource and character have been an inspiration to us all, and you have worthily upheld the great traditions and ideals of your country.

We spent a very pleasant evening with the Findlays, who had kindly asked us to dine at the Legation, and started at half-past seven on Monday morning, the 14th, for Bergen. Owing to some mistake no carriage had been reserved for us, and we had to travel third class for the first three hours of the journey. We only reached Bergen after midnight, and had but a few hours' sleep, having to get up the next morning soon after six. As it was considered advisable to keep our movements a secret from the Germans, we were fetched while it was still dark and smuggled on board the King's small yacht, the *Heimdal*, that was to take us down the fiord to a sheltered bay, close to the point where the cruiser that was being sent for us from Leith, was expected at eleven o'clock. By the time we got there a regular blizzard was blowing and there was no sign of the cruiser. After waiting a couple of hours we were told that as there was now no chance of her arriving before the next morning, we must spend the rest of the day and the night on the yacht. The accommodation on board was very restricted, but the commodore did everything that was possible to make us comfortable. He plied us with food and drink, gave my wife and daughter his own, and me the first lieutenant's cabin, and arranged for the rest of the party to sleep on the floor of the saloon.

Next morning the weather cleared a little, and between eleven and twelve the cruiser *Yarmouth* was sighted and we went to meet her. It was, however, still blowing a gale, so we had to lead her to a sheltered bay where we could tranship. Captain Grace, a son of the famous cricketer, was kindness itself, and did all he could to make what proved to be a very bad crossing as tolerable as possible for my poor wife and daughter, who were both very bad sailors. Not being myself subject to sea-sickness, I readily fell in with his suggestion that we should have luncheon before starting; and, after partaking of beefsteak pie and treacle pudding, retired with a big cigar to my cabin. But I had never before experienced the antics which a light cruiser can play in a heavy sea, and paid the penalty for my imprudence.

On the following morning (the 17th) we got into calm water, reaching Leith in lovely weather about three o'clock, after a passage that had lasted twenty-six instead of the usual fourteen hours. At Leith we found motors waiting to take us to our hotel at Edinburgh, where Admiral Burney, the naval commander-in-chief, kindly came to congratulate us on our safe arrival. After a very cheerful dinner we left by the night express for London, which we reached early the next morning, after having been exactly eleven days *en route*. My friend,

Ian Malcolm, met us at King's Cross with congratulatory messages from the Prime Minister and Mr. Balfour.

In the course of the afternoon I received a most kind and gracious telegram from the King, welcoming us home; and when Their Majesties returned to London we had the honour of lunching with them at Buckingham Palace. The Lord Mayor, Sir Charles Hanson, in a letter inviting us to dine at the Mansion House, was also good enough to express the City of London's admiration for the manner in which I had faced the difficulties of an ever-changing situation under three successive regimes. Everybody indeed, the Press included, was as nice and sympathetic as could be. Invitations to dinners, both private and official, were showered on us, and, as a lady remarked to me, I was for the moment the Ambassador *à la mode*. Besides having several long conversations with Mr. Balfour, I had the privilege of breakfasting with the Prime Minister and of discussing the Russian situation with him. I also attended two Cabinet meetings at No. 10, where I met with a most cordial reception, Lord Curzon assuring me that the telegram which I had received at Christiania expressed the feelings of all the members of the War Cabinet.

I was, however, so tired both in mind and body that, on lunching with Lord Reading, who wanted to know my views about Russia before starting on his mission to Washington, I broke down altogether and had to be taken back to Buckland's Hotel. My doctor told me that I was worn out and ordered me complete rest. As ill luck would have it, there was a bad air-raid that night, and as there was a skylight in the adjoining passage the manager insisted on my coming downstairs, in spite of my high temperature. I felt far too ill to care whether we were bombed or not, but I had to obey and to spend several hours in an armchair in a comatose state.

It was only after a few weeks' rest at Newquay that I was able to resume any active work. Though I had now no regular official duties, my time for the next eighteen months was fully occupied by seconding my wife's efforts to minister to the needs of the British and Russian refugees and by pleading Russia's cause before the British public. I was chairman of some half-dozen committees that dealt with various sides of the Russian question. I was also president of the British Russia Club that had been founded by some of our business men, with vested interests in Russia, who had realized that it was only by co-ordinated and concerted action that they could hope to save anything from the wreck. The club gradually became a rallying point for all who were interested in Russia, and, as most of its members had a practical knowledge of all the conditions of Russia's economic, industrial and financial life, it was able to place much useful information at the disposal of His Majesty's Government. I so deeply sympathized with the losses which most of its members had sustained that I gave it my wholehearted support, and took the chair at its dinners whenever any distinguished guest, such as Mr. Winston Churchill, honoured them with his presence.

In my first conversations with Mr. Balfour and other members of the Government I had deprecated a complete rupture with the Bolsheviks on the ground that it would leave the Germans a clear field in Russia. On the other hand, I had laid stress on the fact that, while we had nothing to hope for from the Social revolutionaries, Lenin and Trotzky, though very big men, represented a destructive and not a constructive force. They could pull down, but they could not build up. Their end and aim was to sweep away all the old so-called imperialistic Governments, and they would never, as I told the Prime Minister at the time, work with a man whom they regarded as the very personification of imperialism.

As the situation changed for the worse, I modified the views which I had originally expressed. The Bolsheviks had dissolved the Constituent and had murdered two ex-Ministers; while Litvinoff had, in a speech at Nottingham, openly preached revolution. To allow an unofficial diplomatic agent to carry on an active revolutionary propaganda in our midst seemed to me inadmissible; yet were we to take disciplinary measures against him Trotzky would retaliate with reprisals against members of our embassy. We had therefore to choose between coming to terms with the Bolsheviks, on the basis of complete reciprocity in all things, or to break with them altogether and to withdraw our embassy. I was strongly in favour of the latter course, more especially as there now seemed some prospect of the Allies affording material assistance to the loyal elements in South Russia, who had not yet submitted either to the Bolsheviks or the Germans.

In all the speeches which I made during the course of the next twelve months, either at the Russia Club or elsewhere, I consistently advocated a policy of armed intervention. The Russian problem, I contended, was the dominating factor in the international situation, and so long as it was left unsolved there could be no permanent peace in Europe. Moreover, to leave Russia to her fate might result in Germany one day securing the control of Russia's vast man power and untold mineral wealth; while to allow the Bolsheviks to consolidate their position would mean the dissemination by their agents of subversive Communist doctrines through the greater part of Asia and Europe. I did not advocate an expedition on a large scale to effect what the opponents of intervention termed the conquest of Russia, but the stiffening of General Denikin's and the other anti-Bolshevik armies by the despatch of a small volunteer force that might easily have been raised among our home and Colonial troops after the Armistice. The Bolshevik army was not then as strong as it is at present, and a mere handful of British troops, with tanks and aeroplanes, would have enabled General Yudenitch to take Petrograd. On the other hand, had we, in addition to supplying General Denikin with war material, sent out a British general at the head of a small expeditionary force to control his operations, and to insist on his pursuing a conciliatory policy towards the peasants, Moscow would also have been captured; and the Bolshevik Government would not long have outlived the fall of those two capital cities. The question of finance had, I readily admit, to be taken into account, for with the income tax at 6s. in the £ we could not lightly embark on an enterprise of this nature; but, had the object of that enterprise been attained, the money which it would have cost would have been well invested. We should have expedited the opening to trade of the richest country in Europe, we should have safeguarded many important British vested interests in Russia, and, with the elimination of the Bolshevik menace to the world's peace, we should have had better reason to face the future with confidence than we have at present.

But few people, I am aware, will take my view of the question, as our intervention proved such a failure in practice that it has been generally condemned in principle as a mistaken policy. Carried out, as it was, in a half-hearted spirit it was undoubtedly a mistake, and the money spent on it was wasted. The Allied Governments, without any clearly defined policy and afraid of committing themselves, had recourse to half-measures which were almost bound to fail. They supported Denikin with one hand and they held out the other to the Bolsheviks. They furnished the former with war material and they invited the latter to a conference at Prinkipo — a proposal that was directly responsible for the defection of a large body of Don Cossacks and for the serious setback in the south that resulted from it. Had intervention been carried out on other lines the result might have been very different. It did not, however, serve, as is so often asserted, to drive loyal Russians into the Bolshevik camp.

Their defection was due to other causes. While the Prinkipo scheme had disheartened many of our friends and sympathizers, the recognition of the Caucasian Republics and of the Baltic States, coupled with the unfounded suspicion that we were encouraging the Poles to annex territory that was ethnically Russian, was resented by many patriotic Russians. It was the fear that the Allies were intent on the dismemberment of Russia, and not intervention, that reinforced the ranks of the Red Army. Nor is the precedent of the French Revolution — that is frequently cited as an argument against intervention — applicable in our case. For, whereas the Austrians and Prussians intervened for the express purpose of replacing the Bourbons on the French throne, we never for a moment contemplated imposing the Romanoffs on an unwilling Russia. We made it clear from the very first that any such idea was far from our thoughts, and that our object was to secure for the Russian people the right of self-determination, so that they might be free to choose whatever form of government they thought best.

Early in October, 1919, I received a most kind letter from Lord Curzon telling me that he had submitted my name to the King for the post of His Majesty's Ambassador at Rome, and expressing the hope that I would accept that office for a term of two years. Having served at Rome as Third Secretary in 1878 and as Counsellor of Embassy in 1900, I was delighted to go back there as Ambassador and to close my career amid familiar scenes which were associated with so many happy memories of earlier years. It naturally entailed my giving up all my Russian work and resigning the presidency of the British Russia Club. In taking leave of its members at a luncheon, at which they were good enough to present me with my portrait by the well-known Canadian artist, Mr. Sheldon Williams, I briefly recapitulated what I had said on previous occasions about the Russian situation. I had not yet kissed hands on my appointment and was still only Ambassador designate, and as this was to be my farewell speech on Russia, I felt perfectly justified in doing so. But the Cabinet thought otherwise, and a couple of days later I was sent for by Lord Hardinge and reprimanded, in their name, for having propounded a policy contrary to theirs. I replied that I had been careful to abstain from criticizing them, and that I had but given expression to my personal views, as I had never been able to make out what their policy really was. At the end of October we left for Rome.

Short as was the duration of my mission to the Quirinal, I had in the course of those two years to treat with three successive Prime Ministers — Nitti, to whom Mr. Lloyd George had given his photograph, with the inscription, "To my kindred spirit"; Giolitti, the oldest in years but the youngest in mind of Italy's elder statesmen; and Bonomi; and with four Foreign Ministers — Tittoni, Scialoja, Sforaa and della Torretta, who is now Italian Ambassador in London. I do not propose to commit the indiscretion of recounting the inner political history of these two very interesting years, and will only record the fact that my official relations with all these distinguished men were throughout of a most cordial character. As I never mixed myself up in Italian party politics, a change of Ministry did not in any way affect me. With Count Sforza, with whom, first as Under-Secretary and then as Minister for Foreign Affairs, I was in constant touch for more than a year and a half, and with the Marquis della Torretta, whom I had known as Counsellor of Embassy at Petrograd, I was, moreover, on terms of close personal friendship.

Lord Curzon showed me throughout the greatest kindness and consideration, but I must admit — and I can do so without betraying any official secret — that I found my position as Ambassador very different from what it had been when I was in Russia. There were now virtually two Foreign Offices in Downing Street, and the precept enjoined by the Scriptures with regard to our exercise of the virtue of charity was applied to the conduct of diplomacy. Though I was brought up in the old school of diplomacy, I am not in the least biased against the methods of the new. On the contrary, I fully appreciate the many advantages which accrue from regular personal intercourse between the Allied Premiers and Foreign Ministers by means of conferences and supreme councils. But an Ambassador can contribute to the success of such meetings by doing the preliminary spadework and by endeavouring to predispose the Government to which he is accredited in favour of the policy advocated by his own Government. In discussing this question with Sir Maurice Hankey when he was staying with us at the Embassy, I pointed out that an Ambassador could only do this if he was taken into his Government's confidence, and that if, on the contrary, he was kept in the dark he might, in his conversations with the Foreign Minister, give expression to views diametrically opposed to theirs.

Though I had not the same interesting work to do as I had in Russia, there were ample compensations outside politics, and the two years which we spent in Rome passed far too quickly. There were old friendships to be renewed and new ones to be formed. There were old haunts to be re-visited and new and more distant scenes, which had not been so accessible in pre-motor days, to be explored. There were walks on the Alban Hills, with the lakes of Albano and Nemi glittering like twin gems in their sylvan setting, with the Campagna at our feet, and with Rome and St. Peter's in the background. There was the Rosebery Villa at Posillipo, overlooking the Bay of Naples, where Nature has blended together all that is beautiful on land and sea to produce one of her greatest masterpieces. Then, when we had time, we wandered among the old Umbrian and Tuscan towns, or, motoring over one of the passes of the Apennines, surveyed the wonderland of Italy.

But, alas! though we did not then know it, our happy days were already numbered. It was during our last visit to Posillipo, in the summer of 1920, that I first read the writing on the wall that told me of the coming of a great sorrow. We spent the month of August at Fiuggi, a fashionable watering-place half-way between Rome and Naples. We still took long motor-drives over the mountain roads, or watched the sunset from one of the many fortress-towns perched on the hill-tops that had played their part in the old feuds of the Colonnas. But I, who alone realized what the future had in store for us, was but too conscious of the fact that "there had passed a glory from the earth."

We returned to Rome early in September, and spent the rest of the autumn there. At the end of November we came home, and on the 25th of the following April, after five months of incessant suffering, my wife found rest and peace.

The generous tributes paid by the Press to her memory and the sympathy shown me by countless friends both touched and comforted me, but it was only in work that demanded a concentrated effort that I could hope to find distraction from the one engrossing thought. The writing of this book has provided me with that work and has served its purpose, though it has also, by waking happy memories of the past, sometimes added to the sadness of the present. But when, as I close its pages, I reflect on the happiness that was mine for thirty-seven years, I can but take to heart the lesson conveyed in Dryden's well-known lines:

Come fair or foul, or rain or shine,
The joys I have possessed, in spite of fate, are mine.
Not Heaven itself over the past has power;
And what has been has been, and I have had my hour.

Other reprints available in this series

Life of Alexander II, F.E. Grahame
Alexander III, Tsar of Russia, Charles Lowe
The Intimate Life of the Last Tsarina, Princess Catherine Radziwill
The reign of Rasputin, M.V. Rodzianko
Collected Works: Once a Grand Duke, Always a Grand Duke, Twilight of Royalty, Alexander, Grand Duke of Russia

Frederick, Crown Prince and Emperor, Rennell Rodd
Letters of the Empress Frederick, edited by Sir Frederick Ponsonby
Between two Emperors: The Willy-Nicky Telegrams and Letters, 1894-1914
Potsdam Princes, Ethel Howard

My Past, Marie Larisch
The Story of my Life (Vols. I-III in one volume), Marie, Queen of Roumania

Richard III, Sir Clements Markham

The Complete Works: The Journal of a Disappointed Man; A Last Diary; Enjoying Life and other Literary Remains, W.N.P. Barbellion

For further details please see *amazon.co.uk/amazon.com*

Printed in Great Britain
by Amazon

67674589R00201